Spiritualism and British society
between the wars

MANCHESTER
UNIVERSITY PRESS

STUDIES IN POPULAR CULTURE

General editor: Professor Jeffrey Richards

Spiritualism and British society between the wars

JENNY HAZELGROVE

Manchester University Press

Manchester and New York

distributed exclusively in the USA by St. Martin's Press

Published by Manchester University Press
Oxford Road, Manchester M13 9NR, UK
and Room 400, 175 Fifth Avenue, New York,
NY 10010, USA

Distributed exclusively in the USA by
St. Martin's Press, Inc., 175 Fifth Avenue, New York,
NY 10010, USA

Distributed exclusively in Canada by
UBC Press, University of British Columbia, 6344 Memorial Road,
Vancouver, BC, Canada V6T 1Z2

British Library Cataloguing-in-Publication Data
A catalogue record for this book is available from the British Library

Library of Congress Cataloging-in-Publication Data applied for

ISBN   0 7190 5558 X   *hardback*
         0 7190 5559 8   *paperback*

First published 2000

07 06 05 04 03 02 01 00   10 9 8 7 6 5 4 3 2 1

Typeset in Monotype Garamond by Lucy Morton & Robin Gable, Grosmont
Printed in Great Britain by Biddles Ltd, Guildford and King's Lynn

For Nick, Jon and Georgia, with love.

STUDIES IN POPULAR CULTURE

General editor's introduction

There has in recent years been an explosion of interest in culture and cultural studies. The impetus has come from two directions and out of two different traditions. On the one hand, cultural history has grown out of social history to become a distinct and identifiable school of historical investigation. On the other hand, cultural studies has grown out of English literature and has concerned itself to a large extent with contemporary issues. Nevertheless there is a shared project, its aim, to elucidate the meanings and values implicit and explicit in the art, literature, learning, institutions and everyday behaviour within a given society. Both the cultural historian and the cultural studies scholar seek to explore the ways in which a culture is imagined, represented and received, how it interacts with social processes, how it contributes to individual and collective identities and world views, to stability and change, to social, political and economic activities and programmes. This series aims to provide an arena for the cross-fertilization of the discipline, so that the work of the cultural historian can take advantage of the most useful and illuminating of the theoretical developments and the cultural studies scholars can extend the purely historical underpinnings of their investigations. The ultimate objective of the series is to provide a range of books which will explain in a readable and accessible way where we are now socially and culturally and how we got to where we are. This should enable people to be better informed, promote an interdisciplinary approach to cultural issues and encourage deeper thought about the issues, attitudes and institutions of popular culture.

Jeffrey Richards

Contents

List of illustrations

General editor's foreword

If there is one character who can be said to dominate popular cultural representations of the Spiritualist medium, it is Noël Coward's Madame Arcati, the elderly, dotty, bicycle-riding spinster so memorably portrayed on stage and film by Margaret Rutherford. But this was only one of a range of images attached to the idea of the medium, as Jenny Hazelgrove explains in this vivid and enthralling study. There was the medium as a type of the Virgin Mary or Joan of Arc, the medium as hysteric and degenerate, the medium as vampire, devouring mother or disturbed adolescent. Hazelgrove examines the origins, development and meaning of this range of images, and relates them both to the complex ideas of authority and power within Spiritualism and to the broader field of social and cultural attitudes towards women in general.

Cultural historians have for the most part concentrated on Spiritualism in the Victorian and Edwardian periods. But Spiritualism continued to flourish in the interwar period, given a massive boost by the Great War, which left many people desperately seeking to contact the spirits of loved ones killed in that conflict. However, Jenny Hazelgrove argues that the popularity of Spiritualism can be explained not simply by mass bereavement but also by its capacity to absorb and explain traditional beliefs and phenomena – ghosts, poltergeists, life after death, alternative healing – and by its deployment of a repertoire of specifically Catholic signs and ideas, such as purgatory, the Mass and guardian angels.

All of this leads her to challenge the secularisation and modernisation thesis which argues for a steady decline in popular religious belief in the twentieth century. She sees popular religious impulses being preserved and diverted for some people into Spiritualism. Her case is persuasively argued and the whole study adds up to a fascinating and revealing insight into an alternative culture and world view that flourished – and still flourishes – alongside more conventional outlets for deep-seated spiritual beliefs and needs.

Jeffrey Richards

Acknowledgements

During the preparation of this project, I have been continually impressed by the willingness of individuals to offer help in whatever way they can – intellectually, emotionally and materially. As it is impossible to name every person who helped in one way or another to mould this study, I should like first to offer a general thank you to all those involved. More specifically, I want to thank Homer Le Grand and Ian Britain, whose complementary approaches to my work have guided, stimulated and encouraged me. Special thanks are also due to Roy Porter of the Wellcome Trust, who helped me immensely during my research period. Conversations with Perry Williams and Logie Barrow helped to get this project 'off the ground', as did the support of friends, especially Tony Bagley (who offered material and emotional comforts), Amanda Whiting, Julie Shaw and Doug McCann. Thanks to Vivien Browning for her reminiscences of the Spiritualist movement and to Doll Lewis for her recollections of interwar Britain.

I have, of course, depended on many library services, but I would like to extend special thanks to Dorothy Sheridan and Joy Eldridge at the Mass-Observation Archive, University of Sussex, and A. H. Wesencraft of the Harry Price Library, University of London. Mass-Observation material is reproduced with permission of Curtis Brown Ltd London. Copyright the Trustees of the Mass-Observation Archive at the University of Sussex. Thanks also to H. Beric Wright for permission to reproduce material from the Helena Wright archive.

I should also like to acknowledge financial support from the Alma Hansen Scholarship.

Finally, I want to thank Roy Hazelgrove, whose unconditional affection and support have made this project possible.

Introduction

I do not remember a time during my childhood in the 1950s and 1960s when I was unaware of legends of the supernatural. Each of these legends established itself in my imagination on a spectrum of safety, colour and odour. Witches were unsafe, of course; they were black and malevolent with a damp, earthy, rotting smell. Fairies, by contrast, brought good luck and resembled fragrant flowers. Mary, the mother of God, wore blue and smelt like a church – musty and old. Images from religion mixed in fantasy with images from folklore. I recall that when I was about seven years old, a nun gave me a postcard picture of Jesus holding a lamp; he was standing in a forest beside a large tree. The wood was wild and dense, with intense colours glowing in the darkness. In that pagan-looking wood, with its Pre-Raphaelite colours, it seemed natural to me that Jesus, as the representative of light in chaotic darkness, should be surrounded by all manner of strange and fabulous creatures. I was born among atheists and lukewarm Congregationalists in a working-class part of South London. Nevertheless, the supernatural seemed to me to be an obvious and uncontested part of existence. Family and school may have espoused the secular 'laws of nature', but the transgressive romance of the supernatural persisted in local legends and superstitions, while encounters with those 'beyond the grave' were a common subject of conversation. Where I lived, acceptance of 'scientific truth' and indifference to formal religion did not necessarily imply disbelief in the supernatural.

Spiritualism, as it was handed down to me through the local community, was similarly ambivalent. The prevailing dogma, which made science synonymous with 'truth', mixed with traditional acceptance of an unseen power and made Spiritualism appear both fraudulent *and* the bearer of some dark, occult knowledge. And it was both dangerous and desirable – dangerous because it tampered with the unseen and desirable for the same reason. It was also vaguely unhygienic. The seance room was airless and furnished in the Victorian style, which to 1960s aesthetics was heavy and ugly. The medium was a woman who dressed in 'old-fashioned' – perhaps Edwardian – clothes. She had long dark hair and wore gypsy earrings, which somehow associated her with sexual seduction.[1] Another version of the medium that circulated in our community and contradicted this one, pictured her as middle-aged and scrawny. Instead of being blowsy and seductive, this medium was neat and 'repressed', a 'dried up spinster', 'not quite right in the head'.

In this study, we shall explore the processes by which these and other legends about Spiritualism and mediums were constructed in interwar Britain. The ideas of scientists and other members of the post-World War I intelligentsia are included in so far as their ideas were influential in shaping popular perceptions, but this is primarily a history of mediumship in relation to the working-class or 'plebeian' culture in which it flourished.

The period covered in this book (1919–39) represents a break with previous studies, because although historical treatments vary considerably, the majority share an explicit or implicit assumption of the dominance of secular society in the twentieth century. Consequently, scholarly interest in Spiritualism has concentrated on the Victorian and Edwardian period, and rarely extended beyond the period of the Great War. Yet we shall see that Spiritualism was every bit as popular during the interwar period as it had been in the previous century. Spiritualism reflected the increasingly democratic values of the twentieth century, and the movement continued to grow. Indeed, the interwar period turned out to be a boom time: Heterodox Christianity and widespread belief in the supernatural simultaneously supplied a rich resource for Spiritualistic thought and a cultural setting where conversion to Spiritualism could feel natural and even inevitable. Spiritualism's preoccupation with the miraculous linked it to popular Catholicism, as did its view of the afterlife and relations to the dead.

Since its beginnings in the 1840s in America, when two young sisters claimed that they talked with the dead,[2] Spiritualism has stimulated fierce controversy on both sides of the Atlantic. Throughout the latter half of the nineteenth century and well into the twentieth, scientists, clergymen, doctors, psychical researchers, occultists, and all manner of interested parties continued to debate its meaning and possibilities for humankind. The historiographical literature is similarly diverse. Frank Podmore, Spiritualism's first chronicler, viewed the subject from the perspective of a disillusioned psychical researcher. Like many middle-class intellectuals of the late nineteenth century, Podmore was disturbed by the social divisions created under *laissez-faire* capitalism and attracted to a kind of spiritually orientated socialism expounded through the works of Henry George, Thomas Davidson and Robert Owen.[3] At first he was inclined to accept Owen's verdict on the existence of a spirit world that had become active in human affairs to mark the coming of what Owen dubbed the 'New Moral World'. In 1875, an article by Podmore appeared in *Human Nature* in which he declared that Spiritualism had come to establish a 'kingdom of a freer life and fuller light, together with a love which would otherwise have come more slowly'.[4]

In 1882, a group of Cambridge intellectuals committed to carrying out investigations into psychic phenomena according to scientific prin-ciples formed the Society for Psychical Research (SPR).[5] Podmore joined the Society in its second year. During the following twenty-seven years, in which he carried out investigative work for the organisation, he developed a deeply sceptical attitude towards Spiritualist phenomena. His strict criteria for proof soon became legendary at the SPR, and he was known as the Society's 'sceptic in chief' – an epithet not always applied in good humour.[6] The title was well earned, for in his history of mediumship, *The Newer Spiritualism* (1910), not one medium passed his exacting tests, and most were dismissed as charlatans.[7] Neverthe-less, Podmore never quite gave up hope of a 'higher' reality. In telepathy, he wrote, may lie 'the germ of a more splendid capacity, or the last vestige of a power grown stunted through disuse'.[8] This cautious and somewhat melancholy search for a vitalistic universe which conformed to a set of 'laws' elaborated through 'science' was opposed by the supporters of scientific materialism, who viewed the research project of psychical research as necessarily doomed to failure. In the decades following the foundation of the SPR, as the boundaries between 'science proper' and theology hardened, psychical research failed to make inroads into orthodox science, and was widely condemned by scientists and non-scientists as a 'pseudo-science'.[9]

If psychical research was labelled pseudo-scientific, mediumship appeared to a range of twentieth-century commentators as an unconscionable fraud, fit only for the fairground. In 1916, *The Umpire* complained that mediums 'preyed' on the emotions of the war dead, a view that was regularly preached by the press and clergy throughout the duration of the Great War.[10] Lamenting the continuing popularity of Spiritualism in the Western world, the psychiatrist C. B. Farrar said in 1921 that mediumship was an 'irregular' profession that preyed on human gullibility, while Spiritualism was a 'deviant' practice that reflected 'the animism of the childhood of the race'.[11] In 1944, George Orwell recommended to the readers of the *Tribune* a book entitled *The Follies and Frauds of Spiritualism*, and expressed surprise at the number of scientists who had been 'taken in' by Spiritualism in the past.[12] Twenty years later, the historian and polemicist Trevor Hall occupied an identical position. In *The Strange Case of Edmund Gurney*, Hall examined the death of the psychical researcher of that name, and considered the knowledge claims of nineteenth-century Spiritualism and psychical research. He devoted the greater part of the book to debunking what he saw as the scientific pretensions of the SPR, and exposing the 'deceits' of mediums. He scoffed at the SPR and their 'higher laws', and wondered how anyone could have been 'taken in' by the 'shifty frauds of spiritualism.'[13]

However, 'crisis of faith' analysis has probably been the most common way of understanding Spiritualism and allied movements. The 'Victorian crisis of faith' denotes the perceived conflict between 'science' and 'religion' in nineteenth-century Europe and America.[14] These historians argue that as science undermined Christian cosmology, people turned to movements like Spiritualism, which seemed to offer concrete confirmation of a metaphysical and moral presence in the universe.[15] The interest in Spiritualism during the Great War is also frequently explained by reference to the effects of social crisis on 'rational judgement'. One historian writes:

> [A]ll who could not come to terms with ever-hovering death, sought mystical shelter elsewhere, in the arms of upstart sciences, old delusions and the charlatanry which offered communion with their dead sons;

a recourse not to be scoffed at in an age which swallows the grossest occult nonsense so long as it is called extra-sensory perception.[16]

In crisis of faith analysis, loss of faith in a metaphysical universe is treated as rational, inevitable and unproblematic, whereas Spiritualism emerges as the pathological outcome of science's triumphant but traumatic shedding of religion. The assumption of the epistemological superiority of 'scientific knowledge' and the inevitability of 'progressive', secular society has frequently blinded historians to the fact that the secularisation process is not nearly as complete in the West as we are sometimes led to suppose. John Hedley-Brooke has questioned the thesis that religious belief *was* as thoroughly displaced by science-based secularism as is normally assumed. He argues that the secularisation thesis is far too simple, and fails to take account of the historical dialogue between secular and sacred thought and the place of religion in the history of science.[17] 'Crisis of faith' analysis also fails to recognise the place of power relations in the construction of Spiritualist belief. Under the influence primarily of Michel Foucault, however, several studies have fruitfully explored Spiritualist epistemology in the context of class and gender relations. Two stand out. Logie Barrow emphasises the nexus between power and knowledge in his depiction of nineteenth-century Spiritualism as a product of plebeian culture that embraced a democratic definition of knowledge.[18] Alex Owen's fascinating study of women and Spiritualism explores issues of power, knowledge and femininity in Spiritualist practice.[19]

As in the previous century, mediums of the twentieth century were likely to be women.[20] Baldly stated, this claim is misleading. Male mediums have always existed in the Spiritualist movement. In the nineteenth century, Daniel D. Home was widely known in Britain and America for his breathtaking feats under trance, which included elongating his body and floating in the air.[21] In this century some famous mediums have been men or boys. Willi and Rudi Schneider, teenage brothers from Austria, were famous for their physical mediumship;[22] and the physicist Sir Oliver Lodge endorsed the mediumship of A. Vout Peters.[23] Nevertheless, male mediums were in the minority.[24] More important, because mediumship was signified as 'feminine', male mediumship was commonly associated with homosexuality. Edward Carpenter, in *Intermediate Types among Primitive Folk* (1914), linked the Uranian temperament, as he put it, with 'divinatory psychic or unusual powers'.[25] Carpenter campaigned vigorously for social acceptance of homosexuals,[26] and his book considered homosexuality in a positive light. Such people, he argued, had fulfilled the function of priest in any number of archaic and primitive societies, and were especially suited to this role. Carpenter occupied a minority position with his positive construction of homosexuality; homophobic attitudes were far more prevalent. Male mediums were often viewed contemptuously as 'cissies' or 'Jessies'.[27] For example, in Anthony Powell's comic novel *What's Become of Waring?* (1939), a male medium is described as 'a slim young man with an inquisitive nose and weak double chin'. He wears a dressing gown for his seance performances and speaks in a 'small high voice like a child's'.[28] A similar impression is created in a report on a Spiritualist meeting for a Mass-Observation survey in 1937. Here, the male medium strikes the observer as 'a cissyish type'; he thinks he is trying to flirt with him, and suspects 'uranianism'.[29] In the British comedy film, *London Belongs to Me* (1948), Alistair Sim plays Squales, a fraudulent medium who is a sponger and flatterer. His profession is presented as integral to his 'failure as a man'.

Mediumship, whether an attribute of women or men, was signified as intrinsically 'feminine' – the obverse of 'masculinity' – and existing studies on mediumship and gender relations have focused on the associations between Spiritualism and feminism,[30] or the subversion of normative femininity through the discourse of the seance.[31] Without denying that mediumship could, at times, be deeply subversive of patriarchal gender divisions and norms, I emphasise the discursive use that twentieth century Spiritualists made of traditional images of transcendent femininity in the construction and subsequent *control* of their mediums.

In the wider community, constructions of mediumistic identity encompassed an extraordinarily large and diverse range. Mediums were variously regarded as the fount of truth, the mouthpiece for demonic disinformation, and the raw material of psychiatric and psychical research. Within these shifting and contradictory narratives, mediumship became charged with moral ambiguity: it was never clear whether a medium was psychically sensitive or crazy, benign or malevolent, or whether she intended to harm or heal. The atmosphere of horror, fascination, deviancy and pleasure that gathered around the figure of the medium intensified as she became entangled with a reordering of the symbolic understanding of feminine sexuality elaborated in the writings of the sexologists and generated through novels, films and newspapers.

What of the medium herself? How did an individual come to accept the mantle of mediumship? The question of how a sense of self is accomplished is a controversial and complex one that cannot be addressed comprehensively in this book, but there is no doubt that the essentialist concept of an original self, governed by biology and existing somehow outside culture, has come under sustained and persuasive criticism. However, as Seyla Benhabib has recently commented, some postmodern authors give the impression that the self is nothing more than 'a position in language'.[32] I stress that in this study I retain the traditional notion of personal autonomy while recognising the embeddedness of the self in culture. As Benhabib comments: 'no matter how constituted by language the subject retains a certain autonomy and ability to rearrange the significations of language, [this] is a regulative principle of all communication and social action'. The self may be constituted through language, but not merely as a 'ventriloquist for discourses operating through her or "mobilising" her'.[33] This claim is demonstrated in the lives of mediums considered here, each of whom selected from a shifting range of meanings offered to them about 'who they really were' and generated, in turn, further meanings. Women who identified as mediums often shared common influences, but each identification was a complex process, involving continual internal dialogue between culture and personal experience. The maintenance of a coherent sense of self, necessary for day-to-day functioning, was not easy for a medium. Even if she received widespread endorsement (which was rare), she was still confronted with a range of constructions concerning all aspects of her life which generated further ambivalence, tension and instability of identity. The authenticity of her identity was continually called into question, and demands were made upon her to produce 'proof', but what counted as 'proof' was itself a subject of doubt and conflict.

In trying to reconstruct the social processes that constituted Spiritualism, mediumship and mediumistic identity, I have been influenced by a variety of theorists from sociological and psychoanalytic schools of thought. I will refer to these theories wherever appropriate in the chapters that follow. I should add, however, that in the research and writing of this project I have found time and again that human behaviour resists tidy theoretical analysis. Theories function heuristically in this project to make way for the idiosyncrasies of human thought and practice in a particular historical period.

Notes

1 In this respect, expectations in my community matched those in northern towns. Doris Stokes, who was to become a medium herself, was under the impression that mediums 'had long dresses and fat hands with rings on every finger'. D. Stokes and L. Dearsley, *Voices in My Ear: The Autobiography of a Medium* (London, Futura Macdonald, 1980), p. 30.

2 C. B. Farrar, 'The Revival of Spiritism', *Archives of Neurology and Psychiatry* (1921) 670–73.

3 See E. Pease, *History of the Fabian Society*, 2nd edn (London, Cass, 1925). Here, Pease mentions Podmore as a fellow member of the Fabian Society; he talks about their friendship and their common interest in the ideas of George, Owen and Spiritualism. See also W. Wolfe, *From Radicalism to Socialism: Men and Ideas in the Formation of Fabian Socialist Doctrines* (New Haven, CT, Yale University Press, 1975); I. Britain, *Fabianism and Culture: A Study in British Socialism and the Arts, 1884–1918* (Cambridge, Cambridge University Press, 1982), ch. 1.

4 Quoted by E. J. Dingwall, 'Introduction' to F. Podmore, *Mediums of the Nineteenth Century*, vol. 1 (New York, University Books, 1962), p. vi.

5 'Objects of the Society', *Proceedings of the Society for Psychical Research*, 1:1 (1882–83) 3–4.

6 As Eleanor Sidgwick noted in her 1911 obituary of him, his sceptical attitude sometimes produced the effect of a 'douche of cold water' on other investigators, and 'made some members of the Society impatient with him' (E. Sidgwick, 'Frank Podmore and Psychical Research', *Proceedings of the Society for Psychical Research*, 25 [1911] 9).

7 F. Podmore, *The Newer Spiritualism* (London, Routledge & Kegan Paul, 1910).

8 F. Podmore, *Apparitions and Thought Transference: An Examination of the Evidence for Telepathy* (London, Walter Scott, 1915), p. 457. See F. Turner, *Between Science and Religion: The Reaction to Scientific Naturalism in Late Victorian England* (New Haven, CT, Yale University Press, 1974) for his analysis of like-minded contemporary figures: Henry Sidgwick, James Ward, Alfred Russel Wallace, Frederick Myers, George Romanes and Samuel Butler. These men shared an acceptance of 'the concepts and theories of science', but denied the 'proposition that all valid human experiences and ideals could be expressed through or subsumed under existing scientific categories and laws' (p. 2).

9 The historiography on psychical research is relatively large. What follows is intended to represent a cross-section of the literature available: B. Inglis, *A History of the Paranormal, 1914–1939* (London, Hodder & Stoughton, 1984); B. Wynne, 'Physics and Psychics: Science, Symbolic Action, and Social Control in Late Victorian England', in B. Barnes and S. Shapin (eds), *Natural Order: Historical Studies of Scientific Culture* (Beverly Hills, CA, Sage, 1979), pp. 167–86; P. Williams, 'The Making of Victorian Psychical Research: An Intellectual Elite's Approach to the Spiritual World' (PhD dissertation, University of Cambridge, 1984); H. M. Collins and T. J. Pinch, 'The Construction of the Paranormal; Nothing Unscientific is Happening', in R. Wallis (ed.), *On the Margins of Science: The Social Construction of Rejected Knowledge* (Keele, Keele University Press, 1979), pp. 237–70; P. Allison, 'Experimental Psychology as a Rejected Science', in Wallis (ed.), *On the Margins of Science*, pp. 271–9; S. E. D. Shortt, 'Physicians and Psychics: The Anglo-American Medical Response to Spiritualism 1870–90', *Journal of the History of Medicine and Allied Sciences*, 39:3 (1984) 339–55; Turner, *Between Science and Religion*; S. H. Mauskopf and M. R. McVaugh, *The Elusive Science: Origins of Experimental Psychical Research* (Baltimore, MD, Johns Hopkins University Press, 1980); A. Gauld, *The Founders of Psychical Research* (London, Routledge & Kegan Paul, 1968). Gauld's *History of Hypnotism* (Cambridge, Cambridge University Press, 1992) also contains interesting material on psychical research.

10 G. Nelson, *Spiritualism and Society* (London, Routledge & Kegan Paul, 1969), p. 156. For other examples of this sentiment, see H. Price, *Search for Truth: My Life for Psychical Research* (London, Collins, 1942), p. 77; E. O'Donnell, *The Menace of Spiritualism* (London, Werner & Laurie, 1920), p. 158.

11 Farrar, 'The Revival of Spiritism', pp. 673, 675.

12 S. Orwell and I. Angus (eds), *The Collected Essays Journalism and Letters of George Orwell, Vol 3, As I Please, 1943–45* (Harmondsworth, Penguin, 1970), pp. 319–20.

13 T. Hall, *The Strange Case of Edmund Gurney* (London, Duckworth, 1964), p. 41.

14 Frank Turner was one of the first to challenge this thesis when he argued that the apparent conflict between these two epistemologies represented the opposing interests of the clergy and the professionalising scientists. See Turner, 'The Victorian Conflict Between Science and Religion; A Professional Dimension', *Isis*, 69 (1978) 356–76.

15 See, for example: J. Oppenheim, *The Other World: Spiritualism and Psychical Research in England 1850–1914* (London, Cambridge University Press, 1985); M. McMackin Garland, 'Victorian Unbelief and Bereavement', in R. Houlbrooke (ed.), *Death, Ritual, and Bereavement* (London, Routledge, 1989), p. 162; R. C. Finucane, *Appearances of the Dead: A*

Cultural History of Ghosts (London, Junction, 1982); R. Brandon, *The Spiritualists: The Passion for the Occult in the Nineteenth and Twentieth Centuries* (London, Weidenfeld & Nicolson, 1983); A. Braude, *Radical Spirits: Spiritualism and Women's Rights in Nineteenth-Century America* (Boston, MA, Beacon Press, 1989); J. Briggs, *Night Visitors: The Rise and Fall of the English Ghost Story* (London, Faber, 1977); A. Gauld, *The Founders of Psychical Research*; David Morris, *The Masks of Lucifer: Technology and the Occult in Twentieth Century Popular Literature* (London, Batsford, 1992). In Morris's analysis of Theosophy in the last century, 'crisis of faith' is invoked only as *part* of a complex of cultural events. A variation on the theme of 'crisis of faith' underpins James Webb's account of European occultism in the twentieth century. In explaining what he sees as the occultists' 'flight from reason', he refers to the theory of 'future shock'. This, according to its exponents, is a condition of anxiety brought on by rapidly changing social conditions. J. Webb, *The Occult Establishment* (La Salle, IL, Open Court, 1976), pp. 7–19.

16 E. S. Turner, *Dear Old Blighty* (London, Michael Joseph, 1980), p. 137. Samuel Hynes takes a similar view with respect to the physicist Oliver Lodge who lost a son during the Great war and was also a convert to Spiritualism: *The Edwardian Frame of Mind* (Princeton, NJ, Princeton University Press, 1968), pp. 145–6. However, Lodge's *Survival of Man* (London, Methuen, 1911) shows that he was convinced of the persistence of life after death several years before the outbreak of war.

17 J. Hedley-Brooke, 'Science in History: Some Problems with the Secularization Thesis', unpublished paper, University of Melbourne, 7 July, 1994. Joy Dixon makes a similar point in the context of her study of the Theosophy movement in England between 1880 and 1935: 'Gender, Politics and Culture in the New Age: Theosophy in England, 1880–1935' (PhD dissertation, Rutgers University, 1993). The historical persistence of the interconnectedness of 'science' and 'religion' in shaping elite culture and gender relations is vividly illustrated in D. Noble's *World without Women: The Christian Clerical Culture of Western Science* (New York, Alfred Knopf, 1992).

18 L. Barrow, *Independent Spirits: Spiritualism and English Plebeians 1850–1910* (London, Routledge & Kegan Paul, 1986). See also J. F. C. Harrison, 'Early Victorian Radicals and the Medical Fringe', in W. Bynum and R. Porter (eds), *Medical Fringe and Medical Orthodoxy* (London, Croom Helm, 1987), pp. 198–215, which links nineteenth-century Spiritualism with utopian socialist politics. Williams, 'The Making of Victorian Psychical Research', ch. 8, contrasts the elite epistemology of psychical researchers with the more democratic epistemology of Spiritualists, and comments on the ensuing conflict between the two groups.

19 A. Owen, *The Darkened Room: Women, Power and Spiritualism in Late*

Victorian England (London, Virago, 1989); Owen, 'Women and Nineteenth-Century Spiritualism: Strategies in the Subversion of Femininity', in J. Obelkevich *et al.* (eds), *Disciplines of Faith* (London, Routledge, 1987), pp. 130–53. Other texts that explore power and knowledge in relation to female mediumship in the nineteenth century include V. Skultans, 'Mediums, Controls and Eminent Men', in P. Holden (ed.), *Women's Religious Experience* (London, Croom Helm, 1983), pp. 27–55; J. Walkowitz, *City of Dreadful Delight: Narratives of Sexual Danger in Late Victorian London* (London, Virago, 1992), ch. 6. Diana Basham explores the Victorian world of the unconscious in the association she makes between interest in the occult and taboos surrounding menstruation: *The Trial of Women: Feminism and the Occult Sciences in Victorian Literature and Culture* (London, Macmillan, 1992).

20 Owen, *The Darkened Room*; Owen, 'Women and Nineteenth-Century Spiritualism', pp. 130–53. See also Skultans, 'Mediums, Controls and Eminent Men'; Walkowitz, *City of Dreadful Delight*, ch. 6; D. Burfield, 'Theosophy and Feminism', in Holden (ed.), *Women's Religious Experience* pp. 27–55; Braude, *Radical Spirits*.

21 Podmore, *The Newer Spiritualism*, Book I, ch. 1. Podmore considered Home to be fraudulent.

22 According to the supporters of the Schneider brothers, caged musical boxes played by themselves and tables bumped about in their presence: Price, *Search for Truth*, ch. XV. For a more recent commentary on Willi Schneider, see Inglis, *A History of the Paranormal*, pp. 105–13.

23 A. Vout Peters was one of the mediums whom Lodge believed had contacted the spirit of his dead son, Raymond, who was killed in the First World War. O. Lodge, *Raymond*, 7th edn (London, Methuen, 1917).

24 George Lawton estimated that four-fifths of mediums practising in Britain in the 1930s were women: *The Drama of Life after Death: A Study of the Spiritualist Religion* (New York, Henry Holt, 1932), p. 181. Muriel Hankey provides a list of mediums who worked at the British College for Psychic Science between 1920 and 1929, most of whom were women: M. Hankey, *James Hewat McKenzie: Pioneer of Psychical Research* (London, Aquarian Press, 1963), pp. 57–9.

25 E. Carpenter, *Intermediate Types among Primitive Folks: A Study in Social Evolution* (London, George Allen, 1914), p. 48.

26 J. Weeks, *Sex, Politics and Society: The Regulation of Sexuality Since 1880* (London, Longman, 1990); *Chushichi Tsuzuki, Edward Carpenter, 1844–1929: A Prophet of Human Fellowship* (Cambridge, Cambridge University Press, 1980).

27 Alex Owen makes a similar point with respect to the perceived 'effeminacy' of the nineteenth-century medium Daniel D. Home: Owen, *The Darkened Room*, p. 10.

28 A. Powell, *What's Become of Waring?* (London, Cassell, 1939), p. 28.

29 Mass-Observation Archive, University of Sussex, Topic Collection: Astrology and Spiritualism 1/B, 'Report on Spiritual Centre, Princess Chambers, Fold Street', 1937.

30 Braude, *Radical Spirits.*

31 See especially Owen, *The Darkened Room*; Owen, 'Women and Nineteenth-Century Spiritualism', pp. 130–53; Walkowitz, *City of Dreadful Delight*, ch. 6.

32 S. Benhabib, 'Feminism and the Question of Postmodernism', *in Situating the Self: Gender, Community and Postmodernism in Contemporary* Ethics (London, Routledge, 1992).

33 *Ibid.*, p. 216.

Spiritualism after the Great War

Most historians treat Spiritualism as a Victorian and Edwardian phenomenon. A proliferation of literature describing how English culture was transformed intellectually and aesthetically under the banner of modernism has perhaps reinforced this assumption.[1] As Jay Winter points out, such literature tends to 'obscure the continuity of traditional forms of thought into the war period and beyond'.[2] In *Sites of Memory, Sites of Mourning*, Winter explores Spiritualism's power to capture the religious imagination of soldiers at the Front. The experiences of the trenches eluded conventional theological explanation, and legends concerning the supernatural abounded. In civilian circles bereavement was to become a national experience, mourning a community activity. In this emotional climate, stories of the return of the dead were common.[3] Some observers at the battlefront saw strange figures who, after tending the wounded, instantly and inexplicably disappeared.[4] Others insisted that a ghostly army helped to defend the British troops at Mons. Arthur Machen originally told this story in *The Bowmen and Other Legends* (1915), and it quickly became a symbol of hope and encouragement to both troops and the civilian population. It is easy to see why, for the rhythmic call of the angelic archers overflows with a passionate religiosity that blends Christian, pagan and patriotic motifs:

> 'St. George! St. George!'
> 'Ha! Messiah; ha! sweet Saint, grant us good deliverance!'
> 'St. George for merry England!'

'Harrow! Harrow! Monseigneur St. George succour us.'
'Ha! St. George! Ha! St. George! A long bow and a strong bow.'
'Heaven's Knight, aid us.'

Then a line of shining archers could be seen beyond the trenches. They drew their bows, and a cloud of arrows flew through the air towards the 'German hosts'.[5] Legends such as these recalled the Spiritualist doctrine of another world from which spirits of the dead returned to help and console the citizens of this world.

Yet Spiritualism's attraction is not explained simply by the exceptional circumstances of mass bereavement,[6] since it continued to gain in popularity at least up to the outbreak of World War II. Geoffrey Nelson, the only historian to comment in any detail on Spiritualism in the postwar period, designates the 1930s as its 'high water mark'.[7] My own research supports this view, and in this chapter I present some thoughts on how and why Spiritualism continued to make converts during the interwar years. My argument is that Spiritualism's success lay partly in its ability to adapt to modern tropes, but chiefly in its capacity to incorporate and co-ordinate traditional thoughts and beliefs.

The rise of Spiritualism between the wars

In the nineteenth century, Spiritualism attracted converts from across the social spectrum, finding its largest body of support among radically minded 'plebeians' – the Owenites, herbalists, and Methodists – of the North of England.[8] In the twentieth century Spiritualism had retained its eclectic membership, with a preponderance towards what one prominent medium described as the 'superior working class',[9] and the number of people who identified as Spiritualists grew rapidly nationwide.[10]

In 1914, there were 145 societies affiliated to the Spiritualists' National Union (SNU); by 1919 there were 309.[11] In 1932, the newly established Spiritualist London-based journal *Psychic News* announced that there were 500 societies affiliated to the SNU.[12] In reply to an enquiry from a committee acting for the Archbishop of Canterbury in 1937, the secretary of the SNU said that there were now 520 affiliated societies distributed throughout Britain. He estimated that there were 'twice as many meeting places' not connected with the Union.[13] These figures did not include attendance at the Marylebone Spiritualist Association, the second largest Spiritualist organisation in the country after the SNU,[14] or meetings at the Queen's Hall, the Grotian Hall and the Aeolion Hall, where famous mediums gave inspirational addresses and psychic demonstrations. Both London and provincial-based meetings were very popular. The medium Helen Hughes regularly addressed an audience of 3,000 or more;[15] while 9,000 people gathered at the Royal Albert Hall for the opportunity to witness Estelle Roberts speaking to the dead. According to the honorary vice-president of the SNU, applications in October 1938 to see Roberts give five further demonstrations totalled 60,000.[16] As well as consolidating their organisational base, many Spiritualists continued to propound the importance of informal home circles for discovering and developing psychic powers. In June 1932, a journalist for *Psychic News* felt confident that there were approximately 100,000 home seance circles operating in Britain.[17]

The Spiritualist press exaggerated,[18] but publications dealing with spirits and the spirit world were undoubtedly popular. Oliver Lodge's *Raymond* (1916), and Arthur Conan Doyle's *New Revelation* (1918) and *The Vital Message* (1919), attained the status of Spiritualist classics in the interwar period. Perhaps the single most successful Spiritualist publication was *On the Edge of the Etheric* (1931), by Arthur Findlay, an enthusiastic worker for Spiritualism and a prolific writer on the subject. In 1920 he founded the Glasgow Society for Psychical Research, and was co-founder of Psychic Press. He was once vice-president of the SNU and president of the London Spiritualist Alliance.[19] *On the Edge of the Etheric* was reprinted twenty-five times between November 1931 and June 1932 and, according to *Psychic News*, sold at the rate of 500 copies per week. In its first year of publication the book ran to thirty impressions, and was subsequently translated into nineteen languages.[20] A reviewer for the *Journal of the American Society of Psychical Research* said that it 'is today the most widely read book on Spiritualism in the world'.[21]

Celebrity conversions to Spiritualism helped to promote public interest in the subject. Doll Lewis, a former domestic servant, now in her eighties, told me that Sir Oliver Lodge's belief in Spiritualism was public knowledge in the 1930s. She and her family used to listen to his wireless broadcasts, in which he talked about his Spiritualist convictions and expressed his views about the nature of the afterworld.[22] Arthur Conan Doyle was just as enthusiastic as Lodge in his support of Spiritualism. He visited many countries on lecture tours, and was president of several Spiritualist institutions.[23] Another influential convert to Spirit-ualism was Hannen Swaffer, a well-known Fleet Street journalist. He succeeded Conan Doyle as president of the SNU, and wrote a regular feature in *Psychic News* detailing the activities of his home circle. In 1925 he published the circumstances of his conversion in *Northcliffe's Return*. More equivocal in his approach to Spiritualism was the contro-versial Harry Price. In 1923 Price founded his National Laboratory of Psychical Research, and proceeded to proclaim his views loudly on every aspect of psychical research. Price proved something of a mixed blessing to Spiritualism, since he claimed to have exposed several promi-nent mediums in fraudulent acts. On the other hand, there were some mediums he wholeheartedly endorsed, including Rudi Schneider, Eileen Garrett and the medium known as Stella C.[24] Price's main contribution to Spiritualism was the publicity it received through him. He repeatedly became embroiled in one controversy or another – sometimes with Spiritualists themselves, sometimes with sceptics who refused to accept the validity of his research. His flamboyant personality and aggressive approach to his opponents made his exploits favourite topics for journalists and wireless broadcasters.[25]

Besides the increased availability of Spiritualist literature, the establish-ment of Spiritualist societies and the regularity of public debates on the subject, we can point to the establishment in the interwar years of some privately controlled organisations founded for developing psychic powers. The most notable of these was the British College of Psychic Science, founded by Hewat and Barbara McKenzie in 1920. The Mc-Kenzies were leading figures in Spiritualist circles, though neither was raised as a Spiritualist. Barbara McKenzie came from a devout Pres-byterian family with Labour Party connections in the north of Scotland. One of her brothers entered the Presbyterian ministry; another was a great friend of Ramsay MacDonald. In 1890, when Barbara was just twenty years old, she left her job as a trainee teacher to join the London Civil Service as a clerk. It was in London five years later that she met and married James Hewat McKenzie.[26]

Hewat McKenzie's early life had some things in common with his wife's. He too came from a devout Christian family in Scotland, 'almost Calvinistic in its harsh discipline'.[27] He left school at thirteen to join his father's ironmongery and tool-making business but, driven by the bourgeois imperative to 'improve', he read avidly of 'the classics'. Hewat left his home for London when he was nineteen – in his case to escape from what his biographer described as 'the petty tyranny of his father'.[28] Once in London he worked long hours, saved, and eventually establish- ed his own building firm and estate agent's business among several other successful business ventures.

Early in their marriage, the McKenzies' main interests centred around their local Presbyterian church and the Adult Education movement. However, Hewat soon rebelled against the religion of his father, just as he had rebelled against other paternal restrictions and expectations, and he and Barbara became converts to Spiritualism.[29] Hewat McKenzie was genuinely committed to Spiritualism, but he was also aware of the commercial possibilities of a college devoted to its study and practice. The McKenzies' resolve to establish a college of this sort was stiffened by an incident with the American medium Almira Brockway. In 1916 they invited Brockway to England to investigate her mediumship. Shortly after her arrival, she was arrested and prosecuted under the existing legislation, Clause 4 of the Vagrancy Act 1824. Spiritualists complained that the existing legislation persecuted mediums and maligned Spiritual- ists. As one prominent Spiritualist, Louise Lind-af-Hageby, said:

> under clause 4 of the Vagrancy Act, those who claim to possess supernormal gifts are classed as imposters. The Act does not make allowance for genuine gifts. It is not cognisant of the 'respectability' of Spiritualism; it assumes that all demands for the exercise of psychic faculties come from rogues and vagabonds. This makes the use of this old Act not only offensive, but ridiculous.[30]

Despite vehement protests from Spiritualists and many attempts by the McKenzies to secure bail for her, Brockway was remanded to Holloway Prison until her trial. She was subsequently convicted of fraud, fined heavily, and deported as an undesirable alien. It was this experience, wrote Barbara McKenzie in later years, 'which decided us to found a centre where mediums could be housed on the premises and as employ- ees of our institution be preserved from such brutal attacks'.[31] The institution flourished until the death of Hewat McKenzie in 1929, and claimed many a successful medium as its own prodigy. Barbara, with some outside help, maintained the college until 1939, when it was amalgamated with the International Institute for Psychical Investigation.[32]

Another indication of Spiritualism's popular appeal was the unease with which conventional religious sects followed its progress in the years following the Great War. Since its inception in the mid-1840s in America, Spiritualism had never received official endorsement from any religious body.[33] As Anglican church membership went into decline in the 1930s,[34] however, certain members of the Church hierarchy began to eye Spiritualism's expanded following with concern. In 1937 the Archbishop of Canterbury appointed a committee of ten, chaired by Francis Underhill, Bishop of Bath, '[t]o investigate the subject of communications with discarnate spirits and the claims of Spiritualism in relation to the Christian Faith'.[35] According to this committee, the parochial clergy continually reported that members of their congregations were attracted to Spiritualism because of the evidence it provided for survival, and because of the consolation and guidance it offered.[36] One witness, described as 'a typical churchman', took up with Spiritualism after suffering a bereavement. He said that 'until he studied spiritualism he was beginning to lose interest in religious life because he did not hear anything that he had not heard many times before. Spiritualism, on the other hand, seemed to bring some new teaching which was alive and which had given him a new interest in spiritual things.'[37]

The committee was divided about the validity and value of spirit communications. The majority of the members felt that if none of the 'fundamental Christian obligations or values' was unchanged by the acceptance of the 'possibility of communication with discarnate spirits', then 'those who have the assurance that they have been in touch with their departed friends, may rightly accept the sense of enlargement and of unbroken fellowship which it brings.' The Minority Report concluded that there was 'no evidence which would convince a scientist or an open minded layman that Spiritualists do communicate with discarnate spirits' and that such 'alleged communications may not only be valueless but may also be misleading and therefore dangerous'.[38] Committee members agreed, however, that Church people had 'drifted towards Spiritualism' because of the Church of England's failure to satisfy their desire to pray for their dead:

> The Church of England, for reasons of past controversy, has been altogether too cautious in its reference to the departed. Anglican prayers for the departed do not satisfy people's needs, because the prayers are so careful in their language that it is not always evident that the departed are being prayed for, as contrasted with the living. In general, we need much more freedom in our recognition of the

living unity of the whole church, in this world and in that which lies beyond death.[39]

Whereas some influential members of the Anglican clergy hoped to combat conversions to Spiritualism by placing renewed emphasis on prayers for the dead, the Catholic Church remained unreservedly hostile to Spiritualists, viewing them as dangerous pretenders to sacred communion. Catholic publications insisted that demonic spirits inspired psychic manifestations, and seance practices threatened the spiritual and mental health of participants.[40] However, the distaste with which Catholicism traditionally viewed Spiritualism was now accompanied by marked signs of anxiety, and special campaigns were initiated to combat the perceived threat Spiritualism posed to religious life. In 1926, a society called the Catholic Crusade Against Spiritualism was formed. Its founders feared that Spiritualism accounted 'for considerable leakage among Catholics', and proposed, by means of lectures, to 'expose the dangers which follow the practice of the cult'.[41]

In more secular circles, Spiritualism's ability to attract new converts in the 1920s and 1930s may have been bound up with its appeal to contemporary democratic values. Radical egalitarianism was characteristic of nineteenth-century Spiritualism,[42] and later generations of Spiritualists continued to uphold democratic traditions. In 1932, Hannen Swaffer reminded the readers of *Psychic News* that 'Spiritualism is never destined, as such, to be a movement possessing power and authority, that its principles are permeative, not exclusive … [It] is a democracy, and every member of every church has a right to his own point of view.'[43] Spiritualism was thus well placed to capitalise on the contemporary cult of the 'average man' or, colloquially, 'the man on the Clapham Omnibus'. The 'average man', imagined as unintellectual, but intelligent; 'independently minded', but with a 'healthy respect for the facts', and endowed with unerring 'common sense', gained currency in the increasingly insistent egalitarianism of the interwar years. D. L. LeMahieu has argued that the identification of commercial culture with its 'lower class' consumers assisted the democratizing process:

> Commercial culture served the self-interest of its producers.
> Yet it also served the self-determined interests of the audience who supported it with their pocket-books. For shrewd business reasons, commercial culture could not afford to alienate its intended public. It could not afford to treat them like subordinates, pupils or

'masses'. It could not afford to ignore or patronize the average individual. Commercial culture was fundamentally egalitarian because it
collapsed the distance between a communicator and a public.[44]

With this new alliance between communicator and public, the discourse
of the 'man in the street' cropped up in all kinds of situations, and
underpinned a variety of political interests. The interwar tabloid newspapers – *Express*, *Herald*, *Chronicle*, *Mail*, *Mirror* and *Daily Sketch* – all
employed the mythical 'man in the street' to support wildly divergent
political positions. The 'common sense' of the 'average man' could be
adapted to collective trade-union interests, or used to underpin the
electoral hegemony of the interwar Conservative Party.[45] Such rhetoric
frequently incorporated a distinct anti-elitist, anti-intellectual flavour.
The following passage from the reminiscences of a retired police
sergeant, Alec Comryn, was typical:

> [L]ately the experts have come to some awesome conclusions about
> these [criminal] youths. The criminologists will tell us they have in-
> herited dangerous gene combinations; the endocrinists will tell us
> they are subpituary, hyper-thyroid or superadrenal; the alienists will
> tell us they are unbalanced; worse than any of these, the moralists,
> amateur and professional, will tell us they are just plain bad and beyond
> redemption.
>   A lot of this is ballyhoo, and we ought to be on our guard against
> it lest it make too deep inroads into our common sense.[46]

The founding of Mass-Observation in 1937 by Charles Madge, Tom
Harrisson and Humphrey Jennings, for the purpose of documenting the
experience of everyday life in Britain, also testified to the growing
importance attached to the opinions of 'ordinary people'. The reports
written for Mass-Observation, said Madge in 1937, 'come largely from
people whose behaviour, language and viewpoint are far removed from
academic science. Sociologists and realist novelists – including proletarian
novelists – find it difficult if not impossible to describe the texture of
this world'.[47] Two years later Madge praised the work of Mass-
Observation's amateur observers, whom he described as 'ordinary
hardworking folk' who are 'also intelligent and interested enough to
help us'.[48]

Spiritualists made full use of the rhetoric of the 'common sense' of
the 'average man'. In 1926, the journal *Light* celebrated Spiritualism's
origins 'among the common people' and the fact that '[o]ur spirit friends

have never been much concerned about convincing scientists, or appealing to the intellectuals, but they have gone all out to help those who had the "intelligence of the heart".[49]

Arthur Findlay's *On the Edge of the Etheric* successfully exploited the legendary good sense of the 'man in the street' on behalf of Spiritualism. The *Morning Post* said that Findlay brought 'a fund of sound common sense to the study of what is now often called Psychics'; the *Birmingham Gazette* considered that Mr Findlay was 'clearly a careful recorder, with a Scotsman's respect for facts'; and the *Aberdeen Evening Express* commented that the book dealt with evidence of survival after death in 'a sound commonsense manner'. Many other reviewers of the book expressed similar sentiments.[50] On the other hand, the voice of 'everyman' could be – and was – employed to discredit Spiritualist claims. Elliot O'Donnell, a prolific writer on ghost-haunting and polemicist on occult subjects, vigorously opposed Spiritualism (from motives that will be addressed in Chapter 4). His polemical technique included frequent mention of the supposed aversion of the 'average man' to Spiritualism. In his book published under the unambiguous title, *The Menace of Spiritualism* (1920), he wrote:

> To the ordinary average man who is neither very religious nor very eminent, but who has plenty of common sense, Spiritualism can only appear as a hotch-potch of imbecility, gullibility, and roguery – a hotch-potch that has been of benefit to no one, saving those who have filled their pockets out of it.[51]

Nevertheless, Spiritualism's appeal to 'common sense' and other popular egalitarian postures helped to enhance its attraction and expand its constituency.

Spiritualist deployment of the 'average man' could counter the hegemony of 'expert' culture; even so, Spiritualists repeatedly associated their own phenomena with scientific concepts and modern technology. Not only did this serve propaganda purposes (in that it aimed to endow the movement with a certain scientific *cachet*), it was also to do with the search for an adequate language to describe Spiritualist ideas and experiences. Mediumship became analogous with the telephone and wireless. Just as people 'tuned in' to wireless broadcasts, so 'sensitives' 'tuned in' to the 'other world'.[52] Throughout the general population, to 'tune in' became a standard means of representing telepathic experience and feelings of empathy. One woman, canvassed by a Mass-Observation survey in 1947, thought that '[s]ome people are so much "in tune" that they often think and speak the same words simultaneously. If you think of someone, they often, if in tune, think of you, hence the tiresome habit letters have of "crossing" each other'.[53] To be 'on the right wavelength' was a favourite synonym for 'tuning in'. Helen Hughes wondered if her ability to hear spirit voices more or less clearly, according to where she was standing, was to do with different kinds of wavelengths.[54]

Seance activity mixed the familiar with the uncanny. As wireless became even more popular as a source of information, entertainment and communication after the Second World War, conversations with the spirit world seemed to follow conversational conventions established in listener participation shows like 'Family Favourites'.[55] The spirit messages relayed by the medium Doris Stokes sounded like those sent via this show by members of the Forces overseas to friends and relatives at home. Stokes wrote about a spirit called Reg, who communicated with his family and friends in the following way: 'First he sent his love to Connie, then he said, "I'd like to be remembered to Mrs Fall who speaks at the church and to my old friend Bill Strickland" ... Then he wished his wife happy birthday in advance, gave his daughter's name, Frances, and his sister-in-law's, Pat.'[56]

Spiritualists struggled to explain – and to justify – their understanding of the indestructibility of human, animal and plant life through reference to scientific terms such as protons, electrons, atoms and the ether. Protons and electrons, explained Findlay, are 'linked together [in the atom] by the invisible ether, which is ... the basic substance of the universe', and the material from which both the physical world and the spirit world are made.[57] More than anything, however, Spiritualists emphasised that their claims were scientifically based on 'the steady accumulation of facts'.[58] Several contemporary observers considered that this attention to empirical evidence gave Spiritualism an advantage over competing religions. Arthur Ponsonby, aristocrat, socialist, rationalist, religious sceptic and Parliamentary MP, was ready to concede that 'the spiritualist cannot be ignored because he declares he has tangible proof of life after death. He has a large following, greatly increased since the war.' Somewhat despondently, Ponsonby added that Spiritualism was 'more in favour' in the 1930s than it had been the generation before.[59]

The afterlife

Historians of nineteenth-century Spiritualism traditionally seize upon the fact that Spiritualists offered to *prove* survival. In view of this, it is often claimed that Spiritualism was symptomatic of widespread feelings of anxiety about the threat posed to the tenets of Christianity by science. Confronted with a scientised universe consisting only of blind matter and force, people, it is argued, turned to Spiritualism in an attempt to rationalise faith and restore the comforts of religion.[60]

Conversion to Spiritualism was a more complex process than a simple rationalisation of irrational impulses. In the rest of this chapter I shall argue that Spiritualism's power of persuasion was rooted in its ability to elicit and co-ordinate a variety of fugitive and fragmented supernaturalisms buried in modernity. The people considered here did not turn to Spiritualism to shore up failing faith in a metaphysical universe. For many, the supernatural realities of their lives were omnipresent; for some, they were burdensome. What Spiritualism offered to such individuals was a way of organising supernatural experiences and assumptions in relation to existing cultural realities.

Let us begin with some childhood experiences of Eileen Garrett, a celebrated medium in the 1930s. Garrett grew up with her Protestant aunt and uncle in County Meath, Ireland.[61] In her autobiography, *Many Voices*, she recalled a turn-of-the-century childhood steeped in a mysticism and theological heterodoxy that extended to her staid and otherwise conventional aunt and uncle. Her uncle, generally regarded as a 'good Christian man', thoroughly believed in the wailing spirit of the banshee. So did her aunt, for she heard them talking about this wailing wraith on several occasions: '"I heard the banshee last night – the time is not far away for someone to depart", they would say, with a certain poetic melancholy, but at the same time with a kind of gentle, objective acceptance.'[62] According to Garrett, the banshee was part of fairy lore, 'which was regarded by the country folk as more potent than their religious practices'. Eileen became deeply involved with the magical powers which, she felt, 'lay hidden all around'. On her way to school she made primrose and cowslip wreaths, and left messages to reassure the spirits of her goodwill.[63] She listened in the evenings to the stories of her neighbours, who believed in creatures who 'surpassed human beings in knowledge and power' – creatures who liked music, dancing and bright colours, and came and went oblivious of time. And she remembered in later years how this ancient belief in a race of fairy beings 'neither divine nor human, existing apart on a "plane" different from humans, but occupying the same space, tended to give one a perpetual sense of never being alone'.[64]

This story of creatures existing on a different plane, yet occupying the same space, is strikingly analogous to Spiritualist and occult conceptions of the relationship between this world and the next. In *On the Edge of the Etheric*, Arthur Findlay set out the Spiritualist theory of this relationship:

> The ether of space can now be taken as the one great unifying link between the world of matter and that of spirit; it is the substance common to both worlds. Both are contained within this substance, both are parts of it, both are formed out of it. The two worlds are part of the same universe.[65]

Theosophists, whatever their theoretical differences with Spiritualists on other matters, tended to corroborate Findlay's view of interacting planes of existence. William Judge explained in his Theosophical teaching text that 'Akaska [meaning ether] is the connecting link between matter on one side, and spirit-mind on the other.'[66] Similarly, Dion Fortune, a well-known occultist[67] and author of many books on the subject, isolated four main planes of existence. Each of these was 'real in every sense of the word; each tangible according to its type; each with its own natural laws; and each interacting with the systems next to it' in ethereal density.[68]

However, it was the famous physicist and convert to Spiritualism Sir Oliver Lodge who was the first to popularise the ether as the means of immortality: In line with the prevailing nineteenth-century view of ether, Lodge described it as the 'universal connecting medium which binds the universe together, and makes it a coherent whole instead of a chaotic collection of independent isolated fragments'. Going beyond the scope of orthodox accounts, he considered that it was by means of this sublime medium that the soul of the 'Unseen Universe' might penetrate and inspire the 'Mind' of humankind.[69]

Just as the ether united matter and spirit in the cosmos, so it linked the human body to its soul or spirit. Hewat McKenzie described this relation in his book *Spirit Intercourse*. He imagined the human as a triune being composed of a material body, a spirit and an 'ethereal counterpart'.

This counterpart was 'so refined in its nature' that it was invisible to ordinary eyesight. The ethereal counterpart and the spirit survived into the next world and were able, under circumstances known to Spiritualists, to return to this world.[70] When Lodge wrote his book *Raymond*, he had accepted that things and humans 'have ethereal counterparts, in an ethereal world'. 'Perhaps everything', he wrote, 'has already an ethereal counterpart of which our senses tell us the material aspect only'.[71] Lodge wrote *Raymond* following the death of his son of that name in the Great War. He devoted several sections to verbatim reports of conversations with Raymond, relayed mostly through the mediumship of Gladys Leonard. Raymond described a spirit world which, in many respects, mirrored our own. The spirits of the dead, in their ethereal form and surroundings, continued to eat, wear clothes, work, live in houses and enjoy gardens. Some even retained their earthly craving for whisky and cigars.[72]

The revelation that Raymond drank whisky and smoked cigars provoked hoots of incredulous laughter from sceptics. Nevertheless, the book was extremely popular and influential. Part of its appeal lay precisely in the fact that Raymond's description of the spirit sphere matched expectations in heterodox pockets of Christianity, where continuity between matter and spirit, earth-life and afterlife, was already assumed. Between 1937 and 1947 Mass-Observation asked individuals from various walks of life about their conception of heaven. Many respondents anticipated that life would continue after death on a 'higher plane' of existence. Some envisaged this new plane of existence in some tangible form. One working-class woman was sure she would see the people she loved in heaven, or 'there wouldn't be any point in it'. She hoped that people would not 'just sit around enjoying themselves', and that work would be available.[73]

In *A Clergyman's Daughter* (1935), George Orwell portrayed a rural community in which Anglicanism shaded off into Spiritualistic notions of the 'other world'. The story, set in the 1930s, concentrates on the collapse of Dorothy's religious faith. Before she succumbs to atheism, in the form of a thoroughgoing attack of amnesia, Orwell pictures her ministering to two of her father's parishioners, Mr and Mrs Pither:

> Mrs Pither talked some more about Heaven. It was extraordinary how constantly Heaven reigned in her thoughts; and more extraordinary yet was the actuality, the vividness with which she could see it. The golden streets and the gates of orient pearl were as real to her as

though they had been actually before her eyes. And her vision extended to the most concrete, the most earthly details. The softness of
the beds up there! The deliciousness of the food! The lovely silk
clothes that you would put on clean every morning! The surcease
from everlasting to everlasting from work of any description!... Her
faith was almost *too* great, if that is possible.[74]

Such beliefs were, of course, passed on to children, and as one contemporary schoolteacher noticed, with so many children bereaved during
the Great War, the subjects of death and the afterlife were at the
forefront of classroom discussion. At this teacher's school in the East
End of London, the comments of children between the ages of eight
and eleven revealed strongly material expectations of the afterlife.
Heaven was a place where one could 'see God', the 'people in Heaven',
'the lovely green grass' and other 'beautiful sights'.[75]

A competition organised by the *Sunday Dispatch* in 1940 revealed that
many people dreamed of postmortem survival and of reunion with dead
loved ones. The newspaper offered to award a prize for what 'readers
considered the best film fade-out they had seen'. Mass-Observation
analysts handled the findings and were struck by 'the emphasis on
supernatural endings ...: 20 per cent of the votes cast were for fade-
outs with the spirits of the dead living happily in the other world though
they could not do so in this'. The most popular fade-out was *The Three
Comrades* (1938), where two dead comrades beckon the third to join
them. *Smilin' Through* (1932), which dealt with the theme of communication between the dead and living, was also popular.[76]

Although Anglican theologians endorsed prayers for the dead, this
did not imply acceptance of Spiritualist or other 'popular' beliefs about
heaven. The battle undertaken by the representatives of both official
Catholicism and official Protestantism in post-Reformation Europe to
dispel 'superstitious' thought[77] persisted into the twentieth century.
Members of the clergy tended to attribute the tenacity of a material
concept of heaven to 'bad education' and the social consequences of
unemployment in the interwar years. One Anglo-Catholic priest remarked of his parishioners:

They talk glibly about heaven and the angels, and think their children
are going to be little angels in a place where some of the frightful
difficulties now besetting them just *are not*. Like Oliver Lodge and
Raymond ... who was supposed to have said there was very good
whisky there, they hope there'll be very good beer.[78]

Another clergyman held similar views: 'Most of them look forward after death to some hope of conditions that are easier – an escape from the troubles of life. And certainly there are a few spiritualistic ideas floating about in their heads.'[79]

In this cultural atmosphere, Spiritualist evidence about the continuity of life after death was redundant. Spiritualism made its appeal to those who recognised in the spirit plane of existence their own vision of heaven. Of more interest to these people than 'proof' of survival was information about the experience of death, the nature of a future life, and the whereabouts and condition of deceased loved ones. The questions put to the spirit of twenty-two-year-old Lester Coltman, killed at Cambrai in 1917, were typical of the kinds of concerns displayed by relatives and friends of the deceased: *'Tell us of your actual death.' 'Please tell us what you can of the pleasures of the world in which you find yourself.' 'Please tell us more as to your Actual Surroundings.' 'Tell us of Your Intercourse with earth.'*[80] A proliferation of literature supplied such information; the authors professed to have gleaned their knowledge directly from spirit-guides. Hewat McKenzie described life on the 'other side' in the most minute detail: the process of death, immediate circumstances of the newly dead, climate, education, housing, marriage customs and working patterns.[81] McKenzie's idea of life 'on the other side' was, in many ways, an idealised version of this life – a version that drew on a well-established utopian tradition, exemplified in William Morris's *News from Nowhere*.[82] Conan Doyle presented a similar view:

> The life has a close analogy to that of this world at its best. It is pre-eminently a life of the mind, as this is of the body. Preoccupations of food, money, lust, pain, etc., are of the body and are gone. Music, the Arts, intellectual and spiritual knowledge, and progress have increased. The people are clothed, as one would expect, since there is no reason why modesty should disappear with our new forms. These new forms are the absolute reproduction of the old ones at their best, the young growing up and the old reverting until all come to the normal. People live in communities, as one would expect if like attracts like, and the male spirit still finds his true mate though there is no sexuality in the grosser sense and no childbirth.[83]

This compensatory, idealised postmortem existence was available to most people. For those who, for reasons of 'bad conduct' in this life, found themselves on the lowest of the seven spirit planes of existence, there was always the opportunity to 'improve' and 'progress' to a higher plane.[84]

The return of the dead

Acceptance of the continuity of mundane existence in another world made communication with that world seem inevitable. Legends about the return, or continued presence of dead relatives and acquaintances flourished in rural and urban areas. In Lincolnshire, right up to the 1950s, it was common for widows to have their photographs taken standing behind their late husband's chair. A Tattershall woman explained that '[o]nce Dad had gone, you still kept his chair for him ... Mam didn't use it because when the chair was empty, part of Dad was still there.'[85] The Irish banshee was also associated with the family, it being a 'disembodied soul' who had reason to love or hate a particular family. If the former, the banshee would sing in tender tones, giving notice of the 'close proximity of the angel of death'; if the latter, 'the cry [was] the scream of a fiend, howling with demoniac delight over the coming death agony of another' of its enemies.[86]

The most ubiquitous supernatural entity in folklore was the ghost. Ghosts, for many people, were a part of daily life – something to be endured or avoided like inclement weather. In Salford during the years leading up to the First World War, houses in Robert Roberts's working-class district rarely 'stood vacant for longer than a fortnight before ghosts got in'.[87] In this setting, Spiritualist theories were easily absorbed. While one of Roberts's neighbours stoically endured the intrusive ghost of her mother, his other neighbour attempted to 'call up' spirits of the departed through the seances he held regularly in his parlour.[88] Publications dealing with the phenomenon of ghosts abounded in the inter-war period. Perhaps no single author exceeded the output of Elliot O'Donnell, who produced over forty books on ghosts and allied subjects. In 1954 O'Donnell recalled how, over several decades, he had given many talks on the phenomenon to 'all kinds of audiences and in all kinds of places'. After these talks, people were always eager to tell him of their own experiences with the supernatural.[89]

Spiritualists thought that spirit entities manifested themselves in various ways. They conveyed messages through the control of a medium's vocal organs, or they controlled the medium's hands during automatic writing. Sometimes a spirit would duplicate poltergeist manifestations by making its presence felt through rapping noises and the movement of furniture. Occasionally, spirit figures were observed; it was in this form that spirits mimicked the traditional ghost. In 1932, a contributor to *Psychic News* described one of these manifestations:

> The [human like] forms manifested on this second occasion were, I thought, a little lacking in clearness and power. Nevertheless, they were essentially of the same type – that is, shining with a curious phosphorescent sheen in the ruby light and entirely self-luminous.[90]

Spirits and ghosts heralded their coming in a similar manner. Cold draughts and the rustle of fabrics often acted as preludes to spirit and ghost activity. Spiritualists sometimes said that the ectoplasm (a denser form of ether) produced at seances was cold and clammy in texture.[91] Gladys Leonard, made famous through her connection with Oliver Lodge, described a spirit manifestation at a seance that was indistinguishable from traditional ghost appearances. First, participants felt a chill in the room. Then appeared an apparition of a woman who looked 'exactly like a lovely statue of marble or alabaster'. She seemed 'to glide over the floor without moving her legs or feet', and she passed through their linked hands. The 'cold became a hundred times more intense'.[92] Similarly, Doris Stokes located the presence of a spirit in a house by sudden drops in temperature. This is how she did it: 'You walk through the rooms, backwards and forwards and if there is anything there, you'll come to a place which feels like cold bathwater. As you stand in this spot, an icy sensation creeps up from your feet over your whole body.'[93]

Whereas Spiritualists insisted that their spirits were for the most part benign, ghosts were usually regarded as malign. According to Elliot O'Donnell, 'evil people' were more likely to attract ghosts, but in certain circumstances 'good people' might find themselves so afflicted.[94] In either case, the prognosis was not hopeful:

> In some houses there is an indefinable, mysterious something in the atmosphere that endangers the morals; in others a something that endangers the mentality; and in others a something that endangers the morality and mentality. Maybe it is the lingering, harboured thoughts of a former occupant, or very possibly an invisible spirit entity.[95]

Thus a ghost, or 'evil atmosphere' perceived in a particular home tended to cast doubt on the sanity and 'moral fibre' of its occupants.

Before she became a Spiritualist medium, sinister 'voices' troubled Helen Hughes. Hughes grew up among Methodists, but this did not prevent her relatives and neighbours from taking supernatural faculties in certain people for granted. Her grandmother reputedly had second sight, which local people regarded as 'vaguely weird', but hardly exceptional.[96] Hughes's own experiences with the supernatural began when she was a child. On her way to school she saw standing by the school window a strange child whom she pointed out to the other children. When the teacher approached, the vision disappeared.[97] After her marriage to a miner, uncanny 'voices' tormented her. During an illness she heard these voices continually calling to her to 'Get up and walk.' Other manifestations accompanied the voices. She heard raps on the wall, her bed shook and sometimes the entity snatched off her bedclothes during the night. To add to her troubles, her acquaintances suspected that she was morally implicated in her own haunting. Terrified by her experiences, she could not prevent herself from telling her neighbours about them. She received little sympathy, and one woman told her: 'You must have a funny conscience.'[98]

The assumption that individuals were culpable in their own haunting was widespread. The occultist Dion Fortune explained the occult view:

> If a mental image be repeatedly visualised and brooded over, it tends to take up an independent existence. Such a thought-form may receive ensoulment from many different sources, attracting to itself that which is congenial to its nature. For instance, a long-brooded thought of hate might attract a ... demon; a long-brooded thought of love might attract ... an angelic presence.[99]

Occultists, Spiritualists and ghost investigators, such as O'Donnell, agreed that like attracted like. Conan Doyle expressed the Spiritualist view when he described the attraction of something to its like as a law of nature.[100] A poor psychic atmosphere that harboured vengeful or 'evil thought' of any kind was likely to produce 'low spirits'.[101]

The idea that like knows its like originated with the Greeks,[102] became incorporated into medieval alchemy and has persisted in various forms down to the twentieth century.[103] Detached from earlier epistemologies, this ancient maxim has persisted as a powerful rhetorical resource in the nineteenth and twentieth centuries,[104] particularly in literature. Henry James's story *The Turn of the Screw*, for example, derives its disturbing power partly through his elusive use of the concept, for we never know who is attracting the ghosts of the former governess, Miss Jessel, and her lover. Is it the children? Is it their present governess? Is it a consequence of the relationship of all three, or are the ghostly manifestations and their baleful effects a token of the present governess's mental instability?[105]

As we shall see, to those afflicted by ghosts, such questions were of real concern. Spiritualists offered a range of services in this respect. They claimed to be able to distinguish between malevolent and friendly spirits, and between normal and supernormal happenings. They knew how to prevent 'low spirits' entering the earth plane, and how to dispel those that did get through. They offered to explain the meaning and purpose of supernatural activity in a way that made sense of people's experiences and provided practical help into the bargain. To illustrate these points, let us first return to Helen Hughes's story.

The 'voices' and physical disturbances continued unabated in the Hughes's home until Helen thought she must go insane. In particular, a vision of an unknown woman frequently appeared. Eventually, Helen persuaded her husband to move to another house, but the phantom continued to appear. Worse, Mr Hughes began to 'see things' too, which brought him to the conclusion that these manifestations were centred on his wife.[106] So far Helen Hughes's ordeal reads like a run-of-the-mill ghost story. But soon an extra element appears in the form of an 'old road-mender'. We are not told his name, nor are we told anything about his life except that he is a Spiritualist. The 'old road-mender' entered Helen Hughes's life in the traditional manner of biblical angels who assume human guise and visit mortals, and Hughes responded to her 'angel' in the manner prescribed by the Bible. One morning, after she had spent another restless night because of the 'voices', there 'came three raps on the door'. She opened it to find an old man who had been working outside. 'He asked her if she would warm his can of tea at the fire', and she told him of her troubles. He explained to her that her 'voices' were benevolent spirits, and predicted that she would become a great medium.[107] Relief overwhelmed her: the unknown man 'mended me, he smoothed my road, and from that day I was slowly led to become a public demonstrator' of mediumistic power.[108]

Helen Hughes's identification as a medium happened by way of a baptism where she was given her 'real' and future identity by an external authority; like Mary, who was named the mother of Christ; or

Moses, who was named Jehovah's prophet. Spiritualism, in Helen Hughes's case, was not a substitute for failing religious belief, nor was it an escape from bleak materialism. On the contrary, the metaphysical features of her life were only too real. The old man, cast in the role of visiting angel, sanctified her experiences, assuaged her fears and gave her permission to cast her 'voices' and visions in a different and positive light.

The story of Edith Clements's conversion to Spiritualism followed a similar pattern. In 1932 she related the circumstances of her conversion to *Psychic News*. Clements was a strict Roman Catholic, and she was acutely conscious of the fear of losing her soul and living for ever in hell. Nevertheless, despite the disapproval of her family, she was aware from childhood of 'presences' that were apparently unseen by other people. Once, she had an unnerving experience that involved a vision of her dead brother. He stood looking at her, she recalled, 'exactly as he was', before his death. '[T]error stricken at this vision', Edith rushed screaming into her mother's arms. She repeatedly insisted that her family had buried the wrong man, because Harry, her brother, was not dead: she had just seen him. Edith's mother, now thoroughly alarmed, took her daughter to a doctor, who prescribed a bottle of medicine and rest in a darkened room.[109] Some years later, following the death of her mother, Clements became deeply depressed. She suffered from poor health, missed her mother's nursing, and worried about the expense of medical treatment. Things came to a head when she began to hear her mother's voice:

> I was simply haunted by my mother's presence. Wherever I went, or whatever I did, I could not get away from her. She continually followed me.
>
> My health became weaker and I wondered why I fancied I saw my mother. Being a strict Catholic, I hoped she was safe in heaven.
>
> At last I thought I would go to my priest for advice. He, surely, ought to be able to help me. I went to him and asked him what it meant. He replied that my mother was not happy, but that perhaps she was 'in purgatory' and needed our prayers.
>
> I was advised by my priest to have masses said 'for the repose of her soul', and to light candles in the church and spend a time praying whilst they were burning.
>
> I carried out these instructions in detail and spent quite a lot of money in having masses said for her.

Whenever I placed the lighted candles in the church and tried to pray for her, my fears grew worse because she used to kneel by the side of me. I still thought I was suffering from delusions.

My health broke down completely and I was sent to Brighton, where I met a gentleman who was a Spiritualist. I found a listener to whom I could pour out my troubles, one who would not think I was suffering from delusions.

He listened carefully to me – and then said, 'Oh! you poor soul. Of course you are not mad – you are a natural medium and your mother has been trying to make you understand, but your religious beliefs are making a barrier to you both.'[110]

In view of theological, medical and popular theories about the activities of the dead, Edith Clements's fear must have been extreme. Maybe her mother was in purgatory, as her priest suggested; or she had attracted a demonic spirit who was impersonating her mother; or she was suffering from delusions and about to become insane. What the Spiritualist interpretation offered immediately to both Edith Clements and Helen Hughes was relief from fears concerning their sanity and moral rectitude. Simultaneously, Spiritualism confirmed their identities as mediums. This confirmation does not seem to have come as a surprise to either woman; both acted as if they were already mediums before taking on the mantle of their mediumship. Each conversion came as a formal recognition of what they would come to perceive as their latent and 'real' identities – identities nourished in a culture steeped in supernatural signs.

The healing art of Spiritualism

Spiritualism gave positive explanations of the meaning and purpose of supernatural occurrences. Spiritualists said that what were normally taken for ghosts were probably the spirits of loved ones who wished to assure relatives and friends of their survival and happiness in the spirit sphere. They also associated spirit visitations with educational purposes, the delivery of prophetic messages, and the 'righting of injustices'.

Some specialised in unwanted spirit manifestations, commonly known as poltergeists. Muriel Hankey, who for many years was an employee and friend of Hewat McKenzie, counted poltergeist-haunting among his special interests. Once in 1932, a family in South London, asked McKenzie to investigate an outbreak of inexplicable disturbances in their home. Hankey and the medium Marie D'eu accompanied

McKenzie on his mission. Having probed the domestic circumstances of the family, McKenzie arranged a seance. D'eu entered a state of trance. In this condition she disclosed the reason for the disturbances: there had been a domestic tragedy in the family that had motivated the haunting. McKenzie judged that an unhappy spirit had tried to 'drain' the ethereal substances of the children of the house. It was the illegitimate use of these substances, declared McKenzie, that was responsible for the disturbances. Working on the Spiritualist assumption that no spirit was wholly evil, McKenzie appealed to this invisible entity. He called attention to the danger of impairing the health of the children by drawing upon them in this way; he pointed to the damage to property, and reminded the spirit of the anxiety it was causing. Finally, he instructed the spirit on how to withdraw from earthbound conditions, and how to become integrated into a new state of being. McKenzie's diagnosis and methods apparently satisfied the family, for from that moment on, the trouble ceased.[111]

Spiritualists believed that human conflict was usually responsible for poltergeist activity. On these occasions the medium acted as mediator between the warring parties in this world and the next. Eileen Garrett worked for McKenzie in this capacity for ten years. She recalled how, in 1927, she and McKenzie became involved with poltergeist disturbances at a farmhouse in a small Sussex village, inhabited by the farmer, his wife and two children by his previous wife, deceased. Garrett went into trance and the farmer's first wife 'came through', by drawing on the etheric substances of her children, and expressed resentments about past and present conditions at the farmhouse. She complained of her husband's adultery with her former nurse, now his wife, and accused the pair of plotting to get her money. She also expressed concern about the welfare of her children. Garrett's revelations enraged the farmer; he ordered her and McKenzie out of his house, but the disturbances continued and the farmer became convinced that he was in the grip of an evil force. He recalled Garrett and McKenzie; his first wife again 'came through' and reiterated her complaints. During this episode, the second wife burst into tears and accused the farmer of treating her badly. She revealed that they were unmarried, and said that she had never wanted to enter an adulterous relationship with him. She added that because of these grievances she was unable to take up the role of mother to the farmer's children.[112]

In Garrett's experience, the emotional tensions at the farmhouse provided the right ingredients for a typical poltergeist case: Here 'was a "departed" personality at work. Here, also, was conflict and anxiety about the children. The loss of the mother, the intrusion of the other woman, the greed of the father, the suppressions', and so on.[113] Eventually the family became reconciled. The farmer regularised his circumstances by marrying his mistress, and distributing property and money according to the wishes of his dead wife. Garrett's intervention was timely in what threatened to become a conflict centred on the stereotypical figure of the 'wicked stepmother'. As mediator, she performed a similar function to that of community priests, or psychoanalysts, in that she helped to 'release' suppressed anxieties, resentments and guilt and prepared the way for the restoration of 'right order'. She initiated rites of passage by which the former wife and mother might 'rest in peace', allowing the new one to take her place.[114]

Mediums performed similarly therapeutic services for the bereaved. As Europeans grieved over the losses in the Great War, the impulse to maintain relationships with the dead was strong. Spiritualism supplied an outlet for this emotion. Noting the upsurge of interest in the movement during the Great War, Gladys Leonard commented that many a distressed relative found relief after receiving assurance through a medium that their husband or son lived on in another place.[115] Geraldine Cummins, a respected medium of the interwar period, saw her work as 'humanly constructive' because, among other things, her psychic gifts 'helped the bereaved over the worst period of their lives'.[116]

Jay Winter has commented on how traditional ceremonies and memorials supplied the means by which communities might remember the fallen, and express their grief and indebtedness to them. Much of postwar commemorative art, religious and secular, entailed everything modernist art rejected: romanticism, sentimentality, duty and honour. Spiritualism acted as a kind of living memorial to the dead, and performed an identical function to such commemorative art.[117] In transcripts of conversations with the spirit world there was no trace of the bitter irony and anger of modernist war poetry and other anti-war literature, such as Richard Aldington's *Death of a Hero* (1929) and Henry Williamson's *The Patriot's Progress* (1930),[118] rather, the tone was of religious commitment, of shared memories and the reaffirmation of conventional family and community values.[119] Winter concludes that the 'savage wit of Dada could express anger and despair, and did so in enduring ways; but it could not heal. Traditional modes of seeing the war, while at times less profound, provided a way of remembering which enabled the bereaved to live with their losses.'[120]

As well as offering healing services to mourners and those troubled by ghosts and poltergeists, mediums advised on health matters and treated diseases. Healing mediums functioned alongside a range of other fringe medical practitioners.[121] Indeed, the term 'fringe' seems to be something of a misnomer, considering the importance of traditional remedies and cures in working-class communities. Despite the expansion of state health care immediately before and after the Great War, including the introduction of a national insurance scheme (which provided sickness benefit and free medical services for contributors), the establishment of the school medical service, and legislation on maternity and child welfare,[122] large numbers of people continued to trust traditional and local remedies. Besides, hospital care and GP services were far from universally available in the interwar period.

Local healers abounded in urban, rural and seaside areas – especially in seaside areas where people from urban areas came to 'take the air'. Along Blackpool's seafront in 1937, faith healers, astrologers and herbalists jostled with Buddhist healers and snake charmers, each of whom promised rude health and longevity for a small fee. Back at home, people commonly treated themselves choosing from a wide range of herbal and patent medicines; maybe they consulted popular publications on health matters, such as the astrologer Ellis's *Book of the Ellis Family*.[123] People in rural Lincolnshire treated ailments with a mixture of herbal remedies and charms. Sufferers from whooping cough were told: '[y]ou must go to the sea and when the tide is going out, cough into it and the tide will take the cough with it'[124] Certain people specialised in the curing of a single ailment. My own father-in-law used to charm away warts in his home town of Brighton by buying them for a small sum – a technique that was also widely known and used in Lincolnshire. Spiritualist mediums also offered therapeutic services. Robert Roberts remembered how Mr Carley, a medium who lived near him in the poorest area of Salford during the Great War, had a reputation for curing varicose veins. 'These and other "women's ailments"', wrote Roberts, 'he professed to cure by "herbs" and the "laying on of hands", a therapy which gave rise to salacious gossip.'[125]

The mixture of psychic and practical therapy offered by Spiritualist mediums was perfectly in accord with popular approaches to medicine. Most mediums practised a variety of diagnostic and healing methods, although some acted purely as 'channels' for spirit-guides, and attributed cures entirely to spirit agency. Others concentrated on what Spiritualists called the personal 'aura' of each subject for treatment. The aura formed the visible part of the etheric body – visible, that is, to the psychically gifted – and looked like a 'shrouded light' surrounding each individual. In disease it appeared speckled with ragged edges. By its appearance, wrote one authority on the subject, 'clairvoyants give their character readings and healers diagnose disease'.[126]

Psychometry was another aid in the diagnosis of disease or emotional disturbance. Psychometrists assumed that objects 'retain the impression of contacts that have been made with them.'[127] At one small psychometry class, held in 1940, the medium asked participants to place objects belonging to them, such as a pen or a key, in a tray. She gave 'readings' about the owner's health and emotional well-being, in the present and in the future, through the 'feel' of the object.[128]

Spiritualist healers did not follow any set method, and routinely combined psychometric and clairvoyant impressions with the help of a spirit-guide; some mediums incorporated the language of popular astrology and numerology in their predictions about physical and emotional health.[129] Just as mediums mingled their techniques in the diagnosis of disease, so they mingled advice about health matters with advice on other subjects such as travel, marriage and friendships. At a Spiritualist meeting in 1938, the presiding medium undertook psychometry while carrying on a conversation with her spirit-guide. Simultaneously, she dispensed advice on the physical and mental health of participants, made clairvoyant predictions and relayed messages from the dead.[130]

Mediums after the First World War increasingly assimilated psychological and psychoanalytic concepts into their already eclectic methodologies. Some – like Geraldine Cummins, who was herself the daughter of a doctor – co-operated with regular physicians in the treatment of mental disturbance. A Fellow of the Royal College of Physicians once contacted her to try a different approach to the treatment of what 'seemed almost an hopeless case of neurosis':

> The idea occurred to him that, in cases of obscure neurosis, or those
> in which physical manifestations were suspected of having a psycho-

logical basis, there might be a short cut to the secrets of the patient's subconscious mind, to hidden complexes, through the methods of memory-divining.[131]

In 'memory-divining', Cummins used psychometric techniques to reveal early memories in the patient's subconscious mind, with the aim of exposing the hidden cause or causes of 'neurosis'.[132] According to her, this method was successfully employed in the treatment of '[p]atients suffering from claustrophobia, asthma, amnesia, melancholia, periodic self-imposed starvation, periodic alcohol craving, a neurosis of choking, various fears that menaced with ruin the careers of able-bodied men.' The physician with whom Cummins worked subsequently published the results of their co-operation under the pseudonym 'Dr. Connell'. After the publication of the book, *Perceptive Healing*, several medical doctors contacted Cummins and asked her to conduct similar experiments with them.[133]

The fact that 'Dr. Connell' chose to publish under a pseudonym reveals something of the continuing antipathy of the medical establishment to irregular competitors. Spiritualism had faced intense opposition in the nineteenth century from orthodox medical men in general and from alienist psychologists – such as Henry Maudsley and William Carpenter – in particular.[134] However, as the notion of unconscious activity grew in importance as an explanatory model of mind in the twentieth century, doctors became increasingly interested in mediums as subjects of research into unconscious processes. From the perspective of theories of the unconscious, mediumship was viewed either as a disturbance of the psyche or as a sign of little-understood psychic ability.[135] Some, like 'Connell', went down this latter road and accepted the existence in some people of a psychic power that could help cure disease, both physical and mental. Other well-known mediums – such as Estelle Roberts and Gladys Leonard – occasionally co-operated with the medical profession. Roberts worked with a physician to compare her psychic diagnostic methods with conventional ones,[136] and Leonard recalled how she worked for a West End doctor as a trance subject to help with the treatment of patients suffering from 'different troubles, usually of a nervous order, such as stammering, stuttering, hallucinations, melancholia, etc.'. She went into a trance and the 'doctor would speak to [her] subjective mind and tell it what was wrong with the patient, and that it must get into touch with the patient's subjective mind so as to eliminate the trouble from it'. However, conflict arose through a paradigm clash, specifically when the doctor in question refused to recognise Leonard's spirit control as an independent entity, insisting that it was an aspect of her personality.[137]

Helena Wright's orthodox medical training as a gynaecologist did nothing to dent her Spiritualist convictions. She attended the London School of Medicine for Women, and was the first woman resident doctor in the Outpatients Department of the Hampstead General Hospital before becoming a gynaecologist. During the early 1930s she became involved with the campaign for women's right to seek advice on contraception, and practise birth control. In the mid-1930s, Margery Spring Rice, niece of Millicent Fawcett and Elizabeth Garrett Anderson, offered Wright the position of Chief Medical Officer at the Women's Welfare Centre in North Kensington. She remained in this position for the next thirty years.[138]

Helena Wright's feminism was of the non-militant variety espoused by Millicent Fawcett, whose feminism Brian Harrison has summarised as unsentimental and reflecting all the 'fierce middle-class commitment to an opportunity society, all the strenuous Liberal faith in liberty and progress'.[139] Despite the influence of her positivist medical training and her contact with rationalist feminists, Wright clung to her Spiritualist beliefs. She held seances with her family after finishing work at the North Kensington clinic, and she and her sister agreed that whoever died first would contact the other.[140] If anything, her belief in Spiritual-ism deepened over the years. She once said to her biographer (who regarded her views on this subject as 'incongruously eccentric at times and in sharp contrast with her scientific background'): 'From my point of view it [the spirit world] is as real as the biscuits on this plate.'[141]

Wright appears to have kept her interest in psychic matters separate from her work at the North Kensington clinic, but in later life she became an enthusiastic member of the Institute of Psionic Medicine, based almost entirely on Spiritualist assumptions. In an approving draft review of a book on Psionic medicine, written by a doctor, a dentist and a philosopher, Wright announced that the first principle of Psionic medicine was:

> the existence of a non material body, called the etheric body, held to
> be an enveloping shape, exactly resembling the physical, and extend-
> ing a short distance beyond it in all directions. Human etheric bodies

are part of the fourth-dimensional world, where every physical type in
the ordinary three-dimensional world has its etheric counterpart.

The Institute of Psionic Medicine required its practitioners to have
paranormal sensitivity for diagnostic purposes. This enabled them to
establish connections 'between physical intelligence and superior knowledge available to the etheric body'. For this purpose, they equipped
themselves with a pendulum that psychically located areas of disease.[142]
Despite its obvious debt to Spiritualism, the Institute of Psionic Medicine effectively excluded most Spiritualists by limiting membership to
officially qualified medical practitioners.[143] This might be an example of
an elite group's attempt to expropriate the knowledge of a competitor,
but on the level of the individual there is no sense of this. Rather,
Helena Wright's Spiritualism peacefully coexisted with her scientised
outlook, demonstrating an individual's capacity to assimilate conflicting
epistemologies within a personal cosmology. We can say the same of
mediumistic encounters with medical orthodoxy. Although the medical
establishment and Spiritualists were historical enemies, individuals in
both camps showed a willingness, at times, to exchange ideas. This
could develop into the kind of co-operative relations described by
Geraldine Cummins and others.

The absorption of a variety of ideas did not detract from Spiritualism's essentially holistic approach to healing. In this respect, healing
traditions in Spiritualist circles had remained unbroken since the previous century. Then, as Alex Owen remarks, 'healing was predicated on
the successful interaction between healer and recipient and a commitment to the key factor of holistic care ... Body and spirit worked in
unison and must be properly addressed if true cure was to take place.'[144]
The unity of spirit and body, mind and matter, all contained within a
living universe, was central to Spiritualist cosmology. In this cosmos
there were no clear boundaries between matter and spirit, between the
living and the dead, or between animals, humans and plant life. The
ether, that vitalistic substance, linked everything. Spiritualists expressed
these connections in virtually every aspect of their beliefs and practices:
in healing, in expectations of the afterlife, in relations with the dead. In
its assumption of the interconnectedness of all things, Spiritualism
locked into existing supernatural thought. Spiritualism after the Great
War was not so much a revival of animist consciousness as a co-

ordinator of existing animist ideas. This is why it fitted so comfortably into the fabric of daily life.

Notes

1 See, for example, D. Lowe, *History of Bourgeois Perception* (Chicago, University of Chicago Press, 1982); S. Kern, *The Culture of Time and Space 1880–1918* (Cambridge, MA, Harvard University Press, 1983).

2 I am grateful to Jay Winter for allowing me to look at his article 'Spiritualism and the First World War', before publication. There is a growing body of literature that argues for this position in different contexts. See, for example, Alison Light, *Forever England: Femininity, Literature and Conservatism Between the Wars* (London, Routledge, 1991); R. M. Bracco, *Merchants of Hope: British Middlebrow Writers and the First World War, 1919–1939* (Oxford, 1993); J. Dixon, 'Gender, Politics and Culture in the New Age: Theosophy in England, 1880–1935' (PhD thesis, Rutgers University, 1993).

3 J. Winter, *Sites of Memory, Sites of Mourning: The Great War in European Culture* (Cambridge, Cambridge University Press, 1995), ch. 3.

4 Winter, 'Spiritualism and the First World War' (from draft copy of *Sites of Memory, Sites of Mourning*).

5 Quoted by I. F. Clarke, *Voices Prophesying War 1763–1984* (London, Oxford University Press, 1966), p. 92. Other wartime legends are recorded by E. S. Turner, *Dear Old Blighty* (London, Michael Joseph, 1980), ch. 12. See also P. Fussell, *The Great War and Modern Memory* (Oxford, Oxford University Press, 1975).

6 James Webb attributes the revival of Spiritualism in the twentieth century to the 'shock of World War I in his *The Occult Establishment* (La Salle, IL, Open Court, 1976), p. 24, but the movement receives virtually no attention beyond this.

7 G. Nelson, *Spiritualism and Society* (London, Routledge & Kegan Paul, 1969), p. 161. According to Nelson, the movement went into sharp decline during the Second World War, then revived slightly. By 1955, Spiritualist numbers had sagged considerably and many Spiritualist organisations had closed down or amalgamated (p. 157).

8 L. Barrow, *Independent Spirits: Spiritualism and English Plebeians 1850–1910* (London, Routledge & Kegan Paul, 1986). See also J. F. C. Harrison, 'Early Victorian Radicals and the Medical Fringe', in W. Bynum and R. Porter (eds), *Medical Fringe and Medical Orthodoxy* (London, Croom Helm, 1987), pp. 198–215.

9 G. Leonard, *My Life In Two Worlds*, 'Foreword' by O. Lodge (London, Cassell, 1931), p. 16.

10 Nelson, *Spiritualism and Society*, pp. 155–60.

11 *Ibid.*, p. 157.

12 Hannen Swaffer, 'Spiritualism's Crisis Now', *Psychic News*, 2 July, 1932, p. 7.

13 'Archbishop's Committee on Spiritualism: Report of the Committee to the Archbishop of Canterbury', chaired by the Right Reverend F. Underhill, D. D. (unpublished, certified copy, 1947), p. 7, Harry Price Library, University of London.

14 N. Blunsdon, *A Popular Dictionary of Spiritualism* (London, Arco, 1961), p. 202.

15 B. Upton, *The Mediumship of Helen Hughes* (London, Spiritualist Press, 1946), p. 37.

16 S. Barbanell, *Some Discern Spirits: The Mediumship of Estelle Roberts* (London, Psychic Press, 1944), pp. 7–8. Barbanell does not supply the date of this performance. See also A. Findlay, *The Psychic Stream* (London, Psychic Press, 1939), p. 1152.

17 H. Swaffer, 'A Home Circle I Know', *Psychic News*, 4 June, 1932, p. 7.

18 Nelson, *Spiritualism and Society*, p. 161.

19 Blunsdon, *A Popular Dictionary of Spiritualism*, p. 83. See also 'Publisher's Introduction' to A. Findlay, *The Psychic Stream*.

20 A. Findlay, *On the Edge of the Etheric or Survival after Death Scientifically Explained*, 25th Impression, 'Preface' by Sir William Barrett (London, Rider, 1932); *Psychic News*, 25 June 1932, p. 6; Blunsdon, *A Popular Dictionary of Spiritualism*, p. 83.

21 N. Fodor, 'A Letter From England', *Journal of the American Society for Psychical Research*, XXX: 11 (1936) 358.

22 D. Lewis in conversation with the author, 27 December 1996.

23 These included the International Spiritualist Federation, the Marylebone Spiritualist Association and the London Spiritualist Alliance. Blunsdon, *A Popular Dictionary of Spiritualism*.

24 H. Price, *Search for Truth: My Life for Psychical Research* (London, Collins, 1942), pp. 142–4, 157–8; *Stella C.: An Account of Some Original Experiments in Psychical Research* (1925) (ed. James Turner) (London, Souvenir Press, 1973).

25 P. Tabori, *Harry Price Ghost Hunter* (London, Sphere, 1974).

26 M. Hankey, *James Hewat McKenzie, Pioneer of Psychical Research: A Personal Memoir* (London, Aquarian Press, 1963), ch. 4. Muriel Hankey was a close friend and the employee of the McKenzie family.

27 *Ibid.*, p. 33.

28 *Ibid.*, p. 11.

29 Frank Turner has commented on this phenomenon with respect to the loss or modification of religious faith among a number of prominent Victorians. In these cases there was a 'frequent psychological conflation between God the Father and the father of the household, and rebellion against God the Father was a way of signalling inde-

pendence from the family circle' (F. Turner, 'The Crisis of Faith and the Faith that was Lost', in *Contesting Cultural Authority* [Cambridge, Cambridge University Press, 1993], pp. 73–100). The McKenzies were probably introduced to Spiritualism through the Education movement. Nineteenth-century Spiritualists were enthusiastic proponents of 'self-help' and self-education; many upheld the kind of political radicalism espoused by Robert Blatchford, Spiritualist and leading figure in the Education movement. See Logie Barrow, *Independent Spirits*, for the association he makes between Spiritualists, autodidacts and socialists. See also J. F. C. Harrison, *Learning and Living 1790–1960: A Study in the History of the English Adult Education Movement* (Toronto, University of Toronto, 1961) for an overview of the Education movement in Yorkshire (also the cradle of English Spiritualism).

30 Lind-af-Hageby (President of the London Spiritualist Alliance), *Light*, LX11:32011 (1942)163.

31 B. McKenzie, *Psychic News*, 10 August 1940, p. 7.

32 M. Hankey, *James Hewat McKenzie*, p. 53.

33 See F. Podmore, *The Newer Spiritualism* (London, Fisher & Unwin, 1910). Podmore was one of the earliest and most enthusiastic members of the Society for Psychical Research. However, he became increasingly sceptical of the authenticity of most forms of psychic phenomena, particularly mediumship.

34 J. Stevenson, *British Society 1914–45* (Harmondsworth, Penguin, 1984), pp. 357–72. Protestant sects in general suffered from declining numbers. See also J. Obelevich, 'Religion', in M. L. Thompson (ed.), *The Cambridge Social History of Britain 1750–1950, vol. 3: Social Agencies and Institutions* (Cambridge, Cambridge University Press, 1990), pp. 348–56.

35 'Archbishop's Committee on Spiritualism', p. 3. The report was published thirty-two years later in the *Christian Parapsychologist*, 3:2–3 (1979).

36 *Ibid.*, p. 5.

37 *Ibid.*, pp. 19–20.

38 *Ibid.*, pp. 29–30, 33.

39 *Ibid.*, pp. 40, 31.

40 For example, Father Knapp, a Roman Catholic priest, launched an attack on Spiritualism in the *Sunday Graphic*. He said that Spiritualism was a 'serious menace to the mental health of the people as well as to their spiritual welfare', and added that its practice had sent a million people mad. His article was reported in *Psychic News*, '1,000,000 Mad Victims of Spiritualism', 4 June 1932, p. 3. See also I. Hernamen, *Spiritualism and the Child* (London, Catholic Truth Society, 1924); Father B. Vaughan, 'Foreword' to Elliot O'Donnell, *The Menace of Spiritualism* (London, Werner & Laurie, 1920), pp. 1–4.

41 Quoted in *The Two Worlds*, 12 March 1925, p. 159.

42 Barrow, *Independent Spirits*, See also: J. F. C. Harrison, 'Early Victorian Radicals and the Medical Fringe', pp. 198–215; A. Owen, *The Darkened Room: Women, Power and Spiritualism in Late Victorian England* (London, Virago, 1989); A. Braude, *Radical Spirits: Spiritualism and Women's Rights in Nineteenth-Century America* (Boston, MA, Beacon Press, 1989).

43 H. Swaffer, 'Spiritualism's Crisis Now', *Psychic News*, 2 July 1932, p. 7.

44 D. L. LeMahieu, *A Culture for Democracy: Mass Communication and the Cultivated Mind in Britain between the Wars* (Oxford, Clarendon Press, 1988), p. 55.

45 See, for example, the distinction made by the interwar Tory press between the 'public' and 'labour', where the 'public' stood for the side of 'common sense' and 'sound' views. R. McKibbin, *The Ideologies of Class: Social Relations in Britain 1880–1950* (Oxford, Oxford University Press, 1990), ch. 9. 'Equality' and 'democracy' served as key signifiers in replies to a Mass-Observation survey on education. The following remark is typical of the views expressed: 'If we believe "that all men and women are born equal" and as a democracy fighting for democracy we must believe that, then we should believe with equal conviction that all men's children have an equal right to be educated in such a way as to fit them for their existence in this world we have raised ourselves.' Mass-Observation Archive (University of Sussex) Directive Respondent, reply to April 1942 Directive; Mass-Observation, *Britain* (London, Penguin, 1939), ch. 2. See also M. Bracco, *Betwixt and Between: Middlebrow Fiction and English Society in the Twenties and Thirties* (Melbourne, University of Melbourne, History Department, 1990), for her analysis of the rise of the 'middlebrow' novel between the wars.

46 Detective Sergeant A. Comryn, *Your Policemen Are Wondering* (London, Gollancz, 1947), pp. 27–8. The narrative covers the period 1938 to 1945.

47 Mass-Observation Archive, quoted by D. Sheridan, '"Ordinary Hard Working Folk": Volunteer Writers in Mass-Observation 1939–50 and 1981–91', *Feminist Praxis*, 37/38, 1993, pp. 1–34.

48 *Ibid.*, p. 5. The discourse of the 'average man' was countered by the discourse of the 'masses'. John Carey argues that 'elite culture', particularly the English literary intelligentsia, employed the rhetoric of 'the masses' to exclude 'newly educated (or "semi educated") readers, and so to preserve the intellectual's seclusion'. Carey claims that the founders of Mass-Observation failed to overcome their own intellectualist and elitist bias in their approach to their project. See Carey, *The Intellectuals and the Masses: Pride and Prejudice among the Literary Intelligentsia, 1880–1939* (London, Faber, 1992), especially p. 25. Whatever difficulties there may be with Carey's thesis with respect to the polarised divisions he makes between 'elite' and 'non elite' culture, the deploy-

ment of the term 'mass' tended to uphold the 'naturalness' of hierarchical social structures against the democratising tendencies of 'average man' rhetoric.

49 W. H. Evans, 'Spiritualism and Commonplace Morality', *Light*, XLVI:2374 (1926) 320.

50 See 'Extracts from some of the Press Reviews of *On the Edge of the Etheric*', Findlay, *On the Edge of the Etheric*, pp. I–VIII. There are seventy-five favourable extracts from reviews in this edition.

51 O'Donnell, *The Menace of Spiritualism*, pp. 213–14.

52 Analogies between spirit communications and the telephone and wireless are ubiquitous in Spiritualist publications. See, for example, E. B. Gill, 'Tuning In', *Psychic News*, 4 June 1932, p. 15; *Psychic News*, 25 June 1932, p. 10; Barbanell, *Some Discern Spirits*, where Estelle Roberts is described as a 'human wireless set' (pp. 95–6); Doris Stokes said that her mediumship worked something like a telephone: D. Stokes and L. Dearsley, *Voices in My Ear: The Autobiography of a Medium* (London, Futura Macdonald, 1980), p. 91.

53 Mass-Observation Archive (M-OA). Topic Collection: Astrology and Spiritualism, 1938–47 (1/F), quoted in an anonymous article, 'Superstition', 1 January 1947, p. 2.

54 B. Upton, *The Mediumship of Helen Hughes* (London, Spiritualist Press, 1947), p. 57. The author was a Spiritualist and the friend of Helen Hughes.

55 This show was broadcast by the BBC at 1 p.m. on Sundays. Listeners passed greetings and made requests for pieces of music to be played for their relatives and friends overseas with the armed forces. Similarly, those overseas made requests and passed messages to family at home. This kind of show was preceded in the 1930s by the BBC Empire Service, which broadcast news, vaudeville, dance music and light music. Empire countries broadcast a limited selection of shows to Britain. See A. Briggs, *The History of Broadcasting in the United Kingdom Volume II: The Golden Age of Wireless* (London, London University Press, 1965), pp. 369–410.

56 Stokes, *Voices in My Ear*, p. 138. See also pp. 114, 184.

57 Findlay, *On the Edge of the Etheric*, pp. 37–8. In the nineteenth century, orthodox physics held that a pervasive medium, the ether, must exist to support the undulations of light waves. J. C. Maxwell, 'Ether' (written for the *Encyclopaedia Britannica*, 9th edm) from W. D. Niven (ed.), *The Scientific Papers of James Clerk Maxwell* (New York, Dover, 1965), p. 767. See also Sir E. T. Whittaker, *A History of the Theories of Aether and Electricity from the Age of Descartes to the Close of the Nineteenth Century* (London, Longmans, 1910); J. Merz, *A History of European Thought in the Nineteenth Century* (New York, Dover, 1965); K. Shaffner, *Nineteenth Century Ether Theories* (Oxford, Pergamon, 1972); B. Wynne, 'Physics

and Psychics: Science, Symbolic Action, and Social Control in Late Victorian England', in B. Barnes and S. Shapin (eds), *Natural Order: Historical Studies of Scientific Culture* (Beverly Hills, CA, Sage, 1979), pp. 167–86.

58 Findlay, *On the Edge of the Etheric*, p. 20.

59 A. Ponsonby, *Life Here and Now: Conclusions Derived from an Examination of the Sense of Duration* (London, Allen & Unwin, 1936), pp. 156–7. There is a short biography of Ponsonby in the *Dictionary of National Biography, 1941–1950*, pp. 683–5.

60 See, for example, R. Brandon, *The Spiritualists: The Passion for the Occult in the Nineteenth and Twentieth Centuries* (London, Weidenfeld & Nicolson, 1983); S. Hynes, *The Edwardian Turn of Mind* (Princeton, NKJ, Princeton University Press, 1968); J. Oppenheim, *The Other World: Spiritualism and Psychical Research in England 1850–1914* (Cambridge, Cambridge University Press, 1985); E. S. Turner, *Dear Old Blighty* (London, Michael Joseph, 1980), p. 136.

61 The circumstances of Eileen Garrett's childhood are rather obscure. In her autobiography, *My Life as a Search for the Meaning of Mediumship* (1939) (New York, Arno Press, 1975), Garrett says that her mother married a Catholic Basque named Anthony Vancho. Her mother's Protestant family refused to forgive this interdenominational marriage, and the couple committed suicide; this was how she came to live with her aunt, Martha Little. Research by Joan Healy, however, casts doubt upon this version of events. According to Healy, Eileen was the daughter of James Savage, an Irish labourer, and his wife Anne. On the death of Anne Savage from epilepsy in 1892, the seven-month-old Eileen, then known as Emily Jane, went to live with her mother's sister, Martha Little, and her husband. Eileen's immediate family continued to live, unknown to her, in County Meath. J. Healy, *Journal of the Society for Psychical Research*, 54:806 (1986) 90–92.

62 E. Garrett, *Many Voices* (London, George Allen & Unwin, 1968), p. 17. Legends of the banshee originated in Ireland, where it is understood to be a 'supernatural being of the wraith type.' The apparition presages death and is 'generally supposed to assume the form of a woman, sometimes young, but more often old'. *Encyclopedia of Occultism and Parapsychology*, ed. L. Sharp, vol. 1, 2nd edn (Detroit, Gale Research Company, 1984), pp. 130–31.

63 Garrett, *Many Voices*, p. 22.

64 *Ibid.*, p. 21.

65 Findlay, *On the Edge of the Etheric*, p. 39.

66 W. Q. Judge, *The Ocean of Theosophy* (1893) (California, The United Lodge of Theosophists, 1915), pp. 14–16. Judge founded the Theosophy movement along with Alfred Sinnett and the more famous Madame Helena Blavatsky. More recent works on Theosophy include

D. Morris, *The Masks of Lucifer: Technology and the Occult in Twentieth Century Popular Literature* (London, Batsford, 1992); J. Dixon, 'Gender, Politics and Culture in the New Age: Theosophy in England, 1880–1935' (PhD dissertation, Rutgers University, 1993).

67 The term 'occult' is intended to be understood in its general sense of characteristic of the magical or supernatural arts.

68 D. Fortune, *Through the Gates of Death and Spiritualism in the Light of Occult Science* (Wellingborough, Aquarian Press, 1987), p. 70.

69 Quoted by B. Wynne, 'Physics and Psychics', p. 171; O. Lodge, *Ether and Reality: A Series of Discourses on the Many Functions of the Ether of Space* (London, Hodder & Stoughton, 1925), pp. 162–3.

70 J. Hewat McKenzie, *Spirit Intercourse: Its Theory and Practice* (1916) (London, British College of Psychic Science, 1936), p. 23.

71 O. Lodge, *Raymond*, 7th edn (London, Methuen, 1917), p. 336.

72 *Ibid.*, pp. 197–8.

73 M-OA, File Report 1315, 'Death and the Supernatural', June 1942, p. 26; Mass-Observation, *Puzzled People* (London, Gollancz, 1947), p. 33.

74 G. Orwell, *A Clergyman's Daughter* (1935) (London, Penguin, 1975), p. 51.

75 E. Rolfe, *The Soul of the Slum Child*, 'Foreword' by Frank Briant (London, Benn, 1929), pp. 37–8, 32.

76 Mass-Observation, *Puzzled People*, pp. 36–7.

77 See, for example, G. Strauss, *Luther's House of Learning: Indoctrination of the Young in the German Reformation* (Baltimore, MD, Johns Hopkins University Press, 1978); P. Burke, *Popular Culture in Early Modern Europe* (London, Temple Smith, 1978), ch. 8; J. Bossy, 'The Counter-Reformation and the People of Catholic Europe', *Past and Present* 47 (1970) 51–70; Bossy, 'The Social History of Confession in the Age of the Reformation', *Transactions of the Royal Historical Society* 25 (1975) 21–38; M. Ingram, 'Religion, Communities and Moral Discipline in Late Sixteenth and Seventeenth-Century England: Case Studies', in K. Von Greyerz (ed.), *Religion and Society in Early Modern Europe 1500–1800* (London, George Allen & Unwin, 1984).

78 Quoted in Mass-Observation, *Puzzled People*, p. 32.

79 *Ibid.*, p. 33.

80 L. Walbrook, *The Case of Lester Coltman*, 'Introduction' by A. Conan Doyle (London, Hutchinson, 1924), pp. 30, 25, 32, 35.

81 Hewat McKenzie, *Spirit Intercourse*. See also Findlay, *On the Edge of the Etheric*; S. Barbanell, *When Your Animal Dies* (London, Psychic Press, 1940); Barbanell, *When a Child Dies* (London, Psychic Press, 1942); Walbrook, *The Case of Lester Coltman*; Lodge, *Raymond*; Air Chief Marshal Lord Dowding, *Many Mansions* (London, Rider, 1943); Leonard, *My Life in Two Worlds*. C. McDannell and B. Lang, *Heaven: A History* (New York, Vintage, 1990), offers a useful comparative study on different

historical versions of heaven, including the Spiritualist heaven. See also P. Ariès, *The Hour of Our Death*, trans. H. Weaver (New York, Alfred Knopf, 1981).

82 W. Morris, *News from Nowhere; or An Epoch of Rest, Being Some Chapters from a Utopian Romance* (London, Reeves & Turner, 1891) As Philippe Ariès has noted, the expectation that dead loved ones would meet in an idealised version of this world was already widespread in Europe in the early nineteenth-century. Both Catholics and Protestants expressed the 'same intolerance of the death of loved ones, the same sadness of a life deprived of its affections, the same desire for and certainty of reunion with the deceased after death' (*The Hour of Our Death*, p. 442).

83 A. Conan Doyle, *The New Revelation and The Vital Message* (London, Psychic Press, 1981), p. 45.

84 Hewat McKenzie, *Spirit Intercourse*.

85 Quoted by M. Sutton, *We Didn't Know Aught: A Study of Sexuality, Superstition and Death in Women's Lives in Lincolnshire during the 1930s, '40s and '50s* (Stamford, Paul Watkins, 1992), p. 137.

86 *Encyclopedia of Occultism and Parapsychology*, vol. 1, p. 131, from D. R. McAnally, *Irish Wonders*, 1888.

87 R. Roberts, *A Ragged Schooling* (Glasgow, Fontana, 1981), p. 131.

88 *Ibid.*, pp. 132–4.

89 E. O'Donnell, *Dangerous Ghosts* (London, Rider, 1954), p. 41. In 1942, a Mass-Observation survey on the subject of the supernatural received a flood of replies from people detailing their psychic experiences with ghosts and the like: M-OA, Respondents to April 1942 Directive. A subsequent summary of the material received found that people gave 'on average more than one supernatural story per person. 28% [were] alleged personal experience, 72% come from acquaintances' (M-OA, File Report 1294, 'The Unknown', June 1942).

90 Quoted by A. Crossley, *The Story of Helen Duncan* (Devon, Arthur Stockwell, 1975), p. 38. The author is a Spiritualist, and appears to be a friend of the Duncan family.

91 *Encyclopedia of Occultism and Parapsychology*, vol. 1, p. 277.

92 Leonard, *My Life in Two Worlds*, pp. 147–9.

93 Stokes, *Voices in my Ear*, p. 152.

94 O'Donnell produced more than forty books on the subject. For his comments on the character of ghosts see his *Dangerous Ghosts* (London, Rider, 1954), p. 15.

95 *Ibid.*, p. 19.

96 Upton, *The Mediumship of Helen Hughes*, p. 20–21.

97 *Ibid.*, p. 22.

98 *Ibid.*, p. 26.

99 Fortune, *Spiritualism in the Light of Occult Science*, p. 122. She repeated

this conclusion in her *Psychic Self Defence* (Wellingborough, Aquarian Press, 1973), pp. 125, 129.

100 Conan Doyle, *The New Revelation*, p. 45.

101 H. Boddington, *Psychic News Booklet 3: Trance States in Relation to Spirit Control* (London, Psychic Press, 1933), p. 32. See also Leonard, *My Life in Two Worlds*, p. 253

102 In, for example, Aristotle's doctrine of natural place and motion.

103 In medieval cosmology, writes Morris Berman, '[t]he world was seen as a vast assemblage of correspondences. All things have relationships with all other things, and these relations are ones of sympathy and antipathy' (M. Berman, *The Reenchantment of the World* [Ithaca, NY, Cornell University Press, 1981], pp. 73–6). The concept of sympathetic attraction was reformulated in seventeenth century physiology as the doctrine of 'mutual feeling between different parts' (C. Lawrence, in B. Barnes and S. Shapin [eds], 'The Nervous System and Society in the Scottish Enlightenment', *Natural Order: Historical Studies of Scientific Culture* [London, Sage, 1979], p. 27).

104 Notoriously for victim-blaming in rape cases. In 1923, for example, a judge concluded that a seven-year-old girl was responsible for the attack upon her because, presumably, the child's 'perverted' sexuality exercised a strong attraction to its like. The case was raised in the House of Commons by Lady Astor. See S. Jeffreys, *The Spinster and Her Enemies: Feminism and Sexuality 1880–1930* (London, Pandora, 1985), p. 64. See also J. Steinbeck, *East of Eden* (New York, Viking Press, 1952), where the anti-heroine's 'inner corruption' means that prostitution exercises an irresistible attraction for her. The concept also appears in Radclyffe Hall's autobiographical novel when Stephen, the lesbian heroine, befriends a homosexual called Jonathan Brockett. Stephen's former governess, Puddle, fears that like has found its like: R. Hall, *The Well of Loneliness* (1928) (London, Virago, 1992), pp. 244, 250.

105 H. James, *The Turn of the Screw* (1898), *The Aspern Papers* (1888), 'Introduction' by K. Murdock (London, Dent, 1960). See also the 1961 film version, directed by Jack Clayton and entitled *The Innocents*.

106 Upton, *The Mediumship of Helen Hughes*, p. 26.

107 *Ibid.*, pp. 28–9.

108 Quoted by Upton, *ibid.*, p. 30.

109 E. Clements, *Psychic News*, 2 July 1932, pp. 5, 14.

110 *Ibid.*, p. 14.

111 Hankey, *James Hewat McKenzie*, pp. 112–13.

112 Garrett, *Many Voices*, pp. 77–80.

113 *Ibid.*, p. 80.

114 See J. Macklin, 'Belief, Ritual, and Healing: New England Spiritualism and Mexican-American Spiritism Compared', in I. Zaretsky and M.

Leone (eds), *Religious Movements in Contemporary America* (Princeton, NJ, Princeton University Press, 1974), pp. 383–417, for an account of North American and Mexican-American healing in Spiritualist circles. In the same volume, E. Fuller Torrey condemns the Western propensity to dismiss mystical healing techniques as 'crackpot', and suggests that shamanistic rituals in so-called 'primitive societies' performed a similar function to psychotherapy. See Torrey, 'Spiritualists and Shamans as Psychotherapists: An Account of Original Anthropological Sin', pp. 330–7. Many anthropological studies on this subject have been carried out since. See, for example, R. Torrance, *The Spiritual Quest: Transcendence in Myth, Religion and Science* (Berkeley, University of California Press, 1994), which also contains an extensive bibliography.

115 Leonard, *My Life*, p. 54.

116 G. Cummins, *Unseen Adventures* (London, Rider, 1951), pp. 18–19. This view of the purpose of mediumship persisted into the post-World War II period. See Stokes, *Voices in My Ear*, pp. 107, 116.

117 J. Winter, 'The Sites of Memory: War Memorials and Bereavement in the Wake of the First World War' (draft of *Sites of Memory, Sites of Mourning*).

118 Historians of the Great War have begun to discern an underlying ambivalence in anti-war literature. John Onions writes: 'First World War literature, as Andrew Rutherford points out, refuses to be simply anti-heroic. Much of it – whether fictional, autobiographical or journalistic – veers between heroic approbation and moral denunciation, between praise of the soldier and rejection of the war' (J. Onions, *English Fiction and the Drama of the Great War, 1918–39* [London, Macmillan, 1990], pp. 2–3).

119 Oliver Lodge's *Raymond* is probably the most famous example of how seance sessions reaffirmed community values, and served to express family intimacies and concerns. See also Walbrook, *The Case of Lester Coltman*; W. T. Pole, *Private Dowding: The Personal Story of a Soldier Killed in Battle* [1917] (London, Spearman, 1966). Private Dowding was the son of Air Chief Marshall Lord Dowding, Spiritualist and author on the subject.

120 Winter, 'The Sites of Memory'. Alison Light, on the other hand, suggests that modernist irony might have been used as a necessary distance from the pain of bereavement. See Light, *Forever England*, especially ch. 2.

121 And had done so since the previous century. See Owen, *The Darkened Room*, pp. 107–38; Harrison, 'Early Victorian Radicals and the Medical Fringe', pp. 198–215; Barrow, *Independent Spirits*, and L. Barrow, 'Anti-Establishment Healing: Spiritualism in Britain', in W. J. Sheils (ed.), *The Church and Healing* (Oxford, Basil Blackwell, 1982), pp. 225–47.

122 Stevenson, *British Society 1914–1945*, ch. 7; Virginia Berridge, 'Health

and Medicine', in *The Cambridge Social History of Britain 1750–1950*, vol. 3, pp. 221–39; *Can We Afford the Doctor? Memories of Health Care*, ed. Pam Schweitzer (London, Age Exchange, 1985); D. Fraser, *The Evolution of the British Welfare State* (London, Macmillan, 1984)

123 G. Cross, *Worktowners at Blackpool: Mass-Observation and Popular Leisure in the 1930s* (London, Routledge, 1990), pp. 75–116.

124 Quoted by M. Sutton, *We Didn't Know Aught*, p. 152.

125 Roberts, *A Ragged Schooling*, p. 134.

126 H. Boddington, *Psychic News Booklet 1: The Human Aura and How to See It* (London, Psychic Press, 1933), p. 1.

127 Barbanell, *Some Discern Spirits*, p. 113.

128 M-OA, TC: Astrology and Spiritualism (1/B), 'Psychometry Class', 31 August 1940.

129 See, for example, M-OA, TC: Astrology and Spiritualism, 1938–47 (1/B) Spiritual Centre Fold Street, February 1938. Here, the Mass-Observation volunteer reported that the medium used psychometric techniques, which she supplemented with astrological-style predictions.

130 M-OA, TC: Astrology and Spiritualism, 1938–47 (1/B) Spiritual Centre, Fold Street, February 1938.

131 Cummins, *Unseen Adventures*, p. 63.

132 *Ibid.*, p. 19.

133 *Ibid.*, pp. 64–5; R. Connell (pseud.) and G. Cummins, *Perceptive Healing* (London, Rider, 1945).

134 See H. Maudsley, *Natural Causes and Supernatural Seemings* (1886) (London, Watts, 1930); W. B. Carpenter, 'Spiritualism and its Recent Converts', *Quarterly Review*, 131:262 (1871) 301–57; 'Dr. Carpenter on Spiritualism', *The Times*, 15 December 1876, p. 6. See also Owen for her commentary on Maudsley and Carpenter and the response of the medical establishment to mediumship: *The Darkened Room*, pp. 139–67.

135 Sometimes it was seen as both, and within the two camps interpretations differed enormously. See chs 7 and 8 below.

136 Barbanell, *Some Discern Spirits*, p. 41.

137 Leonard, *My Life in Two Worlds*, p. 281.

138 B. Evans, *Freedom to Choose: The Life and Work of Dr. Helena Wright, Pioneer of Contraception* (London, Bodley Head, 1984).

139 B. Harrison, *Prudent Revolutionaries: Portraits of British Feminists between the Wars* (Oxford, Clarendon Press, 1987), p. 19.

140 Evans, *Freedom to Choose*, p. 186.

141 *Ibid.*, pp. 9, 205.

142 H. Wright, 'Draft Review' of *Psionic Medicine* by J. H. Reyer, G. Laurence and C. Upton, in the Helena Wright papers at the Contemporary Medical Archives Centre, Wellcome Institute for the History and

Understanding of Medicine, London, CMac: PP/HRW/C5.

143 'Constitution and Regulations of the Institute of Psionic Medicine', Regulation 2. 16 July 1976. Wellcome Institute for the History and Understanding of Medicine, London, CMac: PP/HRW/C.1.

144 Owen, *The Darkened Room*, p. 108.

2

Catholic connections

Part of Spiritualism's strength lay in its ability to produce powerful images in the 'free association' of ideas. Existing concepts found new meaning and new enchantment in the picturesque language of Spiritualism, and its ever-accumulating theory was readily co-opted into personal experience. It was also heavily influenced by a Christian repertoire of signs with a Catholic bias.

In view of the historiography of Spiritualism this claim may seem odd, since Spiritualism is normally associated with the Protestant/empirical tradition – at least in England.[1] Also, Catholicism has traditionally underpinned patriarchal and hierarchical power, whereas Spiritualism privileged 'feminine insight' and propounded the doctrine of equality between souls as a fundamental tenet of psychic law. These two aspects of Spiritualist discourse contributed to the subversion of traditional gender relations, and formed the basis of a vigorous critique of conventional class structures.[2] This much is known. What is often overlooked is the profound ambiguity of Spiritualist discourse. 'Modernity' and 'progress' may have figured strongly in Spiritualism's urban and plebeian culture, but its relation to the dead closely resembled the mutual bonds and obligations characteristic of an earlier, Catholic culture. Similarly, Spiritualism contradicted its egalitarian and feminist tendencies with its acceptance of rigidly hierarchical structures in the other world, where all authority stretched back to God the Father.

In my attempts to show continuities between Spiritualism and Catholicism, I am not concerned with the intricacies of contemporary Roman Catholic debate on theological points, or with the many different shades of Catholic religiosity. My purpose is to compare Spiritualism with what we might label 'everyday' Catholic orthodoxy in interwar Britain – that is to say, those articles of faith given by the clergy to the laity in educational literature such as the penny pamphlets produced by the Catholic Truth Society.

Intended to fulfil propaganda and educational purposes, this society was formally established in 1884, under the presidency of Bishop Vaughan. Its stated aims were: '(1) to spread among Catholics small devotional works, (2) to assist the uneducated poor to a better knowledge of their religion, (3) to spread among Protestants information regarding Catholic faith and practice, and (4) to promote the circulation of good and cheap Catholic literature'. The Society flourished in the twentieth century, and branches extend throughout England, Ireland, Scotland, America and Australia.[3] Among the materials published by the Society, many continuities between Spiritualism and Catholicism may be found.

Admittedly, these continuities are not immediately apparent. There is no evidence that Spiritualism consciously attempted to align itself with Catholicism or, for that matter, any traditional religion. The Spiritualists' attitude to conventional theology remained identical to those of their nineteenth-century counterparts, and continued to express widespread resentment and dissatisfaction with the established churches. In 1933, *Psychic News* issued a booklet on the philosophy of Spiritualism where familiar criticisms of religious orthodoxy were again rehearsed. According to this publication, conventional theology was incorrect, morally bankrupt, and incapable of contributing to social and spiritual advancement: the doctrine of Hell, the Fall, and the Sacrifice of Christ were all immoral doctrines that maligned God, and the doctrine of rewards and punishments merely underpinned clerical power by inducing fear in the faithful.[4] Nevertheless, Spiritualists were immersed in the Christian tradition. Although on an institutional level the Spiritualist movement remained divided (as it had in the previous century) between Christians and non-Christians,[5] the language used by both groups habitually employed Christian metaphors in their descriptions of Spiritualist practice and belief. Before turning to specifically Catholic influences, we should note these ecumenical aspects of Spiritualist belief and ritual.

Spiritualists regularly evoked Scriptural miracles to lend credence to modern psychic events. The levitations, the rushing winds, the tongues of fire described in the Bible, were all recast in the language of modern Spiritualism; so were the healing and clairvoyant powers of Christ and the Apostles. Arthur Conan Doyle, a lapsed Catholic and much-prized convert to Spiritualism, found such phenomena 'absolutely in accord-ance with psychic law as we know it'. In *The New Revelation* (1918), Conan Doyle sought to show how the miracles described in the Bible corresponded to those performed by modern mediums:

> [W]hen Christ, on being touched by the sick woman, said: 'Who has touched me? Much virtue has passed out of me.' Could He say more clearly what a healing medium would now say, save that he would use the word 'power' instead of 'virtue'; or when we read: 'Try the spirits whether they be of God', is it not the very advice which would now be given to a novice approaching a séance?[6]

According to Spiritualism's spokesmen and -women, miraculous events were part of nature. Hewat McKenzie declared that the resur-rection of Christ 'was but the operation of a natural law'.[7] Under this law the dead were conterminous with the living. Nevertheless, the means by which people were supposed to survive death came straight from the mystery of the Trinity. McKenzie, as we know, imagined the human as a triune being composed of a material body, an ethereal counterpart, and a spirit. The spirit and ethereal body survived, while the material body was left behind to disintegrate.[8] Arthur Findlay also relied on the concept of the Trinity when he wrote: 'Man we now know, is a trinity composed of a body of flesh, a duplicate etheric body, and a mind, which latter, through the etheric body, controls the physical body on earth, and the etheric body in the etheric world.'[9]

Spiritualists quoted freely from the Bible, placing special emphasis on the apostolic Scriptures. The early Church represented 'pure Christi-anity'. These were the halcyon days of the spirit, when miracles worked freely through the disciples, and nobody listened to 'those Old Testa-ment prohibitions which were meant to keep these powers only for the use and profit of the priesthood'.[10] The Apostolic Church provided many Spiritualists with their theological framework and political authority. Spiritualists continually cited the Acts of the Apostles in ways that underpinned a socialist agenda, and criticised civic and clerical privilege.[11] The *Scripts of Cleophas*, communicated through the mediumship of Geraldine Cummins, provided the most comprehensive interpretation of the apostolic community in the light of modern Spiritualism.

Community

Geraldine Cummins was one of Spiritualism's most respected mediums. The daughter of Professor Ashley Cummins, she grew up in County Cork, Ireland, in the years leading up to the First World War. She tried many diverse occupations, including librarian, agricultural labourer, athlete, short-story writer, office secretary and woodcutter. While she was still in her teens, she became a 'speech-making suffragette'; this activity led to her 'being stoned through the streets of my native city by the sweated women factory workers whose cause I so ardently espoused'.[12]

When Cummins reached her twenties, she was introduced to Hester Dowden, a Spiritualist medium, and W. B. Yeats, both of whom aroused her interest in psychic matters. They persuaded her to try her hand at telepathy, and during the 1914–18 War she had two experiences of prevision. One of these involved the prediction of the death of her brother, then serving with the Fifth Gurkhas in Gallipoli. In a dream, Geraldine was running with others on an open plain:

> My brother Harry was a little ahead of us, urging us on. Suddenly he flung up his arms and fell forward on his face. Then I heard a voice saying, 'You will never see Harry again.' Trembling and momentarily broken with emotion, I woke up and the voice ceased ... Three weeks later we received the news that Harry had been killed instantaneously while leading his men in an attack against the Turks, across an open plain in broad daylight.[13]

Even so, Cummins's career as a medium did not really begin until 1923, when she met Beatrice Gibbes, who was to become her constant companion and collaborator in psychic experiments. Gibbes acted as investigator, Cummins as medium. Gibbes was a member of the prestigious Society for Psychical Research (famous for its careful experiments with psychics), and so lent extra credibility to Cummins's mediumship. She made her home available to Cummins for eight months of each year, and became the '"guardian–caretaker" of [her] psychic life'.[14]

In 1923, Cummins received through automatic script the first few lines of a manuscript subsequently known as *The Scripts of Cleophas*. The communicating spirit said that his name was 'Messenger', and his task was to supplement the Apostolic Scriptures with a hitherto unknown history of the early Christian Church. The *Scripts* aroused a good deal of public interest and controversy. Many reviewers were sceptical of 'Messenger's' authenticity,[15] but his testimony was cautiously endorsed by several biblical scholars.[16] For Spiritualists, *The Scripts* acquired the status of a second Scripture.[17] 'Messenger's narrative stressed the communal values of the early Christian Church. In one passage, the apostle James appears before an assembly of elders, merchants and priests.

> Let there be a State, and let all men obey its laws. But let all men gather together and hearken to the teachings of those who have the knowledge of Christ within them, and then, when they are filled with the Spirit of Truth, let them form themselves into Brotherhoods, and let those within the Brotherhood share alike and have a common treasury.[18]

The miracles described by 'Messenger' also preserved communal values. In one place, for example, the eleven disciples are pictured together for the purpose of choosing Judas's replacement:

> The twelve had learned from the Master certain practices concerning the invocation of knowledge. He bound them to give those secrets to no man, so they have perished. I can but tell you that they gathered together, and in the midst of them was a table; the Brethren sat about it in silence, and for a space their hands were joined, and they prayed with their whole being for the light. After the loosing of their hands they made certain signs. Of these I may not speak but to say that they were for the freeing of the Body of Light from each of the Eleven. When all these spiritual bodies were set free they blended with one another, making what would seem to mortal eye a rounded pillar that was pure white and which passed into a mist above the heads of the watchers.[19]

This miracle was in complete accord with seance technique and with Spiritualist expectations of the behaviour of psychic phenomena. Because each disciple was a powerful medium, the results were more dramatic than could normally be expected, but the procedures were identical. The participants were seated around a table, they linked hands to form what Spiritualists called the psychic circle, and they boosted the power with prayer. Soon, the psychic energy generated by the circle began to take effect; the etheric bodies rose above their physical bodies and combined to produce a denser kind of etheric substance, visible to the naked eye.

The emphasis on communal effort in the production of phenomena reaffirmed Spiritualism's egalitarian values; it was also in agreement with contemporary Catholic conceptions of the role of community in the production of the miracle of the Mass. The theologian Gerald Ellard considered that the 'living streams of the Saviour's fountains course through – and are in part conditioned by – his own active part in the [Mass and other] rites as received'.[20] In *The Mass in Transition* (1956), Ellard explained that community activity at the Mass was author-ised by the early Church, and emphasised in modern times by Pope Pius X, who held the office of Pontiff between 1903 and 1909. The Church's aims in this respect seem to have been pragmatic as well as spiritual, since as Cardinal Mercier once remarked: 'The most certain means of preserving the people from religious indifference is to give them an active role in the divine services.'[21] According to Ellard, both Pius XI (Pontiff 1909–39) and Pius XII (Pontiff 1939–58) held similar views about the spiritual efficacy of active involvement in the Sacra-ment. In 1940, in a talk on the subject, Pope Pius XII said: 'But for your own spiritual welfare and that of others (who you are striving to assist at Mass more faithfully), you must know that *to assist fully at Mass* means to take part *in the entire sacred "Action"*.'[22]

Catholic sects, like the Liberal Catholic Church,[23] also emphasised the efficacy of collective effort during Mass. In 1942, Bishop Piggott (who presided between 1934 and 1956), asked his readers to consider 'the Mass as a medium between that world and this', as an 'occult force of simply incalculable potency' for good which relied, in part, on human effort. 'All depends', he wrote, 'upon sovereign power, but in our world our effort is also required.' At the Mass our 'part as assistants' of God 'is to follow the ceremony closely and at the appropriate moments to will the distribution of the stupendous force to oppose evil and strengthen good in the world.' In this way, 'God has given us a small share in His work of managing the universe'. Piggott thought the com-munity effort of the Mass was better than private prayer because '[c]ollective effort, as all know, is cumulative and therefore more potent than the sum of individual efforts acting separately'.[24]

Seance techniques expressed parallel sentiments and expectations. The one described in *The Scripts of Cleophas* called first on the power of God, and secondly on the collective effort of participants whose combined power 'amplified' the psychic force and produced the pillar of white.

'Compensation and retribution hereafter'

In accordance with teachings of *The Scripts of Cleophas*, most Spiritualists explicitly recognised an authoritative God figure or Great Spirit at the apex of creation. Interwar Spiritualism was steeped in nostalgia for authoritarian forms of Christianity even while it revolted against them. In the Christian tradition, miracles are the prerogatives of Divine power: saints, seers and prophets cannot perform miracles under their own volition, 'God alone can do that'.[25] Such people act as 'channels' or 'instruments' of the Divine will. Spiritualists claimed no more for their mediums. Mediums did not *own* their psychic abilities, they were 'but the mouthpiece of those in the Beyond',[26] who, in turn, were authorised by the Great Spirit, or God. Spirit visitors repeatedly spoke of the love of the 'Great Father', and the 'Fatherhood of God' appeared as the first of the Seven Principles of the Spiritualists National Union.[27] Even Spiritualists like Arthur Findlay, who conceived of God, strictly speaking, as 'evolving Mind', tended to slip into a more orthodox approach to God's nature when he conversed with the spirit world. The spirit visitors recorded in Findlay's *Way of Life* spoke about the 'homes which the Great Father had prepared on the spirit side of life', and gave sermons about how to 'serve God'.[28] Spirit-guides were also inclined to dispense conventional Christian blessings and advice. One Red Indian guide advised seance sitters to say in times of trouble: '"Come dear Father, into Thy hands I commend my way"; and the spirit friends ... will come and guide you.'[29]

Spiritualism conceived of rigidly hierarchical structures in the 'other world', comprising seven spheres of existence. Each of these was a moral and physical improvement on the one below. The highest sphere was known as the 'Christ sphere', and resembled the biblical version of the topography of Heaven depicted in Revelations. Hewat McKenzie described the Christ sphere as follows:

> Looked at with the human eyes, its foundations seem to be various coloured precious stones, and the streets as if manufactured from

blocks of gold. This description, however, is unsatisfactory, for it has the appearance of crystalline gems congealed, so that as one walks upon it the various facets sparkle with a dazzling radiance as of frosted gold or precious stones.[30]

The 'Christ sphere' was reserved for highly 'evolved spirits', and was the most refined in ethereal density. Spheres below were progressively dense and more 'evil' in character. The lowest sphere housed 'evil doers' from earth. From the perspective of McKenzie's 'plebeian' politics, such individuals were likely to be 'the proud and degraded aristocrats' who, despite every advantage in life, had 'picked up vicious practices and left an evil trail behind [them]'.[31]

Spiritualists may have rejected the doctrine of rewards and punishments, but the idea was apt to reappear under the guise of spiritual evolution. According to McKenzie, individuals after death gravitated by the 'law of attraction' to their appropriate sphere. He suspected that most people would gravitate to the second or third sphere, where life was similar in kind to earthly existence, but free from earthly anxieties. In time, through the 'education of the spirit', the individual rose to a higher plane.[32] Those relegated to the lower planes could expect to suffer in a purgatorial manner:

> The author makes no attempt to describe the mental suffering, which all residents experience before rising from these low spheres. A pen infinitely more capable than his, is necessary to describe the agony of remorse, the ghastly fears, the awful soul efforts that all must undergo before a purified state is reached.[33]

The chain of sin, suffering, cleansing and healing is familiar from Catholic accounts of purgatory. In a booklet by the Reverend G. J. MacGillivray, published by the Catholic Truth Society in 1929, the soul in purgatory is likened to a 'sick man who feels himself daily growing stronger and returning to health' as he 'sees those stains of rust being gradually cleansed away'.[34] Conan Doyle agreed that the idea of 'punishment, of purifying chastisement, in fact of Purgatory, [was] justified by the reports from the other side'. Employing an identical metaphor to MacGillivray, he described the lowest spirit sphere as a 'hospital for weakly souls'.[35]

Spiritualist accounts of the topography of the lowest sphere varied, but generally it was thought to be dark and composed of an extremely dense substance. In McKenzie's words, the lowest sphere 'is extremely gross and solid in nature in comparison with the more distant spheres. The floor or basement of this place is composed of solid rocky sub-stance, honeycombed with deep gorges and chasms, in which are to be found degraded human beings who once dwelt on earth.'[36] Similar associations made between lightness and goodness, heaviness and sin, were produced in Catholic publications of the period. MacGillivray explained:

> Just as heavy bodies fall by their own weight, and light bodies neces-sarily rise because of their lightness, so souls that are in sin are carried inevitably by the weight of their sins to Hell, while those that are in grace as inevitably rise to Heaven, unless they are hindered for a time by the remains of sin, which must be purged away.[37]

Following the ancient assumption that like attracts like, both Spiritual-ists and Catholics expected to find their appropriate place after death. Works on earth played a role in salvation, as distinct from traditional Protestantism where salvation is justified through faith. One could accumulate sin and descend to the lower planes, or alternatively strive for the 'lightness' of virtue and ascend to a higher sphere. One virtue recognised by both Spiritualists and Catholics was the fulfilment of obligations owed to the dead.

Obligations to the dead

Twentieth-century Catholics continued to live in close contact with the 'afterworld'. In the hour of death the faithful were taught to expect the presence of Christ and Mary, and 'a strong company of angels and saints', who together acted as 'the allies of our soul against the enemy', the devil.[38] But it was not only in the extremity of death that links were forged with life beyond the grave. According to the Reverend Mac-Gillivray, souls in heaven and in purgatory watched over their friends and relatives on earth, and took an interest in their progress.[39] The living also retained intimate relations with Mary, guardian angels and the saints, and petitioned them for moral guidance and consolation in adversity.[40]

Spiritualists related to the inhabitants of the spirit world in a similar way. The *raison d'être* of the seance was the opportunity it offered to continue relations with dead relatives. However, Spiritualists distinguished between these spirits and more 'evolved spirits' who existed on a higher plane and often acted as spirit-guides. Such spirits were explicitly identified with the traditional saint or angel. Indeed, the three terms 'evolved spirit', 'saint' and 'angel' were used synonymously. In *The Scripts of Cleophas* there were copious references to angels, and Conan Doyle thought that the 'many higher spirits with our departed' could equally well be called angels.[41] Another Spiritualist author wrote that 'God's angels' were constant visitors to this earthly plane 'on their ceaseless errands of mercy and pity'.[42] Mediums often spoke of their 'guardian angel' and prayed to their spirit-guides as one would pray to a favourite saint. Spiritualists also relied on their spirit-guides for moral teaching and for revelation. At the time of mortal death, 'evolved spirits' adopted the function, and sometimes the name, of 'angel'. At one seance during the Second World War, the spirit-guide informed the seance circle that 'thousands of Ministering Angels' ware engaged in helping the casualties of war: even those 'who were very badly mangled [felt] no pain. Very gently they [were] carried over to the other side by those engaged in this merciful work.'[43]

Less exalted spirits also returned to earth for the express purpose of assisting the living. The reappearance of the dead for the purpose of 'righting wrongs' on earth captured the imagination of Hollywood. In 1926, Fox Film Company made *The Return of Peter Grimm*, adapted from the play of that name by the Spiritualist David Belasco. The film focused on Peter Grimm, who arranged a marriage between his son and his adopted daughter. However, following his death, and from the vantage point of the spirit world, he came to realise the unworthiness of his son. The story dealt with his return as a spirit and his attempts to prevent the wedding. Spiritualists were quite pleased with the results. *The Two Worlds* liked the moral tone of the film, and the photographic effects: 'The spirit of the old man is well produced. It is less shadowy than the usual ghost, and yet sufficiently ethereal to enable the observer to differentiate between the incarnate and discarnate individuals.'[44]

Just as mortals received help from the 'afterworld', so the inhabitants of that world expected to receive help from the living. According to one Catholic Truth Society author: 'God has given us such power over the dead that they seem … to depend almost more on earth than on heaven.'[45] In particular, the souls in purgatory relied on human intervention in divine affairs for speeding their progress to heaven. Several methods were considered efficacious: prayer, good works (which could be transferred into indulgences for those in purgatory) and the saying of Masses. Such duties were essential to the well-being of the dead, because by these means 'we can help them, console them and shorten their time of waiting'.[46] Similarly, Spiritualists did not merely communicate with the spirits of the dead; they cooperated with some and offered to help others. As we have already seen (Chapter 1), the operations carried out to dispel poltergeists were undertaken on *behalf* of the poltergeist, just as much as for those who were afflicted by their presence. While Catholics prayed for the release of souls in purgatory, Spiritualists attempted to release spirits who were 'trapped' in or near the earth plane. The medium Gladys Leonard described in her auto-biography how she helped one spirit who had become 'trapped' owing to his intense craving for his previous earth conditions:

> Many of his spirit friends had tried to help him by attempting to turn his thoughts to their own higher plane, but he would not open his mind to them. When I arrived at the house, these friends were able to contact me, and impressed me to pray for him in a manner and form that would best suit his case. It appeared to be the first time anybody on earth had done so; and, being so much more in touch with earth conditions than he was with any other, he caught the sense of my very definitely worded prayer, and made an attempt to respond, or rather cooperate with it.[47]

Following Catholic teaching on the subject of purgatory, Leonard declared that those spirits on the lower planes 'are *more in our power, more at our mercy, than we are in theirs*'. It was therefore our responsibility to help and uplift these spirits by assisting them to progress to higher planes of existence.[48]

This sense of responsibility for the welfare of the dead prompted Spiritualists to create special 'rescue circles' with the express purpose of helping spirits who, for various reasons, had failed to gravitate to their proper place in the spirit universe. Spiritualists said that some such spirits were asleep, and that others were lost or confused. A *Psychic News* educational pamphlet (1933) said that a lost spirit was often 'more surprised than the sitters to find himself talking through an unaccustomed body'. According to this publication, these spirits invariably dwelt on the manner of their death. If they passed away 'under stress of emotion, this automatically reproduce[d] itself, and carr[ied] on towards its logical conclusion'.[49] Frederick Wood described how his rescue circle aided the 'lost spirits' of people killed in various ways during World War II. In his book, *Mediumship and War*, he explained that the problem for these spirits was the manner of their passing:

> [A]lthough physical pain is ended, the conditions of their passing may affect their mental condition for a long time.
>
> In cases of sudden death by accident or bombs they are often bewildered – lost in a grey mist – until rescued by some spirit-helper; and this is where the real tragedy lies, for often they are unable to perceive the help which is close at hand. In such cases they can *only* be helped *from this side*, and psychic power and mediumship are usually the only means of giving help.[50]

The method employed to help these spirits was quite simple: 'lost' spirits expressed their fears through a medium and the rescue circle responded with reassurances, sympathy and advice on how confused spirits might adjust to their new condition. The more violent the death, the more difficult it was for the spirit to adjust to its new surroundings.

In 1937, the medium Estelle Roberts claimed to be in contact with the spirit of ten-year-old Mona Tinsley, who was reported missing from her home in January of that year. Roberts became involved with the case soon after the child disappeared. Having heard about Mona through the newspapers, and concerned about public speculation over whether the girl was dead or alive, Roberts wrote to the Chief Constable of Newark-on-Trent asking him to send her a garment belonging to Mona. With the permission of Mona's parents, a pink silk dress was sent:

> As I took it from its wrapping and held the soft material in my hands, I knew at once that Mona was dead …
>
> Then, with Red Cloud's help [Roberts' spirit guide] Mona spoke to me, saying she had been taken to a small house where she had been strangled. She gave me a picture of a house, with a water-filled ditch on one side, a field at its back, a churchyard close by, and an inn within sight. In my vision I was taken to a graveyard, over a bridge, and across some fields to a river beyond. There I stopped, unable to go further.
>
> The picture projected to me was so clear that my secretary telephoned the Newark police to check its details with them. Evidently

my description coincided closely with the location of the child's disappearance because before they rang off they invited me to visit the site.[51]

From then on, Roberts co-operated with the police. She wrote that through her clairvoyant impressions she helped them to find Mona's body and confirm their suspicions as to the identity of the murderer.[52]

As far as Spiritualists were concerned, Roberts's part in the affair served the dead as well as the living. Taking up the story, Sylvia Barbanell, a leading propagandist for Spiritualism and author of many Spiritualist tracts, insisted that 'the conflicting thoughts and emotions that were rife in her [Mona's] earthly surrounds, shattered the child's peace and retarded her progress in the spirit world'.[53] Through Estelle Roberts's intervention, Mona's troubled mind 'was eased, and she was able to attain the natural heritage of every dead child – progress and happiness in the spirit world.'[54] So despite Spiritualism's deployment of modern rhetoric – progress, evolution and the attainment of happiness – Mona's use of Roberts as an instrument of justice on earth spoke of the traditional obligation to perform services for the dead to ensure their peace and well-being.[55]

There was a tacit sense of danger attached to all spirits who were dispatched violently to the 'other world', for it was these spirits who were liable to 'take possession' of the living. This is why Spiritualists condemned suicide and capital punishment. Capital punishment, wrote one Spiritualist, launched into the afterworld souls who were full of 'angry passions' and 'vengeful feelings'.[56] These were the spirits who came closest to the 'unclean spirits' of the popular Catholic imagination.

Estelle Roberts recalled an incident where she and her spirit-guide, 'Red Cloud', intervened in a case of possession. This involved a young man who said he was often almost overwhelmed with a desire to kill his mother. A seance was arranged, and 'Red Cloud' 'came through'. Applying the logic of like attracts like, he said to the man: 'Two years ago you visited a house of ill repute in France, and when you left you did not come away alone. An evil spirit accompanied you in your aura, seeing in you a channel for the earthly expression of his own sinful desires.' 'Red Cloud' then performed an exorcism by temporarily allowing the 'evil spirit' to control Roberts. There followed a 'raucous, rumbustious performance' where the 'evil spirit' uttered 'threats and screaming blasphemies' through the medium. The force of 'Red Cloud' and the prayers of the seance circle managed to dislodge the 'unwanted creature', and 'all was silence'.[57]

Roberts performed exorcisms when the need arose, but it was Carl Wickland, founder of the National Psychological Institute, who was the acknowledged authority for Spiritualists on this kind of entity. Wickland became interested in the hypothesis that souls survive, and can enter the minds and bodies of the living, through his work as a psychologist at the Psychopathic Institute of Chicago. Struck by the large number of people who displayed signs of conventional demonic possession following experiments with Ouija boards and the like, Wickland undertook research into psychic phenomena.[58] His suspicion that 'obsessing spirits' caused this condition was confirmed, he wrote, following a routine day at the dissecting laboratory: On his arrival home, his wife seemed to have been 'taken with a sudden illness'. She complained of 'feeling strange, [and] staggered as though about to fall'. As Wickland placed his hand on her shoulder, she:

> drew herself up and became entranced by a foreign intelligence who said, with threatening gesture:
> 'What do you mean by cutting me?'
> I answered that I was not aware of cutting anyone, but the spirit angrily replied:
> 'Of course you are! You are cutting on my leg.'
> Realising that the spirit owner of the body on which I had been operating had followed me home, I began to parley with him, first placing my wife in a chair.[59]

After this encounter with the spirit world, Wickland and his wife collaborated in what one Spiritualist described as the work of 'Waking Up and Saving the Lost Souls of the Dead'[60] – she as medium, he as priest/doctor. They published their experiences in 1924 under the title *Thirty Years among the Dead*. In this book, which quickly attained the status of a Spiritualist classic on the subject of 'possessing' or 'obsessing' entities,[61] Wickland describes the conditions under which spirits can 'attach' themselves to humans. The psychosomatic conditions listed as conducive to obsession comprised stereotypical 'feminine' disabilities, such as 'a depleted nervous system' and lowered 'vitality'.[62] Significantly, all the patients mentioned by Wickland were women. In this discourse, the 'forces of unreason', traditionally inscribed in the female physiology,[63] attracted corresponding forces from the next world: 'Many controlling spirits act as if demented and are difficult to reason with.'[64] In keeping with this popular view of insanity as the binary opposite of reason, Wickland's obsessing spirits were overrepresented by groups who were stigmatised under Enlightenment rationality as the epitome of irrationality: pubescent girls, children, and 'criminal' men.

Wickland's understanding of spirit pathology illustrates the degree of ambivalence in Spiritualist discourse. On the one hand, 'nervous femininity' was constructed negatively as the condition of spirit obsession; on the other, it was 'feminine intuition and feeling' which were the means of contacting and dispersing unwelcome spirit companions. Then again, Wickland invokes the mystical law of like attracts like, only to express Enlightenment anxieties about the sources and dangers of 'irrational forces'.

Wickland's treatments were similarly ambivalent. In dealing with spirits he mixed the methods and language of psychotherapy with traditional Catholic rites of exorcism. The victims of 'obsessing spirits' were labelled 'patients', and considered in need of 'treatment'. But it was the spirit to whom Wickland turned his attention. Typically, the obsessing spirit simulated the behaviour of a traditional devil, causing the 'patient' to deviate from prescribed cultural norms:

> Mrs Fl., a patient who had been declared incurably insane by several physicians, was a refined lady of gentle disposition, who had become very wild and unmanageable, swearing constantly, and fighting with such violence that several persons were required to restrain her.
>
> She was also subject to coma states, again to fainting spells, would refuse food, announce that she had been 'married above by celestial powers' and used extraordinarily vile language.[65]

Wickland frequently used 'electric shock treatment' on such 'patients' – not for conventional reasons, but to 'cast out' obsessing entities. The effect of this was to drive the 'obsessing' spirit into Mrs Wickland's specially sensitive psychic aura, which made it easier for Wickland to address the spirit directly. Adopting the manner of doctor to patient, Wickland questioned the spirit about its previous existence on earth, and instructed it about its present condition. The dialogue that followed owed something to medical categories of mental instability, something to traditional ghost and cautionary tales and also had a distinct flavour of the Catholic confessional.

Mrs McA, for instance, was diagnosed by Wickland as suffering from 'psychic invalidism, chronic illness and lassitude due to spirit obsession'. A curious aspect of Mrs McA's condition was her sudden and uncontrollable desires. One day she developed an intense desire for ice cream, though normally she did not care for it. That evening she attended the Wicklands' seance circle, and it transpired that she was under the influence of a spirit named Harry Haywood, a 'handsome reprobate with a weakness for beautiful women' and ice cream. Harry Haywood talked about his life as an earthbound spirit and about his life on earth: how his indulgent upbringing had resulted in his 'reduced moral sense', how his gambling had left him penniless, and how he arranged life insurance for his lover, naming himself as beneficiary, and then arranged her murder. Harry described his trial and his execution in detail. The spirit showed signs of remorse for what he had done and was, in effect, absolved of his 'sins' by Wickland, who then enlightened him concerning the 'higher life', and thus opened the way for Harry Haywood's future 'progress in the spirit world'.[66]

Sensuous experience

The Spiritualist conception of the 'other side' – its heavens and purgatories, its relations with the dead, its guardian angels and demons – was thoroughly enmeshed in popular Catholic traditions. Similarly, the rituals by which Spiritualists brought themselves into communion with the inhabitants of the 'other side' paralleled the sensuous experience of the Mass – representing another departure from the relative austerities of various brands of Protestantism.

The Mass and the seance opened channels to an unseen world and, as we have seen, the success of each event was dependent, in part, upon the cumulative power of collective participation. In Spiritualist circles, empathic feelings between participants were vital to the success of the seance. Unsympathetic or otherwise unsuitable sitters disrupted the delicate balance of psychic forces and spoilt the seance. Gladys Leonard thought that the sitter played 'almost – perhaps quite – as important' a role as the medium in seance procedure and the successful production of phenomena, and she complained about the casual sitter, who '"blows in" without any preparation whatever'.[67] Among committed Spiritualists, everything possible was done to produce an atmosphere conducive to feelings of union between participants. Hewat McKenzie described the ideal setting in *Spirit Intercourse*:

> Whenever spirit intercourse is to be conducted a room should be set aside as far as possible for this purpose, where quietness and isolation from intruders can be had. A musical instrument, when tastefully played, helps the conditions, for music is a great asset in banishing the thought of besetting cares and in stimulating noble emotions. It also helps to free the spirit of the medium, and attunes the sitters to the finer vibrations of celestial spheres ... No strong light should issue from the windows, therefore a blind is necessary, or better still, the window may be covered with artistic glacier paper. The atmosphere of the room may be freshened by the use of any essence of flowers, or incense if desired, but the particular essence should be restricted to the seance room alone, and not used upon the person, or for any other purpose, as the sense of smell is a very important factor in the association of ideas. This also applies to the music, and as far as possible the particular music used in the seance room should be reserved for this, such songs and hymns being selected as best pleases the worshippers.[68]

Having completed these preparations, sitters would seat themselves around a table and link hands to activate the 'psychic flow'.

Marina Warner has remarked that the 'Catholic Church has always sought to reach the soul through the senses ... The Reproaches of Good Friday or the litanies chanted by the choir and answered by the congregation are intended, like the rosary, to lull the believer into a trance-like state in which spiritual light may more easily flood the soul.'[69] Spiritualist rituals were designed with the same purpose in mind. The physical environment recommended by McKenzie for spirit communication lacked the grandeur and complexity of the Mass, but the seance experience was no less sensuous for that. There was the subdued lighting, the emphasis on smell and sound, the dreamlike atmosphere and the suspension of felt boundaries between 'inside' and 'outside' as sitters linked hands in the darkness.

For many Spiritualists, feeling was explicitly part of cognition.[70] This is why a number of them were attracted to the mystery and magic, the warmth and passion, of the Catholic Church. Eileen Garrett recalled how, as a child, she secretly watched the confirmation of her Catholic schoolmates. Hiding in the gallery of the chapel, she was deeply impressed by the beauty and mystery of the ritual unfolding before her.

After this experience she looked forward to her own confirmation in the Church of England. The event was a disappointment. The appearance and indifferent demeanour of the presiding Bishop repelled her, and the service seemed cold and perfunctory:

> The memory of the Catholic Confirmation I had witnessed flashed back into my mind. I could see again the kindly Catholic prelate placing his hands in gentle blessing on the heads of my schoolmates. I could still remember how deeply moved I had then been, by the mystical setting and the harmonious chanting and intoning of the priests. Here, in this [Anglican] church there was neither beauty or true emotion; everything was hurried, perfunctory and cold.[71]

For Garrett, her confirmation lacked authenticity because the service excluded sensuous experience, and thus the possibility of subjective immersion in events. By contrast, the Catholic Confirmation Mass seemed 'real' to her because it produced a personal sense of full participation.

The importance of sensuous and aesthetic experience in constructing reality is also demonstrated in Clare Sheridan's dual attraction to Catholicism and Spiritualism. Sheridan was born Clare Frewen, daughter of Clara Jerome and cousin to Winston Churchill. She was brought up within the Church of England, but for disciplinary reasons her parents dispatched her to a convent boarding school in France when she was about twelve years old. In other respects she received a conventional upper-class upbringing and made an orthodox marriage, at the age of nineteen, to the aristocratic but financially insecure Wilfred Sheridan. Upon the death of Wilfred, five years later in the slaughter of trench warfare, Clare visited a medium for the purpose of making contact with his spirit.

By the time of Wilfred's death, 1915, Clare was well acquainted with the supernatural. She learned of heaven from her nurse, Nene, and hell from her governess. She perused Spiritualist publications in her father's library, and her convent education increased her sensitivity to spiritual forces. When her eldest child, Elizabeth, became critically ill, she prayed desperately to the Virgin Mary.[72] So she arrived for her seance appointment fully expecting to make contact with Wilfred – and she did! Accurate details of Wilfred's life were revealed by the medium, and Clare was convinced of his continued existence. But although she believed that the medium was genuine, and accepted the existence of a spirit world, there is no sense of her having *felt* anything except a vague dissatisfaction and irritation. The experience, she wrote, was 'undeniably *un*satisfactory'; it was 'exasperating rather than consoling'.[73] When Wilfred's spirit began to adopt the domineering postures characteristic of him in life, she ceased to attend seances. Her next encounter with Spiritualism, however, was an entirely different matter. This time connection with the spirit world grew gradually out of her feelings of affinity with her ancestral home, Brede, and her friendship with a medium.

Clare inherited Brede on the death of her son, Dick, in 1938. She thought of it as her 'true home', and her return in middle life evoked childhood memories. She remembered how she and her brother Peter had transformed the dell in the grounds of Brede into a 'sacred hidden place'; how they built an altar and offered flowers to an unknown god who, Clare believed, had control over the wild things in the dell. In this place, with its evocative memories, smells and sights, the spirit of her dead son seemed to speak to her.[74] Soon after her return to Brede, she received a letter from a woman called Shirley Eshelby, who assured her that Dick survived in another world. Shirley said that she also had a daughter and a son on the spirit plane, and was in constant communication with them. The two women met, and subsequently became friends.

One winter evening, Clare and Shirley were sitting together when suddenly, in the middle of an unfinished sentence, Shirley began to speak with someone unseen. Clare said she could see her friend become drowsy 'as the psychic spell' began to take effect.[75] Shirley's voice went husky; she closed her eyes and went on to describe a clairvoyant vision. However, it soon became clear to Clare that something had gone wrong. Shirley seemed distressed, and her hands went cold. It transpired that the communicating spirit was trying to persuade Shirley to leave her body. Clare struggled to bring her friend back to normal consciousness.

> Again he [the spirit] urged Shirley to come out of her shell [body], and I was witness of this strange thing; Shirley struggling against an unseen hand that had seized her by the arm. There seemed to be only one protection left, and we each made the sign of the Cross.[76]

Unlike Clare's previous contact with the spirit world, this encounter was entirely 'real'. No evidence whatever was offered by the spirit concerning its identity, but Clare was too caught up in the drama of the moment to ask. Instead of accepting the existence of a spirit world in an abstract and distant way, she *experienced* it in the fullest sense of the word. Through Shirley Eshelby's trusted mediumship, Clare contacted other spirits with whom relations were less disturbing, but similarly intense. She had a particularly close relationship with a deceased priest, named 'Father John', who acted as her spirit adviser and confessor.

Clare's ability to enter intense relations with unseen entities harked back to her childhood worship of a pagan god, and to a passionate involvement with the Catholic Church. When she was sent to the convent school in France, her sense of isolation as a foreigner was intensified by her Protestant background (her parents paid for her to eat meat on Fridays) and her lack of interest in games and school work. Her one source of joy was the Chapel, where the 'altar glistened with gold' and where there were 'masses of candles which a nun lit one by one with a long taper before the Angelus':

> Throughout the day I looked forward to the moment of the Angelus, and it seemed all too short. I should have liked to spend hours in the Chapel. I loved High Mass and the unexpected ritual of feast days.
>
>   There was one day in the year when we filed by the High Altar and kissed a crucifix inset with a relic of the Holy Cross. This I approached with an emotion that was almost an ecstasy.[77]

The feeling of ecstatic union that Catholic ritual elicited in Clare Sheridan is identified in Freudian analysis with the resurgence of primary narcissism. In *Civilization and Its Discontents*, Freud links 'religious feeling' with infantile experience. According to this view, the 'oceanic feeling' or 'sense of oneness' with the cosmos represents the restoration of a time when the infant has not yet distinguished its own ego from the external world. Freud constructs this inclusiveness of ego consciousness, this blurring of inside/outside boundaries – summed up in the phrase 'oceanic feeling' – negatively. He interprets the sensation as as a 'regression' or 'escape' into the memory of a sheltering maternal world – a world that threatens to disintegrate personal boundaries.[78]

The weakening or apparent loss of personal boundaries is intolerable to the Enlightenment/scientific project to which Freud is heir. 'Mind', 'individuality', 'objectivity', 'rationality', guarantee 'scientific truth' and stand sentry against the lure of an undifferentiated union, labelled maternal, which threatens the sovereign integrity of the ego.[79] We will return to this stigmatised maternity in Chapter 5, but for now I want to note the importance of the 'maternal unconscious' in the Catholic and Spiritualist imagination.

Some strands of feminism have cautioned us against succumbing to the stereotype of a transhistoric 'Mother Principle'. But, as Jacqueline Rose observes, 'because an image of femininity can be identified as male fantasy, it is not any less intensely lived by women'.[80] In Catholicism, the fantasy of a sheltering, unifying maternity is integrated in the performance of the Mass and celebrated through the devotional figure of the Holy Mother.[81] Spiritualists replicated Catholic representations of archaic union in their seances, while the figure of the Holy Mother was mirrored in the medium. In Chapter 3, I will show how Spiritualists identified their mediums with Mary and the female saints. It was not merely that Mary was offered as an ethical and spiritual model for mediums to emulate; rather, a 'true medium' became the personification of Mary. Through mediumship a bid was made to transcend (or was it comply with?) the patriarchal command that woman must be both virgin and mother.

Notes

1 Kaja Finkler has analysed Mexican Spiritualism in relation to the strongly Catholic culture of Mexico. See his 'Dissident Sectarian Movements, The Catholic Church, and Social Class in Mexico', *Comparative Studies in Society and History* 25 (1983) 277–305. He argues that Mexican Spiritualism 'represents [a historical] movement against Catholicism and its tacit acceptance of class differentiation' (p. 279). Finkler concentrates on the antagonistic aspects of the association. Conversely, June Macklin, 'Belief Ritual and Healing: New England Spiritualism and Mexican-American Spiritualism Compared', in I. Zaretsky and M. Leone (eds), *Religious Movements in Contemporary America* (Princeton, NJ, Princeton University Press, 1974), pp. 383–417, distinguishes between modern-day Spiritualism (North American and Protestant) and Spiritism (Continental, Latin American and folk-Catholic). She concentrates on their healing aspects, and emphasises the religious eclecticism of both Spiritism and Spiritualism, and the many points of sociological comparison between the two. In particular, she argues that the 'ritual dramas of salvation' are to be found in both New England Spiritualism and Mexican-American Spiritism and suggests that 'these dramas do heal the split, [in the twentieth century

between the temporal and eternal order] restoring personal, social and spiritual wholeness – and consequently physical health – to partici- pants' (p. 383). In his exploration of Western attitudes to death in the nineteenth century, Philippe Ariès finds several points of correspond- ence between the Catholics of France and Italy and the Spiritualists of America and England. In Europe and in America there was com- monly an anticipation of the survival of the soul or spirit in another and idealised world and a new emphasis on communication with the dead: Philippe Ariès, 'The Age of the Beautiful Death', in *The Hour of Our Death*, trans. H. Weaver (New York, Alfred Knopf, 1981). However, authors of works on British and North American Spiritu- alism have mostly concentrated on how Spiritualism relates to the Protestant/empirical tradition. Of the relatively recent works, see J. Oppenheim, *The Other World: Spiritualism and Psychical Research in England 1850–1914* (London, Cambridge University Press, 1985). See also R. Brandon, *The Spiritualists: The Passion for the Occult in the Nineteenth and Twentieth Centuries* (London, Weidenfeld & Nicolson, 1983); Laurence Moore, *In Search of White Crows: Spiritualism, Parapsychology, and American Culture* (New York, Oxford University Press, 1977); A. Braude, *Radical Spirits: Spiritualism and Women's Rights in Nineteenth-Century America* (Boston, MA, Beacon Press, 1989), especially ch. 2. Malcolm Kottler, 'Alfred Russel Wallace, the Origin of Man, and Spiritualism' (*Isis* 65 [1974] 145–92), considers Wallace's Spiritualism in relation to his theories of evolution. C. McDannell and B. Lang, *Heaven: A History* (New York, Vintage, 1990) view the Spiritualist heaven as an out- growth of 'progressive' Protestant values of the nineteenth century. See especially pp. 276–303.

2 Logie Barrow's links Spiritualism to radical plebeian politics and to Owenite morality in his fascinating study *Independent Spirits: Spiritualism and English Plebeians 1850–1910* (London, Routledge & Kegan Paul, 1986). J. F. C. Harrison, 'Early Victorian Radicals and the Medical Fringe', in W. Bynum and R. Porter (eds), *Medical Fringe and Medical Orthodoxy* (London, Croom Helm, 1987), pp. 198–215, takes a similar approach. A. Owen, in her *The Darkened Room: Women, Power and Spir- itualism in Late Victorian England* (London: Virago, 1989) and 'Women and Nineteenth-Century Spiritualism: Strategies in the Subversion of Femininity', in J. Obelkevich et al. (eds), *Disciplines of Faith* (London: Routledge, 1987), pp. 130–53, considers gender and the subversion of patriarchal order in Spiritualist practice, as does J. Walkowitz, *City of Dreadful Delight: Narratives of Sexual Danger in Late Victorian London* (London, Virago, 1992). Vieda Skultan explores mediums in relation to their male spirit-guides in 'Mediums, Controls and Eminent Men', in P. Holden (ed.), *Women's Religious Experience* (London, Croom Helm, 1983), pp. 15–26.

3 *New Catholic Encyclopedia*, vol. 3 (New York, McGraw-Hill, 1967), p. 331.

4 W. H. Evans, *Psychic News Booklet 4: The Philosophy of Spiritualism* (London, Psychic Press, 1933), pp. 32–7.

5 G. Nelson, *Spiritualism and Society* (London, Routledge & Kegan Paul, 1969), pp. 148–9.

6 A. Conan Doyle, *The New Revelation and The Vital Message* (London, Psychic Press, 1981), p. 37.

7 J. Hewat McKenzie, *Spirit Intercourse: Its Theory and Practice* (1916) (London, British College of Psychic Science, 1936), p. 5. As Rhodri Hayward has recently remarked, Andrew Jackson Davis had already articulated this tripartite division in nineteenth-century America: R. Hayward, 'Popular Mysticism and the Origins of the New Psychology, 1880–1910' (PhD thesis, Lancaster University, 1996), p. 52.

8 Hewat McKenzie, *Spirit Intercourse*, p. 22.

9 A. Findlay, *The Psychic Stream* (London, Psychic Press, 1939), p. 1132.

10 A. Conan Doyle, *The New Revelation*, p. 38. Spiritualists were particularly critical of an authoritative priesthood. The editor of *The Two Worlds* expressed the standard Spiritualist view, and appealed to the discourse of the 'common man', when he wrote: 'The Romanist Church takes the position that the common people are incapable of judging spiritual values, and its priesthood sets itself up as the censors of the free gifts of God. That is essentially the struggle between us – autocracy or democracy' ('Rome Intends to Fight Us', *The Two Worlds*, 12 March 1926, p. 159).

11 See, for example, Hewat McKenzie, *Spirit Intercourse*; Findlay, *The Psychic Stream*; Conan Doyle, *The New Revelation*.

12 G. Cummins, *Unseen Adventures: An Autobiography Covering 34 Years of Psychical Research* (London, Rider, 1951), p. 18.

13 *Ibid.*, p. 27.

14 *Ibid.*, pp. 38–41.

15 See C. Fryer, *Geraldine Cummins: An Appreciation* (Norwich, Pelegrin Trust, 1990), ch. 7, for an overview of contemporary responses to the book.

16 The editors of *The Scripts*, The Very Reverend W. P. Patterson DD and Professor D. Morrison, were both biblical scholars. The views of the late Dr W. O. E. Oesterley were also included in the 'Introduction'. In the editors' view, 'Messenger' showed detailed knowledge of the Jewish community in Apostolic times. They also noted that the characters of the twelve apostles 'are described with an understanding and sympathy which is remarkable': W. P. Patterson and D. Morrison (eds), 'Introduction', *The Scripts of Cleophas: A Reconstruction of Primitive Christian Documents* [1928] by G. Cummins, 5th edn (London, Psychic Press, 1974), p. xiv.

17 In 1962, *A Popular Dictionary of Spiritualism* described Cummins as 'the

most outstanding Irish automatist of modern times. Her extraordinary scripts, excellently constructed and written unconsciously at terrific speed, are worthy of close study by reason of the detailed information concerning little known periods of history, and certain Biblical and historical characters. Much of her detail has been verified by experts of these times': N. Blunsdon, *A Popular Dictionary of Spiritualism* (London, Arco, 1961), p. 54. One recent critic of Cummins's mediumship said of her: 'Miss Cummins moved in polite society, and appeared to be of a shy retiring nature. She eventually became semi-canonised' in Spiritualist circles: L. Price, 'The Enigma of Geraldine Cummins', *Alpha* 7 (March–April 1980) 21.

18 Cummins, *The Scripts of Cleophas*, p. 35.

19 *Ibid.*, p. 15.

20 G. Ellard, *The Mass in Transition* (Milwaukee, WI, Bruce, 1956), p. 52.

21 D. Mercier, quoted by Ellard, *ibid.*, p. 54.

22 Pope Pius XII, 10 November 1940. Quoted by Ellard, *ibid.*, p. 256.

23 The Liberal Catholic Church derived from the Old Catholics, a schismatical group of autonomous communities formed in 1889 under the Union of Utrecht. The Liberal Catholic Church blends 'theosophical mysticism and Catholic sacramentalism' and was established in 1916, when the Old Catholic Mission in Great Britain was, for various reasons, without a hierarchy. See the *New Catholic Encyclopedia*, vol. 10 (New York, McGraw-Hill, 1967), pp. 672–3; and vol. 8, pp. 679–700.

24 Right Reverend F. W. Piggott MA, 'The Occult Power of the Mass', *Occult Review*, LXIX:2 (April 1942) 58–60.

25 *Ibid.*, p. 60.

26 S. Barbanell, *Some Discern Spirits: The Mediumship of Estelle Roberts* (London, Psychic Press, 1944), p. 96.

27 In 1932, the Seven Principles were listed in *Psychic News*:

(1) The Fatherhood of God.
(2) The Brotherhood of Man.
(3) The Communion of Spirits and the Ministry of Angels.
(4) The Continuous Existence of the Human Soul.
(5) Personal Responsibility.
(6) Compensation and Retribution hereafter for all the good and evil deeds done on earth; and
(7) Eternal Progress open to every human soul. (H. Swaffer, 'Spiritualism's Crisis, Now', *Psychic News*, 2 July, 1932, p. 7)

Air Chief Marshal Dowding, a zealous and influential convert to Spiritualism, thought the first creed of Spiritualists should read: 'Honour and love your Father God'. See his *Many Mansions* (London, Rider, 1943), p. 109.

28 Findlay, *The Psychic Stream*, p. 1157; A. Findlay, *The Way of Life: A Guide to the Etheric World* (London, Psychic Press, 1953), pp. 114, 116.

29 Findlay, *The Way of Life*, p. 215.

30 Hewat McKenzie, *Spirit Intercourse*, pp. 232–3. Compare with Revelations 21: 18–19.

31 Hewat McKenzie, *Spirit Intercourse*, p. 205.

32 *Ibid.*, p. 186. See also Conan Doyle, *The New Revelation*, ch. 3; Dowding, *Many Mansions*, chs VII–X; Findlay, *The Way of Life*, chs VIII–X.

33 Hewat McKenzie, *Spirit Intercourse*, p. 205; see also Dowding, *Many Mansions*, p. 55.

34 Reverend G. J. MacGillivray MA, *What Happens after Death* (London, Catholic Truth Society, 1929), pp. 20–21.

35 Conan Doyle, *New Revelation*, p. 42. One Anglican priest, who undertook investigations into Spiritualism, was so convinced that messages 'from the beyond' proved the existence of purgatory that after a course of instruction he was received into the Catholic Church. See G. Raupert OP, *A Convert from Spiritualism* (Dublin, Irish Messenger Office, 1932), p. 3. Gregory Raupert is referring to his father, J. Godfrey Raupert.

36 Hewat McKenzie, *Spirit Intercourse*, p. 185. See also G. Leonard, *My Life in Two Worlds*, 'Foreword' by Sir Oliver Lodge (London, Cassell, 1931), pp. 114–15; N. Fodor, *These Mysterious People* (London, Rider, 1935), p. 86.

37 MacGillivray, *What Happens after Death*, p. 10. MacGillivray refers to Thomas Aquinas as his authority in this respect.

38 M. Peaks, '*In the Hour of Death*' (London, Catholic Truth Society, 1906), pp. 52–3.

39 MacGillivray, *What Happens after Death*, p. 22.

40 Monsignor Canon Moyes, 'Why We Pray to the Blessed Virgin: An Incident of Catholic Life', in Reverend E. Lester (ed.), *Dialogues of Defence: Collected Publications of the Catholic Truth Society*, vol. CVIII (London, Catholic Truth Society, 1917), p. 3. See also Reverend E. Lester, 'Devotion to Our Lady', *ibid.*, pp. 10–13.

41 Conan Doyle, *New Revelation*, p. 35.

42 F. Wood, *Mediumship and War* (London, Rider, 1942), p. 108.

43 Findlay, *The Way of Life*, p. 108.

44 *The Two Worlds*, XXXIX, 3 December 1926, p. 732. The return of the dead was used as a dramatic device in J. B. Priestley's, *An Inspector Calls: A Play in Three Acts* (London, Heinemann, 1947), where Inspector Goole performs a similar moral function.

45 F. Faber (Priest of the Oratory of St Philip Neri), *Purgatory* (London, Catholic Truth Society, 1926), p. 5.

46 MacGillivray, *What Happens after Death*, p. 21.

47 Leonard, *My Life in Two Worlds*, pp. 265–6.

48 *Ibid.*, p. 266. The influence of Catholic thinking on Spiritualism was not a one-way process; Spiritualism also influenced Catholic thought and imagery. Philippe Ariès writes: 'By the end of the nineteenth

century the iconography of souls in purgatory began to show the effects of the invasion of spiritualism. In certain great academic paintings, as in the cathedral at Toulouse, the soul has become a disembodied spirit whose astral body floats through the air' (Ariès, *The Hour of Our Death*, p. 466).

49 H. Boddington, '*Psychic News' Booklet 3: Trance States in Relation to Spirit Control* (London, Psychic Press, 1933), p. 31.

50 Wood, *Mediumship and War*, p. 105.

51 E. Roberts, *Forty Years a Medium* (London, Herbert Jenkins, 1959), p. 71.

52 *Ibid.*, pp. 70–73.

53 Barbanell, *Some Discern Spirits*, p. 130.

54 *Ibid.*, p. 132.

55 The medium Doris Stokes related a similar incident concerning the murder of some children in a Blackpool hospital: D. Stokes and L. Dearsley, *Voices in My Ear: The Autobiography of a Medium* (London, Futura Macdonald, 1980), pp. 142–3. This theme reappeared in the film *A Place of One's Own* (1944). Here, Margaret Lockwood plays a young Edwardian woman who becomes 'possessed' by the spirit of a murdered girl who is trying to contact her former lover (James Mason) to explain the circumstances of her disappearance. For Freud's discussion on this subject, see his *Totem and Taboo: Some Points of Agreement between the Mental Lives of Savages and Neurotics*, trans. J. Strachey (London, Routledge & Kegan Paul, 1960), ch. 2. See also Philippe Ariès, *The Hour of Our Death*, for concepts of purgatory from the seventeenth century to modern times, and obligations thought to be owed to the dead.

56 Lord Dowding, *Many Mansions*, p. 104.

57 Roberts, *Forty Years a Medium*, pp. 42–3.

58 C. Wickland, *Thirty Years among the Dead* (1924) (London, Spiritualist Press, 1971), pp. 28–9.

59 *Ibid.*, p. 30. Alex Owen argues that the female medium's adoption of a male identity unconsciously subverted normative femininity. See *The Darkened Room*, especially ch. 8. The issue is discussed in ch. 8 below.

60 N. Fodor, *These Mysterious People* (London, Rider, 1935) 'List of Contents' and pp. 83–91.

61 Blunsdon, *A Popular Dictionary of Spiritualism*, p. 230.

62 Wickland, *Thirty Years among the Dead*, p. 17.

63 L. Schiebinger, *The Mind Has No Sex: Women in the Origins of Modern Science* (Cambridge, MA, Harvard University Press, 1989).

64 Wickland, *Thirty Years among the Dead*, p. 34.

65 *Ibid.*, p. 40.

66 *Ibid.*, pp. 122–5.

67 Leonard, *My Life in Two Worlds*, p. 166.

68 Hewat McKenzie, *Spirit Intercourse*, pp. 142–3.

69 M. Warner, *Alone of All Her Sex: The Myth and the Cult of the Virgin Mary*, 2nd edn (London, Picador, 1990), pp. 311, 307.

70 See M. Berman, *The Reenchantment of the World* (Ithaca, NY, Cornell University Press, 1981) for his description of 'participating' and 'non-participating' consciousness in Western cosmology. Berman characterises the former as belonging to pre-scientific culture, where feeling was part of cognition, because the individual was not an alienated observer of the cosmos, 'but a direct participant in its drama' (p. 16). 'Non-participating consciousness', by contrast, refers to a modern scientised outlook, which presupposes radical divisions between subject and object, mind and body, feeling and cognition. If, as some have argued, Berman's history is too schematic and his distinction between a 'scientific' and 'non-scientific' consciousness in Western tradition too polarised, I have nevertheless found his concept of 'participating consciousness' a useful way of understanding the Spiritualist mix of feeling and cognition.

71 E. Garrett, *My Life as a Search for the Meaning of Mediumship* (New York, Arno Press, 1975), p. 55.

72 C. Sheridan, *Nuda Veritus* (London, Thornton Butterworth, 1927).

73 *Ibid.*, pp. 112–14.

74 C. Sheridan, *My Crowded Sanctuary*, 2nd edn (London, Methuen, 1946), pp. 11–14.

75 *Ibid.*, p. 14.

76 *Ibid.*, p. 15.

77 Sheridan, *Nuda Veritus*, p. 34.

78 S. Freud, 'Civilization and Its Discontents', in *Sigmund Freud: Civilization, Society and Religion*, vol. XII of the Pelican Freud Library, ed. James Strachey (Harmondsworth, Penguin, 1985), pp. 251–60.

79 Freudian influence is evident in 'crisis of faith' explanations of the attractions of Spiritualism (discussed in the Introduction to this book), which tacitly rely on an assumption of the Spiritualist's infantile desire for the security and peace of maternal comfort. This (sentimental) return, or 'escape' into the maternal world is then contrasted with the 'masculine', 'face-up-to-reality' world of secular science. But, as Evelyn Fox Keller has pointed out, the framing of a male, or Enlightenment, vision of 'reality' is equally romantic, being a romance about a certain kind of masculinity. See Keller, 'How Gender Matters, Or, Why it's So Hard for Us to Count Past Two', *in Inventing Women: Science, Technology and Gender*, ed. G. Kikup and L. Smith Keller (Cambridge, Polity Press, 1992), p. 56.

80 J. Rose, *The Haunting of Sylvia Plath* (London, Virago, 1991), p. 128.

81 See Julia Kristeva's discussion in 'Stabat Mater', in *The Kristeva Reader*, ed. Toril Moi (Oxford, Blackwell, 1986), pp. 160–87. See also Warner, *Alone of All Her Sex*, Part IV.

3

Virgin mothers
and warrior maids

Mediums in the nineteenth century were likely to be women,[1] and this trend continued into the twentieth century. Between 1938 and 1942, Mass-Observation carried out an intermittent survey of Spiritualist centres in Britain. These included large institutions, such as the Marylebone Spiritualist Association in central London, smaller institutions and gatherings at private homes. All the mediums were professionals; nearly all were women.[2] As I noted above, male mediums did exist, but they were often perceived by onlookers as 'feminine' or 'effete' in character.[3] One interwar student of Spiritualism, George Lawton, looked to a socioeconomic explanation for the predominance of women mediums in the movement:

> [M]ediumship develops more spontaneously among them [women] than among men, it appeals to them more as a profession, they are more contented with the meagre and precarious financial returns of mediumship, and finally they suffer fewer social disabilities by being a medium.[4]

If this passage reproduces familiar assumptions about the 'nature' and 'place' of women, it also raises interesting questions about the construction of mediumship in relation to broader perceptions of femininity.

Mediumistic identity was bound up with contemporary images of femininity encompassing a large and contradictory range. In this chapter, however, I want to concentrate on the Spiritualist gloss on mediumistic identity.

Recent studies of women and Spiritualism have focused on the subversion of normative femininity through the discourse of the seance. Alex Owen, in her study of women, power and Spiritualism in Victorian England, argues that mediumship could involve the subversion of stereotypical feminine qualities. The supposed passivity, nervous sensitivity, physical and intellectual weakness of women, disqualified them from positions of authority, excluded them from participation in the public sphere and circumscribed their influence to the confines of the home. In Spiritualist circles, however, these 'feminine disabilities' had positive connotations and became standard features in the development of mediumistic power. Spiritualists believed that intellectual simplicity and a passive disposition facilitated a clear, unhindered channel to the spirit world and a history of 'nervous invalidism' enhanced spirituality. Mediums were also well placed to appropriate male authority through the revelations of their male spirit-guides.[5] Finally, the seance provided an opportunity for transgressive behaviour, since the responsibility for any 'bad behaviour' was ascribed to the controlling spirit entity.[6] Without wishing to deny that mediumship could, at times, be deeply subversive of patriarchal gender divisions and norms, I want to draw attention to the other side of the coin: the discursive use that Spiritualists made of traditional Christian images of transcendent femininity in the construction and subsequent *control* of their mediums.

The Spiritualist version of 'true' mediumship in the interwar years deployed that supreme figure of patriarchal womanhood – the Virgin Mary. The principal features of Mary's divinity – her virginity and miraculous maternity, her 'voices' and visions, and her intercessional capacities with divine authorities – found full, and literal, representation in the figure of the modern medium.[7] At certain moments, however, Mary was moved aside to make way for Joan of Arc, the 'warrior maid.' Joan was often evoked in times of crisis. Her persona was mobilised against the ridicule of sceptics and, more seriously, against the legal prosecutions of mediums. On a deeper level, it was the fabled life of Joan that structured Spiritualist expectations of the lives of those 'destined' to become mediums. Cast in the transcendent roles of Mary and Joan, mediums occupied a unique and respected position within Spiritualist circles. But the high status accorded to them did not bring comparable power. Governed by all kinds of restrictions, obligations and taboos, the status of a medium was contingent on her powerlessness. Mediums occupied a mythical place apart from 'ordinary mortals' through which other interests were negotiated.

Mary

Veneration of the Virgin Mary saw a resurgence in the nineteenth and twentieth centuries – so much so that Roman Catholic Church leaders have called the years between 1850 and 1950 the Marian age.[8] The cult of motherhood that accompanied this resurgence in the twentieth century was associated with concerns about 'racial purity' and the 'population problem',[9] but it was also one way of dealing with the trauma of war bereavement.[10] Following the carnage of the First World War, official Church publications emphasised Mary's humanity and compassion and her willingness to console the sick, the injured and the bereaved. Catholic mothers were encouraged to talk informally with 'Our Lady', as 'one mother would talk to another' in the knowledge 'that the Mother of ... God would understand, and would not fail to give generously the help of her intercession and sympathy'.[11] As Universal Mother, Mary's comfort is extended to all, but she is particularly associated with the care of the dead and the bereaved. At the 'hour of our death', Mary draws close to perform her function of advocate of the soul at its time of judgement.[12]

Mediumship made a similar appeal to the non-Catholic population. Mediums devoted their attention to the dead and the bereaved; they employed their psychic abilities to aid the transition of spirits from this world to the next, and maintained connections between the two worlds. The mediumistic ability to 'conquer death'[13] was regarded by devotees of Spiritualism as the greatest discovery – or, rather, recovery – of modern times, and as we have seen most mediums saw the comfort of the bereaved as their special mission. Geraldine Cummins saw her work as 'humanly constructive'.[14]

Because of their supernormal abilities, mediums belonged to both this world and the next. Spiritualists explained that the 'two worlds are joined by a uniform etheric substance',[15] but it was the medium who activated that link, bridged the divide and made 'the two worlds one'.[16] Similarly, Mary belonged to both heaven and earth. Although she was only human, Mary was the chosen instrument through which God was made manifest on earth. She was sometimes termed 'the ladder that

Christ used to descend to earth and that man can use to ascend to heaven'.[17] The medieval scholar Bernard of Clairvaux had pictured the Holy Mother as an 'aqueduct that brings the grace of God coursing down through the city of the faithful'.[18] This enduring conception of Mary as a 'channel' of grace was borrowed in interwar imagery of maternity,[19] and found full expression in the Spiritualist medium. The word 'channel' was apposite, because, like Mary,[20] no medium had the power to act independently; she was 'only the instrument' of higher powers.[21] The medium was the 'channel' through which the dead communicate with the living, through which revelations were delivered and psychic healing was performed.[22]

Mediums did not have the power to grant favours by themselves; however, they did work that was akin to Mary's function of intercessor. Mediums often mediated between the dead and the living for clearing up misunderstandings, righting injustices and bringing about reconciliations. Eileen Garrett acted as intermediary in the conflict between the Sussex farm family described in Chapter 1. Estelle Roberts mediated on behalf of Mona Tinsley, for the purpose of bringing comfort to Mona's parents, and healing Mona's injured soul. Once she helped a dead son to contact his mother so that he could explain the extenuating circumstances of his suicide; on another occasion she brought messages from a distraught husband on the 'other side' begging the forgiveness of his wife, and from a father who sought the forgiveness of his son.[23] The Christian tradition that positions Mary as mediator of another's desire, and not her own, is amply fulfilled in the medium. Spiritualism's emphasis on the medium's function as 'instrument', (empty) 'channel', as absence, non-being, is painfully illustrative of a patriarchal system of signs that places the 'feminine' in binary opposition to 'masculine' presence. But if – as some brands of feminism argue – 'woman' does not have a sign under patriarchy, and is nothing more than a 'sort of inverted or negative alter ego' of the male subject,[24] she is nevertheless given a place as mother. Mary, of course, epitomises perfect motherhood. The example of Mary's motherhood was faithfully mirrored in Spiritualist representations of the medium, whose virtues were love, modesty, simplicity, gentleness, faith and the ability to create calm, harmonious conditions.[25] The Spiritualist author and educator Sylvia Barbanell identified Estelle Roberts as the quintessential mother:

Most of the people who have been associated with this medium in her work, refer to her, not as Mrs Roberts, not even as Estelle, but simply as 'Mother'. It does not seem strange, when you know her, to hear her so addressed by individuals who come from all different walks of life. She is 'Mother' to people of position and title. She is 'Mother' to professional men and women. She is 'Mother' to some whose lowly circumstances have been enriched, for all time, by their association with Red Cloud and his medium.[26]

Here is the Universal Mother who presides over supernatural activity, and acts as the catalyst for the free flow of love and empathy. This impression is enhanced by the homely setting of seance procedure. But the identification of the medium with the Holy Mother was more than metaphorical. The drama of the miraculous birth was repeated in the mediumistic production of spirit forms.

In Spiritualist theory, spirits can manifest themselves by borrowing 'vital forces' or 'etheric substances' from the living. This borrowing of etheric substances provides the necessary conditions for spirit entities to become inhabitants of matter.[27] The medium is the principal donor of this substance. In its denser form the etheric substance is known as 'ectoplasm', and it is this ectoplasm that is utilised in material manifestations. According to Hewat McKenzie, the ectoplasm that 'exudes ... from various parts of the medium's body, is of a fluidic and vapoury nature, and under good conditions may be seen with the physical eye as it issues'.[28] While the form is in the process of materialisation, darkness is essential, for 'darkness is in harmony with the creation of all animal ... structures', which require 'the darkness of the womb' for successful development. If the developing form is subjected to light, it 'returns to the body of the medium as an invisible essence'.[29]

McKenzie was not alone in comparing the production of materialised forms to the process of birth. Maurice Barbanell, the editor of *Psychic News* and husband of Sylvia, made the following comments:

You must remember that, in materialisation, what is akin to the whole process of birth is accelerated and takes place within a few minutes. The spirit form which manifests is apparently solid. It has a heartbeat; it has lungs; it can see, hear and talk. To all intents and purposes it is a living, breathing, human being, albeit the manifestation is temporary.[30]

As in biological birth, 'spirit birth' presented a health risk to the 'mother medium'. It could deplete 'the organism of the medium', and lead to

illness and the 'loss of vitality'.[31] Spiritualists said that sudden movements or loud noises could injure a medium engaged in the process of
materialisation. The medium Helen Duncan claimed that she was injured
when a woman screamed during a materialisation seance. In reply to a
question put by a journalist following the incident, Duncan said she felt
'as if someone had given her a blow on the head'. The journalist noted
that there was a trickle of blood issuing from her nostril as she spoke.[32]

The theme of birth persisted in accounts of the production of non-
physical phenomena. Thomas Mann describes a typical seance scene in
his novel *The Magic Mountain*. Here, a medium's efforts to communicate
with the spirit world are identified with the efforts of a woman deep
in labour:

> We men, if we do not shirk our humanity, are familiar with an hour
> of life when we know this almost intolerable pity, which, absurdly
> enough, no one else can feel, this rebellious 'Enough, no more!' which
> is wrung from us, though it *is* not enough, and cannot or will not be
> enough, until it comes somehow or other to its appointed end. The
> reader knows we speak of our husband – and our fatherhood, of the
> act of birth, which [the medium] Elly's wrestling did so unmistakably
> resemble that even he must recognise it who had never passed though
> this experience … One could not regard as anything less than scandal-
> ous the sights and sounds in the red-lighted lying-in chamber, the
> maidenly form of the pregnant one, bare armed, in flowing night-
> robe; and then by contrast the ceaseless and senseless gramophone
> music, the forced conversation which the circle kept up at command,
> the cries of encouragement they ever and anon directed at the strug-
> gling one.[33]

Mann, no advocate of Spiritualism, nevertheless perceived how the
seance atmosphere of tense anticipation and the behaviour of the
medium simulated the drama of childbirth. The jerky movements, the
moaning, the disconnected words reminiscent of a woman in labour,
constituted standard behaviour in trance mediumship. In June and
September 1937, the Society for Psychical Research carried out a series
of tests on Eileen Garrett, with the intention of examining physiological changes alleged to take place during the trance state. Doctor Helena
Wright reported that when Garrett entered trance, her pulse rate increased, her breathing became shallow and uneven, and she rolled her
eyes and clenched her fists. Wright also noted that there was 'marked
abdominal movement'.[34]

Spiritualists made repeated allusions to the 'motherly' aspects of mediumship, while emphasising the virginal purity of their mediums. As we have seen, a medium acted as a 'channel' or 'vessel' for 'higher intelligences' – this was the gift that set her apart from 'ordinary mortals'. Following a logic that belonged to patriarchal Christianity, the value of this 'vessel' lay in its perceived purity or chastity. Spiritualists often employed the language of feminine chastity to vouchsafe the genuine nature of phenomena. Sayings normally associated with maidenliness, virginity and purity were regularly used with reference to mediums. Sylvia Barbanell told her readers that Estelle Roberts's 'integrity' as a medium remained 'inviolate'. In another place she said that 'no breath of suspicion had ever fallen on her psychic integrity'.[35] Helen Hughes was eulogised by her biographer in almost identical terms when he wrote that 'never the faintest breath of condemnation' had touched her life as a medium. Hughes herself wrote that she felt cleansed by her work.[36] The spirit-guide 'Messenger' referred to Geraldine Cummins by the archaic term handmaid. In a culture steeped in Biblical proverbs and phraseology, the natural succession to 'handmaid' was 'of the Lord'.[37]

A 'pure channel' was perceived as a critical component in reliable communication with the spirit world. Spiritualists were anxious to ensure that spirit messages remained uncontaminated by 'subconscious interference' from the medium's own thoughts, or from telepathic interference from sitters. A *Psychic News* booklet on trance states, published in 1933, warned that sensitives who succumbed too easily to hypnotism were rarely reliable mediums, because 'they readily express ideas from the operator or audience, and pass them off as spirit messages'.[38] If easily hypnotised mediums were unsuitable as 'instruments' of communication with the spirit world, mediums who harboured 'impure' thoughts were considered dangerous: for 'if your motives are wholly selfish, or impure, the law of like attracting like mentalities will hold good … God's laws never change. Holy motives attract "holy" spirits. Make your choice.'[39]

A medium's usefulness as a channel for 'higher intelligences' was obtained with difficulty, and required her willingness to live permanently on a 'pure' and 'lofty' plane of thought.[40] Ideally, the trained medium's 'unresisting receptivity' to psychic forces combined with an iron discipline that 'resist[ed] objectionable ideas and actions', which included any form of transgressive behaviour.[41] In other words, a medium should be capable of opening her psychic channels to 'holy' forces, and also capable of closing them down against 'possession' by 'low spirits'.[42]

The 'self-control' required of a medium was not easily come by, and called for a way of life akin to a convent existence. Experienced Spiritualists and mediums advised developing mediums to lead a simple, healthy and prayerful life, and to avoid excitement. In the interests of psychic development, mediums were expected to eschew 'worldly pleasures'. Estelle Roberts, reputedly, only lived 'to serve the spirit world'. Her biographer said she seldom went beyond her home for entertainment, and was hardly ever seen at social gatherings.[43] Successful mediumship, according to authorities like Hewat McKenzie, required complete commitment. This involved the cultivation of purity of mind and asceticism of the body.

In Christian imagery, purity of mind and body is interlinked, and so it was with Spiritualism. A 'pure' diet was thought to aid spiritual development. McKenzie insisted that 'purification of the body' was necessary to reach 'higher spirits'. In his view, mediums should not eat meat, smoke, or consume alcohol.[44] Food should be 'pure and plain, chiefly composed of fruit, vegetables and fish'. Expressly acknowledging a debt to Catholic austerity, McKenzie commented on the spiritual benefits of fasting:

> The Roman Catholic Church has always recognised the importance of diet by setting apart days for fasting, but in modern times this custom has been honoured more in the breach than in the observance. Protestantism has been carelessly negligent on this point, for it has made no protest against a general beef-steak Christianity for all its adherents, evidently not recognising that diet had any special relation to the cultivation of the highest spiritual gifts.[45]

Sexual activity was, in principle, forbidden the medium, although it is impossible to judge to what extent individual mediums followed this ruling. Nevertheless, as we shall soon see, institutions for the development of psychic power often exercised considerable control over the behaviour of mediums in their employ. McKenzie, who owned an important college for the development of psychic gifts, adopted the Pauline dualism that hailed the body as the temple of the Holy Ghost and simultaneously branded it as a treacherous trap of sin,[46] He directed mediums to abstain from sex, because:

> Sex intercourse is disastrous to all highly developed and spiritual states, and those who have not controlled this force and learned to direct it into the channel of spiritual energy, will fail to rise to any advanced state, however much they might desire to do so ... Mere animal enjoyment is a poor substitute for that ecstasy known to the man or woman who by self-purification and sacrifice lives upon the higher realm of existence, such as is frequently known to the poet, the artist, and the mystic.[47]

In the Christian tradition, however, sainthood is rarely achieved simply through chastity and the avoidance of 'animal' or 'worldly' pleasure. What distinguishes the saint is his or her willingness and capacity to suffer.[48] Spiritualists discerned holiness in suffering. Shaw Desmond, Irish poet, journalist and dramatist, wrote prolifically on Spiritualism and psychic matters in the interwar period, and counted suffering as a 'privilege reserved for those who are advancing on the Path'. It was therefore fitting, according to this logic, that mediums should suffer. But in what did their martyrdom consist, and for what purpose? What is immediately evident is that the martyrdom of the medium included the stereotypical feminine trials of endurance and 'sensitivity' to an-other's pain. Desmond argued that it was 'the *power* to suffer which makes us tender to the sufferings of others'.[49] Like the Holy Mother herself, mediums were credited with the ability to share quite literally in the thoughts and feelings of others, whether dead or alive. The *Psychic News* information pamphlet on trance states (1933) considered that the 'discarnate intelligence' had a 'powerful and very important bearing upon the sensations and impressions registered by mediums.' Under the control of a spirit, the medium might be seized with the desire to laugh or cry, depending on the mood of the spirit: 'accom-panying these mental states [were] the purely physical sensations of being hung, crushed, drowned, or some other cause of transition [to the next world].'[50] Frederick Wood, who wrote of the psychic powers of a medium known as 'Rosemary', explained that according to 'psy-chic law the medium must suffer temporarily, all the conditions of the deceased's passing'.[51] Wood described how 'Rosemary' experienced at first hand the pain of a death through suicide, and how she shared the fear of a woman killed by falling masonry during a bombing raid in World War II. As she drifted into trance, the spirit of the woman took control of her body:

[Rosemary] suddenly became dumb and unable to move her legs. The terror shown at first by this 'control' gradually subsided as Rosemary passed into a deep and tranquil sleep. Then the awakening, and my [Wood's] assurances to the released victim that all would be well ... [S]he was no longer trapped in the ruins of her home, but safe with her own spirit-guides, who were now able to make their presence known.[52]

Rosemary said she had once shared in the feelings of Czechoslovakian citizens engaged in an uprising against Nazi occupation, and she experienced their death pangs during subsequent reprisals. While the seance was taking place, participants noticed that Rosemary was under 'great stress of emotion', and that after her ordeal 'she sank into a chair and wept'.[53]

Before meeting McKenzie, Eileen Garrett had a similar experience during the First World War. After her divorce from her husband Clive, she formed a maternal kind of attachment to a young soldier. One day he told her that his regiment had been called to the Front, and asked her to marry him. She said that she had a strong feeling he would not return, and agreed to his proposal because 'it seemed such a little thing to do to marry him, and give him this brief happiness'. About a month later she became aware that her 'husband was going through hours of terrific suffering and fear'. Later in the evening of the same day, the 'vision of [her] husband dying, began to open'. Garrett's description of the scene – two decades later, on the eve of the Second World War – reflects the perspective and expectations of the established medium:

I seemed, for the moment, to have lost my own identity, and was caught in the midst of a terrible explosion. I saw this gentle, golden haired man blown to pieces – I watched the pieces fall; I swam out on a sea of sound. When I came to myself, I was sitting in the foyer of the restaurant [she was visiting] alone ...

Two days later my husband was reported missing. A week later the official word came from the War Office that he was listed as dead.[54]

Joan

The willingness to accept or experience pain on behalf of another is a conventional sign of sainthood, as is suffering for a cause. Spiritualists in the interwar years were not short of representatives of this latter kind of martyr. One *cause célèbre* involved the case of Louise Meurig

Morris, a well-known and well-loved trance medium, whose inspirational platform addresses were legendary among her supporters.[55]

The Meurig Morris case was unusual in that it was she who initiated legal proceedings. In 1932, the *Daily Mail* displayed a hoarding referring to Mrs Meurig Morris that read: 'Medium Found Out'. Meurig Morris sued the *Daily Mail* and the case was heard before Justice McCardie. Although no allegations of fraud were upheld, judgement was made in favour of the defendant on a plea of fair comment.[56] Spiritualists were outraged, and a campaign was launched in Meurig Morris's name calling for the abolition of Clause 4 of the Vagrancy Act. Deploying the rhetoric of 'democracy and freedom', Spiritualist platform speakers, up and down the country, argued that the existing legislation obstructed 'citizens' in their 'right' to worship as they pleased.[57]

The intermittent prosecution of mediums in the 1920s, 1930s and 1940s[58] provided Spiritualists with an opportunity to display their mediums as martyrs and saints. *Psychic News* scrutinised Meurig Morris for signs of strain during her court case, and reported that her ordeal had caused her health to break down. Yet despite her poor-health, the journal triumphantly reported that her spirit-guide, 'Power', had urged the 'continuance of the fight'.[59] Hannen Swaffer, also for *Psychic News*, stressed the courage that was to be expected in 'genuine' mediums:

> But for the woman mediums who, in the past, have often been driven from their homes, thrown out by their own families and ostracised by their own churches, there could never have been a Spiritualist Movement.
>
> Today Spiritualism can boast, in this country more than anywhere, women of whom any movement could be proud.[60]

In another article in the same issue, Swaffer depicted mediums as 'warrior maids' engaged in a ceaseless battle against 'tyrants and oppressors and war mongers':

> Always before they have persecuted our mediums. Always before it has been the mediums that suffered. They are afraid of us …
>
> Now we know where we are. Years ago, mediums were burned; Yes, even Joan of Arc! Now they are merely fined or sent to prison.
>
> But, at whatever cost to its faithful, Spiritualism will go on. Its job to comfort the mourner, to heal the sick, and to stand for Truth – wherever it may lead.[61]

The rhetoric of the 'warrior maid' – imagined as militaristic yet feminine – became a familiar postwar symbol of militant feminism. Using an iconography that both paralleled and appropriated wartime legends of male heroics, the cover of the May issue of *Votes for Women* (1924) shows a woman mounted on a horse, wearing a suit of armour. She holds a medieval standard bearing the inscription 'Legal Prisoners of War'. Immediately under the picture is a verse that resembles the kind of war heroics evoked in the Angel of Mons and, in later years, by David Jones in *In Parenthesis*:

> We wage war, O disciples; therefore are we called warriors.
> Wherefore, Lord, do we wage war?
> For lofty virtue, for high endeavour, for sublime wisdom;
> Therefore we are called warriors.[62]

Spiritualists employed a similarly militarised rhetoric in their battle for official recognition, and 'Joan of Arc' was the epithet commonly applied to mediums who were locked in battle with the law or with hostile critics. Meurig Morris was dubbed 'the Joan of Arc of Spiritualism',[63] as was Helen Duncan during her trial at the Old Bailey for fraud, in 1944.[64] Indeed, it was the legendary life of Joan, more than that of any other saint, that structured the Spiritualist reading of the lives of those 'fated' to become mediums. Joan's childhood voices and visions, her sufferings and ecstasies, her supernormal triumphs, her simplicity and supernatural wisdom, lived again in the mythology of the modern medium.[65]

Many mediums said that they heard 'voices' and saw visions from an early age. As we saw in Chapter 1, both Helen Hughes and Edith Clements heard 'voices' and saw visions as children. The same was true of Estelle Roberts, who saw an apparition of a knight in armour when she was eight years old; and Eileen Garrett, who frequently experienced visions as a child, and played happily with ghostly children. Gladys Leonard said that her nursery years were full of visions of 'beautiful places'. Evoking a nostalgic pastoralism, she described how the walls and ceilings of her home dissolved, allowing her to look out on a rustic country scene.[66]

Childhood visions and voices were not the only experiences these mediums purported to share. In Spiritualist expectations, mediumship followed a rite of passage that included several – almost obligatory –

steps. As an adjunct to their childhood voices and visions, mediums often said that they 'felt different' from other children, and isolated from their families. Parental refusal to recognise their psychic talents compounded this sense of otherness, and the incipient medium passed through a period of self-doubt about her sanity. This period was brought to a close by 'proofs' of supernatural agencies at work. These 'proofs' were often displayed in correct clairvoyant predictions, or through an intellectual feat considered beyond the capabilities of the medium in question. Intellectual simplicity was another sign of personal fitness for a career as a medium.[67] Following 'proof' of supernatural intervention, it was assumed that a medium's fitness for the task ahead would be 'tested' by some unseen force or power. Many mediums said that they faced many trials and troubles, such as an unhappy home life, bereavement, or poverty,[68] before they were ready to commence their appointed task. But like the traditional saint, they did not face these troubles alone: 'guardian angels' frequently sustained them through this period. Finally, most mediums insisted that throughout their lives an 'unseen hand' guided them towards the Spiritualist movement, where their 'true identity' was at last recognised. A personal history that included all – or most of – the above episodes signalled to Spiritualists the arrival of an authentic medium.[69]

Sylvia Barbanell's biography of Estelle Roberts fulfilled in detail the mythology of the developing medium, and acted as a kind of guide on how to recognise the 'real thing'. Barbanell began by noting Roberts's success as a public medium and listing her psychic gifts, which included 'practically all the gifts of the spirit enumerated by Paul in the New Testament'.[70] According to Barbanell, Roberts's mediumship comprised clairvoyance, clairaudience, trance speaking, psychic healing, psychometry, automatic writing, the production of apports, and materialised spirit forms. She could also levitate and 'speak in tongues'. Barbanell emphasised that, despite this staggering list of psychic accomplishments, Roberts was a 'simple and unaffected' person.[71] Roberts's physical features provide another clue to her identity. Barbanell described her as having a slim figure and dark hair. But it was her eyes that commanded attention; they were 'arresting, deep-set and sombre, beneath characteristic brows and high forehead'.[72] Barbanell went on to narrate Roberts's childhood through the lens of sainthood – specifically as the 'warrior maid'.

Roberts's first psychic experience, as narrated by Barbanell, contained all the drama of a biblical moment. One day, when the child Estelle was eight years old, and she and her sister were getting ready for school, she heard a tap on the window. Simultaneously the room darkened and it 'seemed as though a heavy cloud had cast a shadow on the window'.

> Estelle stood, transfixed by the apparition of a knight in shining armour who appeared to be suspended in the air in the window space. In his outstretched hand was a glistening sword ... His deeply penetrating eyes searched those of the young medium to whom he held a beckoning hand. The next moment, he completely vanished.[73]

Retroactively, Estelle's vision emerged as a sign of 'who she was really'. But like those biblical prophets who went unrecognised in their own communities, her experience was disbelieved at the time by her parents, who judged that her knight was really a bat. A struggle with them resulted over whose reality should hold sway:

> She had more than one beating for describing psychic experiences. Naturally, then, she did not understand the meaning of these forces. When, like Joan of Arc, she heard spirit voices, she tried to think, as her parents insisted, that it was merely her imagination. Sometimes she deliberately stifled this clairaudience: at other times, in terror and bewilderment, she listened to the voices, wondering what it all meant.[74]

This disturbing state of affairs continued into her late teens, because the 'hour of enlightenment had not yet struck'. Her 'voices' were a torment to her. In despair, she confided her fears to her new husband. His response was encouraging: he did not attribute her strange experiences to an 'overactive imagination', and pronounced his wife 'fey'. Estelle was encouraged further when one of her visions turned out to be correct: one night she clairvoyantly saw her husband's aunt pass across the room. The vision convinced Estelle that this person was dead. The following morning her husband received a telegram confirming her impression.[75]

Estelle's fortunes took a turn for the worse when her husband died suddenly. Sitting by his bedside, she witnessed his ethereal body withdraw from his material body, and with it the spirits 'who had come to help his transition to the new world'. She still did not understand 'the significance of what she was witnessing'. She obtained work as a waitress at a branch of Lyon's Corner House, London, and tried to support and care for her children simultaneously. Life was very hard. Barbanell's gloss on this episode in Estelle's life was that it was part of a Divine plan. Estelle was being 'tested' and prepared for the work she 'was fated to undertake'. Through her suffering she was able to 'strengthen the bonds of sympathy' between herself and others. And she was helped. While she worked in the bustling café, she could hear the voices and see the 'forms of "guardian angels"' behind the heads of the customers she served.[76] Finally, Estelle came to realise her life's vocation. The 'testing-time was nearing an end', and her 'footsteps were guided towards the organised Spiritualist movement'. At a Spiritualist meeting to which she had been invited by a neighbour, the medium approached her and declared: 'You are a born medium … You have great work to do in the world.'[77]

Estelle Roberts's story conforms to Spiritualism's construction of the proper route to mediumship. The truth effect relied on conventional constructions of the legendary life of Joan, and familiar biblical episodes in the lives of the saints and Mary. In Roberts's story there were hardships and divine tests, angelic visitations and miracles, and a teleological account of existence.

'A race apart'

Cast in the transcendent role of Mary, and allied with the female saints, mediums occupied a unique and exalted position within the Spiritualist movement. But, as we shall see, the high status accorded to them did not bring comparable power. Nineteenth-century Spiritualists insisted that everyone was potentially psychic.[78] In keeping with the democratising impulses of Spiritualism, some twentieth-century Spiritualists considered that psychic power was latent in all humans, and urged its universal development.[79] Nevertheless, it was often noted that there were not enough mediums to keep up with demand.[80] The reasons given for this scarcity varied. *The Two Worlds* complained that too little effort had been made to develop mediums, and that one weakness of modern Spiritualism was the comparative lack of the home circles that had produced the best mediums in the past.[81] Hewat McKenzie thought that clerical prejudice against mediumship and poor remuneration were both responsible for the shortage.[82] Geraldine Cummins agreed that professional mediumship was a very precarious means of livelihood. It was even worse for the amateur, who faced the 'double and exhausting work of earning her livelihood while she carries on experiments'.[83] The payment of mediums was a vexed question within the Spiritualist movement. Some thought that mediums should be paid like the clergy; others insisted that the gift of mediumship was a service to humanity, and should not be treated as a commercial proposition.[84] Maurice Barbanell stood awkwardly between the two camps when he condemned the commercialisation of psychic power, but continued, nevertheless, to advocate 'fair payment' for mediums.[85] Generally, a medium who received low or no payment was regarded as spiritually superior.[86]

Increasingly, though, as the figure of Mary merged with that of the medium, Spiritualists accepted that a shortage of 'good' mediums was 'in the nature of things'. Although they were well aware that the preservation of the movement relied on a ready supply of mediums,[87] the identification of Mary with the medium tended to work against the acceptance of large numbers of psychics. In contrast to the view of nineteenth-century Spiritualism, mediumship came to be viewed as a rare and precious gift, limited to a few chosen individuals. Arthur Findlay, for example, asserted that '[n]ature produced only comparatively few mediums, and they have consequently always been in the minority'.[88] Frederick Wood ventured the opinion that really good mediums were 'perhaps born rather than made',[89] and Muriel Hankey compared them to ancient seers and prophets who were protected in their work and 'treated as a race apart'.[90] An editorial in *Light* in 1935 concurred with this view, and protested against the 'indiscriminate appeal to all and sundry to develop their own psychic faculties', because the possession of profound psychic ability was a 'natural gift, and very rare in its distribution'.[91]

The special status accorded to mediums carried certain obligations, and the persona of Mary imposed its own rules of conduct. The patriarchal discourses that featured motherhood, virginity, sainthood and martyrdom implied a code of living driven by abstinence and sacrifice, and also implied the negation of the individual will. A *Psychic News* pamphlet insisted that the truly spiritual medium was of a retiring disposition, and warned novices, most particularly, against 'wilfulness' and 'egoism'. Egoism, in the language of Spiritualism, compromised the purity of the 'channel' through which spirit-guides communicated, and warped the message. It could even transform 'true mediumship into a form of self-hypnotism'.[92]

Alex Owen has shown that flagrantly transgressive behaviour and language had been features of Victorian mediumship. This was possible, because it was taken for granted that 'wicked' or 'lying' spirits had assumed complete control of the medium and were responsible for anything she might do or say.[93] By the 1930s, however, with the growing influence of Freudian and other theories of the unconscious, this standard explanation for 'bad behaviour' was no longer acceptable. Unwelcome messages were accredited to 'subconscious interference' from the medium's own mind. If an entity was recognised as a *bona fide* possessing spirit, the medium was still culpable. As one educational pamphlet remarked: 'Your secret thoughts and desires constitute the attractive forces which will eventually decide the quality of manifesting spirit controls.'[94] This meant that responsibility for moral lapses could no longer be 'shuffled onto spirit controls', because '[s]ubconsciously we resist all suggestions of which we do not approve'.[95] Deviation from acceptable norms indicated one of several conditions: 'promiscuous' use of psychic power, eventuating in spirit possession;[96] subconscious interference of an unwholesome nature from the medium; temporary or permanent withdrawal of the gift of mediumship; or, in certain circumstances, outright fraud. If a medium fell from grace, Spiritualists could be ruthless in their treatment of her. The Spiritualist press urged publication of the names of 'fraudulent' mediums in the public interest, as well as in the interests 'of honest Spiritualism.'[97]

Hewat McKenzie preserved his own reputation for honesty by making a show of mediums he considered spurious. Muriel Hankey said that he once called on the police to arrest a medium undergoing an audition at his home. At other times he would try to obtain a written confession from the medium in question, and a promise to cease psychic work.[98] In practice, though, a medium was rarely cut off completely from the body of the faithful. A verdict of fraud was never unanimous throughout the movement, and the medium usually found some support. Even so, an accusation of fraud from a powerful figure like McKenzie could be extremely damaging to the reputation of any medium.

McKenzie's vigilance in detecting fraud was matched by the degree of control he exerted over mediums in his employ at the British College of Psychic Science. Here, the virtue of submission was insisted upon. According to Eileen Garrett, she had to 'obey rigid disciplines at the hands of McKenzie'. To keep her mediumistic faculties free from 'subconscious interference', he did not allow her to attend seances with other mediums, or read Spiritualist literature.[99] For the benefit of her mental disposition in relation to the spirit world, he placed her under dietary controls, and emphasised the necessity of leading a quiet and harmonious life, free from alcohol and sex: 'My whole responsibility to myself and my mediumship lay in living this simple and controlled existence.'[100] McKenzie governed appointments for sittings, inside or outside the college, and took charge of financial arrangements.[101] He spoke all the time of training the spirit 'controls', and was in the habit of hypnotising Garrett and intoning the following command: 'It is your duty as a trance medium to give yourself to the care and wisdom of your controls, who in turn are being trained by me.'[102]

Muriel Hankey also wrote about McKenzie's autocratic regime at the British College of Psychic Science – how he demanded 'order and obedience' at all times from those in his employ, he maintained complete control over seance procedure:

> McKenzie had very decided opinions as to the amount of work a medium could or should undertake, beyond which it was unwise to go without danger of damage to the mediumship or to the medium's health. Particularly was this so in the case of physical mediumship, for which there was, therefore, a fairly well-set pattern of work. Usually two or three group seances were held each week to which ordinary members and inquirers were admitted; these seances were always conducted under the direction of a responsible College officer, who kept a watchful eye on the proceedings, but otherwise there were no unusual restrictions. Once a week, however, an extra seance was arranged, attended only by members of the Research Committee, with any visitors invited for special reasons. The conditions pertaining to these research meetings were strict.[103]

McKenzie's establishment acted as a kind of seminary for mediums, and he imposed the kind of discipline normally associated with seminary life. Although mediums were not obliged to undergo training, strong pressure was exerted on them to operate under the control of an accredited Spiritualist institution. Gladys Leonard advised aspirant mediums 'never to attempt to develop the trance condition by yourself'.

She thought 'this might be unwise, and in some cases even a dangerous proceeding', because the inexperienced medium ran the risk of contacting 'low' spirits. Leonard said she always sent novices to some well-known institution 'where classes are held for the purpose, and where the applicants [would] be interviewed by some responsible and experienced person, who will ascertain their qualifications'.[104]

It was not easy for a medium to avoid institutional control. Spiritualist institutions offered some protection against legal prosecution, they paid a salary, and – most important – they ratified the mediumship of their employees. Many – if not most – respected professional mediums of the interwar years trained, or worked for a period, at McKenzie's British College of Psychic Science.[105] The Marylebone Spiritualist Association of Great Britain was another important centre for the development of mediums. For Muriel Hankey, the benefits of institutional mediumship were clear:

> The mediums selected by Mr. McKenzie to work at his College enjoyed … pleasant, quiet rooms. [They] received good fees, with a guaranteed minimum payable also during vacations or times of sickness; they had the assurance that their sitters were genuine inquirers [and not police prosecution witnesses]. The secretarial duties of booking appointments and the collection of fees were undertaken by the College staff. Sitters had the satisfaction of knowing that the sensitives recommended by Mr. McKenzie were genuine, with gifts of good quality; they could make their appointments knowing that they would be arranged with discretion.[106]

The 'protection' offered to a medium meant, in practice, that her life came under surveillance. She was guarded and controlled, disciplined and watched, surrounded with all kinds of restrictions and taboos.[107] For a medium was valuable only as a means of contact with the other world, and this meant arranging her persona in keeping with an image based on the figures of the Virgin Mary and female saints. Failure to do so reduced her seance credibility. Her role as guarantor of life beyond the grave placed her in a position analogous to the priestly kings of *Totem and Taboo*. Here, writes Freud, there was no limit to the care certain tribes devoted to their ruler, and which they compelled him to take of himself:

> [H]is life is only valuable so long as he discharges the duties of his position by ordering the course of nature for his people's benefit. So

soon as he fails to do so, the care, the devotion, the religious homage which they had hitherto lavished on him cease and are changed into hatred and contempt.[108]

A medium could expect similar treatment. Fêted one day, a woman could find herself execrated as a common fraud the next. As I noted above, some Spiritualists championed Helen Duncan, dubbing her the 'Joan of Arc of Spiritualism' during her trial for fraud at the Old Bailey. Others took a different view. One *Light* editorial, published at the height of the controversy over her mediumship in 1944, came down unequivocally on the side of the prosecution. The article concluded that Duncan's phenomena bore 'little relation to spirit intercourse', were 'rarely spiritually uplifting', and merely vulgarised 'the whole Spiritualist position'.[109] Many established mediums, however, enjoyed special privileges. Spirit communications received through them were regarded as revelations, and as the bearers of these communications they were treated with a respect that bordered on adulation. The biographers of Estelle Roberts, Louise Meurig Morris, Helen Hughes and 'Rosemary' all wrote of their subjects in tones usually associated with the sacred.

Through approximation to the persona of Mary, mediums acted as guarantors of spirit truth, but it was only with the elimination of themselves as subjects that they could receive spirit communications. In the disavowal of self as the author of knowledge, and the appeal to a 'higher authority', one of the most powerful symbolic resources in Western culture was mobilised. For 'pure truth', as represented in dominant epistemological traditions, issued from an external and sublime source known as God or, more recently, Nature. Symbolic identification with truth runs: 'It is not I who know, but God who inspires me through the Scriptures.' Or: 'It is not I who know, but the facts of nature that are revealed to me.' Or: 'It is not I who know, but the spirits who speak through me.'

As the bearers of transcendent truth, mediums were potentially very powerful, but the enveloping persona of Mary (modified to some extent by Joan) reproduced patriarchal gender divisions, and muffled subversive inclinations and their emancipatory possibilities. In view of this, it is ironic that mediumship guaranteed an epistemology that privileged 'feminine insight', since it was more likely to be male administrators, like McKenzie, who were in a position to exercise more direct and effective power through the construction of the medium as the Virgin Mary.

Notes

1 A. Owen, *The Darkened Room: Women, Power and Spiritualism in Late Victorian England* (London, Virago, 1989); and 'Women and Nine-teenth-Century Spiritualism: Strategies in the Subversion of Feminin-ity', in J. Obelkevich *et al.* (eds), *Disciplines of Faith* (London, Routledge, 1987). See also V. Skultans, 'Mediums, Controls and Eminent Men', in P. Holden (ed.), *Women's Religious Experience* (London, Croom Helm, 1983); D. Burfield, 'Theosophy and Feminism', in *ibid.*; J. Walkowitz, *City of Dreadful Delight: Narratives of Sexual Danger in Late Victorian London* (London, Virago, 1992), ch. 6; A. Braude, *Radical Spirits: Spiritualism and Women's Rights in Nineteenth-Century America* (Boston, MA, Beacon Press, 1989).

2 Most of the mediums who worked at the British College of Psychic Science between 1920 and 1929 were women. M. Hankey, *James Hewat McKenzie: Pioneer of Psychical Research* (London, Aquarian Press, 1963), pp. 57–9.

3 See 'Introduction', above. There were exceptions. Conan Doyle knew a medium who was a coal miner and another who loaded barges. A. Conan Doyle, *The New Revelation and The Vital Message* (London, Psychic Press, 1981), p. 116. (*The New Revelation* was first published in 1918; *The Vital Message* in 1919.)

4 G. Lawton, *The Drama of Life after Death: A Study of the Spiritualist Religion* (New York, Henry Holt, 1932), p. 181.

5 Owen, *The Darkened Room*. Several other historians have noted that many spirit-guides were male, and have pointed to the paradox that women could 'authoritatively speak spirit' only if they were controlled by men. See Walkowitz, *City of Dreadful Delight*, p. 177; Skultans, 'Mediums, Controls and Eminent Men'. This thesis has only limited application, since it fails to take account of the many spirit-guides who were themselves representative of powerless groups, such as children and Red Indians. W. Sollors, 'Dr Benjamin Franklin's Celestial Telegraph, Or Indian Blessings to Gas-Lit American Drawing Rooms', *American Quarterly*, 3:5 (1983), notes the prevalence of Red Indian guides in nineteenth-century American Spiritualism. For the interwar period in Britain see E. Roberts's autobiography, *Forty Years a Medium* (London, Herbert Jenkins, 1959) – her spirit-guide was a Red Indian – and Gladys Leonard, whose spirit-guide was a child called Feda: *My Life in Two Worlds*, 'Foreword' by O. Lodge (London, Cassell, 1931). The child spirit-guide became something of a stereotype in the inter-war years and beyond. See, for example, N. Coward, *Blithe Spirit: An Improbable Farce in Three Acts* (London, Samuel French, 1941).

6 Owen, *The Darkened Room*, especially ch. 8.

7 In orthodox Catholic theology Mary is not, strictly speaking, divine.

For example, Monsignor Canon Moyes told his readers that the epithet 'Divine Mary' was intended as a metaphor: 'Why Catholics Pray to the Blessed Virgin: An Incident of Catholic Life', in Reverend E. Lester (ed.), *Dialogues of Defence Series: Collected Publications of the Catholic Truth Society*, vol. 108 (London, Catholic Truth Society, 1917), pp. 1–15.

8 B. Carrado Pope, 'Immaculate and Powerful: The Marian Revival in the Nineteenth Century', in C. Atkinson, C. Buchanan and M. Miles (eds), *The Female in Sacred Image and Social Reality* (Boston, MA, Beacon Press, 1985), pp. 173–200. Carrado Pope argues that, as 'nineteenth-century Catholics increasingly saw themselves in a state of siege against the modern world', they turned to Mary as a symbol of comfort (p. 175). See also M. Warner, *Alone of All Her Sex: The Myth and the Cult of the Virgin Mary*, 2nd ed (London, Picador, 1990). For a psycho-analytic approach to the cult of the Virgin Mary, see J. Kristeva, *The Kristeva Reader*, ed. T. Moi (Oxford, Blackwell, 1986), pp. 160–87.

9 J. Weeks, *Sex, Politics and Society: The Regulation of Sexuality since 1880* (London, Longman, 1990), pp. 126–7. See also S. Jeffreys, *The Spinster and Her Enemies: Feminism and Sexuality 1880–1930* (London, Pandora, 1985); A. Davin, 'Imperialism and Motherhood', *History Workshop*, 5 (Spring 1978) 9–65. See C. Haldane, *Motherhood and Its Enemies* (New York, Doubleday & Doran, 1928) for a contemporary expression of the social divisions drawn between mothers and non-mothers, to the disadvantage of the latter.

10 People dealt with bereavement in different ways. Jay Winter explores modernist and more traditional responses to bereavement through the iconography of memorial art in his, *Sites of Memory, Sites of Mourning: The Great War in European Culture* (Cambridge, Cambridge University Press, 1995). See also P. Fussell, *The Great War and Modern Memory* (Oxford, Oxford University Press, 1975), especially ch. XI. Alison Light has noted how Agatha Christie's interwar crime novels, with their emotional detachment from death, helped to distance and protect the reader from the pain of the recent slaughter: *Forever England: Femininity, Literature and Conservatism between the Wars* (London, Rout-ledge, 1991), ch. 2. The issue of bereavement, then and now, is discussed more fully in the 'Afterword' below.

11 Moyes, 'Why Catholics Pray to the Blessed Virgin', p. 3.

12 M. Peaks, *In the Hour of Death* (London, Catholic Truth Society, 1906), p. 7.

13 S. Barbanell, *Some Discern Spirits: The Mediumship of Estelle Roberts* (London, Psychic Press, 1944), p. 199.

14 See, for example, G. Cummins, *Unseen Adventures* (London, Rider, 1951), pp. 18–19.

15 According to Spiritualists, everything in the universe is connected by the invisible ether, which, wrote Arthur Findlay, is 'the basic substance

of the universe', and the material from which both the physical world and the spirit world are made. See A. Findlay, *On the Edge of the Etheric or Survival After Death Scientifically Explained*, 25th Impression, 'Preface' by W. Barrett (London, Rider, 1932), p. 38. Theories of the ether are discussed in ch. 7 below.

16 A. Findlay, *The Psychic Stream* (London, Psychic Press, 1939), p. 1154.

17 According to Marina Warner, the 'sixth century *Akathistos* hymn hails her as Jacob's ladder'. *Alone of All Her Sex*, p. 286.

18 *Ibid.*, p. 286.

19 See E. Bagnold, *The Squire* (1938) (London, Virago, 1989), p. 155, where the heroine sees herself as 'a pipe through which the generations pass'.

20 Warner, *Alone of All Her Sex*.

21 E. Roberts, quoted by S. Barbanell, *Some Discern Spirits*, p. 199.

22 H. Boddington, *Psychic News Booklet 3: Trance States in Relation to Spirit Control* (London, Psychic Press, 1933); and *Psychic News Booklet 2: Psychic Healing* (London, Psychic Press, 1933). See also W. H. Evans, *Psychic News Booklet 4: Philosophy of Spiritualism* (London, Psychic Press, 1933), p. 31.

23 Barbanell, *Some Discern Spirits*, pp. 138, 111.

24 L. Irigaray, *Speculum of the Other Woman*, trans. Gillian C. Gill (New York, Cornell University Press, 1985), p. 22. See also J. Mitchell and J. Rose (eds), *Feminine Sexuality: Jacques Lacan and the École Freudienne* (London, Macmillan, 1982). Taking a more historical approach, T. Laqueur, *Making Sex: Body and Gender from the Greeks to Freud* (Cambridge, MA, Harvard University Press, 1992) shows how the one-sex model in Western culture was replaced (but never quite ousted) by the two-sex model. Both models negate women. In the one-sex model, woman appears as an inverted or imperfect man; in the two-sex model, she is perceived as his opposite.

25 See, for example, Barbanell's representation of Estelle Roberts in her *Some Discern Spirits*. See also B. Upton, *The Mediumship of Helen Hughes* (London, Spiritualist Press, 1946).

26 Barbanell, *Some Discern Spirits*, pp. 198–9.

27 Findlay, *On the Edge of the Etheric*, p. 82.

28 J. Hewat McKenzie, *Spirit Intercourse: Its Theory and Practice* (London, British College of Psychic Science, 1936), p. 44.

29 *Ibid.*, p. 45.

30 M. Barbanell, *The Case of Helen Duncan* (London, Psychic Press, 1945), p. 11. See also D. Cohen, who regarded spirit materialisation as a variation on biological birth: *Price and His Spirit Child Rosalie* (London, Regency, 1965), pp. 20–23. Similarly, the psychical researcher Nandor Fodor wrote: 'Materialisation. That mystery of mysteries … The apparent birth and flowering into full growth of human shapes from

that peculiar bodily substance called ectoplasm. A biological miracle, which is now being forced on the attention of science' (*These Mysterious People* [London, Rider, 1935], p. 28). Physical manifestations reminded Harry Price of biological birth even when the medium was a teenage boy. Reporting on one aspect of the phenomena of Rudi Schneider (a well-known Austrian medium) in 1929, he wrote: All these teleplasmic productions [usually known as ectoplasm] apparently formed inside the cabinet and poked themselves through the openings when "ripe" just like the birth of an embryo' (H. Price, *Search for Truth: My Life for Psychical Research* [London, Collins, 1942], p. 142).

31   Fodor, *These Mysterious People*, p. 74.
32   J. Leigh, 'Mrs. Duncan's Mediumship: Exhibit Two', *The Two Worlds*, XLV:2320 (1932) 307.
33   T. Mann, *The Magic Mountain*, trans H. T. Lowe-Porter (London, Penguin, 1973), pp. 676–7. The book was translated into English in 1928, and awarded the Nobel Prize for Literature the following year.
34   K. M. Goldney and S. G. Soal, 'Report on a Series of Experiments with Mrs Eileen Garrett', Appendix 2, *Proceedings of the Society for Psychical Research*, 154 (1937) 56–9.
35   Barbanell, *Some Discern Spirits*, pp. 152, 94.
36   Upton, *The Mediumship of Helen Hughes*, pp. 41, 52.
37   W. P. Patterson and D. Morrison, 'Introduction', in G. Cummins, *The Scripts of Cleophas: A Reconstruction of Primitive Christian Documents*, 5th edn (London, Psychic Press, 1974), p. xii.
38   H. Boddington, *Trance States in Relation to Spirit Control*, p. 9.
39   *Ibid.*
40   Leonard, *My Life in Two Worlds*, p. 279.
41   Boddington, *Trance States in Relation to Spirit Control*, p. 11.
42   Carl Wickland wrote on the phenomenon of 'possessing' spirits, and was regarded by Spiritualists as an expert on the subject. Typically, the 'possessing' spirit simulated the behaviour of a traditional devil, causing affected persons to scream, swear and tear their clothes. See C. Wickland, *Thirty Years among the Dead* (London, Spiritualist Press, 1924).
43   Barbanell, *Some Discern Spirits*, p. 198.
44   Hewat McKenzie, *Spirit Intercourse*, p. 146.
45   *Ibid.*, p. 148. For historical perspectives on food, fasting and holiness see R. Bell, *Holy Anorexia* (Chicago, University of Chicago Press, 1985); W. Vandereycken, *From Fasting Saints to Anorexic Girls: The History of Self Starvation* (London, Athlone Press, 1994); J. Rubin, *Religious Melancholy and Protestant Experience in America* (New York, Oxford University Press, 1994).
46   For a survey of changing perceptions of the body in Western culture, see A. Synott, 'Tomb, Temple, Machine and Self: The Social Construction of the Body', *The British Journal of Sociology*, 43:1 (1992) 79–110,

especially p. 86. See also M. Berman, *The Reenchantment of the World* (Ithaca, NY, Cornell University Press, 1981); Laqueur, *Making Sex*; Warner, *Alone of All Her Sex*; D. Noble, *A World without Women: The Christian Clerical Culture of Western Science* (New York, Alfred Knopf, 1992). Noble's fascinating study traces the historical processes whereby women were excluded from the masculine culture of learning. He considers the body and sexual desire as sites of struggle and negotiation in this process.

47 Hewat McKenzie, *Spirit Intercourse*, p. 149. The understanding of sex as a resource that can be dammed up, diverted, or spent, began to assume importance in sexual politics from about the turn of the century. See L. Birkin, *Consuming Desire: Sexual Science and the Emergence of a Culture of Abundance, 1871–1914* (Ithaca, NY, Cornell University Press, 1988) Sheila Jeffreys considers perceptions of sexuality as an irresistible energy source which must be 'spent', and analyses its ideological implications for men's access to women's bodies in her, *The Spinster and Her Enemies*. Contemporary ideologies of sexual desire are discussed in ch. 5 below.

48 V. L. Bullough, D. Dixon and J. Dixon, 'Sadism, Masochism and History, Or When is Behaviour Sado-Masochistic?', in R. Porter and and M. Teich (eds), *Sexual Knowledge, Sexual Science* (Cambridge, Cambridge University Press, 1994), reminds us that in the European Christian tradition, 'ecstasy has often been associated with pain' (p. 51). See also P. Gebhard, 'Fetishism and Sadomasochism', in J. H. Masserman (ed.), *Dynamics of Deviant Sexuality* (New York, Grune & Stratton, 1969).

49 Both quotes come from S. Desmond, *Reincarnation for Everyman* (1939) (London, Andrew Dakers, 1943), p. 168.

50 Boddington, *Trance States in Relation to Spirit Control*, p. 30 The same logic applied in psychic healing. During the process of healing it was expected that the symptoms of disease would be transferred to the medium for the purpose of both diagnosis and cure. See Boddington, *Psychic News Booklet 2: Psychic Healing*, p. 9. Many of the mediums included in a Mass-Observation survey on Spiritualism said that they experienced identical symptoms to their patients during healing sessions. See Mass-Observation Archive (University of Sussex): Topic Collection: Astrology and Spiritualism, 1/B, 1938–42.

51 F. Wood, *Mediumship and War* (London, Rider, 1942), p. 107. 'Rosemary' was known for her mediumship in relation to the spirit control known as the 'Lady Nona'. 'Rosemary's' supporters claimed that she was able to speak fluent Ancient Egyptian when she was 'controlled' by the 'Lady Nona'. Much of *Mediumship and War* is devoted to predictions and advice given by this spirit-guide through her medium.

52 *Ibid.*, pp. 108–9.

53 *Ibid.*, p. 106.

54 E. Garrett, *My Life as a Search for the Meaning of Mediumship* (New York, Arno Press, 1975), p. 106.

55 Fodor, *These Mysterious People*, ch. XXV. See also L. Sharp (ed.), *Encyclopedia of Occultism and Parapsychology*, 2nd edn (Detroit, MI, Gale Research Company, 1984), p. 894.

56 'Mrs Morris Vindicated', *International Psychic Gazette*, May 1932, p. 120.

57 See *Psychic News*, 5:25(1932), 'Editorial', p. 11; Ursula Bloom, 'The Way to Freedom: How You Can Help Our Mediums', *The Two Worlds*, 2 September 1932, p. 565. *The International Psychic Gazette* printed an article composed almost entirely of testimonials to Morris from well-known people and institutions: 'Mrs. Meurig Morris's Libel Action', *International Psychic Gazette*, May 1932, pp. 117–18.

58 G. Nelson has recorded the prosecution of mediums in this period in his *Spiritualism and Society* (London, Routledge & Kegan Paul, 1969), pp. 165–7. Each prosecution received a great deal of publicity in the Spiritualist press, and was reported from as far afield as Australia. See *Psychic News*, 14 September 1940, p. 5. The following week, the front page and editorial comment were again devoted to the subject of prosecution: *Psychic News*, 21 September 1940, p. 1. The circumstances of any particular case were often a subject of discussion decades after the event. As we saw in ch. 1 above, Barbara McKenzie spoke to *Psychic News* in 1940 about the prosecution of Almira Brockway just after the Great War. Her reason for doing so was to justify the necessity of colleges like her own where, she said, mediums could be protected against malicious legal action: *Psychic News*, 10 August 1940, p. 5.

59 'Editorial', *Psychic News*, 25 June 1932, p. 11.

60 H. Swaffer, 'Seven Wonderful Women', *Psychic News*, 18 June 1932, p. 7.

61 H. Swaffer, 'The Plot to Destroy Us', *Psychic News*, 18 June 1932, p. 1.

62 *Votes for Women*, V:220, 24 May 1924. D. Jones, *In Parenthesis* (1937) (London, Faber & Faber, 1964), especially Part Seven.

63 'The Joan of Arc of Modern Spiritualism: The Rev. Dr. Lamont and Mrs Morris', *International Psychic Gazette*, May 1932, p. 118.

64 See A. Crossley, 'Author's Preface', *The Story of Helen Duncan* (Devon, Arthur Stockwell, 1975), p. 1. The editor of the Spiritualist journal *Light* noted that Helen Duncan's supporters described her as 'the Spiritualists' Joan of Arc': 'The Case of Mrs. Duncan', *Light*, LXIV: 3288 (1944) 145.

65 The story of Joan, as told by *Light* in two weekly parts, emphasised these aspects of her experience and personality. B. Abdy Collins, 'Joan of Arc', *Light*, LXII:8 (1942) 323, 335. For a recent and compelling account of constructions of the legendary life of Joan, see M. Warner, *Joan of Arc: The Image of Female Heroism* (London, Vintage, 1991).

66 E. Roberts, *Forty Years A Medium* (London, Herbert Jenkins, 1959), p. 17; Garrett, *My Life*, pp. 6–11; Leonard, *My Life in Two Worlds*, p. 11.

67 See, for example, Hewat McKenzie, *Spirit Intercourse*, pp. 14–15.

68 See, for example Garrett, *My Life;* Leonard; *My Life In Two Worlds;* E. Roberts, *Forty Years A Medium* (London, Herbert Jenkins, 1959).

69 See for example: Garrett, *My Life*; Crossley, *The Story of Helen Duncan*; Leonard, *My Life in Two Worlds*; Roberts, *Forty Years A Medium*; Barbanell, *Some Discern Spirits*; Upton, *The Mediumship of Helen Hughes*; Clements, *Psychic News* 2 July 1932, pp. 5, 14; D. Stokes and L. Dearsley, *Voices in My Ear: The Autobiography of a Medium* (London, Futura Macdonald, 1980); Fodor, *These Mysterious People*, chs II, XXV; Wood, *Mediumship and War*; Harry Price, *Stella C.: An Account of Some Original Experiments in Psychical Research* (1925), ed. J. Turner (London, Souvenir Press, 1973).

70 Barbanell, *Some Discern Spirits*, p. 26.

71 *Ibid.*, p. 199.

72 *Ibid.*, p. 12.

73 *Ibid.*, p. 17.

74 *Ibid.*, p. 18.

75 *Ibid.*, p. 19.

76 *Ibid.*, pp. 20–21.

77 *Ibid.*, p. 22.

78 J. J. Morse, *Practical Occultism: A Survey of the Whole Field of Mediumship* (1888) (London, Psychic Book Club, 1956). See also L. Barrow, *Independent Spirits: Spiritualism and English Plebeians 1850–1910* (London, Routledge & Kegan Paul, 1986).

79 An editorial article in *The Two Worlds* expressed the hope that, in time, 'every home will have its own circle, and every family its own medium': 'Concerning Private Sittings', *The Two Worlds*, XXXIX:200 (1926) 160.

80 See, for example, H. Swaffer, 'Spiritualism's Crisis Now', *Psychic News*, 2 July 1932, p. 7. Here, Swaffer said that experienced platform mediums were so scarce that inexperienced mediums were undertaking platform work before they were ready. Similarly, Bernard Upton wrote in his biography of Helen Hughes: 'The demand for good mediums far exceeds the supply, and most of them are seriously overworked' (*The Mediumship of Helen Hughes*, p. 14). George Lawton commented in his study of Spiritualism: 'the scarcity of good mediums present Spiritualists with a permanent and serious problem of which they themselves are acutely aware' (*The Drama of Life after Death*, p. 579).

81 'Concerning Private Sittings', *The Two Worlds*, XXXIX:200 (1926) 161; 'Mediumship – The Foundation Stone', *The Two Worlds*, XXXIX:1992 (1926) 36. However, Spiritualists were unable to agree on estimates of the number of home circles in Britain at any given time.

82 Hewat McKenzie, *Spirit Intercourse*, p. 14.

83 Cummins, *Unseen Adventures*, p. 135. Commenting as an outsider to the Spiritualist movement, George Lawton was convinced that mediumship was a sign of some kind of personal inadequacy, and that only 'mediocre' people would be content with the economic and social lot of a medium: 'The individual fully equipped to meet the stress and strain of life on the outside would not stay. Those who remain in the ministry permanently are the ones who dare not leave' (*The Drama of Life after Death*, pp. 579–80).

84 J. B. McIndoe, president of the Spiritualists' National Union, took up the former position with the following rhetorical question: 'Should I pay people – possibly complete strangers – who have expended their time and trouble at my request in doing me some service? Ask the question about any other profession but mediumship and you will be looked on as either weak-minded or as too mean to be worth answering' ('Should Mediums be Paid?', *The Two Worlds*, XXXIX:1998 (1926) 130). A few weeks later the issue was again discussed in *The Two Worlds*, and similar sentiments were expressed. See 'Concerning Private Sittings', *The Two Worlds*, XXXIX:2000 (1926) 160. The opposite view was put forward by a correspondent to *The Two Worlds* who thought that mediumship should be offered as an unpaid 'service for humanity': 'Should Mediums Be Paid?', *The Two Worlds*, XXXIX:1994 (1926) 147.

85 On one occasion, Barbanell rebuked Helen Duncan for holding too many seances; this, in his view, could lead only to the deterioration of her psychic powers: 'She has been sitting every night for three weeks. The temptation is, of course, the money.' Although 'she must have money … I want to warn Mrs. Duncan that her gifts must not be treated as a commercial proposition' (M. Barbanell, *Psychic News*, 2 July 1932, p. 1).

86 By way of tribute to a male medium, Arthur Findlay wrote that he shunned publicity and always refused payment. See Findlay, *The Way of Life: A Guide to the Etheric World* (London, Psychic Press, 1953), p. 231. See also Conan Doyle, *The Vital Message*. p. 116.

87 For example, Louisa Lind-Af-Hageby, president of the London Spiritualist Alliance, wrote that the growth of Spiritualism was 'inseparably linked with the existence of mediumship'. See Lind-Af-Hageby, 'Prosecutions under the Vagrancy Act', *Light*, LXII: 3201 (1942) 163.

88 Findlay, *The Psychic Stream*, p. 1151. Conan Doyle was one of those who believed that psychic power, in varying degrees, was common to everyone. In his two books later compiled as *The New Revelation and The Vital Message*, he described the mediums he knew as 'average specimens of the community'. On the following page, however, he stressed the moral superiority of mediums compared to the clergy. He

then went on to describe one male medium of his acquaintance as an 'Anthony of Padua type, a walking saint, beloved of animals and children … a figure who might have stepped out of some legend of the Church' (pp. 115–16).

89 Wood, *Mediumship and War*, p. xi.

90 M. Hankey, *James Hewat McKenzie, Pioneer of Psychical Research: A Personal Memoir* (London, Aquarian Press, 1963), p. 93. See also Air Chief Marshal Lord Dowding, *Many Mansions* (London, Rider, 1943), p. 102.

91 An Onlooker, 'Future of Spiritualism: Weaknesses of the Movement and How They May be Remedied', *Light*, LV:2860 (1935) 690.

92 Boddington, *Trance States in Relation to Spirit Control*, pp. 28, 36.

93 Florence Cook, a famous medium who practised in the 1890s, said that she was tormented by a spirit, calling itself 'the fiend', who intended to undo her spirit-guide's good work. See Owen, *The Darkened Room*, pp. 212–13. From the very beginning of her career, Cook's mediumship showed a marked tendency towards transgressive behaviour. It was rumoured that on one occasion she 'was carried dangerously over the heads of the sitters, and invisible hands stripped her of her clothing' (Fodor, *These Mysterious People*, p. 56).

94 Boddington, *Trance States in Relation to Spirit Control*, p. 32. See also G. Leonard, *My Life in Two Worlds*, p. 253.

95 Boddington, *Trance States in Relation to Spirit Control*, p. 24.

96 The sex magic practised by the likes of Aleister Crowley would have been deeply shocking to Spiritualists, and viewed as an invitation to 'low spirits' to possess such foolhardy mediums. For an analysis of Aleister Crowley's forays into sex magic, see A. Owen, 'The Sorcerer and His Apprentice: Aleister Crowley and the Magical Exploration of Edwardian Subjectivity', *Journal of British History*, 36:1 (1997) 99–133.

97 See, for example, 'Fraud at a Seance', *The Two Worlds*, XXXIX:1992 (1926) 37.

98 Hankey, *James Hewat McKenzie*, pp. 27, 76.

99 E. Garrett, *Many Voices* (London, George Allen & Unwin, 1968), pp. 95, 54.

100 Garrett, *My Life*, p. 137.

101 Garrett, *Many Voices*, p. 84.

102 *Ibid.*, p. 55.

103 Hankey, *James Hewat McKenzie*, p. 62.

104 Leonard, *My Life in Two Worlds*, pp. 222, 183.

105 Hankey, *James Hewat McKenzie*, pp. 56–9.

106 *Ibid.*, p. 56.

107 Maurice Barbanell, speaking of Helen Duncan, wrote that her mediumship 'should be guarded and watched, and carefully cultivated. She should not sit more than three times a week. She should put herself in the hands of experienced Spiritualists, wherever she goes' (*Psychic*

News, 2 July 1932, p. 1).

108 S. Freud, *Totem and Taboo: Some Points of Agreement between the Mental Lives of Savages and Neurotics*, trans J. Strachey (London, Routledge & Kegan Paul, 1960), p. 44.

109 H. J. D. Murton, 'Editorial: The Case of Mrs Duncan', *Light*, LXIV:3288 (1944) 147.

4

Possession, dissociation and unseen enemies

Public attitudes to mediums in the interwar years ran parallel to views about the supernatural. Where the supernatural was perceived as benign, so were mediums, but mediums could also be – and commonly were – viewed as dangerous, deluded or mad: sometimes all three. The sign, medium, displayed many characteristics of a taboo in the sense described by Mary Douglas.[1] Ambiguously situated between conscious and unconscious processes, activity and passivity, psychosis and revelation, mediumship eluded a secure and respectable place in the order of things. Mediums were often seen as aberrant people who threatened to bring disorder – and thus harm – to individuals and to society. The expected form of injury varied according to different discursive traditions, but through 'high' and 'low' culture, religious and secular accounts, the medium was routinely placed on the negative side of linguistic oppositions. Catholic representations depicted her as the victim of demonic forces, while medical discourses pathologised her as the victim of mania, delusion, or multiple personality disorder. These associations with disease made her, in turn, a metaphor for human degeneration and urban decay. In occult narratives, possessing demons hovered around this 'psychotic' personality, as if to make a bridge between the hzorrors of the past and those of the present. It was this sense of horror – sustained by contemporary anxieties about unseen 'enemies' 'within' and 'without' – which was the common theme reverberating through different legends about the medium. Yet into the horror that attached to mediumship, fantasies of transgressive pleasure were woven.

Possession

In Chapters 2 and 3, I focused on Spiritualism's debt to Catholic symbols, so it seems apposite to begin with Catholic responses to Spiritualism. Church ratification of Divine visitation or inspiration was difficult to obtain under any circumstances. Traditionally, the Church divided the causes of extraordinary phenomena into three categories: Divine power, natural power, or diabolical influence. However, the rule established by Pope Benedict XIV (1740–58) decreed that no phenomenon was to be attributed to Divine influence until natural or diabolical explanation had been excluded.[2] This rule set the tone for clerical attitudes towards alleged supernormal phenomena in the centuries that followed.[3] During the nineteenth and twentieth centuries, for example, the Church received over 200 applications requesting ratification of visions and other manifestations of the Virgin. It granted only a few, even though the Church specially encouraged veneration of the Virgin at this time.[4]

Despite the many points of similarity between Spiritualist and Catholic practice and thought in the twentieth century, the Church forbade the evocation of the dead,[5] and remained implacably opposed to Spiritualism. In accord with Pope Benedict's ruling, Catholic publications for lay consumption taught that Spiritualist phenomena issued from either natural or demonic causes. Some authors favoured the former, and attributed belief in spirits to fraud, illusion, and naive credulity.[6] Many, however, were inclined to think that after these causes had been considered, there remained a large body of manifestations that were ascribable to some evil agency, wholly external to the medium.[7] These authors condemned mediumship as contrary to Christianity and right order: seance performance had nothing to do with the Grace of God, but was a form of necromancy sanctioned by evil forces. In view of this, attendance at a seance was treated as a sin. Una Troubridge, a Catholic who took up psychical research just after the Great War, recorded in her diary that the veto her Church placed on 'all spiritualistic practices' troubled her. Her partner, Marguerite (John) Radclyffe Hall, felt even more disturbed by this disapproval and felt obliged to mention her own investigations into Spiritualism during her confessions. 'Consequently', wrote Troubridge, Radclyffe Hall 'came for the first time into direct collision with the Priests of her Church ... and it is no exaggeration to say that ... the Father Confessor became a veritable torment.'[8]

Representatives of the Church stressed that Spiritualism was a spiritual, mental and physical danger; its practice compromised the health of participants, even leading to death by suicide.[9] In 1920, one priest wrote: 'This very morning I heard of a girl, who, being told in a seance by her deceased lover that he would not live on the other side without her, drowned herself to join him'.[10] Six years later, a play entitled *The Twin* was produced at the Everyman Theatre, London. The drama centred on a young woman who had cultivated her psychic powers to contact her brother, killed in the war. According to a Spiritualist journalist, the 'girl is shown as falling into a trance (against her will), and being led by a spirit form in the uniform of a British officer … to an open window, and in obedience to the spirit's commands, throws herself into the street below'.[11]

Catholic influence on the subject of mediumship is also apparent in popular films of the period. *The Clairvoyant* (1935) deals with the moral and spiritual dangers of psychic power. The film takes psychic power for granted, but questions its desirability and seeks to display its dangers. The narrative opens with a fake telepath who performs on the music-hall stage with his wife. By accident he discovers that he really does have clairvoyant powers, but only in the presence of a particular woman who seems to be the conductor of a type of psychic–sexual energy. Although the clairvoyant becomes wealthy, his newly found 'gift' does not bring happiness to him or his family. His marriage threatens to break down and he is unable to prevent the disasters he predicts. In the end, the clairvoyant realises that his ability issues from a baleful source; he abandons his gift and returns to his wife.[12]

Alcoholism was another perceived hazard of mediumship emphasised by Catholic authors. The mental and physical pain experienced by some mediums during spirit manifestations was stripped of its associations with martyrdom, and recast as the preliminary symptom of insanity and alcoholism. The alcoholism of various nineteenth-century mediums, such as the famous Fox sisters, was sometimes deployed in support of this claim. Kate and Margaret Fox, from Hydesville, New York, are generally credited with starting the Spiritualist movement in 1848. They and their mother insisted that they heard ghostly rapping at night, which seemed to reply to questions posed by them. The family were given to understand by a series of raps that the disturbances were caused by an 'injured spirit'. From then on, wherever 'either of the daughters happened to be staying, there the mysterious sounds infallibly occurred'. Within a short time, the sisters had become famous.[13] After the death of Kate's husband in 1888, it was rumoured that she had taken to drink. She was arrested in New York for drunkenness and she died in 1892, a confirmed alcoholic. Her sister suffered a similar fate.[14] One Catholic author claimed that the experience of the Fox sisters was a direct consequence of their mediumship: 'The medium often suffers acutely; his or her bodily and mental health is frequently wrecked.' Therefore, it was 'the sacred duty of every man and woman to guard the home from these malign [spirit] influences' who were wreaking havoc on the minds and bodies of those who dabbled with Spiritualism.[15]

Along with alcoholism, questionable morals and suicidal impulses, Catholic writers found evidence of demonic possession in other forms of transgressive behaviour involving deviations in prescribed gender roles. Men, it was frequently implied, were robbed of their will and 'weakened' by a dominating spirit; whereas women were likely to lose interest in their homes and families, and act in disorderly ways. We find an example of each 'condition' in *A Convert from Spiritualism* (1932), by the Catholic writer on Spiritualism and demonic possession Gregory Raupert, who tells of his father's experiences with Spiritualism.[16] The first case involved a woman who, according to her husband, became possessed after experimenting with automatic writing. The initial signs that something was wrong came when she began to experience bouts of insomnia and pains at the back of her head that increased in intensity as the days went by. Soon the entity made it known that he had full command of her body: 'More and more she passed under the control and influence of the invading intelligence, and less and less concern had she in the affairs of everyday life.' The spirit caused her to 'swear and curse, and call [herself by] vile names – names she had never heard in her normal state'. She also felt compelled to run down the street in her nightgown. Once she tried to take her own life.[17]

This description of demonic possession and its effects approximates closely to what Spiritualists called 'obsessing' spirits. Spiritualists, like Catholics, recognised an obsessing spirit by the transgressive behaviour it produced in its victims. Carl Wickland described similar 'symptoms' in the obsession of Mrs Fl, who also became 'wild and unmanageable' and 'used extraordinarily vile language'.[18] However, whereas Spiritualism asserted that obsessions by unwholesome spirits were unusual events, and were controllable, Catholic authors insisted that all spirit manifestations (except, of course, those caused by fraud and delusion) issued from virtually uncontrollable satanic sources.

The worst case of diabolical possession, according to Raupert, involved a man of his father's acquaintance who never answered a question without first addressing some unseen person. Asked about this habit, he replied that he had been consulting the spirits for years, and did nothing without their advice. After some further enquiries, it became clear to all connected with the case that the *'unhappy man had surrendered his will to the "control"'*. An interview with Cardinal Vaughan was organised, and the invading spirit revealed itself with the expected blasphemies and oaths. The man begged the Cardinal to 'free him from this fearful tyranny, promising his sincere co-operation'. Arrangements for a further meeting were made, but he did not keep the appointment – losing, in Raupert's words, the 'grace which might have resulted in complete deliverance from the slavery into which he had fallen.'[19]

Elliot O'Donnell considered the risk of demonic possession in his account of mediumship, *The Menace of Spiritualism* (1920), expressing common misgivings about Spiritualism and the integrity of the medium: 'there is no actual proof that its [the spirit world's] denizens were ever of our flesh and blood'. Nor, in his view, was there any evidence to 'discountenance the possibility, if not, indeed, probability, that they be demons such as are referred to in more than one passage of the New Testament'.[20] Like Raupert, O'Donnell had heard of cases where spirits revealed their satanic identities, and he related a story where a man was hoodwinked by a demon purporting to be a spirit-guide. The demon/spirit told the man that he was to be the second Christ, and the man followed

> the devil's instructions, firmly believing in the Divinity it professed, until foretold events so frequently turned out in direct opposition to prophecy, and he met with such constant failure and disappointment, that his suspicions were aroused and he finally came to the conclusion that this spirit … was something very evil.

Knowledge of the spirit's evil origin, however, did not automatically rid the man of its presence, because 'once you really attract spirit influence, it is extremely reluctant to leave you', and in this instance he had to struggle with 'desperate efforts' to relieve himself of his obsessing demon.[21]

Many occult versions of the activities of 'dark forces' preserved traditional Catholic assumptions about possessing spirits. Sax Rohmer (pseudonym of Arthur Sarsfield Ward), author of many popular novels on the occult[22] and self-styled expert on the subject, gave his views on mediumship in an interview for *Psychic News* in 1932. Spiritualists, he insisted, were uneducated in occult law, and were therefore unaware of the moral and physical dangers of their practices. Mediumistic invocations to the spirit world opened a gateway 'to a kind of spiritual invasion indistinguishable from insanity', which came from demonic sources. Mediums, unbeknown to themselves, practised sorcery, which was neither 'lawful nor profitable'.[23] Similarly, Dion Fortune warned that anyone who dabbled with unseen forces risked setting up a psychological *rapport* with the demons of the abyss. Dion Fortune (pseudonym of Violet Firth), was a prominent London-based occultist and the founder of the Fraternity of the Inner Light (*circa* 1920), which she controlled until her death in middle age in 1946.[24] In her many books about occultism, both fiction and non-fiction, she repeatedly returned to the theme of possession by unseen, malignant forces. In *Applied Magic and Aspects of Occultism*, she spoke of a demoniacal dwelling, named the Quilphoth, which came into existence before 'equilibrium was established' in the world: 'Those who enter the dark portals which lead to the dread subterranean palaces of Quilphoth, … return from this journey with their bias toward evil intensified.'[25] Her book *Psychic Self Defence* (1930) is, as the title suggests, a manual on defence strategies against magical attacks issuing from human and non-human sources.[26]

Both Fortune's and Rohmer's approaches to Spiritualism combined traditional religious objections with the more modern concern with expertise.[27] The occult revival in the twentieth century – in, for example, the establishment of the exclusive Hermetic Order of the Golden Dawn – advanced elite, esoteric knowledge to act as a bulwark against 'mass culture' and the forces of democracy.[28] Reflecting contemporary ideals of professional respectability in other, more orthodox fields, Fortune distinguished between mediums trained in the occult sciences and untrained Spiritualist mediums. In *Spiritualism in the Light of Occult Science*, she claimed that the former knew how to ensure contact with entities on a 'high plane' of existence, whereas the latter were likely to botch the operation and make contact with the unevolved spirits of the lowest planes. These spirits remained in a kind of antechamber between this life and the next, their 'bad' record on earth made them unwilling to face the Judgement which - according to Fortune – all souls must eventually face. It 'is while in this state', she wrote, 'that the soul is most readily contacted by those who would link the living with the dead'. These souls had nothing to offer the living in the way of information about life after death, nor anything in the way of moral guidance, let alone revelation, for here 'souls live[d] among their own thought-forms, the creations of their own imaginations; each in a subjective world of his own.'[29]

Expressions of concern about supernormal possession existed alongside – and were bound up with – World War I anxieties about the invading Other. In the twenty years or so before the outbreak of World War I, the 'Other' usually appeared in the garb of a hostile foreign power poised for the invasion of the British Isles. I. F. Clarke, in his classic history of imaginary warfare literature *Voices Prophesying War* describes how these texts represented and shaped xenophobic sentiments. Such literature typically displayed 'hatred of the enemy, the horror figure of the spy, brutal and violent incidents, fierce nationalistic sentiments, appeals to tradition and to prejudice, the dread picture of the nation alone in adversity and on the edge of defeat, the final swift and facile destruction of the enemy fleet'.[30] The spy was a ubiquitous figure in these narratives. In 1910, William Le Queux published his novel *Invasion*, in which he described the activities of German spies in Britain, 'who having served in the German army, had come over to England and obtained employment as waiters, clerks, bakers, hairdressers, and private servants.'[31] The media received such stories with considerable credence, prompting questions in the House of Commons about the existence of spies in the London area and the Home Counties. Some credited the German advance army with almost supernatural knowledge of British topography. According to one invasion story, *The Enemy in Our Midst*:

> Every registered alien was an authority on the topography and resources of the district in which he dwelt. If there was a *cul-de-sac* into which an enemy could be driven, or trapped and butchered, he knew of it; if there were mews, or garages, he was acquainted with them and their accommodation for horses and vehicles; he knew the resources of every grocer's shop, every public-house, every dairy, every fruiterer's, every butcher's, and every telephone call office.[32]

On the commencement of hostilities in 1914, as war fever infected the inhabitants of Europe,[33] xenophobic sentiments reached new heights. Jay Winter has noted that just as the angels of Mons were thought to aid the British, so the denizens of hell collaborated with the German forces: The 'same minds which conjured up angels had little difficulty in seeing demonic forces at work on the other side.'[34] Atrocities allegedly committed by Germans bore the mark of the devil: Belgian children had their hands cut off; a Canadian soldier suffered crucifixion in front of his compatriots; and a young nurse died in agony, having had her breasts amputated.[35] Some atrocity stories carried more details:

> [S]ome thirty to thirty-five German soldiers entered the house of David Tordens, a carter, in Sempst; they bound him, and then five or six of them assaulted and ravished in his presence his thirteen-year-old daughter, and afterwards fixed her on bayonets. After this horrible deed, they bayoneted his nine-year-old son and then shot his wife.[36]

'The Germans are devils', the wounded told a nurse working in France, 'that's why St. George is fighting for us.'[37] In this climate of xenophobic anxiety, mediums were frequently accused of collaborating with 'the enemy'. Lord Northcliffe's papers suggested that Germany paid British mediums to spread despair among their own compatriots; some others alleged that Spiritualists had become involved in a pro-German conspiracy, known as the 'Unseen Hand'.[38]

After the war, as the story of the full horror of technological combat was brought home from the trenches, war no longer seemed to be a natural or inevitable part of life.[39] Nevertheless, war antagonism persisted in spy stories such as those produced by John Buchan and William Somerset Maugham.[40] Spy films were popular. Alfred Hitchcock's, *Sabotage* (1935), loosely adapted from Joseph Conrad's novel *The Secret Agent*, featured a saboteur with shifty eyes and what was intended to pass for a German accent. Interestingly, German bakeries maintained their sinister reputation in the East End of London during the 1920s and 1930s and were subject to periodical boycotts from local inhabitants. One contemporary cliché asserted that 'the only good German was a dead German'.[41] But public anxiety about conventional military invasion was now being replaced by the spectre of a secret enemy network that planned to dominate the world by more covert means.[42]

Communism and socialism were regular targets for the expression of this concern in postwar Britain. Continuous industrial unrest, the political success of the Labour Party and the recent spectacle of revolution in Russia all helped to aggravate mainly lower-middle-class fears about the rise of the 'dangerous classes' and communist activity.[43] Warwick Deeping's bestselling novel *Sorrell and Son* (1925), expressed the Tory imagination, with its outrage and anxiety about the perceived reversal of right order in 'these Bolshie days'[44] following the war. Deeping's protagonist, Sorrell, an ex-army officer and 'a gentleman', is forced to work as a hotel porter because of his impecunious circumstances. This is a fantasy of the world turned upside down, where covert Bolshevist forces have arranged for the downfall of the nation's 'natural leaders' (middle-class men), and initiated the rule of women and the lower classes.[45] But Deeping's sense of oppression and threat did not take on an occult colouring of the sort to be found, for example, in Nesta Webster's violently anti-Semitic and pro-fascist tract *Secret Societies and Subversive Movements* (1928). Webster singles out five powers which, she claims, are involved in a world conspiracy to destroy Christianity and 'civilisation': Theosophy 'and its innumerable ramifications'; Grand Orient Masonry, controlled by Jewish interests; International Finance; Pan-Germanism; and Social Revolution. Each of these 'desir-[ed] to dominate the world'. She cannot say if these powers work independently or in concert, but she suspects that one power controls the rest, 'either the Pan-German Power, the Jewish Power or what we can only call Illuminism'.[46] In conclusion, she writes:

> [H]ow is it possible to ignore the existence of an Occult Power at work in the world? Individuals, sects or races, fired with the desire for world domination, have provided the fighting forces of destruction, but behind them are the veritable powers of darkness in eternal conflict with the power of light.[47]

Nesta Webster's sense of persecution from the Other was extreme – according to one historian, she used to open her front door with a loaded rifle in her hand[48] – but the themes of her anxieties were scarcely exceptional. On a more local level, the 'threats to civilisation' outlined by Webster were represented in *Strange Cults and Secret Societies of Modern London*, produced six years later by Elliot O'Donnell. O'Donnell wrote these stories in documentary form, and featured 'foreigners' of all kinds:

Asians, Chinese, Southern Europeans and Jews, all engaged in secret and abominable activities beyond the reach of the law or security forces. One 'very dangerous society' made a 'special study of Black Magic', employed 'mesmerism and [astral] projection for nefarious purposes', and consisted 'of Orientals with a sprinkling of Southern Europeans, chiefly Spaniards and Italians'.[49] To this list of dangerous societies O'Donnell added Spiritualist organisations where mediums appeared as more 'foreign' than 'foreigners', and more dangerous since their 'object was to betray and deceive the human race'.[50] Mediums, he fulminated, 'have a baneful influence upon believers, and create discord and confusion; ... [their] teachings inculcate false ideas, approve of selfish individual acts, and endorse theories and principles which, when carried out, debase and make man little better than the brute'.[51]

The 'alien' threat gained new impetus on the outbreak of World War II, and rumours flew through the tabloid press concerning occult collaboration with 'the enemy'. There was talk of mediums engaged in Fifth Column activity[52] and on 18 May 1940 *Psychic News* felt obliged to refute a *Daily Sketch* article, which alleged that Nazi agents attended seances in England to obtain war secrets from dead naval men.[53] Despite being the target of such fantasies, some Spiritualists were quite ready to believe in dark 'Magicians on the Other Side of life, who project and infect the Hitlers and the Mussolinis'.[54] Frederick Wood wrote of an unseen war fought by spiritual forces, which was as real as the conflict between 'democracy and totalitarian states'. In this scenario mediums appeared as assets, because their special powers could be used by 'beneficent spirit-intelligences' for the protection of Britain against 'maleficent spirit-intelligences'.[55]

There was yet another unseen threat that issued from *within* the nation: the degeneracy of the race.[56] In the post-World War I years, fears about the 'quality of the race', the consequences of the loss of the 'nation's best blood' in France and that old subject of middle-class desperation – urban living – found expression in renewed nostalgia for a lost Arcadia. As in earlier decades, promoters of rural living schemes were overrepresented by the anti-materialist middle class with socialist leanings.[57] John Hargrave, for example, founded an organisation named the Kibbo Kift, open to adults and children, which combined democratic principles with the ideal of 'pure', rural living. 'We stood', he wrote, 'for a world brotherhood that would exclude no race or creed or social status ... It meant something to us when we signed the Covenant, taught our tribes the Declaration and unfurled over our camps the flag that showed no local or class or sectarian symbol.'[58] Hargrave's vision encompassed all of society, and he contemplated 're-construction' through the rejection of modern technology and whole-sale return to rural life.

In *The Great War Brings It Home* (1919), Hargrave's postwar urban citizen is surrounded by unseen perils. First, the war has created a dangerous heredity imbalance in the population, since the military se-lection process sent

> our best, our most noble, our finest brains, our strongest limbs [to war] but few are they that come back. The weaklings are left. If we allow them to live they will breed. Yet we cannot kill them. The next generation, bred from defective parents, will be half-sighted, weak-limbed, unmanly, spiritless semi-invalids – a fearful example of a slowly degenerating people! ... It was bad enough *before* the war. But now, with all our best blood and strongly knit muscles lying there upon the war trail – what hope have we?[59]

Urban living exacerbated the 'deterioration of the race' by poisoning the population and reducing fertility – itself a sign of degeneracy. Hargrave also insisted that venereal disease – which, he believed, thrived in the towns – expanded the criminal population.[60] In view of all this, he writes, this 'effete civilisation must crumble away', and be replaced by 'new and virile off shoot[s]'.[61] The only chance for the future, as he sees it, is 'to give our children a hard, clean, outdoor camp-life, and bring them up in a wholesome stimulating and invigorating atmos-phere, both mentally and physically'.[62]

Just as postwar 'reconstruction' was imagined in terms of 'clean', 'hardy' and 'virile' pastoralism, so the seance seemed to be part of 'effete' urban degeneracy. Indeed, the image of Spiritualism as a dark, degenerate and unmasculine activity has endured from the nineteenth century to quite recent times. Nineteenth-century psychiatrists such as Henry Maudsley and W. B. Carpenter were among the most aggressive debunkers of Spiritualism. As Rhodri Hayward has noted, Spiritualism's 'rhetoric of self-abandonment and surrender to external forces described the classic symptoms of insanity'.[63] In accord with the tenets of scien-tific naturalism,[64] psychiatry taught that the 'brain is the organ of mind', and that mediumship, or any other kind of mysticism, was a form of insanity issuing from organic causes, usually of a hereditary nature. These 'mental malformities', as Maudsley put it, presented in such illnesses as hallucination, illusion, mania and delusion.[65]Medical men commonly viewed Spiritualist belief as a predominantly feminine illness or failing. One physician asserted in 1877: 'The community of [Spiritualists] contains a large proportion of weak-minded hysterical women, in whom the seeds of mental disorder, though for a time latent, are only waiting for a new excitement to ripen into maturity.'[66] In 1910, Marcel Viollet described Spiritualism in identical terms. He said that the cult attracted people who were hereditary neuropaths – they suffered principally from those 'stigmas' found in women: '"vapours", moods, nervous attacks, [and] hysterical fits'. Moreover, 'these neuropathic persons [had] a particular character made up of a certain instability in thoughts, opinions, projects, the itch of lying, and the desire, sometimes conscious but more often unconscious, of drawing attention to themselves'.[67]

In the interwar years, such explanations were common coin. Elliot O'Donnell drew intensively on Viollet and medical authorities of the last century to support his views about the effects of Spiritualism on health:

> Spiritualism, with all it comprehends, namely, continually sitting in the dark or semi-dark, in a state of nervous tension, and straining the sight, hearing, and heart almost to bursting point – constantly trying to force on an unnatural condition of trance – peering for hours at a time into a crystal, and always fancying one is hearing spirit sounds or seeing spiritual phenomena – is not only injurious to the health of the strongest, but absolutely fatal to the health of that class of people it especially caters for, and invariably entangles in its meshes, i.e., the abnormal, epileptic, hysterical, and weak-minded; and, secondly, that the majority, at all events, of the phenomena Spiritualists declare to be due to superphysical agency can be shown by medical men to be due chiefly to hysteria, and epilepsy, as well as other physical and mental disease of a similar nature.[68]

According to O'Donnell, Spiritualism was unwholesome in every possible respect: physically, morally, mentally and spiritually. Its practices activated hereditary madness; its mediums were 'unstable', 'unbalanced', and addicted to drugs; many of them were female 'sexual deviants' who used the seance as a cover for their 'unnatural' practices. One 'would like to know', he concluded, 'how many of these trained mediums have ended in becoming hopeless degenerates'.[69]

In recent years a great deal of interesting work has been carried out on the politics of eugenics in a variety of contexts,[70] but it is worth emphasising that fears about racial degeneracy betrayed fundamental feelings of insecurity,[71] amounting sometimes to panic, about unseen dangers. Such fears were simultaneously constituted and expressed in racist, sexist and homophobic ideologies. Worries about degeneracy – perceived as a consequence of urban living, contagious and hereditary disease and the feminisation of the nation and the loss of its 'best (male) blood' – were articulations of widespread anxiety about the ubiquitous 'enemy within', projected in other contexts on to the spy, the communist and the Jew. What these 'enemies' had in common was their capacity to work in unseen and often undetectable ways. Stories about demonic invasion and occult attack flourished in this environment, and the medium became a focus for the attendant anxieties. In this atmosphere of paranoia, it is perhaps not so surprising that Nesta Webster armed herself before answering her front door.

Dissociation

Anxieties about the 'enemy within' were augmented by another internal and uncontrollable 'enemy' – the unconscious self. As the concept of the unconscious grew in importance as an explanatory model of mind and, with it, a cognisance of 'dual' and 'multiple' personalities (most visibly in artistic and psychotherapeutic circles),[72] perceptions of the medium took on another inflection. The state of 'dual consciousness' was noted as early as 1859,[73] but it received much more attention in the latter part of the nineteenth century as the unconscious became the subject of intense interest among European and American psychotherapists. It was variously known as the 'subconscious', the 'subliminal self', 'buried consciousness' and, more generally, the 'unconscious'; psychotherapists debated whether it was normal or pathological, and how to relieve some of its more distressing manifestations such as somnambulism, anaesthesia of various parts of the body, loss of memory, dual and multiple personalities.[74]

Morton Prince was an important figure in the dissemination of established, psychotherapeutic ideas on multiple personality. A leading

Boston neurologist and founder of the *Journal of Abnormal Psychotherapy* (1906), Prince adapted and gave wide circulation to the ideas of Pierre Janet, Edmund Gurney, William James and Alfred Binet, among others.[75] In 1905 he published *Dissociation of a Personality*,[76] which was to capture the public imagination on both sides of the Atlantic.[77] *Dissociation of a Personality* relates the story of Miss Beauchamp, pseudonym of Clara Norton Fowler. When Miss Beauchamp came under Prince's care, she was twenty-three years old and a student at a New England college. She impressed Prince as 'well educated', with 'marked literary tastes and faculties', but he considered that 'her heredity from a neuropathic point of view [was] suggestive of nervous instability'.[78] Neither, in his view, was her emotional history conducive to psychological health. It transpired that her childhood had been unhappy. Her mother ignored her except to reprimand her, and, believing that her 'mother's lack of affection was due to her own imperfections, she gave herself up to introspection'. She never expressed feelings of hunger or fatigue; 'She lived within herself and dreamed.' When Miss Beauchamp was thirteen, her mother died, and in the months that followed she experienced a series of 'mental shocks, nervous strains and frights'. 'It is unlikely', wrote Prince, 'that even a strong constitution would withstand the continuous nervous strain and depressing emotional influences to which her whole childhood was subjected.' Soon attacks of somnambulism occurred, and she would walk out into the street in her nightgown, at other times she fell into spontaneous trancelike states.[79]

When Prince met Miss Beauchamp in the spring of 1898, she complained of headaches, insomnia, fatigue and bodily pains. In view of these symptoms, he categorised her as an extreme 'neurasthenic'. She was also 'suggestible' under hypnosis and plainly, in his view, suffering from aboulia 'an inhibition of the will by which a person is unable to do what he actually wishes to do'.[80] The most striking thing about Miss Beauchamp, however, was that she could be any one of three personalities besides her hypnotic state. These personalities were quite different, and were christened by Prince respectively as 'The Saint', 'The Woman' and 'The Devil'. 'The Saint' – 'the typical saint of literature' – was Miss Beauchamp in her waking state, and designated B I. 'The Woman' (B IV), was the reverse of B I. She personified, in Prince's words, 'the frailties of temper, self concentration, ambition, and self interest, which are ordinarily the dominating factors of the average human being'. Miss

Beauchamp's hypnotic state was B II, and the 'Devil' personality Prince called B III or 'Sally'. Prince viewed 'Sally' as a 'rather mischievous imp, one of the kind we might imagine would take pleasure in thwarting the aspirations of humanity. To her pranks were largely due the moral suffering which B I endured, the social difficulties which befell B IV, and the trials and tribulations which were the lot of both.'[81] 'Sally' was what Prince termed a 'coconscious' personality. She declared that she existed independently of Miss Beauchamp, and claimed to have different knowledge and memories. She held her in complete contempt, disparaged her intensity of thought as 'mooning', and made her life a misery by forcing her to perform socially unacceptable actions such as lying and smoking. 'Sally' also resented any attempt to control her, and she met therapeutic suggestions with characteristically childish opposition.

After a long struggle between Miss Beauchamp's various personalities, Prince amalgamated B I with B II and B IV, to produce the 'real' Miss Beauchamp. Now she no longer suffered from hallucinations, aboulia, or amnesia. As for 'Sally':

> With the resurrection of the real self, she 'goes back to where she came from' imprisoned, 'squeezed', unable to 'come' at will or be brought by command. Automatic writing, speech, and such phenomena cease, and it has not been possible as yet to communicate with her, and determine what part if any she plays in Miss Beauchamp's subconscious, or whether as a subpersonality she exists at all.[82]

Miss Beauchamp's story is analogous to Spiritualist descriptions of mediums. Her personal history coincided with mediumistic rites of passage (discussed in Chapter 3 above). Like them, she suffered early in life, whereupon she gave herself up to introspection. She assumed a saintlike persona, and soon began to see visions. She suffered attacks of somnambulism, and fell into 'spontaneous trancelike states'. Her 'aboulia', 'suggestibility', and inability to remember what occurred while she was in a state of trance or under hypnosis also suggested the mediumistic nature. In her trance state, distinguishable personalities emerged who were united with Miss Beauchamp and yet separate from her. Finally, 'Sally' often played the part of a malicious spirit visitor to B IV's medium. One day, as B IV looked in the mirror, somebody else's expression seemed to come over her face: 'It seemed to her devilish, diabolical, and uncanny, entirely out of keeping with her thoughts.' It occurred to her that she could probably communicate with this thing in the mirror, so she suggested that it wrote answers to her questions:

> Presently her hand began to write, answering the questions that were asked, while B IV, excited, curious, wild for information of the past, kept up a running fire of comment on the answers of Sally, for, of course, the 'thing' was Sally.[83]

Prince insisted that dissociation should be regarded as a mental disorder, with no supernatural content;[84] in 1926 he spoke of automatic writing and crystal visions as established aspects of the dissociated personality.[85]

Prince was not the first to link the concept of dissociation with mediumship; psychotherapy, in association with psychical research, had already made such a connection in the previous century. Theodore Flournoy wrote to William James on the matter in 1895. As keen psychical researchers, both Flournoy and James became interested in the unconscious as representative of a 'higher' or 'subliminal self', which displayed itself in uprushes of genius and was possibly a means of 'tuning in' to 'higher' forces in the cosmos.[86] However, in keeping with the extremely cautious policy of the Society for Psychical Research (SPR), to which both belonged, Flournoy and James were more likely to view mediums as candidates for psychotherapy than as possessors of special powers. In a letter to James, Flournoy wrote that he had met a medium who was

> a veritable museum of all possible phenomena and has a repertoire of illimitable variety; she makes the table talk, – she hears voices, – she has visions, hallucinations, tactile and olfactory, – automatic writing – sometimes complete somnambulism, catalepsy trances etc. All the *automism, sensory and motor*, of Myers,[87] – all the classical hysterical phenomena – present themselves in turn, in any order and the most unexpected fashion, varying from one time to another.

Flournoy noted that this medium's spirit-guides spoke of former events that were generally associated with the ancestors of persons present at the seance. After making some enquiries, he discovered that the parents of those present had known the parents of the medium. From this information, Flournoy judged that the 'great majority of the phenomena were evidently the automatic production of forgotten memories –

or memories registered unconsciously'. He believed that there was 'actually in the nature of this medium a second personality who perceives and recalls incidents which escape ordinary awareness'.[88]

By the interwar period, many psychical researchers accepted this view. Una Troubridge assumed that dissociation accounted for many Spiritualist phenomena; in 1922 she wrote a paper for the SPR comparing mediumistic and non-mediumistic examples of multiple personality.[89] Eric Dingwall, a leading psychical researcher and one-time president of the SPR, took it for granted that mediums were particularly susceptible to dissociation. This conviction led to a quarrell with Hewat McKenzie over the interpretation of one woman's mediumship. Dingwall believed that 'her phenomena were produced by herself in a state of mental dissociation', and was surprised that 'Mr McKenzie took my criticism as a personal affront to his own integrity and after a somewhat difficult interview we parted never to come together again in a spirit of mutual understanding.'[90] In his book *How to Go to a Medium* (1927), Dingwall reiterated his view that 'mediums as a class ... are very easily dissociated in a much more pronounced way than is usual with normal people'.[91]

In his study of Spiritualism for his doctorate degree, George Lawton came to the same conclusion. Mediumship, he wrote, 'has a twofold basis. It depends first on a neurological defect – a mind which readily becomes dissociated and reverts to a trance-like state, and secondly on a desire to utilize this defect in a certain way'.[92] Gregory Raupert was also familiar with this explanation of mediumship. But, as we have seen, he was anxious to show, through the accounts of his father, that Spiritualistic phenomena took shape in the portals of hell, and did not originate in the 'imagination or from any sort of double personality of the medium'.[93]

The debate between supernatural and natural explanations of mediumship continued in the public arena into the 1940s. One respondent to a Mass-Observation survey said: 'A friend who when hypnotised gradually changes personality claims to be the spirit of a free thinker who died about 80 years ago. I do not believe this to be so – I believe it to be dissociation.'[94] The British-made film *Dead of Night* (1945), starring Michael Redgrave and Googie Withers, addressed the question again. The film opens with the protagonists gathered in a farmhouse and about to tell of their experiences with the 'unseen'.

Each story proceeds by way of an unresolved debate between believers in supernatural action and sceptics. One story, told by Joan (Googie Withers), begins with the purchase of a mirror for her husband, Peter, on his birthday. A few weeks after the mirror's installation, Peter can no longer see the reflection of his bedroom in it. As he looks into the mirror he sees another room decorated in the style of the eighteenth century. He soon finds himself drawn into the world of the mirror, and assumes the personality of its first owner, who was injured in a riding accident and left partially crippled. Confined to his room, the first owner began to have paranoid fantasies about his wife's infidelity and eventually strangled her. Peter's personality alters accordingly, and he attacks his wife. When the mirror is accidentally shattered, the spell is broken and Peter returns to normal. The sceptical side of the farmhouse debate is represented by a psychotherapist – complete with German accent – who diagnoses dual personality disorder, but the others remain convinced that supernatural agencies are at work in this and other similar cases.

Spiritualists worried about whether the phenomena produced by their mediums were genuinely psychic or – as a *Psychic News* publication put it – merely the expressions of a 'phase of consciousness normally quiescent'.[95] Some Spiritualists, like Hewat McKenzie, devised ways to avoid 'subconscious interference'. These included asking the spirit control to give information unknown to either medium or investigators, and hypnotising the medium to produce a deeper separation between her conscious and subconscious minds.[96]

The notion of mediumship as dissociated personality was sometimes internalised by mediums themselves. Eileen Garrett had a very unhappy childhood, and she often retreated into a separate world of her own to escape the anger of her aunt, with whom she lived. She recalled how she trained herself to watch her aunt's lips move, 'but hear no sound of the words she spoke', and she thought that this ability 'must have been the beginnings of that separation of personality which later led to the state known as trance'.[97]

When Garrett was fifteen years old, her aunt sent her to London to stay with another relative. Here, a year later, on the eve of the First World War, Garrett married her first husband, Clive. Soon after her wedding trip her husband made it clear to her that he wanted and expected her to be an entirely conventional wife – someone who was always ready to adjust herself to 'his wishes and interests', and was 'well dressed and charming'. He disapproved of her visions and 'voices', and told her that other people did not hear and see such things. He said that if anyone heard her speak of them, they would think her 'unbalanced'. He suggested to her that she had inherited 'unhealthy tendencies' from her parents, whom she never knew. In any event, her way of perceiving was unacceptable, and could lead only to insanity. Garrett accepted his verdict on her mental health and believed herself to be on the brink of madness. From that moment she became 'aware of living in two separate worlds' again. In the first she played out the role of a conventional bourgeois wife – 'gay, superficial and accepting'; in the other, she 'was the sensitive, observant, truly active personality ... belonging only to [herself]'.

> As the division between my two states of mind grew, I chose again to draw in and live with myself alone, as I had done when a child. This now made it easy for me to deal with both my husband and my friends; when I lived in this separated state no one was really able to reach me and they could no longer cause me either hurt or confusion. If this were madness then I had no more fear of it, because in this state alone was I truly peaceful and happy.[98]

Although her husband's speculations about her sanity initially frightened her, she rejected such a negative interpretation of her perceptions, and used her sense of duality as a means of personal expression and defence against a threatening world.

Garrett's understanding of her mediumship evolved over the years. Hewat McKenzie persuaded her that her different trance personalities were genuine spirits of the dead. However, she became uneasy with this explanation (for reasons that will be discussed in Chapter 8) and wondered if her 'controls' were products of her own unconscious. She also considered the possibility that she received information telepathically from sitters. In 1934, she agreed to take part in 'multiple personality' experiments conducted at the University of Oxford by the psychologist William Brown. Garrett made it clear to Dr Brown that she was aware that psychiatrists viewed the mediumistic trance as an expression of the dissociated personality, and that his purpose in undertaking this analysis was to search for the underlying causes of her dissociation. She told him that she was quite 'prepared to risk the loss of the trance condition and the possible disappearance of the *controls*, should these prove to be no more than "a dissociation of my own personality".[99] As it turned out, she accepted neither medical nor Spiritualist constructions of her powers. Her explanation for her visions and 'voices' followed Frederick Myers's concept of the 'subliminal self', and she came to believe that her unconscious was in contact with 'higher' forces in the cosmos. In her view, her spirit-guides were projections of her unconscious. It was this part of the unconscious, however, that permitted her 'to participate and receive knowledge from some ultimate source beyond the limits of personal being'.[100]

In Garrett's conviction of multi-layered consciousness, she was closer to occult than Spiritualist constructions of subjectivity and the unseen. The Hermetic Order of the Golden Dawn 'taught adepts how to develop a second magical self which would conduct lengthy forays into worlds which were conceived as simultaneously inner and outer'.[101] Such forays were not without psychological risk. James Webb relates some instances involving dissatisfied initiates to esoteric groups after the First World War. One man claimed that he 'had become dissociated through using exercises recommended by Rudolf Steiner and was only prevented from suicide by his Christian convictions.' Another student of Steiner said that he had become separated from his ego through doing the same exercises, and suspected that another occultist had stolen it.[102] Accusations like these were common, since it was widely believed among occult groups that unscrupulous magicians could use hypnotism for dominating and manipulating others. The passive condition of trance mediums made them particularly vulnerable to this kind of abuse. Dion Fortune wrote at some length on the subject, and her novel *The Demon Lover* (1927), deals with this hazard for mediums.

The Demon Lover focuses on Veronica Mainwaring, a 'natural medium' who becomes entangled with a powerful and dangerous occult fraternity. She is passive, vague, dreamy, gentle and impossibly naive – indeed, she manifests all those aspects of stereotypical femininity that were valorised by Spiritualists and pathologised by psychotherapy. While she is searching for work, she meets Mr Lucas, who offers her employment as a secretary at an inflated salary. Lucas's plans for her extend beyond her secretarial duties: he has recognised her latent mediumistic abilities, and plans to use them to advance his already considerable knowledge of the occult arts. Veronica remains unaware of her own abilities, and of Lucas's intention to use them for spying on high-grade occult rites. To achieve his ends, Lucas uses hypnotism and other occult techniques to manipulate Veronica's psyche to split the normal union between body and soul. By such techniques, he causes her soul to be pushed out on to the astral planes of existence while her body remains behind in a state of trance. This, according to Fortune, was an extremely dangerous practice, since the soul was not always able to find its way back to its physical host.[103] As Veronica's soul slips out of her body she is conscious of plunging

> downwards into limitless blue-blackness; out between the planets she seemed to fall into stellar space. The curve of her course turned upwards as a diver returns to the surface, the blue grew lighter, it was pale sapphire that precedes the sunrise. Back she came through rosy dawn clouds, and woke up in her chair.[104]

While Veronica's soul travels through astral space, Lucas, in some unknown way, uses her entranced body as a transmitter of occult practices taking place elsewhere.

In *Psychic Self Defence*, Fortune offers advice on how to recognise and avoid occult assaults such as this. She considers that even if one is armed with this information contact with a suspect occult lodge is always dangerous because assaults are often intangible and leave no trace; victims are not even aware that anything is awry in their lives.[105] In *The Demon Lover*, Veronica appears as the innocent victim of malign forces, but Fortune also thought that victims could be implicated in attacks made on them. Like O'Donnell, she believed that it was possible for demonic forces to gain over their victims a powerful hypnotic influence that was difficult to break by effort of will or by orthodox psychotherapy. This was because like attracts like: 'Just as the devout Catholic is inspired by the influences of his patron saint, invoked by prayer, so the neurotic is hag-ridden by his obsessive demon, invoked by the morbid broodings of the dissociated subconsciousness.'[106] There is an example of this blurring of boundaries between internal malaise and supernatural attack in Fortune's description of her own encounter with an ethereal wolf, which she characterises as a product of her own unconscious and simultaneously as a discrete being with its own will:

> I had received serious injury from someone who, at considerable cost to myself, I had disinterestedly helped, and I was sorely tempted to retaliate. Lying on my bed resting one afternoon, I was brooding over

my resentment, and while I was brooding, drifting towards the bor-
ders of sleep, there came to my mind the thought of casting off all
restraint and going berserk. The ancient Nordic myths rose before
me, and I thought of Fenris, the Wolf-horror of the north. Immediately
I felt a curious drawing-out sensation from my solar plexus, and there
materialised … beside me on the bed a large wolf. It was a well-
materialised ectoplasmic form … I could distinctly feel its back pressing against me as it lay beside me on the bed as a large dog might.

I knew nothing about the art of making elementals at that time,
but had accidentally stumbled upon the right method – the brooding
highly charged with emotion, the invocation of the appropriate natural force, and the condition between sleeping and waking in which the
etheric double readily extrudes.

I was horrified at what I had done, and knew I was in a tight
corner and that everything depended upon my keeping my head. I
had had enough experience of practical occultism to know that the
thing I had called into visible manifestation could be controlled by my
will provided I did not panic; but that if I lost my nerve and it got the
upper hand, I had a Frankenstein monster to cope with.

I stirred slightly, and the creature evidently objected to being disturbed, for it turned its long snout towards me over its shoulder and
snarled, showing its teeth. I had now 'got the wind up' properly; but
I knew that everything depended on my getting the upper hand and
keeping it, and that the best thing I could do was to fight it out now,
because the longer the thing remained in existence the stronger it
would get, and the more difficult to disintegrate. So I drove my elbow
into its hairy ectoplasmic ribs and said to it out loud.

'If you can't behave yourself, you will have to go on the floor', and
pushed it off the bed.

Down it went, meek as a lamb, and changed from wolf to dog, to
my great relief. Then the northern corner of the room appeared to
fade away, and the creature went out through the gap.[107]

Images of the 'enemy within' merged with images of the 'enemy
without' in Hollywood's representations of the unseen. *Supernatural*
(1933), directed by Victor Halperin, captures this play between external
and internal attack. Here, Carole Lombard plays a well-to-do woman,
called Roma, whose brother has recently died. She receives a message
from a male medium informing her that her brother wishes to contact
her from 'the beyond'. In her grief, and ignoring her fiancé's warning
about fraud, she agrees to attend a seance with the medium Paul Bavian.
Bavian – as presaged by his overstated furtive looks and sly manner –
is fraudulent and, as it turns out, psychotic; for just before Roma's

party is due to arrive for the seance, he murders his landlady because she tries to blackmail him with his fraudulent activities.

Meanwhile, in another part of the city, a psychical researcher is carrying out experiments in the mortuary on the body of Ruth Rogen, a convicted murderess, recently executed. Asked about the purpose of his experiments by a woman friend, he replies: 'Well, it may sound crazy, but there's danger of contagion. No, dear, not from the body, that's harmless. No, there's something else.' This danger becomes clear when, during his experiments, the psychical researcher accidentally re- leases Ruth's etheric double from her physical body. Free of her bodily constraints, Ruth travels into the atmosphere and is immediately at- tracted to the evil aura generated by Bavian, now conducting a seance with Roma. While he is pretending to be Roma's lost brother, Ruth's etheric double enters the body of Roma, the 'true medium', and as- sumes control of her thoughts and emotions. Roma's demeanour un- dergoes a radical shift as Ruth's personality comes into view. Adopting the sensual, reckless and inebriated postures of Hollywood whores, Roma/Ruth leaves the seance arm in arm with Paul Bavian.

Ruth is the quintessential image of feminine evil, just as Roma rep- resents feminine virtue. Yet it is Roma whom we see drinking, dancing and seducing Bavian; Roma who then takes Bavian by the neck and, with an expression of pleasure, attempts to strangle him. In these scenes, Ruth as a separate entity is lost; she appears as a contamination of Roma's unconscious. This impression of 'evil' desire buried in the vir- tuous woman is reinforced by the fact that the names of both women begin with 'R' – Roma and Ruth, the 'good' and 'evil' twins.[108]

A note on transgressive pleasure

Sociological literature has traditionally held that cultural norms regulate behaviour, and are the basis for group solidarity. Departure from such norms indicates deviancy in functionalist discourse, for example, and revolutionary intent in Marxist understanding. In these otherwise opposed traditions, socially transgressive acts are understood to be in *opposition* to the dominant moral and political code. Since Freud, however, the notion of enjoyment in transgression has become familiar and the concept is used regularly in novels, dramas and historical studies. What Slavoj Žižek has added to this conventional wisdom is the idea that social transgression is a *function* of the 'Law' – its 'underside' rather than its opposite. In this sense, 'Law' is a metaphor for the prohibiting power of patriarchal rule. Žižek argues that such prohibitions are also accompanied by an unacknowledged invitation to transgress. Furthermore, social solidarity is to be found less in adherence to the 'Law' than in the bonds forged in secret infringements of it – the bonds of guilty pleasure.[109] As we have seen, the medium was frequently represented through this double sided 'Law'. And if the medium evoked 'innocence' on the one hand, and 'deviancy' on the other, it was precisely these ambivalent qualities that made her the focus and object of pleasure.

The dramatic impact of Raupert's descriptions of demonic possession (discussed above) relied on the juxtaposition of 'innocence' and 'deviance' – for example, the normally 'well-behaved' housewife who, under the influence of satanic spirits, ran about publicly in her nightwear, swore at people and tried to commit suicide. Then there was the story about a mild-mannered man who was completely dominated by a demon. During clerical attempts to perform an exorcism on this man his demon lifted him out of his chair and threw him violently to the floor. The demon spoke in a harsh rasping voice, claimed that it had been in possession of this 'd[amned] carcass for years', and declared that 'no d[amned] invocation of [theirs] would be successful in dislodging him'.[110] Raupert remembered how these and similar stories about the dangers of Spiritualism, and particularly mediumship, were greeted by audiences with 'breathless excitement'.[111] (Indeed, Raupert's own excitement as he relates these anecdotes is hard to miss.) 'Dual personality', the secular counterpart of demonic possession, followed the same logic of pleasure. B I (Miss Beauchamp) felt continually anxious and, according to Prince, was possessed of a 'morbid' conscientiousness in all her social dealings.[112] 'Sally', the 'Devil', delighted in transgressing the 'Law' represented by B I. She made fun of B I's scruples, played sexual games with Prince, and asserted that *she* was the 'real' Miss Beauchamp. And, from the standpoint of public identity, she *was* the 'real' Miss Beauchamp, for it is much easier to identify with 'Sally's' transgressions than with B I's meticulous conformity to the 'Law'. Significantly, 'Sally' is the only one of the four personalities to whom Prince allowed a proper name.

The symbolic line that separated demonic possession from dual personality was a thin one that was frequently breached. When this happened, there was endless scope for the expression and reception of transgressive enjoyment. The climax of *Supernatural* sees the emergence of Roma's reckless and amorous double. Ruth, as the 'underside' of Roma, is the voyeuristic object of forbidden desire. The pleasure derives not from her social transgressions alone, but also from its proximity to Roma's virtue.

The appeal of Dion Fortune's *Demon Lover* owed much to its un-acknowledged but evident fantasy of sexual transgression exhibited through the medium, Veronica. Veronica's vaunted 'feminine innocence' makes her excursions into sexual masochism and bondage even more delightful. Soon after her capture, she makes several fruitless attempts to escape. Her occult persecutor, Lucas, thwarts further attempts through hypnotic suggestion:

> 'There is something around your neck,' he said. Up went Veronica's hand involuntarily.
> 'Look,' he said, 'it's a steel collar.'
> The image his words evoked flashed into her mind, and as it did so she felt cold hard metal under her hand.
> 'There is a steel chain attached to it,' the man's soft level voice continued. 'A slender steel chain. Run your hand down it.'
> He took her hand in his and drew it towards him, and she felt the links run through her fingers.
> 'And I hold the end of it,' he added significantly. 'If you try to call out, or tell what I do not wish to be told, that collar will contract till it strangles you. Feel it contracting now.'
> Veronica felt something rigid grip her about the throat. The pressure steadily increased. She gasped and fought for air as the trachea closed. Then Lucas touched her forehead.
> 'It has relaxed now,' he said, 'but remember, this will happen again if ever you try to give me away.'[113]

Fortune employed a similar device in a later novel, *The Winged Bull* (1935). Again, the protagonist is a young medium whose passive recep-tivity to occult forces makes her the focus of an occult lodge which wants to manipulate her mediumship in secret black magic rites.[114]

Secrecy is another frequent element in such stories. It is pivotal to the dramatic effectiveness of Robert Louis Stevenson's *Dr. Jekyll and Mr. Hyde* and Oscar Wilde's *The Picture of Dorian Gray*. Dorian hides his grotesque *alter ego* in the attic, and Hyde is the covert 'underside' of Jekyll. In each case the reader is made party to these guilty secrets.

Similarly, in Morton Prince's non-fictional work, the existence of 'Sally' is secret. When Miss Beauchamp begins treatment with Prince, she is reluctant to speak of her personal life at all,[115] and the reader is led into her story by the promise of guilty revelations. The mediumistic governess in Henry James's *The Turn of the Screw* is even more enticingly transgressive, because her secret desire remains enigmatic.[116] It is murky and forbidden, to be sure, but what it might be remains obscure. We are never sure if her desire focuses on the spirits of the former governess, Miss Jessel, and Peter Quint, the dead valet, or on the children in her care, or on the imagined relations of all four.

James's governess embodied the moral ambiguity that gathered around the figure of the medium: was she was innocent or guilty, psychically sensitive or insane, and did she intend to help or harm? So far in this study we have followed the figure of the medium through assorted and contradictory configurations: as the Virgin Mary, the martyr Joan of Arc, the victim of demonic possession, the dissociated personality and the degenerate. And we have seen how these images were shaped through various historical resources and incorporated into the cultural management of pleasure. But we have not exhausted representations of mediumship. In subsequent chapters we shall see how mediumship became enmeshed with images of vampirising maternity on the one hand, and the ideology of 'sour spinsterhood' on the other.

Notes

1 M. Douglas, *Purity and Danger: An Analysis of the Concepts of Pollution and Taboo* (London, Routledge & Kegan Paul, 1966), especially ch. 6.

2 *New Catholic Encyclopedia*, vol. 10 (New York, McGraw-Hill, 1967), p. 172.

3 The rule seems simple enough, but procedures and theological guidelines employed during official investigations into such phenomena were and continued to be complex – down to the present century (*ibid.*, pp. 170–77).

4 M. Warner, *Alone of All Her Sex: The Myth and the Cult of the Virgin Mary*, 2nd edn (London, Picador, 1990), p. 394 n. 25. Of those that were refused, Warner cites the following: 'In 1948, at Lipa in the Philippines, the Carmelite nun Tersita Cactilo saw the Virgin under the aspect "Mary Medriatrix of all Graces".' Other refused petitions included those of Perini Gilli (1946–47) and Bruno Cranacchiola (1947) (p. 394). However, there was a spate of officially recognised visions of the

Virgin in the nineteenth century and again in the 1920s and 1930s. See B. Carrado Pope, 'Immaculate and Powerful: The Marian Revival in the Nineteenth Century', in *The Female in Sacred Image and Social Reality*, eds C. Atkinson, C. Buchanan and M. Miles (Boston, MA, Beacon Press, 1985), pp. 173–200.

5 P. Ariès, *The Hour of Our Death*, trans. H. Weaver (New York, Alfred Knopf, 1981), pp. 467–8.

6 See, for example, W. J. Blyton, *The After-Life: The Truth and Some Modern Distortions* (London, Catholic Truth Society, 1933).

7 See, for example, Reverend G. Raupert, *A Convert from Spiritualism* (Dublin, Irish Messenger Office, 1932); I. Hernaman, *Spiritualism and the Child* (London, Catholic Truth Society, 1924), pp. 1–15; Father B. Vaughan, 'Foreword' to E. O'Donnell *The Menace of Spiritualism* (London, Werner & Laurie, 1920), pp. 1–4; Reverend G. J. MacGillivray, *What Happens after Death* (London, Catholic Truth Society, 1929), p. 2.

8 Quoted by R. Ormrod, *Una Troubridge: The Friend of Radclyffe Hall* (London, Jonathan Cape, 1984), p. 98. Ormrod does not say whether Radclyffe Hall mentioned her lesbian relationship with Troubridge in her confessions, or whether their priest was aware of this relationship.

9 Father Knapp, a Roman Catholic priest, launched an attack on Spiritualism in the *Sunday Graphic*. He said that Spiritualism was a 'serious menace to the mental health of the people as well as to their spiritual welfare', adding that its practice had sent a million people mad. His article was reprinted in *Psychic News*, 4 June 1932, p. 3. See also I. Hernaman, *Spiritualism and the Child*.

10 Father Vaughan, 'Foreword', *The Menace of Spiritualism*, p. 4.

11 *Light*, 10 July 1926, p. 320.

12 *The Clairvoyant* was subsequently reworked into the 1948 thriller *The Night Has a Thousand Eyes*.

13 C. B. Farrar, 'The Revival of Spiritism', *Archives of Neurology and Psychiatry*, V (1921) 670–73.

14 See A. Owen, *The Darkened Room: Women, Power and Spiritualism in Late Victorian England* (London, Virago, 1989), pp. 65–6. Owen suggests that alcoholism might have 'provided a temporary escape from the problem of declining powers and popularity'. It was 'also one way of dealing with the pressure of constant seances and the unremitting demand for exciting phenomena'.

15 I. Hernaman, *Spiritualism and the Child*, pp. 14–15.

16 G. Raupert, *A Convert from Spiritualism*. Gregory Raupert's father, John Godfrey Raupert, took Anglican orders in 1887 and simultaneously developed an interest in psychical research. Within a few years he had become convinced that seance procedure exposed people to demonic invasion. He was received into the Roman Catholic Church, took up their crusade against Spiritualism with gusto, and commenced writing

on the subject. His books are: *Modern Spiritism: A Critical Examination of its Phenomena, Character and Teaching, in the Light of Known Facts* (London, Kegan Paul, 1904); *The Dangers of Spiritualism* (London, Kegan Paul, 1906); *Roads to Rome* (London, Longmans, Green, 1908); *The Supreme Problem: An Examination of Historical Christianity from the Standpoint of Human Life and Experience and in the Light of Psychical Phenomena* (London, Simpkin, Marshall, 1910); *Hell and its Problems* (London, St Anselm's Society, 1912); *Spiritistic Phenomena and its Interpretation* (London, St Anselm's Society, 1913); *Christ and the Powers of Darkness* (London, Heath, Cranton & Ouseley, 1914); *Black Magic and the Truth about the Ouija Board* (New York, Devin Adair, 1919). Gregory Raupert's book is a compilation of his father's experiences.

17 Raupert, *A Convert from Spiritualism*, pp. 15–17.

18 C. Wickland, *Thirty Years among the Dead* (London, Spiritualist Press, 1924), p. 40.

19 Raupert, *A Convert from Spiritualism*; pp. 18–20.

20 E. O'Donnell, *The Menace of Spiritualism*, p. 50. See also E. O'Donnell, *Spiritualism Explained: A Popular Handbook for Inquirers* (London, C. Arthur Pearson, 1920), pp. 86–8.

21 O'Donnell, *Spiritualism Explained*, pp. 92–3.

22 These include *The Romance of Sorcery* (London, Methuen, 1914); *Tales of Secret Egypt* (London, Methuen, 1918); *The Quest of the Sacred Slipper* (London, Pearson, 1919); *Moon of Madness* (London, Cassell, 1927); *She Who Sleeps* (London, Cassell, 1928); *Seven Sins* (London, Cassell, 1944). Rohmer is probably best known for his series of Fu-Manchu mysteries, which are also flavoured with occult themes. The series begins with *The Mystery of Dr Fu-Manchu* (London, Methuen, 1913) and concludes with *Emperor Fu-Manchu* (1959). *Trail of Fu-Manchu* (London, Cassell, 1934) was reissued in 1965.

23 S. Rohmer, 'Spiritualism is Sorcery', *Psychic News*, 28 May 1932, p. 8.

24 A. Richardson details the career of Dion Fortune in *The Magical Life of Dion Fortune: Priestess of the Twentieth Century* (London, Aquarian Press, 1991).

25 D. Fortune, *Applied Magic and Aspects of Occultism* (published posthumously in 1962) (London, Aquarian Press, 1987), especially pp. 50, 112. Fictional works by Fortune that touch on the subject of possession include 'Blood Lust', in *The Secrets of Dr Taverner* (1926) (London, Aquarian Press, 1989); *The Demon Lover* (1927) (Wellingborough, Aquarian Press, 1987); *The Goat Foot God* (1936) (London, Aquarian Press, 1971).

26 D. Fortune, *Psychic Self Defence* (1930) (Wellingborough, Aquarian Press, 1973), especially p. 128.

27 The nineteenth century saw the emergence of technocrats, experts and professionals. The 'professional classes' were well established by

the time of the Great War, and professional management encompassed the environment, family life, work and play. The rise and impact of this new class of professionals is well documented. See, for example, J. Morrell and A. Thackray, *Gentlemen of Science: Early Years of the British Association for the Advancement of Science* (Oxford, Clarendon Press, 1981); F. Turner, 'The Conflict between Science and Religion: A Professional Dimension', *Isis*, 69 (1978) 356–7; J. Lewis, *Women in England 1870–1950: Sexual Divisions and Social Change* (Brighton, Wheatsheaf, 1984); A. Sutcliffe, *Towards the Planned City: Germany, Britain, the Unived States and France 1780–1914* (Oxford, Basil Blackwell, 1981); Harold Perkin, *The Rise of Professional Society: England since 1880* (London, Routledge, 1989).

28 A. Owen, 'The Sorcerer and His Apprentice: Aleister Crowley and the Magical Exploration of Edwardian Subjectivity', *Journal of British History*, 36:1 (1997) 120.

29 D. Fortune, *Through the Gates of Death, and Spiritualism in the Light of Occult Science* (1931) (Wellingborough, Aquarian Press, 1987), p. 80.

30 I. F. Clarke, *Voices Prophesying War 1763–1984* (London, Oxford University Press, 1966), p. 130. See also R. Stott, *The Fabrication of the Late-Victorian Femme Fatale: The Kiss of Death* (Basingstoke, Macmillan, 1993), pp. 19–23.

31 Quoted in Clarke, *Voices Prophesying War*, pp. 123–4.

32 Quoted in Clarke, *ibid.*, p. 149, from W. Wood, *The Enemy in Our Midst: The Story of a Raid on England* (London, John Long, 1906).

33 J. B. Elshtain vividly describes the atmosphere of excitement at the prospect of war and the kind of propaganda current during the war: *Women and War* (Brighton, Harvester, 1987), pp. 111–12.

34 J. Winter, 'Spiritualism and the First World War' (draft of *Sites of Memory, Sites of Mourning*).

35 A. Ponsonby, *Falsehood in Wartime* (1928) (Melbourne, Institute for Historical Review, 1980). As Ponsonby said, these stories were false. Ponsonby was an aristocratic turned socialist. He was a Liberal MP, and in 1914 he sided with Keir Hardie's pacifist stand against the war. See *Dictionary of National Biography*, 1941–1950, pp. 683–5. During the war, atrocity stories were corroborated by government on the flimsiest evidence, augmented by propaganda issued by the Department of Information, which included a Cinema Division, a Political Intelligence Division and a News Division. See J. Stevenson, *The Pelican Social History of Britain: British Society 1914–45* (Harmondsworth, Penguin, 1984), pp. 74–7.

36 It transpired after the war that nobody by the name of Tordens lived in Sempst before or during the war (Ponsonby, *Falsehood in Wartime*, p. 129).

37 Winter, 'Spiritualism and the First World War'.

38 E. S. Turner, *Dear Old Blighty* (London, Michael Joseph, 1980), pp. 246, 144.

39 See Jay Winter for a recent appraisal of postwar sentiment from various sections of the population: 'Sites of Memory: War Memorials and Bereavement in the Wake of The First World War', draft of *Sites of Memory, Sites of Mourning*. See also Paul Fussell, *The Great War and Modern Memory* (Oxford, Oxford University Press, 1975) for his depiction of war experiences from the perspective of the soldiers involved.

40 John Buchan's most famous spy story is *The Thirty-Nine Steps* (London, Blackwood, 1915). The story became more famous with Alfred Hitchcock's film production in 1935. See also W. Somerset Maugham, *Ashenden: Or the British Agent* (New York, Doubleday & Doran, 1928).

41 I owe this information to conversations with my father, Ralph Dodkins, who was born in Bermondsey, London in the early 1920s.

42 This is not to claim that fear of military attack disappeared. B. Bergonzi suggests that two of the most important presences in the 1930s 'were the cinema and the fear of aerial bombing; one an enhancement of life, the other a desperate threat to it; and both products of new technology'. See B. Bergonzi, *The Myth of Modernism and Twentieth Century Literature* (Brighton, Harvester, 1986), p. 125.

43 I say *aggravate*, because the spectre of working-class revolution had haunted middle-class consciousness since the last few decades of the nineteenth century. These concerns were expressed in a proliferation of literature such as H. Mayhew's *London Labour and the London Poor* (1851); A. Mearns and W. C. Preston, *The Bitter Cry of Outcast London* (London, James Clarke, 1883); W. Booth's, *In Darkest England and the Way Out* (1890). The ceaseless attempts of various sections of the middle classes to avert revolution through educational reforms, slum clearance, 'scientific charity', and other devices intended to reform the 'dangerous classes' are described in G. Steadman Jones, *Outcast London* (Harmondsworth, Penguin, 1971). See also A. Wohl, *The Eternal Slum: Housing and Social Policy in Victorian London* (Montreal, Queens University Press, 1977). For an account of class rivalries and ideological struggles in interwar Britain, see R. McKibbin, *The Ideologies of Class: Social Relations in Britain 1880–1950* (Oxford, Oxford University Press, 1990), especially ch. 9; Clarke, *Voices Prophesying War*, pp. 162–6. See also D. L. Le Mahieu, *A Culture for Democracy: Mass Communication and the Cultural Mind in Britain Between the Wars* (Oxford, Clarendon Press, 1988); J. Carey, *The Intellectuals and the Masses: Pride and Prejudice among the Literary Intelligentsia 1880–1939* (London, Faber & Faber, 1992), for associated concerns about urbanisation, consumerism, and social levelling represented in that 'many headed beast' – the 'masses'; R. M. Bracco, *Betwixt and Between: Middlebrow Fiction and English Society in the Twenties and Thirties* (Melbourne, University of Melbourne, History

Department, 1990) gives a description of lower-middle-class anxieties and sensibilities. Alison Light details the Tory imagination in popular fiction in *Forever England: Femininity, Literature and Conservatism between the Wars* (London, Routledge, 1991).

44 W. Deeping, *Sorrell and Son* (London, Cassell, 1928), p. 150.

45 See Light, *Forever England*, for her comments on the perceived 'feminis- ation' of English literature and English society between the wars. See also L. Segal, 'Competing Masculinities I, II, III', in *Slow Motion: Chang- ing Masculinities, Changing Men* (London, Virago, 1990), for 'tough-guy' culture of the interwar period and the appeal of fascism.

46 Illuminism, in this sense, means an occult power controlled by humans: N. Webster, *Secret Societies and Subversive Movements*, 4th edn (London, Boswell, 1928), pp. 351, 352, 402. Pan-Germanism refers to an extreme form of nationalism amounting to imperialist ambitions (*ibid.*, pp. 352 ff.).

47 Webster, *Secret Societies*, p. 405.

48 J. Webb, *The Occult Establishment* (La Salle, IL: Open Court, 1976), p. 129.

49 E. O'Donnell, *Strange Cults and Secret Societies of Modern London* (London, Philip Allan, 1934), p. 39. Similarly, S. Rohmer's *Dr Fu-Manchu* stories played their part in the construction of oriental occultism and its supposed threat to 'civilisation'.

50 E. O'Donnell, *The Menace of Spiritualism*, p. 105. O'Donnell is quoting from an article by A. B. Douglas in *The Sunday Times*, 16 September 1917.

51 O'Donnell, *The Menace of Spiritualism*, p. 102.

52 *Psychic News*, 14 September 1940, p. 1.

53 *Psychic News*, 18 May 1940, p. 1.

54 Shaw Desmond, 'Occultism as Life', *Light*, LXII:3194 (1942) 106.

55 F. Wood, *Mediumship and War* (London, Rider, 1942), pp. xii, xi.

56 The twentieth-century eugenic movement rested on decades of mid- dle-class concern about the perceived physical and moral decline of working people. Such concerns were expressed early in the nineteenth century. J. Oppenheim notes:

> with the emphasis on imperialism, military threats, commercial competition, and the falling birthrate, social commentators before World War I neglected to realise that the debate over the physical and moral deterioration of the British people had been brewing for decades. Long before late Victorian international rivalries provoked a pervasive sense of public insecurity, doctors had been tracing the links between nervous maladies and declining racial standards. (J. Oppenheim: *'Shattered Nerves': Doctors, Patients and Depression in Vic- torian England* [Oxford, Oxford University Press, 1991], pp. 267–8)

See also G. Davison, 'The City as a Natural System: Theories of Urban Society in Early Nineteenth-Century Britain', in *The Pursuit of Urban History*, ed. D. Fraser and A. Sutcliffe (London, Edward Arnold, 1983), pp. 347–70. There are many excellent histories of the cultural construction of eugenics. See, for example, D. Pick, *Faces of Degeneration: A European Disorder* (Cambridge, Cambridge University Press, 1989); J. Weeks, *Sex, Politics and Society: The Regulation of Sexuality since 1880* (London, Longman, 1990).

57 John Ruskin and William Morris were well-known campaigners for the return to rural life. See W. Morris, 'The Lesser Arts', in *Collected Works*, vol. XXII (London, Longmans, 1915), pp. 31–56. See also C. R. Ashbee, 'An Endeavour Towards the Teaching of John Ruskin and William Morris', *A Few Chapters in Workshop Reconstruction and Citizenship*, ed. P. Stansky and R. Shewan (New York, Garland, 1978). For a historical survey of nineteenth-century pastoralism, see P. Brandon, 'Wealdon Nature and the Role of London in Nineteenth-Century Artistic Imagination', *Journal of Historical Geography*, 10 (1984) 53–74. In the twentieth century, socialists such as Edward Carpenter were at the forefront of the movement. See E. Carpenter, *Civilisation: Its Cause and Cure* (London, Swann, 1921) See also Webb, *The Occult Establishment*, for an overview of anti-materialist pastoralism, especially ch. 2.

58 Quoted by J. Webb, *The Occult Establishment*, p. 90.

59 J. Hargrave, *The Great War Brings It Home: The Natural Reconstruction of an Unnatural Existence* (London, Constable, 1919), pp. 51–2.

60 *Ibid.*, p. 47.

61 *Ibid.*, p. 21.

62 *Ibid.*, p. 62.

63 R. Hayward, 'Popular Mysticism and the Origins of the New Psychology, 1880–1910' (Ph.D thesis, Lancaster University, 1996), p. 107.

64 In the previous century, the representatives of scientific naturalism treated accounts of spirit manifestations with contempt. Against the resistance of the clergy and the incursions of popular philosophies, men such as John Tyndall and Thomas Huxley advanced scientific naturalism as the one true knowledge – the key to continuing prosperity and the guarantee of moral progress. See Frank Turner, 'The Conflict between Science and Religion: A Professional Dimension', *Isis* 69 (1978) 356–76. There is quite a lot of literature on the politics of scientific orthodoxy, detailing the social processes involved in marking the boundaries between 'science', 'pseudo-science' and 'nonsense'. See, for example, Roy Porter and Bill Bynum (eds) *Medical Fringe and Medical Orthodoxy* (London, Croom Helm, 1987); Roger Cooter, *The Cultural Meaning of Popular Science: Phrenology and the Organisation of Consent in 19th Century Britain* (London, Cambridge University Press, 1984); Roy Wallis (ed.) *On the Margins of Science: The Social*

Construction of Rejected Knowledge (University of Keele, Keele Sociological Review Monograph No. 27, 1979); P. S. Brown, 'Herbalists and Medical Botanists in Mid-Nineteenth-Century Britain with Special Reference to Bristol', *Medical History*, 26 (1982) 405–20.

65 H. Maudsley, *Natural Causes and Supernatural Seemings* (1886) (London, Watts, 1930); W. B. Carpenter, 'Spiritualism and its Recent Converts', *Quarterly Review*, 131:262 (1871). See also L. Weatherby, *The Supernatural?*, with a Chapter on Oriental Magic, Spiritualism and Theosophy by J. N. Maskalyne (London, Marshall, Hamilton, 1891). As late as 1964, T. Hall evoked an unwholesome atmosphere around Spiritualism in his book about the nineteenth-century psychical researcher Edmund Gurney: 'Gurney was initiated into the seedy darkened rooms and shifty frauds of spiritualism, under the euphemism of psychical research' (*The Strange Case of Edmund Gurney* [London, Duckworth, 1964], p. 41). See also the film *Seance on a Wet Afternoon* (1964), discussed in ch. 5 below. For psychiatric perceptions and treatment of mediums in the nineteenth century, see Owen, *The Darkened Room,* ch. 6. See also J. Oppenheim, *The Other World: Spiritualism and Psychical Research in England 1850–1914* (London, Cambridge University Press, 1985). The historiography on psychiatry is extensive. Some recent texts on its growth and application in nineteenth- and twentieth-century Europe include J. Goldstein, *Console and Classify: The French Psychiatric Profession in the Nineteenth Century* (Cambridge, Cambridge University Press, 1987); Oppenheim: '*Shattered Nerves*'; E. Showalter, *The Female Malady: Women, Madness and English Culture, 1830–1980* (London Virago, 1985); A. Gauld, *A History of Hypnotism* (Cambridge, Cambridge University Press, 1992).

66 Quoted by A. Owen, *The Darkened Room*, p. 147.

67 M. Viollet, *Spiritism and Insanity* (London, Sonnenschein, 1910), pp. 11–12.

68 E. O'Donnell, *The Menace of Spiritualism*, pp. 143–4.

69 *Ibid.*, p. 190.

70 See, for example, Weeks, *Sex, Politics and Society*; Oppenheim, '*Shattered Nerves*'. S. Jeffreys, *The Spinster and Her Enemies: Feminism and Sexuality 1880–1930* (London, Pandora, 1985), ch. 2, gives an account of the marshalling of eugenic assumptions in feminist narratives of female superiority. Conversely, see C. Eagle Russett, *Sexual Science: The Victorian Construction of Womanhood* (Cambridge, MA, Harvard University Press, 1989) for a description of scientific constructions of women as inferior to men. See also E. Richards, 'Darwin and the Descent of Woman', in *The Wider Domain of Evolutionary Thought*, ed. D. Olroyd and I. Langham (Dordrecht, Reidel, 1983), pp. 57–111; Showalter, The *Female Malady*, especially Part Two: 'Psychiatric Darwinism'. The orthodox history of science, which sought to distance science and

Darwin from Social Darwinism, eugenics and racism, was challenged in a spate of articles and books in the late 1970s and 1980s. See, for example, S. Shapin and B. Barnes, in 'Darwin and Social Darwinism: Purity and History', *Natural Order, Historical Studies of Scientific Culture*, ed. B. Barnes and S. Shapin (London, Sage, 1979), pp. 125–39; R. Young, *Darwin's Metaphor* (Cambridge, Cambridge University Press, 1986), ch. 2; J. Moore, 'Socialising Darwinism: Historiography and the Fortunes of a Phase', in *Science as Politics*, ed. L. Levidow (London, Free Association Books, 1986), pp. 38–80.

71 In saying this, I am influenced by J. Cash's account of 'the passions' as constitutive of ideology – the idea that ideologies are 'saturated, indeed suffused, with emotion; emotion informs, shapes and animates them'. This 'involves the recognition that the subject is not merely interpellated by ideology, but rather is an interlocutor, an active party to the discourse' ('Ideology and Affect: The Case of Northern Ireland', *Political Psychology*, 10:4 [1989] 704, 707).

72 There is a growing body of literature which attributes the development of 'fragmented consciousness' to the erosion of Enlightenment rationality and naturalistic perceptions of time and space: D. Lowe, *A History of Bourgeois Perception* (Brighton, Harvester, 1982); S. Kern, *The Culture of Time and Space 1880–1918* (Cambridge, MA, Harvard University Press, 1983). Alison Light has recently noted in her analysis of Agatha Christie's novels that the new dormitory towns of the interwar years 'where neighbours may only have just arrived [were] a seed bed for mistaken or double identities. Exactly what social position is occupied becomes less important than the possible bogusness of it' (Light, *Forever England*, p. 94).

73 Gauld, *History of Hypnotism*, pp. 363–6.

74 *Ibid.*, especially pp. 403–15 for a lucid and interesting account of psychotherapeutic perceptions of the unconscious. In fictional writing, the theme of the divided self gathered momentum apace with psychotherapeutic schools of thought, most notably in modernist literature. The most famous antecedents of this literature are, of course, R. L. Stevenson, *The Strange Case of Dr. Jekyll and Mr. Hyde* (1886) and Oscar Wilde, *The Picture of Dorian Gray* (1891). See K. Miller, *Doubles: Studies in Literary History* (Oxford, Oxford University Press, 1987), pp. 209–44, for his analysis of doubles, seconds and *alter egos* in the work of Stevenson, Wilde, Henry James and William Sharp, among other *fin-de-siècle* authors.

75 Gauld, *History of Hypnotism*, pp. 410–16; N. Hale, 'Introduction' to Morton Prince, *Psychotherapy and Multiple Personality: Selected Essays* (Cambridge, MA, Harvard University Press, 1975), pp. 1–18.

76 Prince wrote on the phenomenon of multiple personality before and after the publication of *Dissociation of a Personality*. Such publications

include 'Miss Beauchamp, The Theory of Psychogenesis of Multiple Personality', *Journal of Abnormal and Social Psychology*, June–September 1920, pp. 67–135; 'Some of the Revelations of Hypnotism: Post-Hypnotic Suggestion, Automatic Writing and Double Personality' (1890), in *Psychotherapy and Multiple Personality*, pp. 37–60. A bibliography of Prince's works is contained in this volume, pp. 317–26.

77 In 1906, *Dissociation of a Personality* was reviewed by a variety of journals ranging from *Catholic World* to *Dial*. The *New York Times* reviewed it on at least five separate occasions. See *Book Review Digest* (Minneapolis, MN, Wilson, 1906). The London-based *Athenaeum* described the book as follows: 'Most excellent reading for the layman, the physiologist, and the student of psychology' (*Athenaeum*, vol. 1, 5 May 1906, p. 549). See also E. Showalter, *Gender and Culture at the Fin de Siècle* (London, Virago, 1991), pp. 121–3.

78 Prince does not say what she studied at college, but noted that she had tried to train as a nurse three times, but 'broke down' each time. M. Prince, *The Dissociation of a Personality: A Biographical Study in Abnormal Psychology* (New York, Longmans Green, 1913), p. 11.

79 *Ibid.*, pp. 12–13.

80 *Ibid.*, p. 15. See Hayward, 'Popular Mysticism', for his comments on nineteenth-century psychiatry and its approach to the presence or absence of will (p. 108).

81 Prince, *The Dissociation of a Personality*, pp. 14–17.

82 *Ibid.*, p. 524.

83 *Ibid.*, p. 361. 'Sally' claimed that she had existed as a separate and independent mind since childhood. In view of this, Prince persuaded her to write her autobiography. 'Sally' wrote some of it as B III and some through the automatic hand of B IV. See *ibid.*, ch. XXIII.

84 B. Inglis, *A History of the Paranormal, 1914–1939* (London, Hodder & Stoughton, 1984), p. 309.

85 M. Prince, 'Automatic Writing Combined with Crystal Gazing', *Journal of Abnormal Psychology*, XX:20 (1925–26) 40.

86 This perception of the unconscious as possibly representative of a 'higher self', capable of contacting correspondingly 'higher' or God-like forces in the cosmos, was promoted by the founding members of the Society for Psychical Research: Henry Sidgwick, Edmund Gurney, and Frederick Myers. The thesis originated with Myers, and it was he who coined the term 'subliminal self'. He wrote widely on psychical phenomena, and was a close and influential friend of William James. See Gauld, *History of Hypnotism*, pp. 391–403. Myers's thoughts on the workings of the unconscious and its relation to psychic phenomena are contained in his *Human Personality and its Survival of Bodily Death*, 2 vols (London, Longmans Green, 1903). A clear overview of the interests and aims of the SPR is given by A. Gauld, *The Founders of Psychical*

Research (London, Routledge & Kegan Paul, 1968). See also Oppenheim, *The Other World*; P. Williams, 'The Making of Victorian Psychical Research: An Intellectual Elite's Approach to the Spiritual World' (PhD thesis, University of Cambridge, 1984). See also *Proceedings of the Society for Psychical Research*, 1882–1890s, in which Myers wrote (and was written about) extensively.

87 See note 86 above.

88 Flournoy to James, 4 September 1985, in *The Letters of William James and Theodore Flournoy*, ed. R. C. Le Clair (Madison, University of Wisconsin Press, 1966), pp. 47–8.

89 U. Troubridge, 'The Modus Operandi in So Called Mediumistic Trance', *Proceedings of the Society for Psychical Research*, XXXII (January 1922).

90 E. Dingwall to M. Hankey, in M. Hankey, *James Hewat McKenzie Pioneer of Psychical Research: A Personal Memoir* (London, Aquarian Press, 1963), p. 139. Hankey does not supply a date for this correspondence, nor does she give any indication as to when this exchange between Dingwall and McKenzie took place. However, most of McKenzie's work with mediums was carried out in the 1920s, so the meeting probably took place then.

91 E. Dingwall, *How to Go to a Medium: A Manual of Instruction* (London, Kegan Paul, 1927), p. 3.

92 G. Lawton, *The Drama of Life after Death: A Study of the Spiritualist Religion* (New York, Henry Holt, 1932), p. 484.

93 Raupert, *A Convert from Spiritualism*, p. 13.

94 Mass-Observation Archive (University of Sussex) Directive Respondent, reply to April 1942 Directive.

95 H. Boddington, *Psychic News Booklet 3: Trance States in Relation to Spirit Control* (London, Psychic Press, 1933), p. 1.

96 E. Garrett, *My Life as a Search for the Meaning of Mediumship* (New York, Arno Press, 1975), pp. 137–8.

97 *Ibid.*, p. 5.

98 *Ibid.*, pp. 84–5.

99 *Ibid.*, p. 182.

100 *Ibid.*, p. 185. See note 86 above and ch. 7 below for details on Frederick Myers.

101 Owen, 'The Sorcerer and his Apprentice', p. 121.

102 Webb, *The Occult Establishment*, p. 71. R. Steiner was a spiritual teacher and founder of the Anthroposophy movement. See S. C. Easton, *Rudolf Steiner: Herald of a New Epoch* (New York, Anthroposophy Press, 1980). The schools he founded and the Anthroposophical Society are still active today.

103 Astral travel was generally regarded as hazardous by occultists. See Owen, 'The Sorcerer and His Apprentice', p. 106.

104 Fortune, *The Demon Lover*, p. 41.

105 *Ibid.*, pp. 144.

106 Fortune, *Psychic Self Defence*, p. 129.

107 *Ibid.*, pp. 52–3.

108 The character of Rebecca in Daphne du Maurier's novel of that name (1938) is similarly ambiguous. So is Rachel, in *My Cousin Rachel* (1951). Here, Du Maurier takes the ambiguity of her character a step further; for Rachel's 'true nature' is never revealed.

109 S. Žižek, 'The Obscene Underside of the Law', lecture delivered at the University of Melbourne, 12 August 1994. See also Žižek, *The Sublime Object of Ideology* (London and New York, Verso, 1989), especially 'Image and Gaze', pp. 105–7. R. Holmes's skilfully executed dual biography of Samuel Johnson and the poet Richard Savage emphasises the excitement, sympathy and empathy that Savage's many social transgressions aroused in Johnson. In Johnson's own biography of his friend, the despised and destitute Savage of eighteenth-century London society is transformed into the outcast genius of future Romantic generations: R. Holmes, *Dr Johnson & Mr Savage* (London, Hodder & Stoughton, 1993)

110 Raupert, *A Convert from Spiritualism*, p. 19.

111 *Ibid.*, p. 6.

112 Prince, *The Dissociation of a Personality*, p. 10.

113 Fortune, *The Demon Lover*, p. 29.

114 D. Fortune, *The Winged Bull* (1935) (Wellingborough, Aquarian Press, 1989).

115 Prince writes: 'Miss Beauchamp – I mean the one who first presented herself for professional care in the spring of 1898 (B I) – is extremely reticent and dislikes intensely any discussion of herself or her circumstances' (*The Dissociation of a Personality*, p. 9).

116 Similarly, in Daphne du Maurier's, *Rebecca*, the reader is unsettled first by the apparent duality of Rebecca's personality and second by the realisation that death must conceal Rebecca's 'true desire' for ever.

5

Mothers, mediums and vampires

The historical fantasy of ideal motherhood contrasted with its mirror-opposite is well known to scholars of nineteenth- and twentieth-century European culture. As one historian has observed, 'the soft breasted mother and steel-taloned destroyer conjoined, was ... one of many chimeras of womanhood expressive of the late nineteenth century's extreme dualistic mentality'.[1] In Baudelaire's poem, 'Metamorphoses of the Vampire' (*circa* 1852), the sexually devouring female appears in the guise of a coiling snake, who, 'once she'd sucked the very marrow from my bones', turned into a 'slime-flanked mollusc full of pus'.[2] Elaine Showalter has noted a similar tendency in Rudyard Kipling's *The Man Who Would Be King*, where the feminine peril to men was imagined through the metaphorical use of the vampire. Showalter writes:

> The representation of women in the story ... underlines female power to threaten male bonds, to create rivalries between men, and to sap male strength. Women are nameless, divisive, and potentially deadly. In the first Kafiristani village Dan and Peachey reach, a fight is underway over a woman who has been abducted, and eight men have lost their lives. Peachey has had a liaison with a Bengali woman who taught him the lingo, but then ran off with the Station-master's servant and half his month's pay. The symbolic wound inflicted on Dan by his bride – 'The slut's bitten me!' he cries – leads to his death, linking here with the castrating vampire-woman of other *fin-de-siècle* stories.[3]

Examples such as these from the literature and iconography of the nineteenth and twentieth centuries have been multiplied by feminist scholars, and their meaning has been discussed at length.[4] My purpose in this chapter is to explore how such signs became incorporated in portrayals of the interwar medium – specifically, I am interested in how the figure of the medium became entangled with fantasies about engulfing, devouring maternity, the obverse of Spiritualist representations of her as the Madonna. In taking this approach, we shall consider some of the psychological and ideological imperatives that contributed to images of ideal and dangerous maternity between the wars.

Seance on a Wet Afternoon

The way in which public perceptions of mediumship became bound up with fantasies and fears about the devouring woman is well illustrated in the film *Seance on a Wet Afternoon*, based on the novel by Mark McShane.[5] The film was made in 1964, but I shall argue that the logic and coherence of the plot relied on a stereotype of mediumship developed in the prewar era.

Seance on a Wet Afternoon is about Myra Savage, played by Kim Stanley, and Billy, her husband, played by Richard Attenborough. The couple are middle-aged and childless. Myra is a medium, who holds weekly seances in her parlour for a small fee, and she dominates the asthmatic Billy. Although the film is set in the 1960s, a Gothic atmosphere is introduced through the couple's home, a large Victorian town house with gables and turrets, filled with Victorian furniture. We know also that the house is airless and stuffy, and possibly not very clean, because the dust aggravates Billy's asthma. Myra's spirit-guide is the couple's dead son, Arthur, who transmits advice and instructions to Myra, sometimes through trance and sometimes through a kind of telepathy. It is obvious from the beginning of the film, however, that Arthur's spirit is a figment of Myra's imagination. Billy knows this, but collaborates with the fiction to please her.

Myra is dissatisfied with her lack of public recognition as a medium. To remedy this situation, and on the instructions of Arthur, she plans to kidnap the ten-year-old daughter of a wealthy couple. She reasons that nobody could deny her worth as a psychic when she correctly identifies the whereabouts of the missing child. For Myra this is sufficient justification to stage the kidnapping; it is not intended to harm anybody; its purpose is to draw attention to the 'truth' of her 'gift'. Thus, although Myra is prepared to resort to deception, she remains convinced of her own psychic powers. Billy feels deeply uneasy about the whole plan, but Myra part-bullies and part-persuades him into carrying it out. After all, she says, 'we will only be borrowing her for a little while' and it is for 'a good cause'. So Billy snatches the child from her school; she is then drugged and installed in Arthur's old bedroom. When she wakes up, Billy tells her she is in a hospital. He pretends to be a doctor and Myra dresses up as a nurse. Billy makes ransom demands to the child's parents, Mr and Mrs Clayton, so that the kidnapping looks as if it has been carried out for the usual financial gain. Meanwhile, Myra makes contact with them in her capacity as medium, and gives them a little personal information about their daughter that she claims to have received in a dream. Mr Clayton is unimpressed, but Mrs Clayton is desperate and wants to know more. To Billy's horror, Mrs Clayton attends one of Myra's seances seeking information about her child who, unbeknown to her, is lying in the room next door. Myra is unconcerned by all this and, under trance, she assures Mrs Clayton that her child is safe and well. But as the seance is ending, Myra faints and says the word 'die!'

Things move quickly after this. Billy successfully collects the ransom, but the child seems unwell and he starts to panic. Myra, however, becomes more dreamy and preoccupied with Arthur. Finally, she tells Billy that Arthur's plans have changed. Arthur has become so attached to the girl in his room that he wants her to be with him, always. They must kill her. At this point, Billy violently resists Myra's fantasies, and for the first time we learn that Arthur was the Savages' stillborn baby. Shouting, Billy reminds Myra that Arthur is dead, was born dead, and that it is she, not Arthur, who wants to keep the child by killing her. Myra insists tearfully that Arthur's spirit really does speak to her, and the girl must die. In the following morning scene we see Billy carrying a still, child-shaped bundle, which he leaves by a tree in a wood. We are left uncertain about whether the child is dead or alive, but in the final scene, the fate of the girl and the sources of Myra's madness become clear.

The police arrive at the Savages' home late that afternoon, ostensibly to solicit Myra's help as a medium in the continuing search for the missing child. This is what Myra has been waiting for, and she eagerly agrees to hold a seance for this purpose. However, the tense bearing of the three police officers tells us that Myra is a suspect. The seance starts: Myra enters trance, and her repressed pain and desires are made manifest. She relives moments from her unhappy childhood, and the experience of giving birth to a stillborn baby: 'They won't let me see him … All that waiting, all that time … Nothing to hold', she says repeatedly. Myra's mood switches abruptly as she suddenly becomes aware that Billy has not carried out her orders to kill the Clayton child: 'I said die! … Take her Billy, kill her, Arthur's waiting.' Myra's trance concludes as she rocks an imaginary baby in her arms. As one contemporary critic observed of the film:

> [The plot] is rather risky, in that it concerns a hairbrain scheme concocted by a woman who is evidently mad and carried out by her husband for hopeless love of her. Everything, clearly, depends on our belief and interest in the heroine, for if we do not believe in her and care about her the film will have no point at all.

In this critic's view, it is Kim Stanley's brilliant portrayal of the deranged Myra that lends plausibility to the story: 'We accept the character of the woman who conceived [the scheme and her relationship with her husband Billy] and that is enough.'[6] But *is* it enough? Why do Myra's obsessions seem to 'ring true' in the context of her mediumship, and why do we accept that Billy, who is not mad, should be prepared to go along with her crazy schemes, even at great personal risk? We shall see that the dramatic plausibility of Myra's personality and her relationship with Billy depend on several well-established narratives, or chains of signifiers concerning the medium. The character of Myra is not a random portrayal of madness (which would make no sense) but is formulated through a cultural legacy, developed in the interwar years, concerning the personality of the medium, which is in turn bound up with constructions of feminine sexuality.

The physical aspects of the film reflect some medical and literary conventions regarding Spiritualism and mediumship.[7] The Gothic setting is meant to convey the atmosphere of an earlier, 'more superstitious age', far removed from modern 'enlightened' times. The Victorian building and furniture, the dingy light and airless, claustrophobic rooms imply Myra's unhealthy mental disposition as well. Her incessant playing of Mendelssohn's 'Hear My Prayer' on a scratchy old gramophone intensifies the impression that we are dealing here with an extreme neurasthenic.

Myra is portrayed not only as mentally unbalanced but also as a calculating trickster, capable of endless intricate manoeuvres in self-justification. The view of the medium as a deliberate and cunning fraud, who 'preyed' on the bereaved and the gullible, has been current since the nineteenth century. Indeed, this assumption was enshrined under Section 4 of the Vagrancy Act, which stated that any claim to psychic or occult power must be pretence.[8] After the First World War, mediums were frequently accused of 'preying' on the relatives of the war-dead. Elliot O'Donnell expressed a common view when he wrote:

> [T]he war has made people so anxious to glean tidings of another world that they will jump at anything, however remote and trivial … and of this the mediums are thoroughly well aware. They know they have only to weave even the barest semblance of truth into one of their messages, and their poor, half-demented clients will joyfully accept all that follows, convinced that it is of spirit origin.[9]

This representation of the medium as a predator who abuses the trust of vulnerable people was – and still is – widespread. In *Seance on a Wet Afternoon*, Myra 'preys' on her victims; she mercilessly exploits the Clayton family as a means to her ends. Her predatory impulses are made even more graphic in the kidnapping of the Clayton child, and ultimately in her wish to kill her. But it is also made apparent that Myra's actions are motivated by 'good' maternal impulses. There is her enduring distress at Arthur's death, her refusal to admit that he *is* dead, her wish to protect and please him. Reference to Myra's 'frustrated maternity' is made throughout the film. The bedroom that was to have been Arthur's is preserved for him; there is a new pram wrapped in cellophane stored in the garage; and Myra's behaviour towards Billy oscillates between childish entreaty and that of the stereotypical matriarch who will brook no opposition. Most graphically, in the final scene Myra caresses and nurtures an imaginary baby.

Dion Fortune creates some similar impressions in her novel *The Demon Lover*, published thirty-seven years earlier, about the medium Veronica. In Chapter 4 I mentioned that Veronica's employer, Lucas, is killed by an avenging occult fraternity. But this is not the end of the story. Lucas's spirit remains after death and he attempts to become an inhabitant of matter by drawing on Veronica's etheric substances. Veronica experiences intensely maternal feelings during this process:

> [N]ow he was dependent on her for his very existence, part of her substance had gone to build up his form, and in some curious way her mother-instinct went forth to this being who was made of her own life. His very dependence upon her gave him his strongest hold over her. Veronica, in her new-found mother spirit, might resist aggression, but, on the other hand, she would cherish fiercely anything that depended upon her, and Lucas in his half-materialised condition was as dependent upon her as an unborn child.[10]

This sheltering maternity is immediately transformed into destructive vampirism. Veronica's uncanny maternity is, like Myra's, potentially deadly. Veronica and Lucas are sharing, as it were, one portion of vital substances between two. They augment their supply of etheric substances by vampirising those of several children in the neighbourhood; this results in the children's death. For Veronica, this night-time vampire expedition is carried out as if in a dream.

Thus Veronica's desires are signified as ambivalent; the same is true of Myra, whose predatory intentions are countered by her desire to nurture and protect. *Seance on a Wet Afternooon* makes a double split: its depiction of Myra's internal duality is mirrored in the social domain where 'normal', 'healthy' maternity is represented in the figure of Mrs Clayton, and contrasted with Myra's distorted and dangerous fantasies. As I have already noted, this depiction of sheltering maternity, constantly overshadowed by its deadly opposite, is a recurrent theme in the Western tradition. The vision of idealised motherhood embodied in the Virgin Mary alternates with that of Eve, the cause of human mortality, or the 'ancient [pagan mother] of fright and lust', whose embrace, in Robert Graves's imagination, 'is death'.[11] What are we to make of this ambivalent image of motherhood, and how was its inter-war incarnation woven into narratives about the medium?

Freud analysed the mother of love and dread through his theory of primary narcissism. In early life, according to Freud, the infant exists in symbiotic relation to the mother. Individuation is accomplished partly through the breaking of these maternal ties that threaten to stifle even as they protect.[12] The process of individuation and gender identity is completed in the Oedipal stage for the boy when he is made aware, through the figure of the prohibiting father, that his incestuous love

for his mother is forbidden him. He must renounce his desire to receive her exclusive love and identify with the father, his former rival.
Through separation from the mother, and identification with the father,
the boy 'achieves' a proper 'masculine' sense of self.

As feminist scholarship has pointed out, Freud's gloss on the primal
scene is rooted in patriarchy. The paternal figure stands for the process
of individuation, 'freedom' and 'reason', while the mother represents
the undifferentiated, retrogressive and, for these reasons, dangerous
maternal territory of primary narcissism.[13] Recent theorists have attempted to explain the dread of motherhood – which seems inescapable,
even necessary, in Freud's theories – through radical revisions of his
work. In my view, the persistent representation of motherhood as both
sheltering and predatory in modern Western culture is made intelligible
through object relations theory, where stress is placed on early development and the dynamic relations between parents and child.[14]

Although theorists diverge considerably among themselves, the
individuation/separation process is normally understood (with Freud)
to produce ambivalent feelings. The infant, in Jane Flax's words,
'explores and continually develops its separateness, then returns to the
mother for "emotional refuelling"'. The 'child both wants to return to
the symbiotic state and fears being engulfed by it'. In 'good enough'
child–mother relations, the child comes to accept its ambivalent feelings towards the mother and *recognise* that it is *both* bonded to her and
separate from her. Under patriarchy, however, this synthesis cannot be
satisfactorily achieved.[15] For the girl, the father is unavailable as an
object of identification, and so unavailable as a means of separation
from the mother.[16] The boy, on the other hand, must identify fully
with the father 'to consolidate' his difference and, in so doing, reject
and repress the 'feminine' parts of himself.[17] The point here is that the
boy must renounce not only his incestuous love for his mother, but
also his *identificatory* love for her. As Jessica Benjamin points out, the
'oedipal injunctions say, in effect: "you may not *be like* the mother, you
must *wait* to love her as I do"'. The boy is thus pushed 'away from
dependence, vulnerability, and intimacy with the mother. And the
mother, the original source of goodness, is now located outside the
self, externalised as a love object … the boy can only return as an
infant, with the dependency and vulnerability of an infant.' The mother
figure is idealised as a lost paradise, on the one hand, and feared on the

other, because her nurturance also threatens to engulf and overwhelm him: 'Once the unbridgeable sexual difference is established, its dissolution is threatening to male identity.'[18] In the Oedipal/patriarchal model, masculine identification *means* the denial of dependency and the repudiation of anything that is constructed as feminine. Individuation is constructed solely in terms of separation from the mother. Thus, 'even when the mother is envied, idealized, sentimentalized, and longed for, she is forever outside the masculine self'.[19] In this process, 'woman' is doubly stigmatised: first as radically other to the male 'self', and second as a threat to personal boundaries.

Psychoanalytic perspectives have served feminist projects well in so far as they have provided insights into a variety of questions posed about gender relations. But this kind of approach can take us only so far. Such insights need to be integrated more fully with the study of ways in which gender relations are sustained and institutionalised, subverted and resisted in *specific* historical contexts. The following comment from Lynne Segal visualises future analytical directions:

> Once we ask what social processes underlie gender relations and representations, we must move towards a complex integration of psychoanalytic accounts of family dynamics and unconscious motivations, on the one hand, and sociological analysis of social structures, practices and relationships, on the other.[20]

What follows is a discussion of ways in which unconscious fears about maternity became encoded in developing representations of the medium in the interwar period.[21] In taking this approach, we shall consider how existing ideologies about motherhood and feminine sexuality helped to promote polarised gender divisions at this time, thus placing increasing demands on men to repress and repudiate 'the feminine' in themselves.

The medium as monstrous mother

'Good motherhood' was an essential component in the ideology of racial health and purity in the years following the Great War. High infant mortality and the reputed mental and physical deterioration of the race were seen by various sections of the ruling, professional and 'respectable classes' as a consequence of biologically unfit mothers and inadequate mothering.[22] As 'good mothering' came to be viewed as the key to a healthy population, the nineteenth-century emphasis on woman as wife shifted to woman as mother.[23] Women who were physically and mentally healthy and who did not want children were perceived, paradoxically, as pathologically selfish. Olga Knopf, a populariser of Albert Adler's psychology with respect to women and sexuality, stated the prevailing sentiment of the interwar period: 'any woman – except those whose lives would be positively endangered by childbirth – can be brought to a point [through judicious psychology] where she wishes to have children, where her social interest is aroused, where she can be cured from her egocentricity'.[24] Similarly, Dion Fortune, when she was still known as Violet Firth, took it for granted that 'home and children *is* the ultimate goal of every normal' woman.[25]

The idealisation of maternity was accompanied by a readjustment in perceptions of female sexuality. The ideology of uncontrollable male sexual urges (promoted by sexologists such as Havelock Ellis and the biologist Walter Heape) assimilated an expectancy of female delight in heterosexual sex,[26] in contrast to the supposed nineteenth-century portrayal of the 'good' woman as sexually anaesthetic.[27] Lynda Nead points out that the 'asexual respectable woman was only one strand in the complex production of female sexualities during the nineteenth century',[28] but the impression that Victorian society ascribed fully to the notion of feminine asexuality in respectable women, conformed to more modern assumptions about Victorian 'prudery' and 'repression', and underpinned campaigns for sexual 'freedom', 'enlightenment', and the 'emancipated individual'. In his introduction to a book that condemned the sexual repression of the older generation, and advocated 'free love', the philosopher Robert Briffault wrote that it was 'difficult to imagine' that modern women would 'ever resume the mental corsets any more readily than the steel corsets of the Victorian age'.[29] And Morris Ernst, in his foreword to Havelock Ellis's *Studies in the Psychology of Sex*, celebrated the 'free' discussion of sex in the modern era and the shedding of old 'hypocrisies' and 'taboos'.[30]

In the hands of such influential and varied writers as D. H. Lawrence, Marie Stopes and Havelock and Edith Ellis, sex took on mystical proportions.[31] In John Cowper Powys's words, the 'mystic-sensuous embrace … binds lovers together' and 'isolates them in a heavenly loneliness'.[32] In the early years of the twentieth century, such expectations about sex belonged mainly to the *avant-garde* elite,[33] but after the

First World War, narratives about the mystical properties of love and sex flooded the popular market.[34] Bart Carrel's 'Dreams End', published in *Great Stories of Love and Romance* (1936), is typical of the genre. Here, the hero, an artist called Kent, 'seemed to give off a sort of vital emanation – a sense of strength and power'.[35] The heroine's sexuality is represented when she invites Kent to rework one of her own paintings:

> Slowly the character of the canvas began to change under his hand. Pamela watched absorbedly. Without altering the form of the picture significantly, he was creating a new atmosphere in it. The colouring took on an inner intensity in place of the surface brilliance that had troubled her. He subdued the gleaming sunlight that she had painted in and gave it a gentle, rather sleepy quality that almost made her cry out aloud with pleasure.[36]

The same volume carried a story about reincarnation and the reuniting of a pair of eternal lovers.[37]

In occult circles, the magical power of sex was often emphasised. In 1941, one contributor to *The Occult Review* stressed the sanctity of sex in relation to the process of reincarnation: 'For, preceding each act of coition, we must ask of the other, "For whom are we opening the doorway to earth?"'[38] The perceived purpose of the mystical powers of sex varied. Whereas the writer for *The Occult Review* retained traditional notions of sexual morality within a magical framework, Aleister Crowley was a notorious exponent of exploitative sex in magical rites, and it was rumoured that he presided over midnight orgies for this purpose.[39]

As motherhood became more 'radiant' and sex more 'ecstatic', images of the sucking, engulfing woman grew proportionately. Significantly, the term 'vamp', depicting a woman who enslaves men with her beauty and sucks their 'vitality', became current after the First World War.[40] 'Woman' appeared as a threat in her domestic and sexual form. It is well known that a key element in modernist art was its violent rejection of 'woman', who threatened to tame, stifle, confine, and drain the mystic vitality of the sovereign (male) individual.[41] The misogyny of Nietzsche and the predatory woman of Strindberg's sexually embittered plays found equally virulent representatives in 'popular culture'. Warwick Deeping's *Sorrell and Son* is probably one of the best-known examples. Here, 'woman' is the 'natural enemy' of 'man' – a harpy who 'emasculates' him by draining him of his 'vitality'. Sorrell's first employer, Mrs Palfrey, the proprietor of the Angel Hotel, appears as a sexually insatiable and predatory woman. Seen through Sorrell's eyes, she suggests 'immense strength, a brutal and laughing vitality'. After his first encounter with her, he is left with 'a feeling of having been crushed against the wall'.[42] Mrs Palfrey's husband shuffles about wearing slippers, bemused, beaten – 'a husk of a man, a man who had been devoured by [his wife]'. One day he says to Sorrell: 'Don't you ever marry, Steve; don't you ever let a woman get you. She'll eat you up.'[43]

At the cinema, too, the financially independent and predatory woman had became a stock figure by the end of our period. In, for instance, *The Wicked Lady* (1945),[44] Margaret Lockwood plays a high-born Restoration woman who becomes the mistress and partner of a highway robber. The film version of *Madame Bovary* (1947) portrays Emma as the victim of her own sentimental hopes and of sexual exploitation by her first lover, Rodolphe. She is also viewed as a predator who depletes the sexual and financial resources of her husband and lovers. In one scene, Emma goes to ask Rodolphe for money to pay off her debts, and he tells her that he is afraid of her because 'she consumes while she burns'. One can chart the growth of this persona in earlier films, such as *The Blue Angel* (1930). Here, Marlene Dietrich plays a 'vamp' called Lola, who brings financial ruin and humiliation to a respectable teacher because he is unable to resist her sexual appeal.[45]

Dread of the sexually active and devouring woman found endless scope in literature and films of the supernatural. In *Family Ghosts*, published in 1933, Elliot O'Donnell relates the story of beautiful 'man-hating' ghosts who seduced and then destroyed mortal men.[46] He presented his *Strange Cults and Societies of Modern London* (1934) in documentary style and told of various London societies, such as The Cult of Cruelty, composed exclusively of women. This society was devoted to witnessing 'depictions of cruel and savage acts, listening to narrations of unusually horrible murders and executions, and zealously upholding all kinds of blood sports'.[47] Another society, named The Gorgons, was again limited to women, and worshipped the High Priestess Medusa. A London club, associated in some vague way with goats, employed the sexual attractiveness of one of its female members to draw unsuspecting young men into the cult, whereupon they were divested of their wealth and psychologically assaulted. One man ended up in a lunatic asylum.[48] The female vampire appeared again in the semi-silent film *Vampyr* (1932), where the principal vampire was an old woman whose nocturnal excursions, according to the film's storyboard, 'seeped a whole village in desolation'. The villagers used a traditional remedy: an iron stake was plunged through her heart, thus nailing her 'repulsive soul' to the earth. Vampire themes also found their way into narratives of illness in occult literature. Dion Fortune devoted one section of *Psychic Self Defence* (1930) to different kinds of vampirism – human and non-human. Mixing Freudian terminology with occult myth, Fortune warned that where 'morbid attachment' existed between two people, whether they were mother and daughter, mother and son, or two female friends, and where one half of the pair was dominant and the other in a debilitated condition, it was likely that a kind of psychic vampirism was in operation. According to Fortune, a relationship of this kind was possible '[w]herever there is a close and dominating bond between two people'. 'There is', she wrote, 'a leakage of vitality going on, and the dominant partner is more or less consciously lapping it up, if not actually sucking it out.'[49]

In saying this, Fortune was not merely expressing the view of the (occult) 'lunatic fringe'; respectable sexology placed a similarly mystical gloss on sexual intercourse. Even as heterosexual sex was celebrated by sexology as the realisation of 'mutual need', it was simultaneously charged with an implicit danger for men. The sexology of Krafft-Ebing and Havelock Ellis associated sexual intercourse with the depletion of nervous energy – men 'spent' their energy on women.[50] The implied vampirising of male 'vitality' in sexual intercourse emerged again in the theories of Walter Heape. Heape insisted that love between a man and a woman created a 'great vital force', and that this 'generation of vitality in consequence of the conjugation of complementary bodies or of the interweaving of complementary forces, is a law of nature'.[51] However, these 'vital forces' were not equal. The 'complementary'[52] aspects of the sexes dictated that the male was active and the female passive: man was an 'expender of energy',[53] woman a consumer. The American William J. Robinson MD expressed the anxiety this assumption elicited in his popular guide *Married Life and Happiness* (1922). According to this publication, normal wives are 'satisfied with occasional relations – not more than once in two weeks or ten days', in contrast to

> the opposite type of woman, who is a great danger to the health and even the very life of her husband. I refer to the hypersensual woman, to the wife with an excessive sexuality. It is to her that the name

vampire can be applied in its literal sense. Just as the vampire sucks the blood of its victims in their sleep while they are alive, so does the woman vampire suck the life and exhaust the vitality of her male partner – or victim. And some of them – the pronounced type – are utterly without pity or consideration[54]

At its most vulgar, fear of the castrating woman found expression in the 'saucy' postcards sold at such seaside resorts as Brighton and Blackpool, before and after the Second World War. These postcards depicted small 'emasculated' men, contrasted with their overpowering wives, who sported huge breasts, bellies and buttocks.

Despite modernist trends against 'confining domesticity', it was not the 'patriotic mothers' of the nation who bore the ideological brunt of this ubiquitous dread of the devouring and victimising woman. Just as the nurturing and engulfing mother was split in the psyche, so 'good women' (the mothers) and 'dangerous women' (the non-mothers) were similarly polarised in the social domain and encoded in ideology. The fantasy of devouring maternity was split off from the cult of idealised motherhood, and projected on to mystics, mediums, 'vamps', 'man-eating', ambitious women, and other allegedly powerful (because childless) women. The developing stereotype of mediumship which we see at its apogee in *Seance on a Wet Afternoon* exemplified the contradictory construction of the devouring mother who was not a mother. Like the childless and dominant Mrs Palfrey of *Sorrell and Son*, the 'vamps' and vampires of the interwar imagination, and the sexually insatiable and non-maternal Emma Bovary, who 'consumes while she burns', Myra seemed to sap the 'vitality' of her husband Billy, leaving him weakened, 'emasculated', and unable to defend himself.[55]

James Leuba, an influential psychologist of mysticism and religion in the interwar period, elaborated the perceived social dangers of female mysticism in *The Psychology of Religious Mysticism* (1925).[56] Leuba's analyses of Western mysticism drew almost exclusively from female examples and extracted from a range of psychotherapeutic theories,[57] including those of Maudsley, Charcot, Janet, Ellis, and occasionally Jung and Freud. In the opening chapters, Leuba made use of orthodox assumptions about the nature of the mystic. Like the alienists, he was inclined to view mysticism as a hallucination induced by drugs, or a delusion 'arising on the basis of a disordered visceral sensitivity'.[58] He was also influenced by more recent psychotherapeutic theories relating to mysticism and hysteria.[59] Thus, a mystical trance could be caused by a variety of pathologies associated with stereotypical feminine emotionalism: nervous instability, hysterical autosuggestion[60] and, critically, a willingness to dissolve the self through union with God, resulting in the well-known ecstasy of the saint. In this respect, mystics had 're-verted' to a 'savage'-like state.[61] There was, he asserted, 'a continuity of impulse, of purpose, of form, and of result between the ecstatic intoxication of the savage and the absorption in God of the Christian mystic'. Both were characterised by 'surrender of self-restraint' and 'fascination of belief in the superhumanness of the experience'.[62] Leuba's stress on the 'self-surrender' involved in the mystic's union with her God returns us again to the underlying theme of a maternity that threatens to stifle and overwhelm the 'sovereign individual'. According to Leuba, it was the willingness to dissolve the self in God which was the definitive trait of mysticism. In solidarity with his class, his sex, and their Enlightenment traditions, he pathologised the mystical immersion of self with other as a moral and intellectual weakness, in binary opposition to 'purposive, rational thinking.'[63]

The traditional mystic's pathological and dangerous propensity to blur the distinction between Self and Other was easily grafted on to the figure of the modern medium. This danger was implied in *Seance on a Wet Afternoon* through the claustrophobic atmosphere of Billy's and Myra's home, and made explicit in Myra's mad trances, where she entered into identity with the spirit of her stillborn son, Arthur. Similarly, in *The Demon Lover*, Self–Other distinction had been lost as the 'available life forces' were shared out between Veronica and Lucas: '[T]hey faced each other, the man partly materialised, and the girl partly dematerialised', the individuality of both lost in this strange union.[64]

The medium's distorted maternity seemed to find physical expression in the production of etheric substances. Dion Fortune elaborated the link between mediumship and maternal vampirism through the character of Veronica, who shared her etheric substances with Lucas and supplemented her own supply by draining those of sleeping children. Ironically, this literal rendering of the medium as vampire relied directly on Spiritualist theories about mediumship and spirit visitation. As we have seen, Spiritualists and occultists conceived of humans as triune beings composed of a soul or mind, a body of flesh and a duplicate etheric body. Spirits, according to this theory, become inhabitants of matter by supplementing their own etheric substances with those of the medium. Gladys Leonard implied the vampirish undertones of such a procedure when she wrote that the spirits often found 'the quiet of the night very suitable for drawing out [human] power to materialize' themselves.[65] This process was inherently ambiguous: Was it the spirit-guide who depleted the etheric substances of the medium, or the medium who 'sucked in' the spirit, making it 'one' with herself?

The impression of deviant maternity surfaced again in 'spirit birth', which Spiritualists explicitly made continuous, if not synonymous, with biological birth;[66] and photographs purporting to show ectoplasmic productions displayed some kind of soft substance. Numerous spirit photographs were produced, as part of the drive to 'prove' survival. Significantly, although the etheric or ectoplasmic substance could in theory issue from any part of the body, many spirit photographs showed it issuing from the orifices of the medium. The seance photographs of the sexologist and psychical researcher Baron Von Schrenck Notzig (published in England in 1921) showed ectoplasm coming from the ears, mouth and breasts of the medium Eva C.[67] In photographs from what was known as the Goligher Circle, also published in 1921, a substance emerged from between the legs of the medium.[68] One photograph of the famous materialisation medium Helen Duncan showed similar material issuing from her nose, purportedly forming a spirit baby.[69] These photographs inadvertently but unavoidably recalled the stigmatised female body – the soft, sticky, wet body of menstruation, lactation and maternity. One woman, on being simply shown a photograph of a medium, was reminded of 'wet steam and a wet smell'.[70] The following observation made by one sitter during a seance with the medium Stella C. demonstrates the analogous relationship that was frequently drawn between physical mediumship and monstrous birth. The incident was reported by the psychical researcher Harry Price:[71]

> By far the most interesting phenomenon of the teleplasmic [meaning ectoplasm] type was witnessed by a sitter (he was actually lying on the floor, with his head poked between the legs of other sitters) at a seance on June 7, 1923. This gentleman arrived late and no chair could be found for him. He saw a white, opaline, egg-shaped body crawl from under the medium's clothes into the rays of red light that I had placed under the table. The egg-like body had attached to it a

thin white neck like a piece of macaroni. The body crawled or wiggled
into the rays of the light, which apparently was too strong for it, and
it then rapidly withdrew into the shadow.[72]

Repellent maternity was exemplified in the mediumship of Mrs Forbes
(of whom we shall hear more in later chapters), who produced an array
of psychic phenomena between 1938 and 1939. After one sitting, carried
out at the International Institute for Psychical Research, during which
a new spirit-guide had manifested itself, her stomach swelled until her
normally thin girth reached thirty-four inches.[73] At another seance with
Mrs Forbes, Eileen Garrett, one of the sitters, had 'a psychic presenti-
ment in the region of her diaphragm. She could feel something sucking
and drawing almost like a vampire'.[74]

Such representations of the medium conformed to contemporary
myths concerning maternity and the female body. Expressions of revulsion for the female body extended from 'high' through 'middle' to
'low' culture: from Jean-Paul Sartre and Simone de Beauvoir,[75] to
Graham Greene's portrayal of the part-time medium and prostitute Ida
in *Brighton Rock* (1938),[76] to Stephen's revulsion for her body in *The
Well of Loneliness* (1928).

Sergeant Alec Comryn displayed a marked and direct distaste for
maternity in one of his anecdotes about everyday policing in Northern
England. He described with disgust – though not without sympathy –
the agony of a woman giving birth in an ambulance: how she moved
into the final stages of labour with a 'great convulsive heave', and with
a 'cry that lashe[d] every nerve in [his] body'. Afterwards, Comryn
could not bring himself to touch either the mother or the baby: 'The
child lies still, a raw, amorphous, monkeyish thing curled up on itself
near the soggy mass that has nourished it and to which it is still attached.'[77] He then fantasised about the possibility of a different, 'cleaner'
form of birth: 'How different the egg birth. No blood, no pain … A
blue ribbon round the egg for a boy, a pink one for a girl.' He concluded
that evolution, in discarding the egg birth for mammals, made one of
its biggest blunders, for 'viviparous birth meant the complete domination of the offspring by its parent during its most impressionable
years'.[78]

It is, perhaps, with this troubled terrain of maternity in mind that
articulations of distaste about Spiritualist physical manifestations may

be understood. The common belief, recorded by Oliver Lodge, that Spiritualism was 'unclean' in some way,[79] or his own insistence that physical manifestations accounted for the 'lowest class' of psychic phenomena,[80] or William James's wish to 'turn from phenomena of the dark-sitting and rat-hole type' to the 'calm air of delightful study' of the mental phenomena,[81] all seem to testify to this reading. While he was carrying out trials on Eva C., the medic and philosopher Gustave Geley witnessed a similar phenomenon to that described by Harry Price: A substance exuded from 'the natural orifices'; it was 'soft, and somewhat elastic, while spreading; hard, knotty or fibrous when it forms cords', and it moved over the medium with 'a crawling reptilian move-ment'.[82] Geley compared this manifestation with 'nature's failure always to produce perfect specimens at birth, resulting in the occasional monstrosity'.[83] James Hyslop, another prominent psychical researcher in the interwar period, also found physical phenomena repulsive.[84] Such feelings of repulsion were strongly evoked by Thomas Mann in the monstrous maternity of the medium Ellie in *The Magic Mountain*. There was the darkened room, the glow of a red lamp, the noisy vulgarity of the sitters, the scandalous birthing postures adopted: 'Madness! What maternity was this, what delivery, of what should she be delivered?' Equally scandalous were Ellie's exertions in this state:

> [S]he would start with a moan, throw herself about, strain and wrestle with her captors, whisper feverish, disconnected words, seem to be trying, with sidewise, jerking movements to expel something; she would gnash her teeth, once she even fastened them into [her neighbour's] sleeve.'[85]

Finally, the birth – the arrival of a phantom, appearing as he looked in his last days on earth. With the appearance of this apparition, the record player stopped playing; no one turned off the machine, and the 'needle [went] on scratching in the silence'.[86]

Yet, as we shall see in the next chapter, if mediums were stigmatised by association with repellent and devouring maternity, they were also tainted by the stereotype of the frustrated spinster. The nexus created in language between femininity, virginity, sexual frustration and religion signified the bitter shadow of ideal motherhood in the figure of 'the old maid'.

Notes

1   B. Dijkstra, *Idols of Perversity: Fantasies of Feminine Evil in Fin-de-Siècle Culture* (Oxford, Oxford University Press, 1986), p. 333.

2   *Ibid.*, p. 334.

3   E. Showalter, *Sexual Anarchy: Gender and Culture at the Fin de Siècle* (London, Virago, 1991), p. 94.

4   See, for example, Dijkstra, *Idols of Perversity*, who associates fantasies of female danger at the *fin de siècle* with male anxieties about women's refusal to behave 'within their appointed station in civilization' (p. viii). See also N. Hertz, 'Medusa's Head: Male Hysteria under Political Pressure', *Representations* (Fall 1983), pp. 27–54. R. Stott, *The Fabrication of the Late-Victorian Femme Fatale: The Kiss of Death* (Basingstoke, Macmillan, 1993) explores ways (and resists offering a single way) of understanding why the *femme fatale* was a recurring figure in the literature and art of the *fin de siècle*. D. Glover ('The Lure of the Mummy: Science, Seances and Egyptian Tales in *Fin-de-Siècle* England', paper delivered at the Australasian Victorian Studies Association, 6–10 February 1995) examines Bram Stoker's deployment of the concept. Psychoanalytical feminist analysis has dealt extensively with the apparently ubiquitous desire for, and dread of, the mother. See, for example, J. Kristeva, *Powers of Horror: An Essay on Abjection* (New York, Columbia University Press, 1982); J. Rose, *The Haunting of Sylvia Plath* (London, Virago, 1991). Other psychoanalytical and feminist approaches to the issue of devouring maternity are explored later in this chapter.

5   M. McShane, *Seance on a Wet Afternoon* (London, Cassell, 1961).

6   'Unusually Intelligent Thriller', *The Times*, 4 June, 1964, p. 20.

7   See ch. 4 above.

8   See ch. 1 above.

9   E. O'Donnell, *The Menace of Spiritualism*, 'Foreword' by Father B. Vaughan (London, Werner & Laurie, 1920), p. 158. In his *Search for Truth: My Life for Psychical Research* (London, Collins, 1942), p. 77, Harry Price said that relatives of soldiers in the First World War were besieged by 'charlatans who offered to hold seances and put them in touch with the spirit world. This damnable trading on the most sacred emotions of the bereaved was finally stamped out by the military authorities.' In 1916, *The Umpire* also accused mediums of preying on the relatives of the war-dead. See G. Nelson, *Spiritualism and Society* (London, Routledge & Kegan Paul, 1969), p. 156. Such accusations were also current during the Second World War. *Psychic News* reprinted one article from the *Methodist Recorder* where such sentiments were expressed, and another the following week from *The Daily Telegraph*. See *Psychic News*, 2 November 1940, p. 4; *Psychic News*, 9 November

1940, p. 5.

10 D. Fortune, *The Demon Lover* (Wellingborough, Aquarian Press, 1987), p. 163.

11 R. Graves, *The White Goddess: A Historical Grammar of Poetic Myth* (1946) (London, Faber & Faber, 1961), p. 24. For a recent analysis of the Great Mother myth in the light of Julia Kristeva's theories, see Rose, *The Haunting of Sylvia Plath*, especially pp. 151, 370, 371.

12 S. Freud, 'Civilization and its Discontents', ch. 1, in *Sigmund Freud: Civilization, Society and Religion*, vol. XII of the Pelican Freud Library, ed. J. Strachey (Harmondsworth, Penguin, 1985), pp. 251–60.

13 Jessica Benjamin comments: 'This polarised structure of gender difference leaves only the alternatives of irrational oneness and rational autonomy. In the wake of this splitting, the image of feminine connection appears the more dangerous, the goal of masculine separation the more rational' (*The Bonds of Love: Psychoanalysis, Feminism, and the Problem of Domination* [London, Virago, 1990], p. 184).

14 Some of the more influential works of feminist theorists within the frame of object relations include N. Chodorow, *The Reproduction of Mothering* (Berkeley, University of California Press, 1978); D. Dinnerstein, *The Mermaid and the Minotaur: Sexual Arrangements and Human Malaise* (New York, Harper Colophon, 1977). For a useful overview of object relations theory in relation to masculine responses to the mother figure see L. Segal, *Slow Motion: Changing Masculinities, Changing Men* (London, Virago, 1990), ch. 3. Klaus Theweleit's *Male Fantasies* (Cambridge, Polity Press, 1987) explores the dread of women in the context of fascist ideology.

15 J. Flax, 'The Patriarchal Unconscious', in *Discovering Reality: Feminist Perspectives on Epistemology, Metaphysics, Methodology, and Philosophy of Science*, ed. S. Harding and M. B. Hintikka (Dordrecht, D. Reidel, 1983), p. 252.

16 Benjamin, *The Bonds of Love*, ch. 3.

17 Flax, 'The Patriarchal Unconscious', pp. 252–3.

18 Benjamin, *The Bonds of Love*, pp. 161–4.

19 *Ibid.*, p. 163.

20 Segal, *Slow Motion*, p. 94. This work has already begun in Segal's study.

21 In my approach to ideology and the unconscious, I am influenced by John Cash, who has analysed certain ideological formations in Northern Ireland from a Kleinian perspective. See J. Cash, 'Ideology and Affect: The Case of Northern Ireland', *Political Psychology*, 10: 4 (1989) 703–24.

22 For an account of official investigations relating to infant health before and after the Great War, see J. Stevenson, *The Pelican Social History of Britain: British Society 1914–45* (Harmondsworth, Penguin, 1984). J. Weeks considers the ideological motivations for these investigations

in *Sex, Politics and Society: The Regulation of Sexuality Since 1880* (London, Longman, 1990), pp. 126–7. As he points out, although eugenic ideas may have originated in the professional classes, 'they were presented as a strategy for the whole ruling class to adopt, and support was gained from outside the professional classes, just as opposition to eugenics came from within it' (p. 132). And although eugenic ideology was often mobilised against the 'vulgar masses', this did not prevent 'popular literature' from assuming eugenicist attitudes itself. See ch. 4 above.

23 Weeks, *Sex, Politics and Society*, p. 126; A. Davin, 'Imperialism and Motherhood', *History Workshop*, 5 (Spring 1978) 9–65. See C. Haldane, *Motherhood and its Enemies* (New York, Doubleday & Doran, 1928) for a contemporary expression of the social divisions drawn between mothers and non-mothers, to the disadvantage of the latter. Segal notes a similar trend in Nazi Germany where the feminist movement was coupled with triumphant motherhood (*Slow Motion*, pp. 120–23). G. Boch, however, stresses that National Socialist policy emphasised pro-natalism and the cult of motherhood much less than it emphasised racist anti-natalism and the cult of fatherhood: 'Equality and Difference in National Socialist Racism', in *Beyond Equality and Difference: Citizenship, Feminist Politics and Female Subjectivity*, ed. G. Bock and S. James (London, Routledge, 1992), pp. 89–109. See S. Jeffreys, *The Spinster and Her Enemies: Feminism and Sexuality 1880– 1930* (London, Pandora, 1985), especially p. 166, for further discussion of the birth control movement in interwar England in relation to eugenic ideals. Jeffreys notes that even 'fallen' women were forgiven in the euphoria that surrounded motherhood. It was reasoned that illegitimate children of soldiers were the heroes of tomorrow. In the nineteenth century, by contrast, female eroticism was controlled by the threat of disgraceful maternity. S. V. Finzi writes: 'From puberty on, women came to think of maternity as a punishment that befell them when they freely expressed their sexuality' ('Female Identity Between Sexuality and Maternity', in *Beyond Equality and Difference*, p. 135).

24 O. Knopf, *The Art of Being a Woman* (London, Rider, 1932), p. 221.

25 V. Firth, *The Psychology of the Servant Problem: A Study in Social Relations* (London, C. W. Daniel, 1925), pp. 84–5. Despite her deviations from the norm in other respects, the future Dion Fortune continued to cleave to this belief. See, for example, the closing pages of her novel *The Winged Bull* (1935) (Wellingborough, Aquarian Press, 1989).

26 Jeffreys, *The Spinster and Her Enemies*.

27 Some relatively recent histories also create the impression that the Victorian middle classes *always* divided women into two, mutually exclusive categories: 'good', sexually inactive women and 'bad', sensual women. See, for example, E. Trudgill, *Madonnas and Magdelens* (New

York, Holmes & Meier, 1976), p. 56; J. Walkowitz, *Prostitution and Victorian Social Reform* (Cambridge, Cambridge University Press, 1980).

28 Doctors were divided on the issue. In 1840, a member of the Royal College of Surgeons, Dr R. J. Culverton, 'claimed that sexual desire in woman was healthy'. See L. Nead, *Myths of Sexuality: Representations of Women in Victorian Britain* (Oxford, Basil Blackwell, 1990), pp. 19–20. The notion that modern sexual values represent a heroic break with Victorian prudery has remained remarkably stable into the present time. See, for example, P. Ferris 'Bromide in the Tea', in *Sex and the British: A Twentieth Century History* (London, Michael Joseph, 1993). See Michel Foucault, *The History of Sexuality Volume I: An Introduction*, trans. R. Hurley (Harmondsworth, Penguin, 1976) for his powerful counter-arguments to the thesis of Victorian sexual 'repression'.

29 R. Briffault, 'Introduction' to V. F. Calverton, The *Bankruptcy of Marriage* (London, John Hamilton, 1929), p. 9. See also R. Briffault, *Sin and Sex*, 'Introduction' by B. Russell (London, George Allen & Unwin, 1931); B. Russell, *Marriage and Morals* (London, George Allen & Unwin, 1929). Some argued from Darwinian and biological tenets; see R. de Gourmont in *The Natural Philosophy of Love* (1926), trans. and 'Introduction' by E. Pound (London, Neville Spearman, 1957). H. G. Wells, *Anne Veronica* (1909), 'Introduction' by J. MacKenzie (London, Virago, 1980), deals with the 'naturalness' of female desire and the constraints of Victorian 'prudery', and is one of the best-known fictional works of the genre.

30 M. Ernst, 'Foreword' to Havelock Ellis, 'Auto Eroticism', in *Studies in the Psychology of Sex*, vol. 1, Part 1 (New York, Random House, 1936), p. viii.

31 See M. Stopes, *Married Love* (1918) (London, Putnam's, 1924); E. Ellis, *The New Horizon in Love and Life*, 'Preface' by E. Carpenter, 'Introduction' by M. Tracy (London, Black, 1921). The book is heavily influenced by Edith's husband, Havelock.

32 J. Cowper Powys, *In Defence of Sensuality* (London, Victor Gollancz, 1930), p. 142.

33 R. Brandon, *The New Women and the Old Men: Love Sex and the Woman Question* (Glasgow, Flamingo, 1991).

34 *The Green Hat*, by Michael Arlen, was among the most popular. Here the adultery of Napier and Iris is justified by virtue of their 'great love' for each other. Even Napier's wife, Venice, is moved by it. At one point in the novel, she cries: 'I'd stuff all our marriage-laws down a drain-pipe rather than keep them [Napier and Iris] apart for another minute' (M. Arlen, *The Green Hat* [London, Collins, 1925], p. 321).

35 *Great Stories of Love and Romance: A Daily Express Publication* (London, Syndicate Publishing Company for the *Daily Express*, 1936), p. 130.

36 *Ibid.*, p. 133.

37 *Ibid.*, pp. 347–70.

38 R. Charleston-Rae, 'The Origin and Idealism of Sex', *Occult Review*, LXVIII:1 (1941) 37.

39 J. Webb, *The Occult Establishment* (La Salle, Il, Open Court, 1976), p. 61. Alex Owen insightfully explores Crowley's forays into sex magic as 'a self-conscious exploration of subjectivity' in 'The Sorcerer and His Apprentice: Aleister Crowley and the Magical Exploration of Edwardian Subjectivity', *Journal of British History*, 36:1 (1997).

40 E. Jones, 'On the Vampire', in Christopher Frayling (ed.), *Vampyres: Lord Byron to Count Dracula* (London, Faber & Faber, 1991), p. 410 – although images of female vampirism existed in the mid-nineteenth century: see Dijkstra, *Idols of Perversity*, ch. X.

41 R. Williams, *The Politics of Modernism: Against the New Conformists*, 'Introduction' and ed. T. Pinkney (London and New York, Verso, 1989), p. 57. See also A. Light, *Forever England: Femininity, Literature and Conservatism Between the Wars* (London, Routledge, 1991), ch. 2, especially pp. 70–75.

42 W. Deeping, *Sorrell and Son* (London, Cassell, 1928), p. 18.

43 *Ibid.*, p. 38. As we shall see in ch. 6, portrayals of characters like Mrs Palfrey represented not only sexual anxieties but also those anxieties associated with female militancy and the perceived economic independence of women after the war.

44 *The Wicked Lady* was the most commercially successful film of the Gainsborough costume dramas: L. Halliwell, *Halliwell's Film Guide*, 10th edn, ed J. Walker (London, HarperCollins, 1994). It was based on the novel by Magdalen King Hall, *The Life and Death of the Wicked Lady Shelton* (London, Peter Davies, 1944).

45 Arlen's novel *The Green Hat* (1925) presents a variation on the oppositional categories of 'vamp' and ideal woman through the notion of mistaken identity. Iris Storm is execrated by her family and friends as a 'destroyer of men' when her first husband commits suicide. But this perception is deliberately cultivated by Iris herself, who sacrifices her own reputation to preserve her husband's. She refuses to reveal that he suffered from syphilis, and had killed himself as a result of the disease. In this case, the 'vamp' turns out to be the ideal woman.

46 E. O'Donnell, *Family Ghosts and Ghostly Phenomena* (London, Unwin, 1933), pp. 117–18.

47 E. O'Donnell, *Strange Cults and Secret Societies of Modern London* (London, Philip Allan, 1934), pp. 167–8.

48 *Ibid.*, pp. 164–82, 233–9, 249–67.

49 D. Fortune, *Psychic Self Defence* (1930) (Wellingborough, Aquarian Press, 1973), p. 57.

50 H. Ellis, *Studies in the Psychology of Sex*, vol. 1; R. von Krafft-Ebing, *Psychopathia Sexualis* (1887) (New York, Physicians and Surgeons Book

Company, 1931). The understanding of sexual desire as an energy source that can be spent, diverted or, with difficulty, controlled began to assume importance in sexual politics from about the turn of the century. See L. Birkin, *Consuming Desire: Sexual Science and the Emergence of a Culture of Abundance, 1871–1914* (Ithaca, NY, Cornell University Press, 1988). See also S. Jeffreys, *The Spinster and Her Enemies.* Recent literature on the subject has also emphasised that it was common among sexologists and sociobiologists to view sexual imperatives as a 'heterosexual instinct in which the sexual energy of the male finds its natural object in the receptiveness of women': J. Weeks, 'Masculinity and the Science of Desire', in *Sexual Difference* (Oxford, Oxford Literary Review, 1985), p. 24. However, Weeks cautions against exaggerating the importance of sexology in inculcating these assumptions. As I have tried to indicate, and as he notes: 'they did not create the assumptions they set out to theorise, many of which were indeed part of the commonsense of the age' (*Ibid.*, p. 24).

51 W. Heape, *Preparation for Marriage* (London, Cassell, 1914), p. 11.
52 For a detailed discussion of the theory of complementarity in Enlightenment thought and nineteenth-century science see L. Schiebinger, *The Mind Has No Sex: Women in the Origins of Modern Science* (Cambridge, MA, Harvard University Press, 1989), ch. 8. See also T. Laqueur, *Making Sex: Body and Gender from the Greeks to Freud* (Cambridge, MA, Harvard University Press, 1992), ch. 6, for his account of the way the two-sex model came into being in Western Europe between the eighteenth and early twentieth century.
53 Heape, *Preparation for Marriage*, p. 99.
54 Quoted by Dijkstra, *Idols of Perversity*, p. 334.
55 See also Strindberg's plays, where the devouring woman is represented as the 'cheating wife' (*The Creditors*) and the 'man-eating', 'mannish', ambitious female who intrudes into properly masculine domains (*Comrades*).
56 The book received favourable reviews from authorative critics in both Britain and America. See, for example, A. W. Hinshaw's review in *The New York Times*, 21 June 1925, p. 22; *The Times Literary Supplement*, 26 February 1925, p. 132; *Literary Review of the New York Evening Post*, 12 September 1925, p. 11; *Nation and Athenaeum*, vol. 37, 18 April 1925, p. 80.
57 For a recent chronological account of nineteenth- and twentieth-century European approaches to psychotherapy, see A. Gauld, *A History of Hypnotism* (Cambridge, Cambridge University Press, 1992).
58 J. Leuba, *The Psychology of Religious Mysticism*, revised edn (London, Kegan Paul, 1929), pp. 56, 15, 27–9.
59 Leuba cites the following texts: H. Ellis *Studies in the Psychology of Sex*; A. Moll, *The Sexual Life of the Child*, trans. Dr Eden Paul (London,

George Allen, 1912); T. Flournoy, 'Une Mystique Moderne', *Archives de Psychologie de la Suisse Romande*, XV (1915).

60 J. Goldstein has shown that *fin-de-siècle* psychiatry – centred in France, with Charcot at its apex – reclassified as hysterical phenomena previously construed as angelic or demonic: *Console and Classify: The French Psychiatric Profession in the Nineteenth Century* (Cambridge, Cambridge University Press, 1987). For a description of French psychiatry in relation to hypnotism, see Gauld, *History of Hypnotism*, pp. 297–380. For English applications, see J. Oppenheim, *'Shattered Nerves': Doctors, Patients and Depression in Victorian England* (Oxford, Oxford University Press, 1991).

61 It was quite common in the medical literature of nineteenth-century Europe to equate 'womanly nature' with a 'less evolved' state of 'savagery'. See C. Eagle Russet, *Sexual Science: The Victorian Construction of Womanhood* (Cambridge, MA, Harvard University Press, 1989).

62 Leuba, *Psychology of Religious Mysticism*, pp. 8, 13.

63 *Ibid.*, p. 31.

64 Fortune, *The Demon Lover*, p. 163.

65 G. Leonard, *My Life in Two Worlds*, 'Foreword' by O. Lodge (London, Cassell., 1931), p. 163. A few Spiritualists were aware that the drawing of etheric substances by spirits amounted to a kind of psychic vampirism. See N. Fodor, *On the Trail of the Poltergeist* (London, Arco, 1959), p. 189.

66 See ch. 3 above.

67 Baron Von Schrenck-Notzig, *Phenomena of Materialisation: A Contribution to the Investigation of Mediumistic Teleplastics*, trans. E. E. Fournier d'Albe (London, Kegan Paul, 1920), figs 45, 73, 78, 127, 128. Eva C. was the pseudonym of Marthe Beraud.

68 W. J. Crawford, *The Psychic Structures at the Goligher Circle* (London, John M. Watkins, 1921) fig. W.

69 A. Crossley, *The Story of Helen Duncan: Materialization Medium* (Devon, Arthur Stockwell, 1975), Plate 1. The explanatory text of the plate reads as follows:

> *The medium roped and her hands held by the two sitters on either side of the [seance] cabinet. The emergence of the ectoplasm is from the nostril. The materialization clearly shows an attempt to materialize a baby. Note the face of the baby which appears in the ectoplasm.*

None of this is really apparent from Crossley's reproduction of the original photograph; only a shapeless substance can be seen issuing from Duncan's nose.

70 Fodor, *On the Trail of the Poltergeist*, p. 174.

71 The relationship between Harry Price and Stella C. (Stella Cranshawe) is discussed in ch. 7 below.

72 H. Price, *Search for Truth: My Life for Psychical Research* (London, Collins,

1942), pp. 146–7.

73 Fodor, *On the Trail of the Poltergeist*, p. 203. According to Fodor's account, this phenomenon occurred regularly during a particular stage in her mediumship. Once her stomach swelled so much that she was unable to keep her balance when walking (*Ibid.*, pp. 189–90).

74 *Ibid.*, p. 174.

75 See T. Moi, 'Existentialism and Feminism: The Rhetoric of the Second Sex', in *Sexual Difference* (Oxford, Oxford Literary Review, 1985), pp. 88–95. Moi considers the stigmatisation of the female body in De Beauvoir's philosophy, and shows how De Beauvoir slips into patriarchal discourse in her attempts to appropriate for feminism the notion of the 'free' and self-defining individual.

76 Ida is portrayed as maternal, vulgar and repulsive the spiritual and intellectual inferior of the Catholic gangster, Pinkie. The lapsed Catholics, Pinkie and Rose, writes Bernard Bergonzi, are characterised as 'conscious of Good and Evil, as opposed to the stupid, good-natured humanist, Ida Arnold, who is concerned only with Right and Wrong' (B. Bergonzi, 'The Decline and Fall of the Catholic Novel', in *The Myth of Modernism and Twentieth Century Literature* [Brighton, Harvester, 1986], p. 177). See also J. Carey's comments on Greene's portrayal of Ida in 'Pinkie: Out on the Dangerous Edge of Things', *The Independent*, 2 January 1993, p. 26.

77 Detective Sergeant A. Comryn, *Your Policemen Are Wondering* (London, Gollancz, 1947), p. 76.

78 *Ibid.*, pp. 81–2.

79 O. Lodge, *Past Years* (London, Hodder & Stoughton, 1931), p. 352.

80 *Ibid.*, p. 310.

81 Quoted by A. Gauld, *The Founders of Psychical Research* (London, Routledge & Kegan Paul, 1968), p. 246.

82 Quoted by B. Inglis, *A History of the Paranormal, 1914–1939* (London, Hodder & Stoughton, 1984), p. 96.

83 *Ibid.*, p. 97.

84 *Ibid.*, p. 25.

85 T. Mann, *The Magic Mountain*, trans. H. T. Lowe-Porter (London, Penguin, 1973), pp. 678, 677.

86 *Ibid.*, p. 680.

6

Frustration, repression and deviant desire

The medium evoked prevalent anxieties about maternity and the maternal body; she was also associated with 'deviant' sexuality. The medium as vampire mother existed alongside other narratives that proclaimed the madness of the mystic and located this madness in 'emergent', 'traumatic', 'thwarted' and 'perverted' sexuality. Female stereotypes – the delinquent adolescent, the spinster whose 'juices had turned sour', and the lesbian 'degenerate' – all found representation in images of female mysticism that were easily transposed on to the medium.

The adolescent

In psychiatric discourse, mystical impulses were often traced to adolescent sexuality in girls. James Leuba remarked that religious revivals usually produced a 'crop of sex-delinquencies', and adolescents were among those most likely to succumb. This was because 'the newly wakened sex impulse' was suppressed in 'civilised countries', and channelled instead into religious feeling.[1] This view corresponded to Carl Jung's early work, where he took a more medically orthodox approach to psychic phenomena than he did later in life.[2] In 1917 he related the case of Miss S. W., a Spiritualist medium, whom he met when she was fourteen-and-a-half. He attended a series of seances with the girl and her family, and kept detailed notes of events and his impressions of them. According to Jung, the whole of Miss S. W.'s immediate family was disadvantaged in some way by a hereditary illness. Miss S. W.'s hereditary deficiencies were comparatively light, and she was described by Jung as 'slenderly built, skull somewhat rachitic, without pronounced hydrocephalus, face rather pale, eyes dark with a peculiar penetrating look'. Her family were artisans, and she received an irregular education. She heard about table-turning at home and from friends, and took part in sessions with her family. 'It was then discovered that she was an excellent medium.'[3]

As she passed into trance, Miss S. W. would shut her eyes, become very pale and then sink into a chair. After drawing several deep breaths, she began to speak. The spirits of her dead relatives spoke through her. She had visions and premonitions, wrote automatically and was subject to forebodings. She was often sad and depressed after what Jung called her 'attacks', especially 'when any unpleasant indiscretions had occurred'.[4] During his analysis of this case, Jung considered a variety of psychological factors, but he attached great importance to the fact that Miss S. W. was entering puberty when her phenomena appeared:

> One must suppose that there was some connection between the disturbances and the physiological character-changes at puberty … Vacillating moods are recognisable; the confused new, strong feelings, the inclination towards idealism, to exalted religiosity and mysticism, side by side with the falling back into childishness, all this gives to adolescence its prevailing character.[5]

Jung sought the genesis of S. W.'s 'disease' in the 'teeming sexuality of this too-rich soil'. Taking a Freudian stance, he wrote: '[T]he whole creation of Ivenes, [S. W.'s spirit-guide] … is nothing but a dream of sexual wish-fulfilment, differentiated from the dream of a night only in that it persists for months and years.'[6]

The presence of pubescent girls, especially those of the working class, became a popular blanket explanation for psychic phenomena in the interwar years, especially in poltergeist cases. Young women were regularly censured for pretending to cause, or unconsciously causing, poltergeist phenomena. Muriel Hankey recalled the story of an unfortunate young woman who worked at a mill towards the end of 1924. Equipment was always breaking when Miss G. was in the vicinity. She was sent to another department, and more breakages occurred. Accidents and breakages followed wherever she went. At home, windows rattled and ornaments fell off her mantelpiece until at last her landlord gave her notice to quit. She was rehoused with a friend, but the disturbances continued. Finally, somebody called the local doctor. He 'ascribed the occurrences to hysteria', and told her that 'if she did not give over being such a fool', she would end up in a lunatic asylum.[7] Similarly, a doctor known to Dion Fortune said that 'whenever he came across a case of bell-ringing, knocks, the dripping of water and oil from ceilings, and other untoward happenings, he always looked for the hysterical maidservant'.[8] So too did the psychical researcher Harry Price, who wrote: 'it is a fact that often a young person – usually a girl – is the unconscious "inducer" of these intriguing phenomena'.[9]

The common belief that the malicious power of poltergeists was somehow manipulated by the emergent sexuality of adolescent girls (arguably one of the least powerful groups in Western society) may be another example of an unconscious projection that became encoded in ideology.[10] The reputedly destructive power of the poltergeist (whether viewed as real or as a manifestation of the unconscious) was a psycho-social device that blamed young women for any sexual excitement and fear they aroused in others. The supposedly uncanny power of girlish sexuality inspired the film *Stop Press Girl* (1949), with Sally Anne Howes in the lead role. Here, a young woman has the unconscious ability to stop any kind of machinery. Significantly, the power leaves her when she falls in love and marries, thus bringing her (dangerous) sexuality under the controlling norm of the family.

The notion that poltergeist occurrences were associated with the conscious or unconscious manipulations of adolescent girls remained stable and widespread in the 1930s and 1940s. One contributor to a Mass-Observation survey believed that 'supernatural happenings' were attributable to the 'deceit of "power seeking" people – e.g. adolescents in "poltergeist" phenomena'.[11] The onset of menstruation figured in Harry Price's interpretation of the weals that spontaneously appeared on various parts of a young girl's body during experiments with telekinetic phenomena. This time, however, the arrival of puberty apparently stopped the phenomena, and the stigmata effect ceased.[12]

The victim

Psychic occurrences were also associated with sexual trauma in women. Nandor Fodor made this connection when he carried out a lengthy investigation of a poltergeist case. Fodor was a Spiritualist and an experienced psychical researcher of the 1930s. Between 1933 and 1935 he was the assistant editor of *Light*, and in 1935 he published *These Mysterious People*, in which he generally endorsed Spiritualist theories of supernatural phenomena.[13] He was also a member of the SPR and director of the International Institute for Psychical Research between 1934 and 1938.[14] In 1938 he undertook the investigation of poltergeist disturbances at a house in Thornton Heath, London. His subsequent book, *On the Trail of the Poltergeist* (published twenty-one years later, in 1959), is an account of this investigation; it is strongly influenced by Freudian thought and thus represents a radical break with Fodor's previous Spiritualistic outlook.[15]

The Thornton Heath poltergeist gained notoriety in February 1938, when the following headline appeared in the *Sunday Pictorial*: 'GHOST WRECKS HOME FAMILY TERRORISED'.[16] The occupiers of the house, a family called Forbes, were immediately besieged by journalists and psychical researchers, all eager to witness poltergeist activity for themselves. They were not disappointed; phenomena were produced on a spectacular scale. Eggs flew about the rooms, china ornaments spontaneously shattered before their eyes, and a heavy wardrobe was flung to the ground. Fodor, who was one of the first on the scene, was cautiously convinced of the supernormal character of these occurrences, but not necessarily of their discarnate causes. The phenomena were centred around thirty-five-year-old Mrs Forbes, and Fodor eventually came to believe that they originated with her. During the course of his investigations Fodor discovered that Mrs Forbes had been at the centre of psychic events since early childhood. She saw ghosts, and was clairvoyant and clairaudient; she had premonitory dreams, had previously been visited by poltergeist phenomena, and once fell into a trance - she awoke 'with a cross mark on her breast'. In view of all this, Fodor hypothesised that the origin of 'the upheaval in her house' lay in 'her mediumistic make-up'.[17] Throughout the rest of 1938, Mrs Forbes's list of psychic accomplishments multiplied. Several spirit-guides emerged; birds appeared from under her skirts, she was showered with violets and claimed to be able to project herself through space. She was continually assailed by the smell of decomposition, suffered from periodic bouts of blindness, and spontaneous burns appeared on her neck. She was mutilated again by claw wounds on her back and vampire-like bites on her neck. Once she had a vision of a man with an 'evil leering face'.

Her spirit-guide, 'Bremba', said that this was a vision of a man who had been hanged for molesting small children. As she returned to consciousness, Mrs Forbes said: 'I have got a tightening on the throat now. I feel I am being pulled.' Fodor tells us that as she spoke, 'strangulation marks appeared on her throat, two half circles, overlapping a quarter of an inch thick and even in depth, as if cut into her flesh by a noose … The mark lasted about 40 minutes.'[18] During this period, the poltergeist phenomena grew even more violent, and seemed to be directed at her husband.

Under 'test conditions'[19] at the International Institute for Psychical Research, many of Mrs Forbes's phenomena turned out to be fraudulent, and as the tests progressed, Fodor became increasingly interested in their possible psychological causes. As his investigations drew to a close, he became more and more convinced that both the genuine[20] psychic happenings and the fraudulent issued from Mrs Forbes's unconscious motivations. He repeatedly hypnotised her and carried out free-association tests in an effort to retrieve an early trauma, or traumas, that could conceivably account for the form her phenomena took. One day he asked Mrs Forbes to free-associate with the word rape. She replied:

> HORROR. DOUBT. DEATH. TREES. DARKNESS. DAMP. HORRIBLE FACE. A PAIR OF BIG GLASSES. (I don't know anybody who wears such things.) SOMETHING VERY COLD. A SLITHERING MOVEMENT. SOMETHING WITH SCALES ON. FLESH IS HARD. A CHURCH. A TERRIFIC LOT OF PEOPLE.[21]

Fodor's analysis of Mrs Forbes's mediumship and the phenomena she produced fitted well – rather too well – with the circumstances of her forgotten – or, in Freudian terms, 'repressed' – childhood rape.[22] According to Fodor, she had clearly 'suffered unspeakable horror in a place where there were trees' and a church.[23] The self-mutilation proclaimed the crime and the poltergeist phenomena, directed at Mr Forbes, dramatised Mrs Forbes's wish for revenge. Mr Forbes was the 'victim of a ghastly mistake'. His wife 'blam[ed] him for crimes of which he [was] entirely innocent'. The shock of sexual intercourse on her wedding night 'led her to make a fatal error of identification. In the mental confusion which resulted from the stirring-up of the vague horrors of the past, the transfer of her desire for retaliation to her husband was inevitable.'[24] '[T]he smell of decomposition', in Fodor's words, stood for 'the ghastliness of Mrs Forbes' injury. It meant death, annihilation of her innocent soul', and the phantom violets (of the kind that comprised her bridal bouquet) attested further to her misplaced and unconscious hatred of her husband.[25]

Fodor's psychoanalytic account of the Thornton Heath episode was controversial. Such an interpretation was unwelcome to Spiritualists,[26] and to the Council of the International Institute for Psychical Research (IIPS), which wanted to confine investigations to the traditional realm of psychical research: the collection and classification of evidential material. Fodor broke his association with the IIPS and devoted himself to the investigation of psychic occurrences entirely in the light of Freudian psychoanalysis. In one paper in this vein, published in the *Psychiatric Quarterly* in 1948, he wrote:

> I consider [poltergeist phenomena] to be the manifestations of major mental disorder of schizophrenic, though temporary, character, not the product of anything supernatural. I became convinced that they could be understood only in the terms of the dynamic psychology which is based on the discoveries of Freud and I am interpreting the case here accordingly.[27]

As the Thornton Heath episode demonstrates, the presumed pathology of the mystic was sometimes associated with traumatic sexual encounters, but it was more commonly associated with *thwarted* sexual instincts.[28]

The spinster

Havelock Ellis, in his highly influential *Studies in the Psychology of Sex*, stressed the relationship between mysticism and disturbed sexuality. In one case history, titled 'The Auto-Erotic Factor in Religion' (1897), he paid particular attention to the patient's mystic passion and her desire to preserve her 'purity'.[29] Similarly, mystical rapture, modern or ancient, was, according to Leuba, a form of insanity composed chiefly of unsatisfied and distorted sexual impulses. He described the relationships of Catherine of Genoa, St Teresa and other virgin mystics with Christ as 'clearly morbid'. 'Not one of the prominent representatives of mysticism', he wrote, 'lived a normal married life. The kind of love bestowed on them by God and Christ is apparently incompatible with normal conjugal relations'.[30] Later in the book he wrote:

> It has become more and more recognised that a prolific, if not the most prolific, source of psycho-neurosis is an ab-normal sex-life. None of our great mystics enjoyed a normal sex life; either they lived un-married and under an exciting love-influence – the women in contem-plation of the Heavenly Bridegroom, the men of the Holy Virgin; or, they were married without finding in that relation the physiological and the moral satisfaction which it should give.[31]

In contrast to Spiritualist constructions, the 'feminine vices' were, according to Leuba, exemplified in the virgin mystic. They were pos-sessed of a 'silly scrupulosity, a diffidence, and inability to act, a desire to simplify one's life, an inordinate craving for the support of author-ity'; they were obsessive and mentally vacuous.[32]

In keeping with Leuba and Ellis, the psychologist Charles de Coti insisted that sexual and maternal frustration had led both Joan of Arc and Mary Tudor to religious fanaticism. This 'type', according to De Coti, was represented in modern times by the 'soured spinster' who

> takes an abnormal amount of interest in local church affairs and who tries to manage the business of everyone, with a resulting nervous bitterness and constant unrest. This management of other people's business is the maternal instinct which, having been thwarted in one direction, becomes active in a 'mirrored' form in another direction.[33]

The discourse of the 'old maid' also informed the plot of Somerset Maugham's *Vessel of Wrath*, filmed in 1938. Here, Elsa Lanchester plays a Christian missionary, Martha Jones, who harasses Ted (Charles Laughton), a beachcomber, about his intemperate drinking habits. Ted's retort is that she is a 'corked up old hen' who is 'afraid of normal virility in a man'. Following a scene replete with 'hostile natives', where Ted displays his virility and his mastery over both Martha and the 'natives', the pair marry and return to England to run a country pub. Within marriage Ted becomes responsible and temperate, while Martha is cured of her 'sexual frustration', and thus of her religious enthusiasm.

Such expressions of dislike for the spinster/virgin[34] can be traced to the place of the single woman in interwar culture. This figure, formerly the object of Victorian pity and contempt,[35] took on in the early twentieth century threatening proportions which reached a peak in the interwar period.[36] One obvious source of male discontent was the lack of employment for returned soldiers, for which working women were routinely blamed. Letters to the press frequently complained that women were doing 'men's work', leading to widespread male unemployment. Feeling ran so high that a Bill was passed making it a criminal offence to employ women in 'male industries'.[37] The widespread concern that women were in the process of usurping male authority[38] was exacerbated by the spectacle of shell-shocked, neurasthenic men, which made the traditional image of assured masculinity difficult to sustain.[39] Further-more, the refusal of some women to conform to contemporary patri-archal values concerning gender relations and the organisation of the family escalated into what one historian has described 'as a war on women'.[40] To say that men waged a discursive war on women may be putting the case too strongly, but 'war' accurately describes the voci-ferous attack launched on spinsters by both men and women.

The marriage contract and the ancient 'conjugal rights' of men were important components in the construction of the 'sour virgin'. The marriage contract represented an anomaly in the ideology of the uni-versally free individual, because (as feminists of the period pointed out) although a woman was said to freely and equally enter the contract of marriage, having done so she became the sexual slave of her husband by virtue of his conjugal rights.[41] As we have seen, the narratives of sexologists and novelists idealised motherhood and endowed hetero-sexual sex with mystical properties.[42] In this discourse, the issue of women's sexual subjugation to men was evaded, and virginity came to represent a form of deviant sexuality.

The 'patriotic mothers' whose enhanced social status was gained at the expense of non-mothers were among the foremost critics of 'devi-ant' femininity.[43] Charlotte Haldane, a novelist and former suffragette turned champion of motherhood, treated feminists, spinsters, lesbians and mystics as interchangeable, and attacked them as a single entity. In *Motherhood and its Enemies* (1928) – where Leuba is frequently cited as an authority – she complains that lesbian and 'old maid' influence on public opinion through suffragette endeavour has 'grown alarmingly' since the war: 'Their fanaticism and their crankiness have caused them to take up freak science, freak religions, and freak philanthropy.' 'In the past', she adds, 'when parental authority and that of the Roman Catholic

Church were still strong, the public was protected against their activities. The '"old maid" was kept down with an iron hand'. [44] Similarly, Maud West, a detective and journalist who wrote for *Pearson's Weekly*, insisted that 'a good deal of the trouble between married couples' was caused by the disruptive influence of 'man-hating' feminists. [45]

Such politics received scientific endorsement, for example in the writings of Walter Heape. In a publication entitled *Sex Antagonism*, which was transparently fearful of feminist emancipatory movements, he complained that the 'natural balance' between the sexes was being disturbed by the women's suffrage movement. Feminism represented a return to a 'primitive condition', and if it were allowed to succeed, the 'authority and power hitherto held by the mothers of the nation would be largely usurped by spinsters' who formed the bulk of the movement. Heape described – or, rather, abused – spinsters in a language similar to that used by Leuba with respect to mystics: They were 'a dissatisfied, and we may assume, an unsatisfied class of women', sexually abnormal, possessed of a 'weak intellect', and subject to degenerative illnesses. [46] If political power were extended to women it would result, wrote Heape, in the 'waste products of our Female population gaining power to order the habits and regulate the work of those women [mothers] who are of real value to us as a nation'. [47]

As this quotation suggests, the women 'deviants' who opposed or were placed in a position external to the controlling norm of the family were suspected in some misogynist quarters of conspiring against the state. Lesbians were perceived as particularly threatening to the moral and physical health of the community. According to one MP in 1921, the 'falling away of feminine morality' through lesbian relations, destroyed civilisation. [48] Seven years later, a journalist for the *Sunday Express* echoed this view in his review of Radclyffe Hall's *The Well of Loneliness*. The novel explores lesbian love and sexuality, and he considered it unfit to be sold. He 'would rather give a healthy boy or a healthy girl a phial of prussic acid than this novel. Poison kills the body, but moral poison kills the soul.' The publisher of *The Well of Loneliness* was subsequently prosecuted under the Obscene Publications Act, and the book was declared obscene. In his summing up, the judge spoke of 'filthy sin' and 'moral and physical degradation'. [49]

Mediums were sometimes associated with lesbian activity. In Elliot O'Donnell's mind, this was 'a fact that [could not] be got away from'.

In support of this claim, he recounted an anecdote, allegedly from a woman Spiritualist:

'We were told [at a seance] … not to have anything to do with men, that men are all beasts and tyrants, and that we must oppose them in every possible way, and try and oust them from all their positions of power and prominence. We were further told that a man's love is a very poor thing compared with a woman's, and that women should only select friends and confidants among their own sex.' The lady went on to inform me that the same spirit 'control' had assured both her and her club mates that the Creator was a woman and not a male, as one had always been led to suppose from the Scriptures, and that the Divine feminine mind, which controlled everything, was strongly opposed to the male sex, which it regarded as the source of all wrongs for which mankind in general had suffered. Now one would be in- clined to regard all this lightly were it but an isolated example, but unfortunately it is not.[50]

O'Donnell warned his readers that the 'unnatural friendships' prevalent among women Spiritualists split the family circle, and would soon lead to 'wider havoc', perhaps a 'sex war involving the wholesale and final destruction of the British, as well as other races'.[51]

O'Donnell's views on this matter may have been bound up with the storm at the SPR in 1920 over Radclyffe Hall herself. This was the same year as O'Donnell published his *Menace of Spiritualism*, and eight years before the publication of *The Well of Loneliness*. Radclyffe Hall and her partner, Una Troubridge, became interested in Spiritualism after the death of Hall's former lover, Mabel Batten (Layde), in 1916. Troubridge and Hall held regular seances with Gladys Leonard (some- times on a daily basis) for the purpose of communicating with Layde's spirit. In 1918, Hall delivered to the SPR a paper about these sittings which, on the whole, was favourably received. However, George Fox Pitt, a friend of Una Troubridge's discarded husband, pointedly left the meeting muttering that the paper was 'scientific rubbish'.[52] When Rad- clyffe Hall attempted to gain election to the Council of the SPR, Fox Pitt vigorously opposed her candidature. He objected that she was a 'grossly immoral woman' who had 'wrecked' Admiral Troubridge's home. He said that if her nomination was not withdrawn, he would make these allegations public. Hall immediately issued a writ for slander. In 1920 the action came to trial and attracted wide publicity. The jury found for the plaintiff. But as Lovat Dickenson, Radclyffe Hall's biographer, points out: 'It was a verdict with which neither side could be really satisfied. Radclyffe Hall's character had been far from cleared. In addition to the charge of homosexuality there now lay the strong implication of "nuttiness" about spiritualism.'[53]

Containment through satire

In this chapter (and in Chapters 4 and 5) I have concentrated on the construction of the medium as a figure of horror. Her name hinted at satanic intervention, degenerate sickness and incipient madness; it crept into images of abusive, emergent and 'deviant' sexuality; it evoked the suffocating embrace of the vampire mother and simultaneously the 'sexually frustrated' ill-will of the 'old maid'. So it is perhaps surprising that these constructions did not expose mediums to the kind of organised persecution to which, for example, anti-Semitic discourse subjected Jews. Mediums were harassed and humiliated under the existing vagrancy laws, but such intermittent prosecutions scarcely constituted purposeful persecution. It is therefore worth recalling at this stage that Spiritualism was also signified positively, and that its attraction worked on both a conscious and an unconscious level. As Daphne du Maurier once noted, the boundary line between aversion and attraction is a thin one,[54] and it should be clear by now that this is especially true of mediumship. In this chapter I have focused on ways in which mediumship evoked fears and aversions concerning feminine sexuality. A possible refuge from such concerns lay in the deployment of satire. The kind of satire used against Spiritualism and mediumship defused any perceived threat by reducing mediumistic power to everyday banality, and holding it up to ridicule. Alec Comryn, who wrote about his experiences as a police sergeant before and during the Second World War, used this variety of satire as a means of distancing himself from the proceedings at a seance he attended some time in the early part of the war.

The seance in question is held by The Rent Veil [seance] Circle, a 'developing circle' where participants, who are almost exclusively women, are encouraged to develop their own psychic powers. Comryn is invited along by his friend Madge, who is a part-time worker in the canteen of a local factory. 'Coming from anyone else', writes Comryn, 'such an invitation would have scared me if anything, and I should have hastily excused myself and moved on. Coming from a woman of such humour and practicality as Madge, I am intrigued.' Despite this declaration of good faith, Comryn has committed himself from the outset to the role of satirical debunker; accordingly, he makes much of the unromantic fact that the ground floor of the building where the seances take place is occupied by a jobbing builder who is 'jobbing' when Madge and Comryn arrive. On entering, he immediately identifies the principal medium, Melita, through the discourse of the 'old maid':

> Madge introduces me to the leader of the Circle, a tall, limp, sallow-complexioned woman with very large eyes and a fluttering solicitous manner who, despite her middle-age, speaks in a girlish treble and continually wrings a silk handkerchief between her hands as she does so. She is delighted to see me and wishes more men would attend. Men are so wonderfully responsive she finds … I may sit where I please and must not be afraid of the ladies – they will not eat me. She accompanies this last remark with another wring of her handkerchief across her bosom and regards me under drooping eyelids in a manner I should have described as coquettish rather than occult had she been a little younger and I a little easier on the eye.[55]

Comryn attempts to highlight what he sees as the mundane and absurd aspects of the meeting. Working-class accents are imitated, bodily imperfections, such as stoutness, are noted and the credulity of the women present is emphasised. The arrangement of the circle provides another opportunity for humour:

> I squat with my knees out and my trouser tops immoderately elevated, clownishly facing two rows of elderly women who add nothing to my composure by regarding me with a mixture of distaste and astonishment as though I had just dropped through the roof covered with soot and plaster.[56]

The only other man present is not behaving as a 'proper man' should. Comryn tries to 'catch his eye and offer him a friendly nod as one male to another, but he will have none of it, and instead, screws up his features in perplexity and begins alternately rubbing his hands and knees and folding them across his chest'. He is told later that this man was developing his mediumistic powers and that '[s]omebody big on the other side [was] trying to contact him'.[57] Having described various botched and ludicrous attempts to make contact with the 'other side', Comryn concludes with another allusion to the 'frustrated' sexuality of

Melita. She takes his hand, implores him to come again, and tells him that he is the quiet type. Comryn continues:

> She prefers my type to the talking type. She gets some of the talking type at her meetings sometimes, but they are not responsive. She would like to see more of the quiet, thinking type at her meetings; they are definitely responsive ... When am I coming again?[58]

Despite his flippant and debunking tone, Comryn's message is ambivalent. His use of satire only partially conceals an unease that seeps into the narrative at various unguarded moments. The embarrassment and shame he feels at finding himself the only 'real man' among women is easily discernible. Soon after entering the seance room, and having appraised the situation, he wants to make a speedy exit. Failing this, he elects to sit as near to the door as possible, 'but Madge will have none of it and bullies me into the inner one'.[59] He gives the impression that he feels browbeaten by these 'flutter[ing]'[60] women, but is incapable of resisting them; he has entered a feminine world where he is no longer 'his own master'. Not only is he incapable of escaping, but he also finds himself colluding in their fiction about the afterlife: 'At last happens the thing I have been dreading all along – somebody sees something over my head.' His 'tormenter' is a 'stout young woman' sitting opposite him: 'How I detest her now!' The woman sees the letter 'J' over Comryn's head:

> I turn round to face a battery of eyes and that silly, podgy, intimidating finger. I am possessed right enough, but hardly by spirits. Something warm and scarlet is being pumped into the lobes of my ears at the same time something leaden and cold is being lowered into my stomach. I feel a deep-down urge to yell out and break the spell, but I am restrained by another urge, deeper down, to lie low and not make an ass of myself ... Am I, the big, bold, blustering agnostic, going to strike a blow for reason or am I not? I am not. My leaden stomach mockingly tells me as much; my tingling ears invite me to try it and see; my rooted tongue asks me jeeringly how I propose setting about it.[61]

Comryn is persuaded to accept 'J' as his dead Uncle Joe, complete with quiff, gardening shears and braces, even though he never knew of such a person. When the ordeal is over, he feels unfit to rejoin the company of men. He considers approaching the other man at the seance, and demanding to know what 'his game was but not now. After my episode with Uncle Joe, who am I to approach him man to man?'[62] The anxiety that this encounter with Spiritualism elicits in Comryn culminates in his description of Melita's farewell. If she fulfils the stereotype of the 'old maid' she also stands for the devouring mother: she grasps his hand, effuses over him, congratulates him, 'implores him to come again' – all the time the reader gains the impression that she is standing too close to him, and breathing into his face. Comryn finds relief from her oppressive presence not only in the 'fresh air and sanity'[63] of the mundane world outside the Rent Veil Circle, but also in his satirisation of the episode.

The dangerous chain – spinster, mystic, predator – is similarly undercut in Noël Coward's popular play *Blithe Spirit* (first produced in 1941), and the medium is transformed into a patronised object of amusement. The play is set among the well-off classes in Southern England. The plot revolves around the supercilious Charles and his two wives. Charles's first wife, Elvira, is dead and when the play opens he has married his second wife, Ruth. Charles and Ruth have decided to hold a seance with a local professional medium for the purpose of supplying material for a book Charles is writing, and as a form of entertainment at a dinner party they are about to hold. Just before the guests are due to arrive there is the following exchange between Ruth and Charles:

> RUTH: I have a feeling that this evening is going to be awful.
>
> CHARLES: It'll probably be funny, but not awful.
>
> RUTH: You must promise not to catch my eye. If I giggle – and I'm very likely to – it will ruin everything.
>
> CHARLES: You musn't. You must be dead serious and if possible a little intense. We can't hurt the old girl's feelings, however funny she is.[64]

The medium, Madame Arcati, fulfils conventional notions of 'old-maidish' eccentricity: she rides a bike, refuses to eat red meat, dresses with a '*decided bias towards the barbaric*';[65] she talks 'nervously', and too much, while habitually using a rousing jolly-hockeysticks phraseology, of the type that Margaret Rutherford was to perfect in her role as Agatha Christie's Miss Marple. Indeed, in the 1941 production of the play, Rutherford *did* play the role of Madame Arcati.[66] And here again, in Madame Arcati's motherly treatment of her child control Daphne (who, significantly, never grows up), and in Elvira's distaste for the medium, the silhouette of oppressive motherhood lingers. In one scene, Madame Arcati sentimentally questions Elvira about her life on the 'other side': 'Are you happy, my dear? … Was the journey difficult? Are you weary?' To which Elvira answers: 'Tell the silly old bitch to mind her own business!'[67]

Satirisation of the medium also extended to children's stories of the period. In one of Richmal Crompton's William stories, class status (as in Comryns's narrative) is an important element of the farce. William meets the vulgar, overpowering, *nouveau riche* Mrs Porker, who tells him about her pet dog, now dead:

> 'My dear, dear little four-footed friend,' said Mrs. Porker, wiping away a tear; ''e crossed over last week.'
>
> 'Crossed over?' said William. 'What was he? Oxford?'
>
> 'What d'you mean?' said Mrs. Porker indignantly.
>
> You said he crossed over,' said William. 'I thought you meant from Oxford to Cambridge or from Lib'ral to Conservative, or something like that.'
>
> 'I meant 'e died of course,' said Mrs. Porker irritably, and then returned to her lamentations.[68]

Mrs Porker shows William her late dog's kennel:

> There was a wooden erection, made in the shape of a doll's house, with little windows and curtains and a large front door.
>
> 'The door 'ad to be made larger once or twice as 'e got stouter,' said Pongo's mistress tearfully. ''E was a good eater for his size an' 'e'd stoutened up considerably, lately. I come 'ere to 'is little kennel,' she went on, 'every night, I do, so's to let 'im know I've not forgotten 'im.'
>
> 'Thought you said he was dead,' said William.
>
> 'Well, 'is spirit isn't dead, is it?' said Mrs. Porker tartly. ''E's got a spirit, 'asn't 'e?'[69]

Armed with this information, William, with the assistance of a ventriloquist, tricks Mrs Porker into believing that the spirit of her dead dog has spoken to her. Given Mrs Porker's preconceptions about the 'other world', this deception is an easy matter. Here, the threat of engulfing maternity that mediumship evoked is rendered harmless.

Instead of the mother of 'fright and lust', there is the absurd and 'ill bred' Mrs Porker, whose motherly attentions are focused on a dead dog – a dog whose return from the grave is engineered by an eleven-year-old boy.

In other 'William' stories, the 'nervous old maid' who fancies she can communicate with the 'other world' is a stock figure. In 'The Haunted House', for example, (*Still William*, 1925), a group of spinsters, members of The Society for Higher Thought, become convinced that an empty house, utilised for play by William and his gang, is visited by spirits. The Society for Higher Thought is composed entirely of women who are credulous and nervous in equal degree; one or other of them is always 'having hysterics'; they fuss about issues of propriety, and seem to be under continuous nervous strain. There is also an intimation of an underlying perverse sexuality in the members' concern with the supernatural. Miss Hatherby, for instance, trembles with eagerness at the prospect of being contacted by the spirit of the dead Colonel Hanks.[70]

In Anthony Powell's *What's Become of Waring?*, this 'dried-up' figure appears again in the shape of Miss McKechnie, a regular sitter at seances, who is described as a 'withered lady'. The story proceeds in the first person and the narrator is attending his first seance with his friend, Hugh. The seance takes place in a large house with furnishings that look as if they have been bought 'wholesale from a reliable antique dealer'. The medium, an effete young man with a 'weak double chin', sits wearing a dressing gown, flanked by an ex-military man and Miss McKechnie. George Eliot is the spirit-guide; she speaks in a high child's voice, seems unable to commit herself on any matter, and for some unspecified reason likes to be addressed as 'Mimi'. The seance drags on for two hours, during which time the narrator feels as if Miss McKechnie's 'mummified paw' has become part of him.[71]

Comryn, Coward, Crompton and Powell include most of the stereotypical pathologies ascribed to the spinster/psychic in their stories. But in their satirisations the atmosphere of horror, morbid fascination and deviancy that gathered around the medium is dissipated (for the moment), and she becomes tame and innocuous. As we shall see in Chapter 7, however, the medium emerges yet again as the focus of anxieties about threatening femininity in the discourse of psychical research.

Notes

1 J. Leuba, *The Psychology of Religious Mysticism*, revised edn (London, Routledge & Kegan Paul, 1929), p. 149, note 2.

2 See C. G. Jung, *Memories, Dreams, Reflections*, ed. A. Jaffe, trans. R. and C. Winston (1963) (London, Flamingo, 1983) for his later theories and speculations about mysticism, especially pp. 119–20.

3 C. G. Jung, 'On the Psychology and Pathology of So-Called Occult Phenomena', in *Collected Papers on Analytical Psychology*, 2nd edn, ed. C. Long (London, Baillière, Tindall & Cox, 1917), pp. 17, 18.

4 *Ibid.*, pp. 18–20. Jung does not comment on these 'unpleasant indiscretions'.

5 *Ibid.*, pp. 67–8.

6 *Ibid.*, p. 74.

7 M. Hankey, *James Hewat McKenzie, Pioneer of Psychical Research: A Personal Memoir* (London, Aquarian Press, 1963), p. 117.

8 D. Fortune, *Psychic Self Defence* (1930) (Wellingborough, Aquarian Press, 1973), p. 30.

9 H. Price, *Search for Truth: My Life for Psychical Research* (London, Collins, 1942), p. 35.

10 Projection, in this sense, entails the 'projection' of one's own feelings (desires, dislikes, fears, etc.) on to another.

11 Mass-Observation Archive (University of Sussex) Directive Respondent, reply to April 1942 Directive.

12 H. Price, *Fifty Years of Psychical Research: A Critical Survey* (London, Longmans, 1939), pp. 80–81.

13 N. Fodor, *These Mysterious People* (London, Rider, 1935); N. Blunsdon, *A Popular Dictionary of Spiritualism* (London, Arco, 1961), p. 85.

14 N. Fodor, 'The Poltergeist Psychoanalysed', *Psychiatric Quarterly*, 22 (April 1948) 196.

15 Fodor did not identify publicly with Freudian psychoanalysis until the late 1940s, but some Freudian influences are evident in his work as early as 1935. In *These Mysterious People*, pp. 165–74, where Spiritualist tenets of thought are generally upheld, Fodor turns to the haunting of Esther Cox. Here, he associates the violent ghost she describes with a rape attack she had suffered.

16 N. Fodor, *On the Trail of the Poltergeist* (London, Arco, 1959), p. 15.

17 *Ibid.*, p. 29.

18 *Ibid.*, pp. 138–9.

19 The nature of these tests and their impact on Mrs Forbes are discussed in ch. 8 below.

20 In Fodor's judgement, an event was genuinely psychic when all natural causes had, to the best of his knowledge, been disqualified.

21 Fodor, *On the Trail of the Poltergeist*, p. 213.

22 P. Hutton reminds us that in Freudian psychoanalysis it is an article of faith that the 'unconscious mind retains all of life's memories. The problem of forgetting – of gaps in memory – is due to repression' ('The Art of Memory Reconceived: From Rhetoric To Psychoanalysis', *Journal of the History of Ideas*, XLVIII:3 [1987] 387). But Freud did, of course, take account of the role of fantasy, 'screen memories' (which act as defences against the memory of painful experiences), and 'suggestion' by the therapist. The reliability of repressed memory, and the role of fantasy and suggestion, have again come under scrutiny in more recent allegations of childhood rape and other forms of sexual and physical abuse. See F. Crews, 'The Revenge of the Repressed', *The New York Review of Books*, XLI:19 (1994) 54–60.

23 Fodor, *On the Trail of the Poltegeist*, p. 213.

24 *Ibid*, pp. 216–17.

25 *Ibid.*, p. 219.

26 See Hankey, *James Hewat McKenzie*, p. 111.

27 Fodor, 'The Poltergeist Psychoanalysed', p. 196.

28 The associations made between sexuality and psychic power became increasingly elaborate after the Second World War. See P. Tabori and P. Raphael, 'Sex and the Occult', in *Beyond the Senses: A Report on Psychical Research and Occult Phenomena in the Sixties* (London, Souvenir Press, 1971). 'Sexual shocks', the onset of puberty or menopause, 'sexual frustration' and 'hyper'-sexuality are all given as the motivating, or actual, 'force' behind psychic phenomena.

29 H. Ellis, 'Appendix C: The Auto Erotic Factor in Religion', 'Auto Eroticism', in *Studies in the Psychology of Sex*, 'Foreword' by M. L. Ernst, vol. 1, Part 1 (New York, Random House, 1936), pp. 316–17.

30 Leuba, *The Psychology of Religious Mysticism*, p. 119.

31 *Ibid.*, p. 193.

32 *Ibid.*, p. 201.

33 C. de Coti, *Hitler Psycho-Analysed* (London, Rider, 1940), p. 8.

34 'Old maidishness' was widespread as a term of abuse in the interwar period. Novelists regularly consigned scorned professions and scorned art to the metaphorical company of 'old maids'. W. H. Auden complained that far too many schoolmasters were 'silted up old maids' (quoted by B. Bergonzi, *Reading the Thirties: Texts and Contexts* [London, Macmillan, 1978], p. 28; from Auden's *The Old School*) And according to Raymond Chandler the interwar whodunit resembled 'a cup of lukewarm consomme at a spinsterish tea-room' (quoted by A. Light, *Forever England: Femininity, Literature and Conservatism between the Wars* [London, Routledge, 1991], p. 75).

35 In the nineteenth century, 'surplus women' – that is to say, those without 'male protectors' – were encouraged – or, more often, forced, because of the lack of employment opportunities – to emigrate to the

colonies. A. J. Hammerton writes: 'From 1832 to 1836 the bulk of the colonial emigration fund was expended on the emigration from Great Britain of single women' ('"Without Natural Protectors": Female Immigration to Australia, 1832–36', *Historical Studies*, 16 [1974–5] 539). See also P. Clarke (ed.), *The Governesses' Letters from the Colonies, 1862–1882* (London, Hutchinson, 1985).

36 S. Jeffreys, *The Spinster and Her Enemies: Feminism and Sexuality 1880–1930* (London, Pandora, 1985).

37 L. Lind-af-Hageby, *Unbounded Gratitude! Women's Right to Work* (London, Women's Freedom League, 1928), pp. 1–11. Against the thesis, adopted by some historians, that the Great War was a watershed in the *emancipation* of women, J. McCalman concluded that the war 'essentially did little to emancipate British women. Although average wage for women had risen above subsistence level', and changes in the economy increased job choice, 'their status as workers had not significantly risen. In fact, equality in the true sense was even further off, for the war reinforced in both tertiary and secondary sectors of the economy the trend for women to perform only "women's work", thus rendering even more difficult the achievement of equal pay for equal work' ('The Impact of the First World War on Female Employment in England', *Labour History*, 21 [November 1971] 47).

38 This fear is expressed in W. Deeping, *Sorrell and Son* (London, Cassell, 1928) in the character of Mrs Palfrey.

39 For recent commentary on returning 'war heroes' who did not look or behave as expected, see E. Showalter, *The Female Malady: Women Madness and English Culture, 1830–1980* (London Virago, 1985), ch. 7; Light, *Forever England*, pp. 170–71.

40 B. Dijkstra, *Idols of Perversity: Fantasies of Feminine Evil in Fin-de-Siècle Culture* (Oxford, Oxford University Press, 1986), p. vii.

41 Jeffreys, *The Spinster and Her Enemies*. For a detailed analysis of social contract theory and its uses in excluding women from citizenship, see Carole Pateman, *The Sexual Contract* (Cambridge, Polity Press, 1988).

42 As S. Jeffreys observes, the ideology of 'mystical love' could underscore oppositional politics. On the one hand, mystical love supported the notion of male sexual need and the husband's 'conjugal right'. On the other, many feminists argued that sex should not take place unless an ideal bond had been formed between the partners. In 1895 Elizabeth Wolstenholme Elmy wrote:

> Seeing there still existent unjust conditions legal or social, in marriage and noting the misery so frequently the lot of the wife – too usually led or left to accept marriage ignorant of the actual incidents of matrimony, and with no word of forewarning as to marital physical intimacies, which unless of reciprocal impulse, may prove repugnant and intolerable to her; involving moreover the sufferings

and dangers of repeated and undesired childbearing – the conviction is everyday growing that under no plea or promise can it be permissible to submit to the individuality, either mental or physical, of the wife, to the will and coercion of the husband. (quoted by Jeffreys, *The Spinster and Her Enemies*, p. 30)

43 See Jeffreys, *The Spinster and Her Enemies*. C. Koonz makes this point in her study of Nazi women, *Mothers in the Fatherland* (London, Methuen, 1988).

44 C. Haldane, *Motherhood and its Enemies* (New York, Doubleday, 1928), p. 153.

45 M. West, 'Why Sex Hate is Growing', *Pearson's Weekly*, 31 May 1919, p. 711.

46 W. Heape, *Sex Antagonism* (London, Constable, 1913), pp. 206–7.

47 *Ibid.*, p. 208.

48 Quoted by Jeffreys, *The Spinster and Her Enemies*, p. 114.

49 Quoted by R. Ormrod in *Una Troubridge: The Friend of Radclyffe Hall* (London, Jonathan Cape, 1984), pp. 177, 183; L. Dickenson, *Radclyffe Hall at the Well of Loneliness* (London, Collins, 1975), ch. 12.

50 E. O'Donnell, *The Menace of Spiritualism*, 'Foreword' by Father B. Vaughan (London, Werner & Laurie, 1920), p. 99.

51 *Ibid.*, p. 100.

52 Dickenson, *Radclyffe Hall.*, p. 85.

53 *Ibid.*, p. 93. See chs 6 and 7 of Dickenson's biography for a more detailed account of the trial and the events leading up to it. See also R. Ormrod, *Una Troubridge*, for an account of Radclyffe Hall and Troubridge's life together, and the oppositions they faced.

54 D. du Maurier, *Jamaica Inn* (1936) (London, Pan, 1976), p. 126.

55 Detective Sergeant A. Comryn, *Your Policemen are Wondering* (London, Gollancz, 1947), pp. 140, 142, 143.

56 *Ibid.*, p. 143.

57 *Ibid.*, pp. 144, 146.

58 *Ibid.*, p. 159.

59 *Ibid.*, p. 143.

60 *Ibid.*, p. 151.

61 *Ibid.*, pp. 156–7.

62 *Ibid.*, p. 160.

63 *Ibid.*, pp. 159–60.

64 N. Coward, *Blithe Spirit* (London, Samuel French, 1941), p. 3.

65 *Ibid.*, p. 10.

66 *Ibid.*, 'Cast List'. She also played Madame Arcati in the 1945 film version of the play.

67 *Ibid.*, p. 67.

68 R. Crompton, 'William Puts Things Right', in *William's Happy Days* (1930), abridged edn (London, Armada, 1977), p. 206.

69 *Ibid.*, p. 207.

70 R. Crompton, 'The Haunted House', in *Still William* (1925), abridged edn (London, George Newnes, 1964), p. 124.

71 A. Powell, *What's Become of Waring?* (London, Cassell, 1939), pp. 28, 27, 28, 29.

7

The dual agenda of psychical research

For I wish to point out that the *emotional* creed of educated men is becoming divorced from their *scientific* creed; that just as the old orthodoxy of religion was too narrow to contain men's knowledge, so now the new orthodoxy of materialistic science is too narrow to contain their feelings and aspirations; and consequently that just as the fabric of religious orthodoxy used to be strained in order to admit the discoveries of geology or astronomy, so now also the obvious deductions of materialistic science are strained or overpassed in order to give sanction to feelings and aspirations which it is found impossible to ignore ... [T]he time is ripe for some such extension of scientific knowledge as we claim that we are offering here – an extension which, in my view, lifts us above the materialistic standpoint altogether, and which gives at least a possible reality to those subtle intercommunications between spirit and spirit, and even between visible and invisible things. (Frederick Myers, 1886)[1]

We must remember that our raison d'être is the extension of the scientific method, of intellectual virtues – of curiosity, candour, care, into regions where many a current of old tradition, of heated emotion, even of pseudo-scientific procedure, deflects the bark which should steer only towards the cold, unreachable pole of absolute truth ... We must continue to demolish fiction as well as to accumulate truth, we must make no terms with hollow mysticism, any half-conscious deceit. (Henry Sidgwick, 1900)[2]

These passages from two founding members of the Society for Psychical Research (SPR) illustrate contrary epistemological ideals within the discipline. The passage from the classical scholar Frederick Myers moves towards a vision of an integrated cosmos. He attempts to bridge conceptual divisions erected between rationality and intuition, the dead and the living, matter and spirit, science and faith, and between heaven and earth. The one from Henry Sidgwick, Cambridge philosopher and first president of the SPR, corresponds to a dualist or *dis*integrated cosmology where faith and science, matter and spirit, feeling and knowing, operate as oppositions. In this chapter, I will first consider ways in which these polarised trends structured the discourse of psychical research in the nineteenth and twentieth centuries, I will then discuss their implications for relations between psychical researchers and mediums.

Psychical research attracted those members of the intelligentsia who were dissatisfied with the limitations imposed upon scientific knowledge by dominant materialist explanations of the cosmos and of mind.[3] Simultaneously, most researchers looked to the 'scientific method' as a means of transcending these perceived limitations. This paradigmatic cleavage had been present since the founding of the SPR by a group of Cambridge scholars in 1882. In its trend towards integration, or 'participating consciousness',[4] psychical research responded to what Myers and his followers perceived as a living, vital universe imbued with Divine consciousness. For Myers, the individual was linked to transcendent realities through the hidden life of the 'subliminal self'. Here, the consciousness of everyday life was but one layer in multiple layers of consciousness – a fraction of a larger whole. To the surface layer Myers accorded 'no primacy'; it was the hidden life in its union with the Divine – a union that had expressed itself through time in outpourings of genius and in the religious instinct – that he considered of momentous importance for humankind.[5] Myers strove until his death in 1901[6] to make the reality of his subjective experience objectively comprehensible to himself and to a largely hostile scientific community. But it was in intuitive religious experience and personal intimacies – in, for instance, the warmth of his relationship with Josephine Butler and her evangelical Christianity, or his ecstatic love affair with his cousin, Annie Marshall – that Myers was really sure there was something in existence 'that was striving upwards into life divine'.[7]

Scientists of the nineteenth and early twentieth centuries did not always view this sense of mystical involvement with the cosmos as inimical to science (though proselytisers for scientific materialism like Tyndall, Huxley and Clifford and their successors could make it seem so).[8] In a quest parallel to that of Myers, the mathematician Peter Guthrie Tait and the philosopher Balfour Stewart posited 'an essential continuity between the phenomena of this world and an unseen realm beyond it'.[9] At the turn of the century, this fourth dimension, as it became known, was often at the centre of speculations about the nature of the universe and our place within it. In *The Fourth Dimension* (1904), C. H. Hinton suggested 'that we might possess 4D souls despite being limited to 3D sense experience'.[10] Time,[11] though not of another dimension, was central to the philosopher and psychical researcher Henri Bergson's concept of *élan vital*, where, the individual's unconscious mind includes the memory of his or her evolutionary past. In this way, people are connected to the rest of creation and have intuitive knowledge of it.[12]

It was the theory of ether, however, that held out the greatest hope of postmortem survival for many nineteenth- and early-twentieth-century psychical researchers. Orthodox physics in the late nineteenth century held that a pervasive substance existed to support electromagnetic waves. Various attempts were made to describe this substance. James Clerk Maxwell, the originator of electromagnetic theory, regarded the ether as 'capable of transmitting energy … possessing elasticity similar to that of a solid body, and also having a finite density'.[13] More whimsically, Lord Kelvin wrote: 'What can this luminiferous ether be? It is something that the planets move through with the greatest ease. It permeates our air; it is nearly in the same condition, so far as our means of judging are concerned, in our air and in the inter-planetary space.'[14]

The ether filled blank space, and permeated all things. For the purposes of psychical research, it was the presumed pervasiveness of the ether that made it of vital interest, since, as one historian has observed: '[T]he ether took on a transcendent, *unifying*, role within science. It was simplicity lying behind diversity, coherence behind disorder. It established continuity and connection between disparate particular events.'[15] It fused the physical plane with the metaphysical realm and promised to be the basis of a moral and teleological account of existence. This was the hope and expectation of Oliver Lodge. In his understanding of ether, Lodge complemented and reinforced Myers's theory of the subliminal self, since it was by means of this sublime medium (neither wholly matter nor wholly spirit, but a combination of both) that the soul of the 'Unseen Universe' might infuse and inspire the mind of humankind.[16]

While the SPR sought to delineate the unifying principle (or principles) in the universe, it remained committed to orthodox scientific procedures[17] – procedures that already assumed the absence of a metaphysical presence in the universe. The scientific naturalists' attempts to destabilise the hegemonic power of the clergy involved replacing the authority of the Bible with the authority of 'scientific fact', and 'cleansing' natural knowledge of all subjective or metaphysical content. Rationality, dispassionate observation, and the careful collection of facts under controlled conditions increasingly formed the basis of reliable knowledge.[18]

Unwavering commitment to the 'scientific method' and the elimination of feeling seemed necessary if the SPR was to have any hope of achieving scientific respectability and professional status. But researchers were aware that such an approach would inhibit the production of the very phenomena it was intended to investigate. In 1886, Edmund Gurney expressed the concerns of many psychical investigators: 'Questions of mood, of goodwill, of familiarity may hold the same place in psychical investigation as questions of temperature in a physical laboratory; and until this is fully realised it will not be easy to multiply testimony to the extent that we should desire.'[19] It was the 'higher' aspects of mind – love, intuition, the emotions, ethical values and spirituality – which, according to the founding members of the SPR, linked humankind to transcendent realities. But it was these very aspects of mind that orthodox science stigmatised as pollutants in the securing of genuine knowledge. Time and again investigators expressed their ambivalent feelings. Myers stressed the virtues of impersonal detachment in research procedures, yet he entertained high hopes for the psychic powers of the medium, Eva Fay, because of her 'courage and kindness'.[20] Lodge insisted upon the 'cold blooded' gathering of facts, yet could assert at other times that 'LOVE BRIDGES THE CHASM' between this world and the next.[21] Even Frank Podmore, a founding Fabian member and psychical researcher, who earned the title 'sceptic in chief' at the SPR, wrote to tell Sidgwick that he had 'at bottom some kind of inarticulate assurance that there is a unity and a purpose in the Cosmos'.[22]

This painfully felt ambivalence at the core of psychical research has scarcely gone unnoticed by historians, but it has been interpreted in different ways.[23] Among relatively recent interpretations is the idea that the SPR's search for an integrated cosmos was part of an upper-class strategy to counter the hegemonic aspirations of the predominantly middle-class scientific naturalists. In the end, according to this historian:

> psychical research turned out to be a naturalization of the super-natural – a form of *scientific* supernaturalism which attempted to trump the naturalism of the professionalizers with a more comprehensive, 'transcendent' naturalism. It wanted scientific authority for its own metaphysical cravings and social ambitions.[24]

Perry Williams, by contrast, argues that the spiritual values of the founding members of the SPR

> meant more [to them] than simply support for the existing social order ... Because Sidgwick, Myers and Gurney identified with these 'spiritual' things, they could not deny their reality without denying themselves. Inwardly they still knew there were such things as duty, art and love, but inward knowledge was no longer sufficient once they were committed to the liberal epistemology:[25] the reality of spiritual things had to be proved by the scientific method.[26]

Williams shows how the SPR's elite scientism distanced it from the more plebeian Spiritualists. It was the tendency, if not the policy, at the SPR to dismiss most Spiritualist evidence as non-expert, and therefore unreliable. Spiritualists, in their turn, regarded the SPR as insufferably condescending in its attitude, and needlessly sceptical. Profound truths, according to Spiritualists, were grasped through simplicity of thought and emotion rather than formal learning and were thus readily available to the uncluttered intellect of 'ordinary people'.[27]

This conflict persisted and, if anything, deepened in the interwar years. In the 1920s and 1930s the SPR centred round the respected figure of Mrs Eleanor Sidgwick, who had helped her husband Henry to found the Society in the 1880s. Her small coterie of intimates agreed with her conception of psychical research: 'low-key, rigorous, con-servative, and respectable'.[28] In keeping with this approach, the leader-ship made every effort to distance the work of the Society from Spiritualist activity. Spiritualists were exasperated with this cautious-ness.[29] Nevertheless, they still hoped for ratification from psychical research (particularly from the elite SPR), and psychical researchers needed phenomena to work with. Thus Spiritualists and psychical researchers remained unwilling, but necessary companions in the inter-war years.[30]

Despite its commitment to the 'scientific method' and its leader-ship's disdain for Spiritualism, psychical research was excluded from mainstream scientific circles. In considering experimental parapsychology (a term coined for psychical research in the 1930s by J. B. Rhine[31]) as a rejected science, Paul Allison points again to its apparent contra-dictions, and the problems they posed for its relations with scientific orthodoxy. The 'hard-nosed' empiricism of psychical researchers seemed to sit awkwardly with their metaphysical concerns and their emphasis on the bankruptcy of mainstream, materialist science.[32]

Psychical research between the wars countered materialism with a whole range of vitalist theories. The success of the theory of relativity had made the concept of transcendent ether less significant in psychical research by this time,[33] but there were plenty of other vitalist or meta-physical theories to choose from. In 1920, the psychologist and psychical researcher William Brown suggested in his King's College Lecture that Bergson's theory had the potential of 'opening the door' to knowledge of our own past lives, and to telepathic communication.[34] For Brown, such theories reinforced his own traditional Christian values and assumptions:

> At every moment of our existence, in our work, and at all times, we are in contact with the eternal, so far as we are doing what we think we ought to do, opening our hearts to the good and the noble and repudiating fear wherever we meet it – especially as we show courage and are unafraid.[35]

Brown's religious feeling echoed the sentiments of a pre-World War I generation for whom words like nobility, honour and heroism still held stable meaning.[36] Such values may have seemed hackneyed and even offensive in cynical modernist quarters after the war, but they remained powerfully meaningful in memorial art,[37] and persisted in such war poetry as David Jones's, *In Parenthesis*, where the romantic language of Arthurian legend is interspersed with the jagged effects of contempo-rary oaths and blasphemies.[38] Also, the language of mysticism helped to render the experiences of the trenches comprehensible. In the litera-ture of the Great War, writes Paul Fussell, the dominant movement 'was towards myth, towards revival of the cultic, the mystical, the sac-rificial, the prophetic, the sacramental, and the universally significant.'[39]

Psychical research drew on a culture infused with supernatural signs – signs that acquired new significance and new urgency in the aftermath of war. Cosmic consciousness, an idea developed by Richard Bucke in the previous century, came into vogue just after the war.[40] Like psychical research, cosmic consciousness addressed bourgeois concerns about the renewal of a degenerate world through spiritual or mystic awareness.[41] In the face of the evident irrationality of the recent slaughter, cosmic consciousness seemed to ensure humanity's capacity for advancement and expanded understanding. For Bucke, it implied contact with the life and order of the universe, and denoted a new hereditary faculty in humans. Such diverse figures as the Buddha, Jesus, Spinoza, Walt Whitman and Edward Carpenter were, according to Bucke, the possessors of such a faculty, and the forerunners of a new age of similarly enlightened or inspired people.[42]

Intuitive knowledge of the cosmos was also explored by J. W. Dunne, whose *Experiment with Time* (1927) aroused a good deal of popular and scientific interest.[43] Dunne claimed that it was quite normal for dream material to mingle images and events from the past, the present and the future. This is possible, according to Dunne, because part of the unconscious has access to a timeless cosmos and can apprehend what *seem*, in everyday, linear time, to be future events.[44] J. B. Priestley was interested in the 'problem of time',[45] as he put it, and helped to popularise Dunne's theories in his famous play *Time and the Conways* (first produced in 1932 at the Lyric Theatre, London). Act 1 is set in 1919 and revolves around the Conway family who are presented as wealthy, popular and attractive. In Act 2, however, one of the daughters, Kay, has a dream in which she receives a glimpse of the grim future awaiting the family. The third act returns to 1919, but is coloured by Kay's half-remembered knowledge of future events. During the 1932 London production of *Time and the Conways*, Dunne was invited to explain his theories to the actors.[46]

A view that amalgamated Bergson's, Dunne's and Myers's theories, and explicitly incorporated bourgeois expectations about continual human progress, was advanced by Dame Edith Lyttelton, daughter of Arthur Balfour, member of the Council of the SPR and president from 1933 to 1934. In *Our Superconscious Mind* (1931) she distinguished between subconscious and superconscious mind. To the former she assigned 'desires, impulses, and egoistic emotions which are in the main concerned with our physical nature, including fear and various kinds of unremembered facts and feelings, some racial, some individual, not normally held in consciousness'. To the latter she assigned

> forms of perception, not acquired through the senses, such as knowledge of what is passing, or has passed, at a distance in time or space: what is about to happen; and the kind of vision which is either called prophecy or inspiration.[47]

She suspected that the 'superconscious faculties', whether employed or not, were the property of all human beings. Such faculties not only gave humans the potential of contacting the 'conscious and superconscious part of other living minds, but also ... another field of existence where time is different from our time'.[48]

Lyttelton viewed telepathy as an aspect of superconsciousness, but the belief that humans can contact each other in this way had long been an established tenet of psychical research. Although there was little agreement about how it worked, psychical researchers generally accepted that telepathy acted as a means of connecting people and events. Some defined telepathy as 'the communication of impressions of any kind of one mind to another, independently of the recognised channels of sense',[49] and assumed that *rapport* or affinity between people was a necessary condition.[50] Others – like Whatley Carington, a member of the Council of the SPR since 1920 – were inclined to think that telepathy operated through a common subconscious. 'Suppose we have a common subconscious', he wrote, 'suppose we can both draw on a common repository, so that associations formed by me are affective for you.'[51] In *Telepathy: An Outline of Its Facts, Theory and Implications*, Carington adopted the neutral, impersonal tone typical of SPR documents, but the content of his theory expressed, again, the hunger for an integrated cosmos where Self/Other boundaries were traversed. Telepathy, for Carington, was 'essentially a matter of sharing rather than of transference.'[52]

Mauskopf and McVaugh note the same tendency in the thought of the psychologist and leading psychical researcher William McDougall:

> Throughout his career, in fact, McDougall was uncomfortably placed between two positions. Philosophically and morally he was predisposed to accept psychical research; yet his professional training [as a scientist] compelled him to adopt a sceptical and critical attitude towards

psychical phenomena, particularly towards any spiritualistic explanation for them.[53]

The strain of maintaining this dual agenda produced friction within
the community of psychical researchers. At the SPR it was expressed
in the formation of opposing camps, dubbed Right and Left by Oliver
Lodge or, more cumbersomely, the High-and-Dry-School and the
Not-High-and-Dry-School by J. G. Piddington in 1924. The former
represented the more sceptical – or, as they preferred to think, more
'scientifically rigorous' – branch of research. The latter encompassed
those – like Lodge himself, or Conan Doyle – with Spiritualist convictions. But, as Mauskopf and McVaugh note, '[t]hese distinctions sometimes made for strange alliances',[54] and individuals repeatedly crossed
– or were seen by others to cross – into the opposing camp. Controversy over which theories and methods should guide research was as
prevalent among psychical researchers as it was in other disciplines,[55]
but the traffic between the two camps was as much to do with the
inherent ambivalence at the root of psychical research as it was to do
with the usual methodological shifts and conflicts: ambivalent drives[56]
and intentions continued to underpin the entire enterprise of psychical
research in the 1920s and 1930s.

I think that the key to this duality is to be found in psychosocial
imperatives: the desire for integration and simultaneous repudiation of
it. In the remainder of this chapter I will concentrate on how these
ambivalent drives at the heart of psychical research were worked out
on the body of the medium in the interwar years. I will save for Chapter
8 discussion of how attempts by psychical researchers to control that
body were received by the mediums involved.

The experimental body of the medium

In Chapter 5, I discussed how the Western, bourgeois unconscious is
structured under modern patriarchy to experience the maternal body
simultaneously as the source of both goodness and danger. The psyche
is split in its desire for symbiotic union and its equally powerful desire
for individuation. Morris Berman puts it thus: 'I resolve the problem
of Self vs Other by protecting myself from invasion (which is what,
dialectically, I secretly yearn for).'[57] And we have seen how these primordial processes became encoded in ideological forms related to the

maternal body,[58] producing that familiar two-sided coin: the idealisation and the denigration of women.

The symbiotic/individuation split is observable, even caricatured, in the discourse of nineteenth- and twentieth-century psychical research. On the one hand, integration is desired. The desire for union is suggested in the mystical experience and anticipation of a spirit world that is connected with our own. It is present in the concept of the ether – a substance perceived as permeating our bodies and the whole universe, which, in so doing, quite literally blurs Self/Other distinction. It appears in Bergson's *élan vital*, in cosmic consciousness, in Edith Lyttelton's conception of superconscious mind and in telepathic communications that promised to erase the gap between Self and Other. On the other hand, the drive towards separation in the culture of psychical research was strong. The adoption of 'the scientific method' by psychical researchers meant that 'feeling' was rigorously excluded from the domain of proper research, while mediums were objectified as experimental material and subjected to control and manipulation. What implications does this split have for power relations between psychical researchers and mediums? In response to this question, we shall need first to review studies of masculinist bias in the history of science.

In recent years, historians have fruitfully explored class and gender relations through the study of scientific culture. Many of these studies have focused on the development of mechanical philosophy in the early modern period in the context of religious upheaval and nascent capitalism. Such texts have made us aware of the complex political motivations behind the mechanical philosophers' repudiation of Hermetic and 'popular' animist traditions, and their ambition to dominate 'wild nature' and bring it under scientific control.[59] Many historians have noted the analogous relation drawn between 'nature' and 'woman' in the mechanical tradition. 'Woman' was commonly represented as sexually rapacious, crafty and deceitful – a threat to male self-control and spirituality.[60] Nature was often conceived as a cunning and dangerous feminine force that constantly threatened to encroach on the frontiers of civilisation – a force that must be tamed and made to yield up its secrets. In the anticipated 'taming' of nature, metaphors of domination and rape abounded. Brian Easlea writes: 'Bacon … explicitly advocated among other things a masculine science … which would consist of a united male attack on female nature, described in aggressive metaphors, and which would give birth to products that would undeniably demonstrate successful male power and control over nature.'[61]

Fears about a nebulous and dangerous female power did not abate with the victory of scientific materialism and the rise of the desexualised 'angel of the hearth' in the nineteenth century. As one historian has noted, representations of female sexuality encompassed more complex productions than the stereotype of the 'angel of the hearth'.[62] 'Woman' was child, savage,[63] beast[64] and (mother) nature. As well as representing the known territory to which loyalty is due, as in the 'mother country', she was the unknown territory that must be conquered and colonised. One gynaecologist who experimented with a speculum in 1845 imagined himself as a 'colonizing and conquering hero'.[65] Later, in the following century, Freud, with his concept of primary narcissism, situated the 'feminine realm' as the 'dark continent'. Metaphors of bonded and colonised femininity appear again in the history of the development of atomic power.[66]

The deployment of such metaphors is not, of course, confined to scientific discourse. As dread of the sexually active and devouring woman increased in the post-World War I years, literature and films countered this dread with allegories of masculine domination of 'feminine nature'. In the film of Somerset Maugham's *Vessel of Wrath* (1938), for example, 'woman', 'nature' and 'savage' are conflated as Ted proves his virility by assuming a position of mastery over all three.[67] Here 'Woman' is 'nature', 'Man' is 'culture', and the latter rules the former. Ludmilla Jordanova has observed similar metaphors in the famous silent film *Metropolis* (1927): Frederson, the factory boss who dominates Metropolis, seeks to reduce Maria's (feminine) influence over his workers by commissioning the scientist/sorcerer Rotwang to make a disruptive robot in her likeness. Rotwang kidnaps Maria and imprisons her in order to learn her secrets, so that he can produce a bogus Maria to mislead the workers.[68] Here, however, as Jordanova notes, 'this passion for knowledge' and control is critically depicted. Rotwang's overweening desire for knowledge leads to illegitimate projects, as it does in Mary Shelley's *Frankenstein* (1818), and again in Nathaniel Hawthorne's *The Birth-mark* (1843), where the scientist ends up killing his wife in his attempts to make her physically perfect.[69]

Scientific mastery of 'feminine nature' was not always viewed positively, and neither was scientific practice driven purely by uncomplicated impulses to dominate and control. Many scholars have recognised the diversity of values, goals and styles in scientific methods, and they have also recognised that creativity, emotional commitment and passionate involvement have (and continue to be) regulative, if disavowed, features in the dynamics of scientific research.[70] Peter Medawar pointed out in 1963 that the impersonal and neutral tone of the orthodox scientific paper '*does* embody a totally mistaken conception, even a travesty, of the nature of scientific thought.'[71] Nevertheless, emotional removal from the object of research, and the ambition to exercise dominion and control over it, have been key features in scientific discourses.[72] All three elements were present in the practice of psychical research between the wars. The impersonal and 'dispassionate' manner in which psychical researchers strove to carry out their research with mental mediumship is an example of how 'proper scientific procedures' served to place the medium at an emotional distance from themselves. Eileen Garrett found this to be the case in the experiments carried out on her by J. B. Rhine at Duke University in 1933.

Rhine was a respected figure in psychical research in both England and America.[73] In the early 1930s he carried out many tests on volunteers, using specially designed cards to test clairvoyant and telepathic ability.[74] Cards with certain symbols were placed in a sealed envelope, and participants were asked to guess their contents. The purpose of his experiments with Garrett was to compare her results, as an established medium, with those already carried out with volunteers. However, Rhine's impersonal approach to the experiment bothered Garrett, and she performed poorly. In her biography she wrote that she could not perform clairvoyance to order, and that the cards lacked what she called 'energy stimulus' (a kind of 'life force') which, she believed, radiated from people and objects in the right circumstances. 'Affirmation, faith and desire are', she wrote, 'the *energy stimulus* needed to produce results, in science as well as in art and life.'[75] Rhine's control over experimental procedures, and his unwillingness to take into account the empathic conditions she considered necessary for psychic sensing, presented obstacles to Garrett. To her, his experiments attempted to '*force supernormal sensing into especially selected and quite arbitrary channels, in order to answer certain specific and quite limited questions*'.[76]

However, the impulses to dominate and control embedded in the culture of psychical research are best illustrated through the investigative

Harry Price

procedures adopted with physical mediumship. Many psychical researchers avoided physical mediumship. As we saw in Chapter 5, the striking
correlation they (among others) perceived between the process of birth
and the production of ectoplasm in mediumship elicited feelings of
abhorrence in many. Correspondingly, there was a tendency to avoid
physical manifestations altogether, and concentrate on mental phenomena, which included telepathy, clairvoyance, telekinesis (moving
objects at a distance through force of will), and written or spoken

communications through a medium from the spirit world. Nevertheless, physical mediumship fascinated some workers in the field. One of these was Harry Price.

Price, who was one of the best-known psychical researchers in Britain between the wars, said that over a hundred people claiming supernormal powers (many of them physical mediums) passed through his hands at his laboratory for psychical research between 1923 and 1937.[77] Price maintained a lifelong interest in all forms of supernatural phenomena. One of his earliest and happiest recollections was of a market fair he attended in Shropshire just before his eighth birthday in 1889. He remembered standing 'open-mouthed at this display of credulity, self-deception, autosuggestion, faith-healing, beautiful showmanship, super-charlatanism, and "magic". The miracles of the market-place left me spellbound.' Price subsequently moved to Brockley, London and entered his father's paper manufacturing business, but psychical research commanded most of his time and attention. In 1925 he became the Foreign Research Officer for the American SPR and worked at times with SPR members in England,[78] but his flamboyant, self-advertising style was not to the taste of the more conservative among them.[79] Moreover, the SPR leadership disapproved of paying mediums in the belief that it encouraged cheating, and Price was prepared to pay them relatively large sums of money. In 1923, Price wrote to Oliver Lodge about the suspicion that he, Price, encouraged fraudulent mediums:

> I hope Dr. Geley will not continue to entertain suspicions about my Bona fides in relation to psychical research. Because I was palmed off with a very obvious trick, after having paid two guineas for a genuine phenomenon, am I to be suspect because I continue my researches with other mediums? It is a most ridiculous attitude for a critic to take up.[80]

The leadership of the SPR viewed Price as something of a liability to respectable psychical research, and when, in 1933, he offered to merge his National Laboratory for Psychical Research with the SPR, they rejected his proposal out of hand.[81] He ran into conflict with sceptics and believers alike, and was always issuing challenges to his opponents. In 1932, for example, he offered Father Knapp, a polemicist on psychic matters, a thousand pounds if he could produce a conjurer who could equal the performance of mediums that Price was currently testing.[82] If Price appeared hopelessly credulous to some, he appeared too sceptical to others. The editor of *Psychic News*, Maurice Barbanell, attacked him on both counts. In *The Case of Helen Duncan*, Barbanell strenuously refutes Price's claim that Duncan's mediumship was fraudulent,[83] but he regarded his investigations into the existence of witches as pure superstition.[84]

The confusion over what Price's convictions might have been can be traced to his duality of purpose, which, I have argued, was endemic to psychical research. He insisted that the creation of a 'sympathetic "atmosphere"' was 'requisite for successful work in the seance-room'.[85] In the same publication he wrote: 'an atmosphere of emotionalism … is inimical to the cool, dry light in which scientific investigation ought to be conducted'.[86] This split was mirrored in the way he experienced different mediums – a split we have already encountered in previous chapters. Some stood for predatory femininity, which must be control-led, punished and subdued; others represented ideal femininity, which should be wooed, cherished and coaxed into submission.

Stella C.

Ideal mediumship appeared for Price in the shape of Stella Cranshawe. Price met Cranshawe, later known as Stella C., on a train in 1923. In his biography he described his first meeting with her in detail:

> [I]n the opposite corner to me was seated a young lady on her way to her home at Southsea. By the time we arrived at Horsham, both she and I had exhausted our respective piles of literature. She then asked me if I would lend her my copy of *Light* that I had placed on the seat beside me. As I handed her the journal, I inquired what her interest was in psychic matters. She told me she was not particularly interested in such things, but that she, herself, was, on rare occasions, the focus of curious manifestations which were perhaps of a psychic nature.
>
> To say that I was interested would be putting it very mildly. I plied her with questions, and the upshot of our chance meeting was that she consented – very reluctantly – to place herself in my hands for some tests. I had hopes that the spontaneous physical phenomena that she had described to me might be induced, under scientific con-ditions, in the seance-room. Actually, she eventually became one of the most brilliant physical mediums with whom I had ever experi-mented and our seances with her made history.[87]

This passage suggests the tone of Price's relations with Stella Cranshawe. He presented her as the embodiment of 'gentility', passivity and petal-like femininity. 'She is a very ladylike sort of girl', he wrote to the psychical researcher Baron Von Schrenck-Notzig,[88] soon after some initial seances with her – 'very sensitive, and very tractable if approached in the right manner'.[89] When Cranshawe remarked that flowers swayed in her presence, Price speculated that she had established a 'subconscious connection with flowers'.[90] Price's attitude towards Cranshawe was that of a suitor or lover. 'It had always been his ambition', writes Price's biographer, to discover an inexperienced medium, 'watch the growth of the phenomena and direct the emanations into predetermined channels for experimental purposes … And Stella C. came into Price's life when he was getting weary of fraudulent mediums.'[91] But in the manner of a contemporary love story, Cranshawe was not to be 'had' so easily. Their correspondence reveals a parody of traditional courtship rituals. While he pursued her and tried to persuade her to take part in his seances, she repeatedly evaded his advances. On 14 September 1923 he wrote the following desperate note, after she had again failed to turn up for an appointment with him:

> Dear Stella,
>
>   I have made careful inquiries here this afternoon as to the letter you say you posted to me last Tuesday, and no trace of it can be found. Of course letters go astray sometimes, and to-day it was particularly unfortunate as it kept me waiting at the 'Popular' for 1 [and a half] hours. But of course it cannot be helped. If you cannot get up West for your lunch (and I quite appreciate your position), let me meet you at Islington or wherever it is you have lunch; or I could meet you any where else. But I want to talk over what we are going to do, as we are all ready to start [the seances]. Will you please give me the opportunity of discussing it with you? If you cannot manage any lunch time, I could meet you after business hours – in fact, at any time convenient to yourself. Hoping you are well, and with kind regards.[92]

There are few letters from Cranshawe to Price in the Price archive, and even in these she is strangely missing. By this I mean that she seems to write with the purpose of defending herself against Price's desire, rather than asserting her own. It is as if she wanted to refuse him but was afraid to offend. On 19 June 1923, she wrote that she was 'awfully sorry to have to disappoint' him, but she 'felt so very queer last evening'.

Stella C. (Stella Cranshawe)

On 23 August, she was again 'so sorry' to miss her appointment with him, but her nephew was crying and she had to take him home. Her letter in September, cancelling another appointment, had unaccount-ably gone astray, and her job, she pleaded, was an obstacle to seance work.[93] Finally, in September she told Price that she could attend no further sittings. She legitimised this action with a male authority:

> I am very sorry I had to disappoint you all last Thursday, but I have decided to give up the sittings altogether.
>
> You see I am engaged to be married and had the sittings been entirely business it would have been different, but under the circumstances it is not fair to either of you, if I see you again.
>
> Thanking you for all you have done for me. I remain
> Yours sincerely
> Stella Cranshawe.[94]

For the first time Cranshawe explicitly revealed her sexual discomfiture with Price's attentions, but she blamed herself and thanked him anyway.

Cranshawe's evasions, refusals and lack of interest in psychical matters seems to have made her even more desirable to Price, both sexually and as a medium. He read her indifference to psychical matters as a *disinterestedness* that vouchsafed the genuineness of her phenomena.[95] Conflating her personal virginal desirability with her mediumistic interest for science, Price wrote that Stella C. fulfilled his ambition to 'secure a medium before the development of the psychic faculties had taken place'.[96] And he acted out the part of a jealous suitor. While their association lasted, he was fiercely possessive of 'his medium'.

The first sittings with Stella Cranshawe were at Hewat and Barbara McKenzie's premises, the British College of Psychic Science. From the outset, Price assumed control over the seances through his role of president. The rules that regulated the Stella C. research stipulated that no one should introduce tests to the seances without the permission of the president. No one was allowed 'to ask questions of the operating "force", "entity" or "controls"' except those appointed by Price, who also vetted visitors. Finally, no report of the circle was to be published '*without the written permission of the President*'.[97] Price arranged for many other psychical researchers and scientists to witness Cranshawe's psychic powers but took care to retain control over her mediumship. Proposals to her concerning her mediumship were filtered through him. In reply to an offer from Malcolm Bird, of the journal *Scientific America*, for Cranshawe to visit America, Price agreed on the condition 'that you give me your word of honour, that as far as you can prevent it, Stella is not approached by anyone on your side with a view to securing her services in the States'.[98]

No doubt Price's determination to maintain control over Cranshawe's mediumship was partly motivated by business interests, but his correspondence regarding her deals only incidentally with financial matters, and with only small sums of money. Moreover, Price was a wealthy man, and he spent far more on psychical research than he ever made.[99]

The management of Cranshawe's mediumship caused friction in the communities of psychical research and Spiritualism. In a letter to Price (8 September 1923) Barbara McKenzie wrote that she and her husband objected to Price's taking 'exclusive control of "Stella"' while they paid her salary and provided seance facilities.[100] Price also came into conflict with the SPR's research officer, Eric Dingwall, over Cranshawe. In April 1923, Price complained to Lodge that Dingwall had tied to 'poach' her services for the SPR: 'He considers that I should hand her over to the S.P.R., and at the same time admits that I should have no control over her. This I will not agree to.'[101]

Price exercised direct control over Cranshawe's body in the seance. The seances he recorded in his book *Stella C.* were complicated procedures designed to monitor occurrences and eliminate fraud. Lighting was carefully arranged, and the temperature of the room was measured before and after the seance. The medium's temperature was taken, and her pulse rate while under trance was monitored. The door of the seance room was locked and the key removed. In addition, Cranshawe's movements were controlled: 'It was arranged', wrote Price,

> that Mrs L. E. Pratt, on account of her experience in nursing, should be placed on the right of the medium, controlling her right hand and foot. I took up a position on the left of the medium, controlling her left hand and foot. The remaining sitters took up various positions, and at every sitting we linked hands and kept contact with our feet.[102]

'Never was a medium easier to control', sighed Price appreciatively. 'She did exactly as she was requested, made no comments – in fact, she hardly spoke at all.'[103]

Price's treatment of Stella Cranshawe may have been oppressive, and his pursuit of her mediumistic services could be construed as harassment by present-day standards. Nevertheless, his letters to her remained courteous in tone, as far as I am aware he never subjected her to invasive or degrading controls during trials, and he tried to create a sympathetic atmosphere at seances by playing music.[104] Although there is no evidence that he included her in the negotiations (acrimonious or otherwise) that he was conducting with various individuals and institutions over the management of her mediumship, he did tell her beforehand about the controls and apparatus to be used at seances, as the following note to Sir Oliver Lodge shows:

> I took Stella to the Institut [Métapsychique, in Paris] in order to make her acquainted with the apparatus in use there. It is my intention – providing I can find suitable accommodation – to equip a laboratory for psychical research, and I wanted this medium (who knows nothing at all about the work), to know beforehand what apparatus we were going to use and what she would be expected to do.[105]

'I am positive', wrote Price, at the close of the first series of sittings with Cranshawe, 'that with a sympathetic environment, and with suitable sitters, Stella could produce the whole *gamut* of psychic phenomena.' As he once said when he was ridiculed for using incense at sittings for its pleasant odour: 'I am not suggesting that the burning of incense at a sitting is helpful in the production of phenomena; *but it pleased* Stella, which was my constant aim.'[106] The same cannot be said of his stance towards Helen Duncan

Helen Duncan

If Stella C. was for Price ideal medium, ideal experimental material and ideal woman rolled into one, Helen Duncan was her antithesis. Cranshawe and Duncan produced similar phenomena, although Cranshawe's psychic repertoire was larger. In Cranshawe's presence chilly winds swept the seance room, tables levitated and bumped about, and a sprig of lavender once appeared. Both mediums produced ectoplasm and were controlled by spirit-guides. Cranshawe's guide was an Indian child called 'Palma'. Duncan had two guides: an adult male called 'Albert' and a child called 'Peggy Hazeldine'. However, the two mediums were different in important respects. Cranshawe came from the southern counties, was young, middle-class and virginal – 'a typical specimen of the modern, well educated English girl', wrote Price.[107] Helen Duncan, by contrast, was born in a poor working-class area in Perthshire, Scotland, and had given birth to nine children by the time she met Price in 1931.[108] Her husband, Henry, was a cabinet-maker whose business had gone bankrupt early in their marriage.[109] He took a job as a postman,[110] but gave up this work to manage and help develop his wife's mediumship.[111] Cranshawe and Duncan had markedly different physical characteristics. Whereas the former was slim and in good health, the latter had been in hospital several times, and was very much over-weight. Only five foot six inches tall, she weighed over seventeen stone.[112] The differences in characteristics and status between the two mediums coincided with the way Price visualised each woman. One reminded him of flowers, the other of a cow. As we shall see, one hypothesis put forward by Price about Duncan's mediumship was that she concealed objects by way of a secondary stomach.

Unlike Cranshawe, Duncan was an experienced medium by the 1930s. While she was still at school, she gained a reputation in her village, Callander in Perthshire, for having 'dark powers'. The local Presbyte-rian minister formalised this reputation when he accused her from the pulpit of being a witch. After her marriage to Henry, she began to develop her powers through spiritualist techniques at their home circle, and she eventually became well known in spiritualist groups for her physical manifestations of various spirit forms.[113] The influential Mau-rice Barbanell endorsed her mediumship.[114]

Helen and Henry Duncan came to London between 1930 and 1931 for a series of demonstration sittings with some Spiritualists. Price heard of this, and approached the Duncans about doing some experiments with the National Laboratory. A seance was arranged for 4 May 1931. Something of Price's adversarial stance towards Helen Duncan is re-vealed in his comment that this initial seance was not to 'be a rigid test – merely a friendly demonstration'.[115] The use of the term 'friendly' in its sporting context[116] implied that future seances would be organised in the atmosphere of a contest. As we shall see, they were.

Price dealt with Helen Duncan alternately as passive object and active cheat. His treatment of her was simultaneously more impersonal and more physically intrusive than his treatment of Cranshawe. In the first seance, according to Price, Duncan offered to strip and be thor-oughly searched. That Price would have insisted on these precautions against fraud anyway is implied by his decision to make no 'vaginal inspection' because 'it would have been rather out of keeping with a "friendly" seance'. She was dressed for the seance in a pair of black sateen knickers, a coat, and a pair of black stockings: 'All these articles were minutely examined, turned inside out and held up to the light.'

Finally, the medium entered the seance 'cabinet' (a recess with an armchair and closed curtains), and the sitting commenced.[117] Within a few seconds she fell into a trance; the curtains moved and the sitters saw 'ectoplasm' – or what Price termed 'teleplasm' – issuing from her mouth and nose.[118] Soon, it had 'spread out like an apron – still coming out of her mouth and nose – [it] bunched on her lap, entwined round her feet and touch[ed] the floor'.[119]

When the curtains of the 'cabinet' closed again, Duncan's spirit-guides, 'Peggy Hazeldine' and 'Albert', began to speak in the manner of music-hall players. 'Albert' joked with the sitters; he reminded Price of Mose, a well-known radio comedian. Henry Duncan suggested that 'Albert' try to materialise himself beside the medium. 'Albert' replied: 'Mind your own business.' Then the 'Peggy Hazeldine' voice cut in, saying that she was 'coming in a minute', but hadn't 'got a frock on yet'. Again, Henry Duncan asked 'Albert' to show himself and was told not to 'try it on'. After more jokes and conversations with Duncan's spirit-guides and the production of more 'teleplasm', the seance ended.[120]

It is evident from Price's 'Notes, Comments and Impressions of the First Seance', recorded on 9 May, that he was extremely suspicious of Helen Duncan's phenomena. Of the 'teleplasm' he wrote: 'It was exactly as if it had been placed in the mouth and the ends tucked into the nostrils. That same evening I secured a piece of gossamer and produced the identical effect in my own mouth and nostrils in the way I have indicated.'[121] The Research Council suggested two more hypotheses:

(1) that the 'teleplasm' was really some fine fabric such as cheese cloth, capable of being compressed into a small compass and then secreted in the genital passages; and (2) that the medium possesses a false or secondary stomach ... like the *rumen* or first stomach of a ruminant, and that she is able to swallow sheets of some material and regurgitate them at leisure like a cow with her cud.[122]

These questions occupied Price's thoughts when he arranged another seance with Helen Duncan for 14 May.

On the night before the seance was due to take place, Henry Duncan telephoned Price to tell him that his wife was unwell. She had vomited all night, following a seance with some Spiritualists where a woman had accidentally trodden on the ectoplasmic mass Duncan had produced. She was, moreover, extremely depressed and talking about

Helen Duncan, aged 32 (c. 1931)

suicide. According to Price, she 'appeared highly strung and nervous on the night of our second experiment'.[123] Nevertheless, the seance went ahead. For this demonstration, the Research Council asked the medium to undergo a 'medical examination' to eliminate fraud. Price wrote:

[We] did the job very thoroughly. The doors having been locked, the medium was placed upon a large settee … and in the presence of Dr. William Brown, Mrs Goldney (who has trained and worked for many months in a midwifery hospital) made a thorough vaginal and rectal examination. The rectum was examined for some distance up the alimentary canal and a very thorough vaginal examination given.

The medium was then completely undressed and sewed into a one piece garment.[124]

Revealing the kinds of pressure brought to bear on mediums who showed reluctance to undergo such indignities, Price noted that her submission to that 'unpleasant duty … was vital to any scientific report of her mediumship'. After the seance, which was similar in type to the previous one, Duncan was again subjected to the euphemistic 'medical examination'.[125] Nothing was found, but Price was now convinced that her phenomena were fraudulent. Referring to plates of photographs taken during the seance, he recorded that the material purporting to be ectoplasm was 'obviously a woven one, such as butter muslin or cheese cloth: again there is the appearance of a hem or selvedge, especially on the edge falling down the right front of the medium. Also, many "rents" are visible, as if the material had been pulled apart or worn.'[126]

The question uppermost in Price's account of further investigations into Helen Duncan's mediumship was: how was the fraud perpetrated? As Price lost interest in her mediumship, and became preoccupied with exposing her methods of deception, Duncan's status, already partly dehumanised as an experimental object, was reduced further to a thing-like adversary to be hounded, dominated and exposed. And we shall see that the more Duncan conceded to the Research Council's de-mands, the more she seemed to acquiesce in the loss of her own subjectivity and agency.[127]

As far as I can see from Price's records, he did not tell the Duncans of his doubts about Helen's mediumship, and they agreed to take part in another sitting on 21 May. At this, the third seance, the Research Council seriously considered introducing X-ray equipment to look for Duncan's hypothetical secondary stomach. However, Price had already contacted several 'electron-medical experts', and they all informed him that 'the X-rays would *not* reveal a secondary stomach or anything soft which it contained'. The Research Council also 'decided not to repeat the severe medical examination that Mrs Duncan underwent on 14th

May … [W]e decided it was not necessary at every experiment.' She was, nevertheless, asked to strip naked in the presence of three women, who examined the exterior parts of her body and dressed her in a specially prepared seance garment.[128] The seance went as before, with the addition of a 'spirit hand', which Price strongly suspected was a rubber glove. Having described the seance and reiterated his conviction that Duncan's mediumship was fraudulent, Price considered various technologies as aids in exposing her deception:

> If X-Rays will not reveal swallowed objects such as muslin or rubber gloves, I am told that such articles would put out of action (through being sucked into a tube) a stomach pump and so reveal their presence. I am also informed that a line of small rubber-covered hooks, like *fish hooks*, could be let down into the stomach and that they might catch any substance like a piece of muslin. But you would have to be sure that your line and hooks were going into the right place. This regurgitation problem will have to be settled one way or another.[129]

And so he arranged a fourth seance. Despite the apparent inability of an X-ray examination to expose a 'secondary stomach', a piece of cheese cloth, or a rubber glove, the Research Council decided that 'this should now be done after the sitting, but without previously informing the medium or her husband as to [their] intention'.[130] Halfway through this seance, 'Albert' told Price to 'put up the white light quickly'. Dr William Brown discovered blood running from the medium's nostril. He wiped the blood from her face, and the seance continued. A few moments later, while Price was pleading with 'Albert' to part with a piece of ectoplasm, the blood began to pour from both nostrils, and she started to retch. The seance came to a close.[131] Then, without warning, a battery of X-ray apparatus was brought into the room where the medium was resting. Henry Duncan agreed to have her examined, but Helen refused categorically:

> Mr. Duncan then spoke to the medium advising her to submit. The approach of her husband seemed to infuriate her, and she became hysterical. She jumped up and dealt her husband a smashing blow on the face; she then made a lunge at Dr. William Brown, who fortunately avoided the blow. She then said she wanted to retire to the lavatory, and (so that she could still be kept under observation) Mrs. Goldney said she and Dr. William Brown (being a medical man) would accompany her.

Mrs. Goldney and Dr. Brown then led Mrs. Duncan out of the *seance*-room into the hall in which was the door leading to the street. The medium found that she did *not* want to go to the lavatory, and sat down on a chair. Thinking she wanted a drink, Dr. Brown went to fetch a glass of water.

Suddenly, without the slightest warning she jumped up and pushed Mrs. Goldney aside, unfastened the door and dashed into the street where she had another attack of hysterics. Her husband dashed after her, followed by other sitters. She was found clutching the railings, screaming, and Mr. Duncan was trying to pacify her.[132]

Despite Helen Duncan's distress, Price's mind was still on the test, which, he wrote, 'had now absolutely broken down'. This was because Helen and Henry were alone together in the street, allowing ample time for Helen to pass any hidden object to Henry. However, Helen now agreed (demanded, according to Price) to be X-rayed, and to undergo vaginal and rectal examinations. These were done, but nothing was found. Price then called Henry Duncan into his office to pay him, and demanded that he allow himself to be searched. William Brown was present; he told Henry that only a second was required to enable the medium to 'pass, say a handful of cheese cloth onto her husband if she so wished'. He urged Henry 'to help him make the test as scientific as possible by turning out his pockets', but he refused.[133]

Although this seance was evidently unsatisfactory from the point of view of both parties, Price suggested – and Henry Duncan agreed to – a final test. Maybe, since the Duncans were not told of the Research Council's view of Helen's mediumship, they still hoped for ratification from the National Laboratory. Price's motivation for persisting with tests was less opaque: he wanted to know how the muslin or cheese cloth was secreted away, then produced at will. For this seance Price asked a gynaecologist and an obstetrician to carry out the 'necessary, bodily examinations' on the medium.[134] They examined her nose, mouth, throat, teeth, and the 'axillae folds under the breasts, groin, buttocks and perineum'. A vaginal examination revealed nothing abnormal; neither did the rectal examination. She was then dressed in her seance suit, tapes were tied round her ankles, and she was led to the seance room and left in the seance cabinet.[135] The examination did show, however, that Helen was in a very poor physical condition. She was suffering from infections in her nose and both ears, and she had an abscess on her arm so bad that she needed to go into a hospital for a few days after the seance.[136] That day, at the seance, 'Albert' allowed a piece of teleplasm that dangled from the medium's mouth to be cut off. The rest of the seance was a fiasco. 'Albert', according to one sitter, seemed discouraged by events. Then 'his distressed voice announc[ed]: "She is in an awful mess here."'[137] Helen Duncan was found with her face covered in blood.

Meanwhile, Price had a piece of the 'teleplasm' chemically analysed by several experts, all of whom declared it to be wood pulp of some kind. On 12 June, the Research Council confronted Henry Duncan with the evidence against Helen. Obviously cornered, Duncan admitted that his wife might have cheated, but suggested that she did so subconsciously.[138]

On 23 June, Price offered to give Henry Duncan a hundred pounds if he could induce his wife 'to swallow and regurgitate the cheese cloth, in full light, in the presence of the Council'.[139] But Price never discovered *exactly* how Helen produced her phenomena. The Duncans ignored the offer, and boarded the train for Leith on the following day. Helen gave no further seances at the National Laboratory.

Power relations governing the series of seances with Helen Duncan were clearly unequal. On the level of class, economics and gender, she was seriously disadvantaged and badly placed to defend herself against the incursions of Price and the Research Council. Their failure to recognise Duncan as a subject led to the abuse of her objectified body.[140] The fact that some male mediums, such as the teenage Schneider boys, Willi and Rudi, were subjected to similar, if less harsh,[141] procedures as those suffered by Duncan does not reduce the place of gender in relations between psychical researchers and mediums. Mediumship was constructed as intrinsically negative and passive; thus to be a medium was to occupy the subordinate female position. And as we have seen, male mediums were commonly regarded as having 'womanly' or negative characteristics.

Spiritualists complained bitterly about the treatment of mediums like Helen Duncan at the hands of psychical researchers. In 1932, Maurice Barbanell censured Harry Price's approach to the Duncan mediumship:

> In her, [Duncan] we have one of the most powerful physical mediums this century has produced. Yet she has had to face hostility, accusations of fraud, the indignities of being searched, the submission to rigorous medical examination, in order to prove her powers.

Harry Price claimed to expose her, but Mrs Duncan's position today is stronger than ever it was.[142]

Spiritualists' antagonism to the methods of psychical research did not
prevent them using the same methods when they thought the occasion
justified it. Indeed, such procedures fell within the range of standard
ways of investigating physical mediumship, whether committed Spiritualists or sceptical psychical researchers were carrying out tests.
According to Muriel Hankey, such procedures were routine for 'test
seances' at Hewat McKenzie's British College of Psychic Science.
Hankey remembered:

> Before the seance the medium would be thoroughly examined – often
> stripped and biologically examined [another euphemism for vaginal
> and rectal searches] – and then probably clad in a specially-designed
> one-piece garment, fastened at the wrists (or even covering the hands)
> and ankles, and round the neck, fastened at the back, and all ties were
> properly sealed with an identifying seal. The medium was never out
> of sight of the controllers until the end of the experiment.
>
> If the medium had to be tied to a chair (the usual wooden one with
> arms), generally several pieces of rope or cord would be used, so that
> the wrists and ankles were fastened separately to different parts of the
> chair. Sometimes the thumbs of the medium would be linked with
> cotton, and the tie of the cotton would be sealed.[143]

Here is the bound, subdued and penetrated body, justified in the name
of fraud prevention. I think, however, that it would be wrong to view
the treatment of Helen Duncan and others simply as the product of
unequal power relations between researchers and mediums, fuelled by
eroticised impulses to dominate, control and conquer. Invasive procedures were not confined to research endeavours, but owed something
to an already established tradition, associated with mediumistic performances in music-hall entertainment before the First World War,
where the exposed and constrained body of the medium was offered
as (titillating) amusement.

Price regularly attended such performances before the war. In 1910
one stage performer, a Mr Thomson, described his wife, with theatrical
hyperbole, as the 'greatest medium in the world'. He invited members
of the audience to examine everything on stage, and asked four more
people to take the medium into the dressing room, 'strip her, examine
her, and put on the special garment provided'.[144] Stage acts such as

these disappeared after the war. With so many lost on the battlefields, nobody was in the mood for theatrical spirit visitations.[145] However, the vaudeville legacy of binding and stripping mediums, combined with the demand for scientific carefulness from psychical research institutions, made such practices seem a largely conventional and acceptable part of investigative procedure. Helen Duncan was perhaps unlucky that her spirit-guide 'Albert' reminded Price of a radio entertainer.

On another level, the adversarial attitude adopted towards Duncan by the Research Council was permitted, even sanctioned, through a discourse that pivoted on a notion of 'truth', where 'truth' appeared not only as an attainable 'state' but as the *highest* priority. To this end, the 'testing' of Helen Duncan by the National Laboratory was undertaken in the atmosphere of a secular inquisition where some kind of 'verdict' *must* be decided upon. Indeed, the sense of a legal proceeding is unmistakable in Price's account of the Duncan investigation. There are the 'female warders' who take her away, undress and search her; she is restrained during investigation, and there are the psychical researchers who act as judges and 'weigh the evidence'. The Research Council at the National Laboratory (unlike some other contemporary investigators discussed below) recognised only two possible explanations for Helen Duncan's phenomena: either they were genuine or they were fraudulent, and she became an obstacle to be overcome in the pursuit of that chimera, 'truth'.[146]

The extreme mistrust that surrounded physical mediumship meant that psychical researchers could, at times, find themselves implicated in allegedly 'fraudulent' practices. This happened to Price on several occasions. His good faith and veracity were questioned with respect to the Stella C. mediumship[147] and, most notoriously, when he endorsed the apparent appearance of a naked spirit child at a suburban home in south-east London in his *Fifty Years of Psychical Research*.[148] In *Four Modern Ghosts* (1958), Trevor Hall and Eric Dingwall accuse Price of inventing the story to 'make an enthralling and sensational chapter in his book.'[149] The potential loss of personal credibility through hasty endorsement of psychic phenomena made psychical researchers even more wary of accepting evidence relating to physical phenomena.

As it turned out, Helen Duncan was prosecuted for fraud in 1933 and again in 1944, when she was sentenced to nine months' imprisonment.[150] Her opponents condemned her mediumship out of hand,[151] while her supporters took up the opposite position. Any suspicious aspects of the Duncan mediumship – the wood-pulp 'ectoplasm', the 'ectoplasmic' drapery that resembled torn cheese cloth – were glossed over by her followers in the interests of producing a wholly idealised picture of her life and mediumship. Alan Crossley, for example, wrote that she was an 'innocent and highly gifted woman' who was unjustly persecuted.[152] Similarly, Maurice Barbanell wrote a book on Helen Duncan's 1944 trial at the Old Bailey with the purpose of vindicating both her psychic powers and her integrity.[153]

This is not to suggest that all psychical researchers divided mediums into the oppositional categories of 'honest and 'dishonest'. Many explanations were given to account for phenomena. These explanations might include anything from an acceptance that the phenomena were genuine, through to a verdict of 'subconscious deception' – termed hysteria or dissociation. Muriel Hankey wrote about the phenomena of one medium, 'tested' by McKenzie: '[E]ight of the manifestations were genuine, four types were doubtful and two were artificial.' Hankey continued: 'This word *artificial* is particularly useful in bridging the gulf of doubt between genuine and fraudulent demonstrations, for much that is doubtful may be due to psychological or other causes and not deliberate cheating.'[154]

If psychical researchers were often sensitive to the nuances and idiosyncrasies of different mediums, this did not detract from the main purpose of psychical research: to sift 'truly' supernormal phenomena from normal or fraudulent occurrences. Henry Sidgwick's ambition, cited at the beginning of this chapter, that psychical research 'should steer only towards the cold, unreachable pole of absolute truth', was never possible, but in the pursuit of this goal, mediums were often casualties. Jacqueline Rose's remarks about the continuing controversies and anxieties about who is to define the 'real' Sylvia Plath seem apposite in this context:

> Whom to believe, how to know, what is the truth of the case? Behind the self-interest of the protagonists lies a drama about the limits and failure of knowledge and self-knowing. We can settle it, like indeed the proceedings of a divorce case, but only by entering into the false and damaging forms of certainty for which these settlements are renowned.[155]

Notes

1 F. Myers, 'Introduction', in E. Gurney, F. Myers and F. Podmore, *Phantasms of the Living* (1886), vol. 1 (Florida, Gainesville, 1970), pp. 1iv–1v.

2 H. Sidgwick, *Proceedings of the Society for Psychical Research*, vol. XV, 1900, pp. 456–60.

3 F. Turner, *Between Science and Religion: The Reaction to Scientific Naturalism in Late Victorian England* (New Haven, CT, Yale University Press, 1974).

4 'Participating consciousness' is a term coined by Morris Berman: the individual or culture is not an alienated observer of the cosmos, 'but a direct participant in its drama'. M. Berman, *The Reenchantment of the World* (Ithaca, NY, Cornell University Press, 1981), p. 16.

5 Myers made several attempts to define what he meant by the subliminal self: in 'The Subliminal Self', *Proceedings of the Society for Psychical Research*, II (1891–92) 301; in *Phantasms of the Living*, p. 1viii; and, most comprehensively, in *Human Personality and its Survival of Bodily Death*, 2 vols (London, Longmans Green, 1903).

6 The circumstances of Myers's death are described in A. Gauld, *The Founders of Psychical Research* (London, Routledge & Kegan Paul, 1968), pp. 332–4.

7 J. J. Cerullo, *Secularisation of the Soul: Psychical Research in Modern Britain* (Philadelphia, PA, Institute of the Study of Human Issues, 1982), pp. 48–50. See also P. Williams, 'The Making of Victorian Psychical Research: An Intellectual Elite's Approach to the Spiritual World' (PhD Thesis, University of Cambridge, 1984), pp. 125–7; Gauld, *The Founders of Psychical Research*, pp. 116–24. Gauld writes that Annie Marshall was to Myers:

> a small hint of the divine in an otherwise godless Universe; and soon his love for her became inextricably blended with his newly found religious hopes. She became at once a symbol and a manifestation of a hidden world of timeless realities, a world once apprehended by Plato, and now obscurely revealed by the strange phenomena of Spiritualism. (pp. 118–19)

For a sensitive appraisal of Butler's Christianity and philanthropy, see N. Boyd, *Three Victorian Women Who Changed Their World* (Oxford, Oxford University Press, 1982). See J. Oppenheim, *The Other World: Spiritualism and Psychical Research in England 1850–1914* (London, Cambridge University Press, 1985) for an account of Butler's crusade against child prostitution, undertaken with the journalist and Spiritualist William Stead.

8 F. Turner, 'The Conflict between Science and Religion: A Professional Dimension', *Isis*, 69 (1978) 356–76; B. Wynne, 'Physics and Psychics: Science, Symbolic Action, and Social Control in Late Victorian

England', in B. Barnes and S. Shapin (eds), *Natural Order: Historical Studies of Scientific Culture* (Beverly Hills, CA, Sage, 1979), p. 174.

9 R. Jann, 'Christianity, Spiritualism, and the Fourth Dimension in Late Victorian England', *The Victorian Newsletter*, 70 (1986) 24. The ideas of P. G. Tait and B. Stewart are elaborated in their books *The Unseen Universe* (London, 1875) and *Paradoxical Philosophy: A Sequel to the Unseen Universe* (London, 1878).

10 R. Jann, 'Christianity, Spiritualism, and the Fourth Dimension in Late Victorian England', p. 26.

11 For a comprehensive account of rapidly changing perceptions of a time and space at the *fin de siècle* in, for example, technology, medicine, the arts and philosophy, see S. Kern, *The Culture of Time and Space 1880–1918* (Cambridge, MA, Harvard University Press, 1983).

12 P. A. Y. Gunter, 'Bergson and Jung', *Journal of the History of Ideas*, 43 (1982). Bergson had an interest in psychical research, and became the president of the SPR in 1913. For his Presidential Address, see *Proceedings of the Society for Psychical Research*, XXVI (1912–13) 462–79.

13 J. Clerk Maxwell, 'Ether' (written for the *Encyclopaedia Britannica*, 9th edn) from W. D. Niven (ed.), *The Scientific Papers of James Clerk Maxwell* (New York, Dover, 1965), p. 767.

14 W. Thomson (Lord Kelvin), 'The Wave Theory of Light', in *Popular Lectures and Addresses*, vol. 1 (London, Macmillan, 1989). p. 327.

15 Wynne, 'Physics and Psychics', p. 170.

16 O. Lodge, *Ether and Reality* (London, Hodder & Stoughton, 1925), pp. 162–3. See also Lodge, *Making of Man* (1924) (London, Hodder & Stoughton, 1938); *Life and Matter: A Criticism of Professor Haekel's 'Riddle of the Universe'* (London, Norgate & Williams, 1906); *Past Years* (London, Hodder & Stoughton, 1931).

17 H. Sidgwick made this abundantly clear in his inaugural presidential address for the SPR See his 'Presidents Address', *Proceedings of the Society for Psychical Research*, I (1882–83). See also O. Lodge, *The Survival of Man* (London, Methuen, 1911), pp. 7–12, where he writes: 'Our primary aim is to be a Scientific Society, to conduct our researches and record our results in an accurate and scientific manner.' These kinds of sentiments from members of the SPR can be multiplied almost indefinitely, and they underscore the Society's own professionalising intentions. Lodge looked forward to the day when 'the psychical sciences would afford the same sort of scope to a career, the same sort of opportunities of earning a living as do the longer recognised sciences' (p. 19).

18 J. C. Greene, *Science, Ideology, and World View: Essays in the History of Evolutionary Ideas* (Berkeley, University of California Press, 1981); Turner, 'The Conflict Between Science and Religion', pp. 356–76; Wynne, 'Physics and Psychics', p. 184; J. Moore, '1859 and All That:

Remaking the Story of Evolution and Religion', in R. Chapman and C. Duval (eds), *Charles Darwin 1882–1982: A Centennial Commemorative* (Wellington, Nova Pacifia, 1982), pp. 167–94; J. Morrell and A. Thackray, *Gentlemen of Science: Early Years of the British Association for the Advancement of Science* (Oxford, Clarendon Press, 1981), ch. 5; Berman, *The Reenchantment of the World.*

19 Gurney *et al.*, *Phantasms of the Living*, p. 30.

20 Quoted by Gauld, *Founders of Psychical Research*, p. 106.

21 Lodge, *The Survival of Man*, p. 32; *Raymond*, 7th edn (London, Methuen, 1917), p. 83.

22 Quoted by Gauld, *Founders of Psychical Research*, p. 316.

23 Some historians simply dismiss psychical research as a 'pseudo-science'. See, for example, T. Hall, *The Strange Case of Edmund Gurney* (London, Duckworth, 1964). 'Crisis of faith' analysis makes similar assumptions about the scientific status of psychical research, but seekd to explain the metaphysical yearnings of psychical researchers through reference to the trauma (personal and social) of the loss of faith experience. In these texts, psychical researchers' avowed commitment to 'the scientific method' merely conceals their craving for traditional Christian comforts and rationalises their flight from rationality. See 'Introduction', above. The work of Thomas Kuhn has occasioned a change in approach to psychical research. See T. Kuhn, *The Structure of Scientific Revolutions* (London, University of Chicago Press, 1970). In view of Kuhn's ideas, some scholars began to explore the possibility that psychical research might represent an alternative paradigm to that governing mainstream science. See, for example, H. M. Collins and T. J. Pinch, *Frames of Meaning: The Social Construction of Extraordinary Science* (London, Routledge & Kegan Paul, 1982); S. Mauskopf and M. McVaugh, *The Elusive Science: Origins of Experimental Psychical Research* (Baltimore, MD, Johns Hopkins University Press, 1980). The growing influence of Foucauldian theory has led to further questions about issues of knowledge and power. How and why do some knowledges 'acquire the mantle of objective scientific truth', while others are marginalised or rejected? How and why do some scientific projects achieve professional status, while others do not? Roger Cooter explicitly poses these questions in *The Cultural Meaning of Popular Science: Phrenology and the Organisation of Consent in Nineteenth-Century Britain* (Cambridge, Cambridge University Press, 1984), p. 35. Alex Owen takes a similar approach from a feminist perspective in her *The Darkened Room: Women, Power and Spiritualism in Late Victorian England* (London, Virago, 1989).

24 Wynne, 'Physics and Psychics', p. 177.

25 'Liberal epistemology' refers to the epistemology represented by the scientific naturalists. H. Kuklick uses the phrase 'meritocratic ideal' to denote this elitist epistemology in *The Savage Within: The Social Meaning*

of British Anthropology (Cambridge, Cambridge University Press, 1991). Logie Barrow has coined the phrase 'democratic epistemology', which refers to Spiritualism's egalitarian theory of knowledge. See L. Barrow, *Independent Spirits: Spiritualism and English Plebeians 1850–1910* (London, Routledge & Kegan Paul, 1986).

26 Williams, 'The Making of Victorian Psychical Research', pp. 119, 135.

27 *Ibid.*, ch. 8. See also ch. 1 above.

28 Mauskopf and McVaugh, *The Elusive Science*, p. 17.

29 In 1932, a leading Spiritualist expressed the frustration felt by many Spiritualists with the whole business of psychical research:

> They [psychical researchers] seem vaingloriously proud of their lame and impotent conclusions, but note the results.
>
> They hold up the march of progress, permit honourable men and women to be treated as rogues and vagabonds, prevent mankind from adopting a truer and saner out-look on after-death states and the reforms consequent thereon. They withhold from the masses the joy and consolation of knowing there is no death and that love and all noble desires live on forever and become veritable treasure in heaven. (H. Bodington, *Psychic News*, 25 June 1932, p. 10)

30 See B. Inglis, *A History of the Paranormal, 1914–1939* (London, Hodder & Stoughton, 1984), for an account of the kinds of experiments and activities undertaken by psychical researchers between the wars in England. See Mauskopf and McVaugh, *The Elusive Science*, for an analysis of psychical research in America.

31 Mauskopf and McVaugh tell us that Rhine adapted the German term 'parapsychologie' to denote the field of psychical research. He intended to indicate 'not that it was *outside* psychology, but that it was "beside psychology in the older and narrower conception"' (*The Elusive Science*, p. 117).

32 P. D. Allison. 'Experimental Parapsychology as a Rejected Science', in R. Wallis (ed.), *On the Margins of Science: The Social Construction of Rejected Knowledge* (University of Keele, Keele Sociological Review Monograph No. 27, 1979), p. 288.

33 Whatley Carington, a former president of the SPR and member of its Council since 1920, wrote in 1945: 'No one to-day, [in psychical research] except possibly one or two die-hards believes in the "substantial existence" of the aether' (Whatley Carington [formerly Smith], *Telepathy: An Outline of Its Facts, Theory, and Implications* [London, Methuen, 1945], p. 60). Oliver Lodge, by contrast, continued to promulgate the theory of ether until his death in 1940. See Lodge, *Past Years*.

34 W. Brown, 'Immortality in the Light of Modern Psychology', in *Kings College Lectures on Immortality* (London, University of London Press, 1920), pp. 124–65.

35 W. Brown, *Mind, Medicine and Metaphysics: The Philosophy of a Physician* (Oxford, Oxford University Press, 1936), p. 227.

36 P. Fussell, *The Great War and Modern Memory* (Oxford, Oxford University Press, 1975), pp. 135–44.

37 J. Winter, *Sites of Memory, Sites of Mourning: The Great War in European Culture* (Cambridge, Cambridge University Press, 1995).

38 Sometimes – disconcertingly – Jones combines a modernist style with romantic sentiment. See, for example, the battle scene in Part 7:

> Who's these thirty in black harness that you can see in the last
>   flash,
> great limbed, and each helmed:
> if you could pass throughout them and beyond
> – and fetch away the bloody cloth:
> whether I live
> whether I die ['whether I die' from Launcelot at the Chapel
>   Perilous]
> But which is front, which way's the way on and where's the
>   corporal and what's this crush and all this shoving you
>   along, and someone shouting rhetorically about
>   remembering your nationality-
> and Jesus Christ – they're coming through the floor,
> endthwart and overlong:
> Jerry's through on the flank … and : Beat it! –
> that's what that one said as he ran past:
> Boshes back in Strip Trench – it's a
> monumental bollocks every time
> and we avoid wisely there is but death.

D. Jones, *In Parenthesis* (1937) (London, Faber & Faber, 1964), Part 7, pp. 180–81. See also Fussell's discussion: 'The Honourable Miscarriage of *In Parenthesis*', in *The Great War and Modern Memory*, pp. 144–54.

39 Fussell, *The Great War and Modern Memory*, p. 131.

40 The 1923 edition of *Cosmic Consciousness* was reviewed internationally. See L. Harris, *Canadian Bookman*, 6 (1924) 38; *Monist*, 3 (1933) 320; G. W. Cunningham, *Philosophical Review*, 41 (1932) 96.

41 See also such *fin-de-siècle* organizations as the Hermetic Order of the Golden Dawn. See A. Owen, 'The Sorcerer and His Apprentice: Aleister Crowley and the Magical Exploration of Edwardian Subjectivity', *Journal of British History*, 36:1 (1997) 102.

42 R. M. Bucke, *Cosmic Consciousness: A Study in the Evolution of the Human Mind* (1901) (New Jersey, Citadel Press, 1961).

43 See Mauskopf and McVaugh, *The Elusive Science*, pp. 224–5, for scientific interest in Dunne's theory. Although scientific concern with Dunne's work was short-lived, his ideas received popular recognition over the next twenty years. Detective Sergeant Alec Comryn discussed Dunne's

version of precognition in dreams in *Your Policemen Are Wondering* (London, Gollancz, 1947), pp. 189–92. In a Mass-Observation survey dealing with belief in the supernatural, Dunne's theory was mentioned frequently. Mass-Observation Archive (University of Sussex), replies to April 1942 Directive.

44 J. W. Dunne, *An Experiment with Time* (London, A. & C. Black, 1927).

45 J. B. Priestley, *Three Time Plays: Dangerous Corner, Time and the Conways, I Have Been There Before* (London, Pan, 1947), p. vii. In his 'Author's Note', Priestley explains that each play rejects ordinary linear time and introduces a different way of understanding it. *Dangerous Corner* assumes the possibility of a split in time 'to produce two alternative series of events'; *Time and the Conways* makes use of Dunne's theories; and *I Have Been There Before* posits the possibility of circular time (pp. vii–x).

46 *Ibid.*, pp. 93–180, p. viii.

47 E. Lyttelton, *Our Superconscious Mind* (London, Philip Allan, 1931), p. 8.

48 *Ibid.*, pp. 269–70.

49 F. Myers, quoted by Eric Dingwall in his 'Introduction' to Rudolf Tischner, *Telepathy and Clairvoyance* (London, Kegan Paul, 1925), p. v.

50 Mauskopf and McVaugh, *The Elusive Science*, p. 30; Carington, *Telepathy*, p. 67.

51 Carington, *Telepathy*, p. 58.

52 *Ibid.*, p. 140.

53 Mauskopf and McVaugh, *The Elusive Science*, p. 59. McDougall was voted president of the SPR in 1920.

54 *Ibid.*, p. 26.

55 *Ibid.*, for an account of the internal conflicts of the British SPR and the American SPR.

56 By 'drive', I mean something akin to Freud's *Triebe* (usually understood as sexual energy), combined with a discursive trend. Thus 'drive', in this context, denotes the dynamics of unconscious impulse and discourse. It could be read as emotionally invested discourse. See J. Cash, 'Ideology and Affect: The Case of Northern Ireland', *Political Psychology*, 10:4 (1989) 703–24. For a clear and concise discussion of the development of Freud's thought on the subject of sexual energy see P. Hirst and P. Woolley, *Social Relations and Human Attributes* (London, Tavistock, 1982), pp. 143–9.

57 M. Berman, *Coming to Our Senses: Body and Spirit in the Hidden History of the West* (New York, Simon & Schuster, 1989), p. 54.

58 This is not, of course, to suggest that unconscious processes are the sole determinants of ideology.

59 See, for example, B. Easlea, *Witch Hunting, Magic and the New Philosophy: An Introduction to Debates of the Scientific Revolution 1450–1750*

(Brighton, Harvester, 1980), ch. 5; C. Merchant, *The Death of Nature: Women, Ecology and the Scientific Revolution* (1980) (San Francisco, Harper, 1990); E. Fox Keller, *Reflections on Gender and Science* (New Haven, CT, Yale University Press, 1985), ch. 3; K. Thomas, *Man and the Natural World: Changing Attitudes in England 1500–1800* (Harmondsworth, Penguin, 1983); Berman, *The Reenchantment of the World*.

60 Easlea, *Witch Hunting, Magic and the New Philosophy*, p. 242. See also T. Laqueur, *Making Sex: Body and Gender from the Greeks to Freud* (Cambridge, MA, Harvard University Press, 1992); Merchant, *The Death of Nature*; Fox Keller, *Reflections on Gender and Science*, ch. 4. J. Klaits, *Servants of Satan: The Age of the Witchhunts* (Bloomington, Indiana University Press, 1985), ch. 3.

61 B. Easlea, *Fathering the Unthinkable: Masculinity, Scientists and the Nuclear Arms Race* (London, Pluto, 1983), p. 21. The gendering of scientific knowledge (where, when and how?) remains a controversial topic. David Noble agues that misogynist science was not born with the establishment of the mechanical tradition. The anti-female stance of Western science took root in the medieval ecclesiastical academy – an all-male homosocial culture where chastity was insisted upon and women were regarded as spiritual pollutants. D. Noble, *A World Without Women: The Christian Clerical Culture of Western Science* (New York, Alfred Knopf, 1992). Other perspectives include L. Schiebinger, 'Feminine Icons: The Face of Early Modern Science', *Critical Inquiry*, 14 (Summer 1988) 661–91. Schiebinger distinguishes two traditions which both vied for the power of representation in the age of the Enlightenment. One was the 'feminine', neo-Platonist tradition which dominated on the Continent before and after the early modern period. The other was the more familiar Baconian tradition, dominant in England – 'virile, ready to act and command' (p. 663). E. Fox Keller introduces further complexity to the topic by pointing to the ambiguity of Bacon's sexual metaphors (*Reflections on Gender and Science*, ch. 2). For a close contextual analysis of sexual allegories in medical writings and their myth-making capacities between the eighteenth and twentieth centuries, see Ludmilla Jordanova, *Sexual Visions: Images of Gender and Medicine between the Eighteenth and Twentieth Centuries* (Hemel Hempstead, Harvester Wheatsheaf, 1989).

62 L. Nead, *Myths of Sexuality: Representations of Women in Victorian Britain* (Oxford, Basil Blackwell, 1990), pp. 19–20.

63 C. Eagle Russet, *Sexual Science: The Victorian Construction of Womanhood* (Cambridge, MA, Harvard University Press, 1989); L. Schiebinger, *The Mind Has No Sex: Women in the Origins of Modern Science* (Cambridge, MA, Harvard University Press, 1989.

64 Images of animal life permeated scientific perceptions of femininity in the nineteenth and twentieth centuries. 'The bitch in heat', wrote

the physician Augustus Gardiner in the 1930s, 'has the genitals tume-
fied and reddened, and a bloody discharge. The human female has
almost the same' (quoted by Laqueur, *Making Sex*, p. 213).

65 Quoted by E. Showalter, *Sexual Anarchy: Gender and Culture at the Fin
de Siècle* (London, Virago, 1991), p. 129.

66 Easlea, *Fathering the Unthinkable*, ch. 2.

67 This film is described in ch. 6 above. See A. Light, *Forever England:
Femininity, Literature and Conservatism between the Wars* (London,
Routledge, 1991), for other representations in literature.

68 Jordanova, *Sexual Visions*, ch. 6.

69 *Ibid.*, pp. 125–7.

70 Sometimes referred to as 'counter-norms'. See M. Mulkay, *Science and
the Sociology of Science* (London, Allen & Unwin, 1979), chs 2 and 3. Fox
Keller argues that the geneticist Barbara McClintock has forged a new
approach to scientific research through her rejection of the traditional
divisions in science between subject and object, and her degree of
empathy with plant life. See Fox Keller, *Reflections on Gender and Science*,
ch. 9.

71 P. Medawar, 'Is the Scientific Paper a Fraud?', *The Listener*, 12 September 1963, p. 377.

72 Fox Keller, 'Dynamic Objectivity: Love, Power, and Knowledge', in
Reflections on Gender and Science.

73 Mauskopf and McVaugh, *The Elusive Science*, ch. 4.

74 The results of this research were published in 1934 in Rhine's book
Extra-Sensory Perception (Boston, MA, Boston Society for Psychic Research, 1934).

75 E. Garrett, *My Life as a Search for the Meaning of Mediumship* (New York,
Arno Press, 1975), p. 177.

76 *Ibid.*, p. 178.

77 H. Price, *Search for Truth: My Life for Psychical Research* (London, Collins,
1942), pp. 95–6.

78 *Ibid.*, pp. 12, 16, 84–5.

79 Mauskopf and McVaugh, *The Elusive Science*, p. 211.

80 Harry Price to Sir Oliver Lodge, 28 April, 1923, 'Stella C. File', Harry
Price Library, University of London.

81 Mauskopf and McVaugh, *The Elusive Science*, p. 211.

82 *Psychic News*, 25 June 1932, p. 5.

83 M. Barbanell, *The Case of Helen Duncan* (London, Psychic Press, 1945),
ch. 2.

84 M. Barbanell, 'Editorial', *Psychic News*, 25 June 1932, p. 6.

85 Price, *Search for Truth*, p. 83.

86 *Ibid.*, p. 123.

87 *Ibid.*, p. 83.

88 Baron Von Schrenck-Notzig was a respected scientist and psychical

researcher who worked with continental mediums. His most famous publication in the field was: *Phenomena of Materialisation: A Contribution to the Investigation of Mediumistic Teleplastics*, trans. E. E. Fournier d'Albe (London, Kegan Paul, 1920). See also P. Tabori, *Harry Price Ghost Hunter* (London, Sphere, [1950] 1974); Inglis, *A History of the Paranormal*.

89 Harry Price to Baron Von Schrenck-Notzig, 14 April, 1923, 'Stella C. File', Harry Price Library, University of London.

90 H. Price, *Stella C.: An Account of Some Original Experiments in Psychical Research* (1925), 'Introduction' by J. Turner (London, Souvenir Press, 1973), p. 62.

91 Tabori, *Harry Price Ghost Hunter*, p. 82.

92 Harry Price to Stella Cranshawe, 14 September 1923, 'Stella C. File', Harry Price Library, University of London.

93 Stella Cranshawe to Harry Price, reproduced in J. Turner, 'Introduction' to Harry Price, *Stella C.*, pp. 27, 31, 34.

94 *Ibid.*, p. 36.

95 Price's gloss on the Stella C. mediumship was taken up by James Turner,who wrote that the low priority she accorded to seance work in her life was 'further proof (if any is needed) that she was genuine': Turner, 'Introduction' to Harry Price, *Stella C.*, p. 26.

96 Price, *Stella C.*, p. 61.

97 'Rules for Regulating the Stella C. Research Sittings', H. Price, *Stella C.*, Appendix 4, pp. 163–4.

98 In 1922, *Scientific America* offered a $2,500 prize for a satisfactory manifestation of physical phenomena under test conditions (see Mauskopf and McVaugh, *The Elusive Science*, p. 22). It seems that Price considered entering Cranshawe for this competition, because he suggested deducting her expenses for the American trip from the prize money in a letter to Malcom Bird. See Price, *Stella C.*, Appendix 5, pp. 168–9.

99 Tabori, *Harry Price Ghost Hunter*.

100 Price, *Stella C.*, Appendix 9, p. 173.

101 Harry Price to Sir Oliver Lodge, 28 April 1923, 'Stella C. File', Harry Price Library, University of London.

102 Price, *Stella.C.*, p. 74.

103 *Ibid.*, p. 75. A parallel situation to that of Price and Cranshawe might be found in the relationship between William Crookes and Florence Cook. In the nineteenth century, the physicist and pioneer psychical researcher William Crookes idealised the young medium Florence Cook and her materialised spirit guide, Katie King. He formed a sentimental attachment to Cook and, some implied, a sexual one too. See T. Hall, *The Story of Florence Cook and William Crookes* (London, Duckworth, 1962). Hall's somewhat scurrilous version of events is balanced by Owen, *The Darkened Room*, pp. 228–30.

104 Price, *Stella C.*, p. 71.

105 *Ibid.*, p. 165.

106 *Ibid.*, pp. 119, 71.

107 *Ibid.*, p. 61.

108 H. Price, *Regurgitation and the Duncan Mediumship* (London, Council at the Rooms of the National Laboratory of Psychical Research, 1931), p. 11.

109 A. Crossley, *The Story of Helen Duncan: Materialization Medium* (Devon, Arthur Stockwell, 1975), p. 20.

110 *Ibid.*, p. 21.

111 Price, *Regurgitation and the Duncan Mediumship*, p. 11.

112 Price, *Stella C.*, p. 61; Price, *Regurgitation and the Duncan Mediumship*, p. 11.

113 Crossley, *The Story of Helen Duncan.*

114 B. Maurice, *The Case of Helen Duncan* (London, Psychic Press, 1945).

115 Price, *Regurgitation and the Duncan Mediumship*, p. 13. Price does not reveal his financial arrangements with the Duncans. We know, however, that the National Laboratory must have paid something for Helen Duncan's services because Price writes about paying Henry Duncan (*ibid.*, pp. 61–2).

116 The term 'friendly' is intended in the colloquial sense, as in 'friendly football match'.

117 *Ibid.*, pp. 13–14.

118 *Ibid.*, p. 16. Price said he preferred the term 'teleplasm' to ectoplasm because 'ectoplasm was a term long used to denote the outer layer, or hyaloplasm, of a vegetable cell' (p. 94).

119 *Ibid.*, pp. 16–17.

120 *Ibid.*, pp. 16–18.

121 *Ibid.*, p. 21.

122 *Ibid.*, p. 25.

123 *Ibid.*, pp. 27–8.

124 *Ibid.*, pp. 30–31.

125 *Ibid.*, pp. 30–33. Eric Dingwall of the SPR also claimed that 'genuine mediums never object to tests' in his *How to Go to a Medium: A Manual of Instruction* (London, Kegan Paul, 1927), p. 11.

126 Price, *Regurgitation and the Duncan Mediumship*, p. 36.

127 For a convincing psychoanalytic interpretation of this kind of sado-masochistic process, see J. Benjamin, *The Bonds of Love: Psychoanalysis, Feminism, and the Problem of Domination* (London, Virago, 1990), ch. 2.

128 Price, *Regurgitation and the Duncan Mediumship*, pp. 39–41.

129 *Ibid.*, pp. 49–50; emphasis added.

130 *Ibid.*, p. 55.

131 *Ibid.*, p. 60.

132 *Ibid.*, p. 61.

133 *Ibid.*, pp. 61–2.

134 *Ibid.*, p. 69.

135 Appendix D: 'Report by Dr. X., M. D., F. R. C. S., of —— Hospital Concerning his Examination of the Medium at the Fifth *Seance*, Thursday, June 4th, 1931 (*ibid.*, p. 106).

136 *Ibid.*, p. 72. For some unknown reason, information about the infections in Ducan's nose and ears was omitted from the published report. Dr X's full report is available in the 'Helen Duncan File', Harry Price Library, University of London.

137 Appendix E: 'Impressions of Two *Seances* with Mrs Duncan held on May 28th, 1931, and June 4th, 1931, by Professor D. F. Fraser-Harris, M.D., D.Sc., F.R.S.E.' (*ibid.*, p. 110).

138 *Ibid.*, p. 80.

139 *Ibid.*, p. 81.

140 Alex Owen notes that the Sidgwick group, comprising Sidgwick, Myers, Gurney and Leaf, also bound mediums with straps and padlocks in the interests of fraud prevention. 'Here', she writes, 'the motif of male mastery surfaced around the relationship between psychical researchers and lower-class mediums in an expression of sexual and class difference' (*The Darkened Room*, p. 231).

141 H. Price, *Fifty Years of Psychical Research: A Critical Survey* (London, Longmans, 1939), ch. V.

142 M. Barbanell, *Psychic News*, 2 July 1932, p. 1. Another contributor to *Psychic News* complained about the treatment of Helen Duncan by a psychical researcher in Belfast:

> 'It is all very well to be stripped and searched', said an 'investigator' to Mrs Duncan in Belfast the other day, 'but I would like you to put your fingers down your throat and be sick, so as to be quite certain.' Mrs Duncan looked at her … Then, she did as she was asked, and was sick. Indeed, she vomited right throughout the seance. How long must we tolerate stupid vivisection by ignorant psychic researchers? ('Vivisecting Mediums', *Psychic News*, 18 June 1932, p. 6)

143 M. Hankey, *James Hewat McKenzie, Pioneer of Psychical Research: A Personal Memoir* (London, Aquarian Press, 1963), p. 81.

144 Price, *Search for Truth*, pp. 62, 39, 57, 58.

145 *Ibid.*, p. 58.

146 J. Rose, *The Haunting of Sylvia Plath* (London, Virago, 1991), ch. 3, makes similar points with respect to the many constructions placed on the 'true character' of Sylvia Plath and the meaning of her work.

147 P. Bond, 'The Mediumship of Stella C.', unpublished manuscript, *c.* 1970, Harry Price Library, University of London.

148 Price, *Fifty Years of Psychical Research*.

149 Quoted by D. Cohen, *Price and His Spirit Child Rosalie* (London, Regency,

1965), p. 16. Cohen's own book is devoted to the vindication of Price in general and the 'Rosalie' episode in particular. For further commentary on Rosalie, see Tabori, *Harry Price Ghost Hunter* and 'The End of Rosalie?' in P. Tabori and P. Raphael, *Beyond the Senses: A Report On Psychical Research and Occult Phenomena in the Sixties* (London, Souvenir Press, 1971), pp. 150–68. This publication contains a long letter to the editors which purports to tell the 'true' story of Rosalie in the form of a confession. The anonymous writer claims that her father persuaded her to pretend to be the spirit of the dead child, Rosalie, in order to please, by this deception, Rosalie's mother, to whom he owed money (pp. 150–61).

150 G. Nelson, *Spiritualism and Society* (London, Routledge & Kegan Paul, 1969), pp. 165–7.

151 See, for example, H. J. D. Murton, 'Editorial: The Case of Mrs Duncan', *Light*, LXIV (April 1944) 144–7.

152 Crossley, 'Author's Preface', *The Story of Helen Duncan*.

153 M. Barbanell, *The Case of Helen Duncan* (London, Psychic Press, 1945).

154 Hankey, *James Hewat McKenzie*, p. 80.

155 Rose, *The Haunting of Sylvia Plath*, p. 98.

8

Becoming a medium

From a purely utilitarian perspective, mediumship was not without its attractions and advantages. Spiritualists cherished and respected their mediums; they occupied an authoritative position in Spiritualist circles at a time when other women were being returned to the home, or confined to low-paid, low-status 'women's work' in the post-World War I backlash against women in the 'male' workforce. Mediums also benefited from Spiritualism's democratic, anti-elitist outlook and its privileging of feminine insight – seance conventions fostered the speaking woman, even if they disowned subjective agency. On the other hand, successful mediumship entailed operating within prescribed limits associated with traditional images of transcendent femininity. Neither did mediumship offer financial rewards, or public respect. On the contrary, mediums were marginal figures in the larger community, with ambiguous status: silent speech-makers who were neither wholly Christian nor pagan, mother nor maid, experimental object nor full subject, they continually evaded classification, and thus a secure place in the order of things. Like other ambiguous groups and individuals, mediums were often treated as if they brought harm in some vague way:[1] they 'preyed' on the bereaved; maybe they acted for satanic or 'enemy forces'; they were 'sexual deviants' or the bearers of some strange and mad sickness. Generally pilloried and disbelieved, yet suspected of cultivating and manipulating murky and unhealthy powers, they could not have led very comfortable lives. But from what we have seen, utilitarian gains and losses do not seem to have figured much in the development of a medium. Neither Spiritualists nor initiates regarded mediumship straightforwardly as a profession.[2] Rather, they perceived it as fundamental to the personality – a 'state of being' rather than a function, duty or job.

I want to begin this chapter by briefly reviewing the cultural components which, I have argued, contributed to the construction of the mediumistic identity. I shall then move on to a discussion of the impact of power relations – specifically the role of the powerful other – on this identity. In taking this approach, I stress that the mediumistic 'self' was not a stable product of private conviction but a contingent and profoundly unstable identity that grew and developed – or, alternatively, was damaged and undermined – in relations with others. Such relations were mediated by hierarchical structures, such as class, gender and family organisation. Disturbingly, a common thread in the construction of the mediumistic persona was the fantasy of inevitable feminine subordination. In the final section, I attempt to deal with the question of why mediums commonly adopted a submissive role in their relations with both humans and spirits.

Identification as a medium was a complex process with no overriding determinants. Each interpellation[3] was bound up with cultural background, personal experience and the giving and receiving of the name 'medium'. As we saw in Chapter 1, mediums usually came from communities where supernatural activity was taken for granted and woven into daily life. In material visions of heaven, in the folklore surrounding ghosts, poltergeists and the banshee, or in Catholic quarters where it was assumed that the departed 'pray for us' and 'do know … what goes on earth',[4] people expressed their continuing relations with the dead. These relations gained new poignancy and urgency in the wake of the First World War. Attempts to make the experiences of the trenches and massive loss of life comprehensible relied partly on existing currents of animistic and mystical thought.[5] Clare Sheridan learned of a concrete heaven and equally concrete and terrifying hell from family servants, and she built a pagan altar of her own in a secret part of her father's estate. Following the death of her husband, Wilfred, in the Great War, she turned to Spiritualism as a way of maintaining contact with him. Eileen Garrett grew up in a heterodox household amid the rich magical lore of County Meath, where the wail of the banshee warned of impending death. Helen Duncan and Helen Hughes came from communities where it was expected that certain people should have supernatural ability. Edith Clements knew of the survival of the dead through her Catholic upbringing and visions she had as a child. Moreover, all the mediums discussed in this book claimed to have encountered the supernatural world in direct and intense ways before becoming mediums.

In Chapter 2, I noted Eileen Garrett's and Clare Sheridan's intense involvement with Catholicism and Spiritualism. For them, feeling was explicitly part of cognition; *participation*, rather than *observation*, structured their understanding of psychic reality. The same can be said of many other mediums. Spiritualists insisted that mediums were passive channels of spirit messages, but this was never true of the mediums discussed here as far as their *early* experiences of psychic life were concerned. Far from being passive at these times, each medium became passionately immersed in the drama of the moment. Frequently these passions revolved around catastrophic events. Edith Clements repeatedly saw visions when she was in a condition of despair about the death of her mother and worried about her own health. Clare Sheridan had recently lost her adored son, Dick, when she experienced the spirit world through the mediumship of her friend, Shirley Eshelby. Before becoming a medium, Estelle Roberts had one of her most intense encounters with the spirit world on the death of her husband, Hugh. A few years into their marriage, Hugh was suffering from Bright's disease and could not work. Estelle supported the family on the money she received from part-time domestic work. On returning home from work one lunch time, she found to her horror that Hugh was dying. While neighbours looked after their children, she sat with him through the night. He died looking at her, and she saw his spirit leave his body.[6] Spiritualism intervened in Gladys Leonard's life soon after a family catastrophe following the death of her grandfather. When Gladys's uncle and father discovered that they had been left nothing in his will, her uncle committed suicide with his wife, and her father became so erratic in his behaviour that, according to Gladys, he 'made it impossible for us to remain with him'. Her mother sold the house, furniture, yacht and children's toys, and the remaining family tried to adjust to what seemed to them 'the absolute squalor of a new condition of things'.[7] In Spiritualism, she found relief from childhood fears about death and from her current situation. 'Sitting in the cheap wooden chair' at a local Spiritualist meeting, 'I felt reassurance and peace steal over me, such as I had never felt before.'[8] Similarly, Geraldine Cummins's first experience of prevision occurred in the midst of her wartime anxiety about her brother Harry, then serving with the Fifth Gurkhas in Gallipoli. Her prevision took the form of a dream in which a voice told her: 'You will never see Harry again.' She awoke in deep distress.[9]

The powerful other

Bereavement and anxiety were hardly the only emotional contexts in which encounters with the unseen occurred. Contact with the supernatural world could be discovered through a variety of human relations, ranging from love to hate, and were often constituted in division, conflict and feelings of powerlessness.

Doris Stokes's involvement with the spirit world came about through her relationship with her autocratic, but benevolent father – a relationship which, for her, continued after his death when she was thirteen years old. She remembered him during his lifetime as the undisputed authority and 'guiding light in our family'. Her mother, she thought, was 'very practical when it came to housework – but for everything else she leaned on father. He was the one with ideas.'[10] Before the Great War he worked as a blacksmith in the Midlands town of Grantham. Having been gassed in the war, he was unable to work much afterwards, and the family was desperately poor. By the time Doris was born, in 1919, he had given up work altogether. The family survived on his ten shillings a week sickness benefit, and his wife took in washing.[11] For Doris Stokes, his authority came from his status as head of the household, his moral integrity, and her belief in his uncanny ability to know the thoughts and intentions of others.[12]

Stokes's description of her father and her relationship with him was mediated through the ancient discourse of 'the Father' (exemplified in the Christian Scriptures) who has the power to save, punish and demand sacrifice. As a child of six or seven in the 1920s, Stokes became ill with impetigo and rheumatic fever. It was then that she became dramatically aware of this paternal power to save. As the days wore on, her illness grew worse, and soon it seemed to reach crisis. Aware of her mother's sobs and the prayers of the curate beside her bed, she heard 'somewhere in the shadows' her father's voice declaring: 'No! she shall *not* die':

> From that moment on father devoted himself to curing me. He'd stood by and let the doctors do their best, now he was going to take over. He scoured the fields for special plants and herbs and brewed up concoctions, one of herbs and one of coal tar. My head had been shaved and father rubbed his concoctions into my scalp three times a day. The neighbours might have scoffed but slowly, to everyone's amazement, I began to recover.[13]

The next time Stokes's father appeared in the role of saviour, he was dead. Stokes had just married and her husband, John, was away fighting in the Second World War. After receiving official notice that her husband was missing in the Arnhem operation, she became frantic: 'I thought I'd die of suspense. The constant wear on my nerves, the violent swings from hope to despair were driving me mad. Anything must be better than this endless worrying.' She visited a Spiritualist church, where the medium told her that John was dead,[14] and she returned home in a state of panic. In the midst of her trauma, a voice said: 'My child, I've come to tell you your husband's not with us on this side of life and on Christ's birthday you will have proof of this.' Stokes said to herself: 'I'm going round the twist.' Then the bedroom door swung open:

> My mouth dropped open. He looked as real and as solid as he did when he was alive. The years rolled back and I was thirteen again.
>   'Dad?' I whispered.
>   'I never lied to you, did I Doll?' he asked.
>   'I don't think so,' I said.
>   'I'm not lying to you now. John is not with us and on Christmas day you will have proof of this.' Then as I watched, he vanished.[15]

On this occasion, Stokes's subordinate position to her father, emphasised by the remark 'I was thirteen years old again', brought comfort, hope and security. Her next encounter with paternal power called for sacrifice.

As it turned out, Stokes's husband survived, but she lost her baby son, John Michael. The spirit of her father warned her of his death. This occurred one evening. As she bent over the tub to bath her baby, she began to feel a prickle at the back of her neck, and a voice said: 'He's done his time on earth, … He's got to come back to spirit.'[16]

Stokes tells us that soon after this incident, she saw her father standing by the door; he said to her: 'He has to come back. At quarter to three next Friday I'll come for him and you must hand him over to me. Don't worry, I'll take good care of him.'[17]

John Michael did become ill, and his mother took him to a hospital. On the Friday of his predicted death, a policeman called to tell the family that John Michael's condition was worse. Stokes felt her 'heart drop to the bottom of [her] shoes'; she felt that she was 'trapped in a nightmare and … couldn't wake up'. Time seemed to stop: 'I gazed for hours, or maybe only seconds [at John Michael] and when I raised my head, my father was standing on the other side of the cot.' In the final minutes of John Michael's life, Stokes and her dead father faced each other:

> He didn't say a word. He looked steadily at me and then silently held out his hands. I clutched John Michael more tightly, but still my father held out his hands. There was a long pause. *I just didn't have a choice.* Slowly, reluctantly, I passed my baby across, and at that very instant father took my son in his arms, I looked down and saw my little John Michael was dead.
>
> When I looked up again my father was gone. The spell was broken. Tears were streaming down my face and terror, panic, pain were flooding through me.[18]

Stokes's conflation of paternal power with God is complete at this time of crisis. The authoritative father demands the sacrifice of her child, and simultaneously moves to protect her against the pain of her sacrifice by promising the child's survival in another world.

Stokes's experiences with the spirit world were mediated through her relationship with a powerful other whose demands seemed undeniable. Eileen Garrett also came to know the spirit world through her emotional responses to a dominant other. But if Stokes touched the unseen world in trust, despair and sacrifice, Garrett's early contact with psychic events and the afterlife was fashioned in feelings of loneliness, powerlessness and, finally, hatred and revenge.

I noted above that Garrett grew up in unhappy circumstances in the home of her aunt and uncle, Martha and William Little.[19] She remembered her aunt as a cold and distant person. The child Eileen would run up to her, 'but her firm hands would take hold of [her] shoulders and turn [her] quietly aside'. Garrett wrote: 'She never pushed me from her roughly, but simply removed my fingers from her hands and turned away.'[20] Starved of the company and affection of her aunt, the child wove romantic fantasies around the objects and photographs in her room. And – as we saw in Chapter 4 – she learned to protect herself against her aunt's disapproval of her 'too lively imagination' by shutting out her voice.

Divisions at home deepened as Garrett grew older. She was intractable and unpopular at school; she saw children who were invisible to everyone else, and her aunt accused her of telling lies. These 'failings', as well as her attraction to the Catholic religion, angered her fiercely Protestant aunt.[21] As Garrett's conflicts at home and school increased, so did her sense of connection with nature. She felt that she was closer to 'the animals and growing things around the farm' where she lived than she was to the human world.[22] Her way of perceiving and acting upon the world embarrassed and exasperated her aunt:

> As a child I deeply resented the fact that no grown-up believed anything I said. When I expressed dislike of people from their touch or smell, I was always reprimanded by my aunt. When I said that someone hurt me who had in reality only stroked [my] hair or touched my face, I told the truth; but the horror produced on my aunt's face by such statements made me realise that she considered I had committed a misdemeanour; I was bewildered by this treatment. I was constantly tearful and wondered why no one believed me when I described exactly what I saw and felt. I could not understand why no one seemed to like me. My only peace came from being alone; no wonder my room became my haven of safety, and 'My Children' and the growing things, my only companions.[23]

This conflict culminated with Garrett's taking violent revenge on her aunt following a quarrel between them over one of Garrett's visions: a lifelike vision of her other aunt, Leon, who appeared to her when she was sitting on the porch of Aunt Martha's house. Leon had a baby in her arms, and she seemed tired and ill. Believing that she had come to visit, Garrett ran to fetch her Aunt Martha. By the time they had returned to the porch, Leon and her baby had disappeared. Martha Little questioned Garrett closely on the matter and declared that she did not believe a thing she described; she had been cruel to play such a joke, and would be punished. The following morning Garrett awoke with her head aching and with feelings of 'cold hate' towards her aunt.

She was too ill to go to school, and went to rest in the garden. When she saw her aunt's beloved ducklings floating on the lake beyond the garden, she knew they were the means of her revenge:

> Bending over the edge of the water at the shore I caught each baby bird as it passed close by me, and in quick succession I held each one under the water until I drowned the entire brood. Then I laid the dead ducks in the grass beside me and was immediately overcome with a terrible dread of my aunt's wrath. I began to think, as I wondered, how she would punish me, that now God must come and His punishment would be greater than any my aunt might visit upon me. I remained rooted to the spot, frozen with fear, waiting for God's wrath to fall. I felt that my life would surely be wiped out after this last grave wrongdoing. The very intensity of my fear produced a strange state of suspended quiet, in which I waited.[24]

As Garrett waited for some terrible punishment to fall upon her, she saw movement around the ducks. Soon 'a grey smoke-like substance' seemed to rise from their bodies: 'This fluid stuff began to move and curl as it rose and gradually … take on new shape as it moved away from the bodies of these little dead ducks.' It dawned on Garrett that the ducks were 'coming alive' again.[25]

Few of Garrett's early experiences with the supernatural occurred while she was in repose or otherwise passively disposed; rather, when she was in the grip of intense feeling. The episode with the ducks produced a sensation of dread that was so profound that it seemed to take her into another mode of consciousness where the boundaries between the dead and the living were traversed. When she saw the ducks escape death, she, too, seemed to escape (or resist) her powerless position, because 'fear had now given way to amazement in the face of this spectacle'.[26]

Dion Fortune's first experience of the supernatural was also constituted in fear of an authoritative other, and in resistance to that authority. In her remarkable semi-autobiographical *Psychic Self Defence*, Fortune gives a vivid description of her emotional disintegration under conditions of continual anxiety and powerlessness. When she was twenty years old, and known as Violet Firth, she was employed in some kind of educational establishment – possibly a private girls' school. Her employer, known as 'the Warden', liked to dominate her staff; this she accomplished, in part, by getting them to testify against one another.

It so happened that the Warden 'wished to get rid of' one of Fortune's close colleagues, and she called upon her to corroborate a series of groundless accusations against him. Her method of collecting evidence was to look into Fortune's eyes 'with a concentrated gaze and say, "Such and such things happened"'. Fortune was fully aware that the Warden's accusations were spurious, but to her extreme surprise she found herself supporting her against a 'man [she] had no reason to believe was other than perfectly straight'. This experience so disorientated her that she seemed to feel the carpet move under her feet. She went to her room and fell asleep.[27] Following this incident, and another involving the Warden and financial fraud, Fortune sought to end her employment. The institution required a term's notice, so she 'watched for an opportunity that would justify [her] in walking out'.[28] This was not long in coming, since the Warden had a very bad temper. Fortune prepared to leave, and the Warden said to her:

> 'Very well, if you want to go you shall. But before you go you have to admit that you are incompetent and have no self-confidence.'
>
> To which I replied, being still full of fight, that if I were incompetent, why did she not dismiss me herself, and anyway, I was the product of her own training-school. Which remark naturally did not improve matters.
>
> Then commenced the most extraordinary litany. She resumed her old trick of fixing me with an intent gaze, and said:
>
> 'You are incompetent and you know it. You have no self-confidence, and you have to admit it.'[29]

The Warden kept chanting these two statements like a mantra. The battle between the two women continued for four hours, until 'everything began to feel unreal'. Fortune thought that once she agreed to the other woman's suggestions, she 'was done for', but she was getting 'near the end of [her] resources'. Finally she broke the deadlock by pretending to be beaten. She went down on her knees to the Warden, and begged forgiveness for all her supposed wrongdoing.[30] Finally, the Warden released her. Returning to her room, Fortune fell into an exhausted sleep, and woke with feelings of fear that overwhelmed her:

> All I know was that out of the depths of my mind a most terrible state of fear was rising up and obsessing me. Not fear of any thing or person. Just plain fear without an object, but nonetheless terrible for

that. I lay in bed with all the physical symptoms of intense fear. Dry mouth, sweating palms, thumping heart and shallow hasty breathing. My heart was beating so hard that at each beat a loose brass knob on the bedstead rattled ... My mind was a blank. I was thoroughly cowed and very exhausted, and my one desire was to get away.[31]

Fortune's family removed her from the institution, but she did not recover and came to believe that the Warden possessed baleful occult powers that she used to deplete Fortune's 'vital energies'. Afraid of being attacked again (by this version of a vampire mother), she took steps to protect herself by entering an occult order: 'Within an hour of the ceremony I felt a change, and it is only upon the rarest occasions since then, after some psychic injury, that I have a temporary return of those depleting attacks of exhaustion.'[32]

Interpellation

Although Fortune, Garrett and Stokes apparently had the supernatural world forced on them through the sheer emotional intensity of their experiences, this did not mean automatic identification as mediums. In all the cases described in this book, the women were unsure what their early visions, 'voices' and uncanny feelings meant, or how to deal with them. Some, like Edith Clements, were afraid that satanic forces governed their perceptions; most suspected that madness lay at the root of their abnormal faculties, and few welcomed the presence of unseen forces in their lives.

Given the negative connotations attached to the supernatural – superstition, madness, badness, immorality (sexual and otherwise), fraud, delusion, illusion, – it is not so surprising that many women who had psychic experiences chose to align themselves with the Spiritualist movement and become mediums. Even so, this did not happen as a simple consequence of choice. Each medium was ideologically 'called into being' (interpellated) through *recognition* from an authoritative individual or group, who functioned as the bearer of news concerning a medium's identity. Sometimes an individual's authority derived from high status within the Spiritualist movement, sometimes from their apparently fated entrance into a medium's life. Sometimes the naming of a medium issued from nobody in particular, but was bestowed by reputation in the local community.

Of all the mediums considered here, not one identified as one until her powers were acknowledged or 'discovered' by an external authority. As we have seen, an old man informed Helen Hughes of her 'destiny'. His seemingly providential visit secured her identity as a medium. A providential stranger also entered Edith Clements's life at a time of crisis, and told her the meaning of her visions. While she was still at school, Helen Duncan gained a reputation in her village for having 'dark powers'. The local Presbyterian minister formalised this reputation when he accused her from the pulpit of being a witch. And when a young man from the village was mysteriously found dead, some villagers asserted that Duncan had put a curse on him.[33] After her marriage, her husband Henry encouraged her to develop her powers through Spiritualist techniques at their home circle. Gladys Leonard and Estelle Roberts were both told by established mediums that they, too, had psychic powers.[34] Eileen Garrett's husbands and aunt denied her encounters with the unseen world, but they were affirmed elsewhere.

When Garrett was ten years old, gypsies set up camp near her home in County Meath. She visited them and an old woman, who appeared to hold an important position within her community, told her stories about her youth in Poland and Spain. She received Garrett's own stories about the 'children' and the ducks and her way of perceiving with equanimity, and told her: 'I was born with the "seeing eye" and have the power to heal and kill. The things you see and hear are therefore not strange to me.'[35] Garrett's experiences with the supernatural continued throughout the rest of her childhood and into adulthood, and became a cause of conflict in two out of her three marriages (her second husband died in the Great War shortly after their wedding). Husbands one and three believed that her visions and voices showed that she was on the verge of insanity,[36] and persuaded her to visit physicians and psychiatrists who, wrote Garrett, 'obviously understood nothing of my condition of mind'.[37] It was not until she met the socialist and seer Edward Carpenter[38] that she achieved a degree of security about her mental state. They met in London after the war through their mutual interest in the Labour movement. When she told him about her experiences, he explained to her that she was of a new breed of humans gifted with cosmic consciousness.[39] Her range of vision and hearing was, consequently, greater than most people's; this was why she heard sounds and saw colours that were imperceptible to others. He urged her to take up one of the arts, presented her with the Oriental Scriptures and the writings of Walt Whitman, and introduced her to Theosophists and the followers of Rudolf Steiner.[40] In reinterpreting her life in the light of cosmic consciousness, Carpenter gave Garrett a 'sense of being reborn and set free … He truly made me understand that my *sensing* and *visioning* were not the products of an unbalanced mind, but the positive powers of knowing and understanding, beyond the range of ordinary comprehension.'[41]

Neither Theosophy nor the teaching of Steiner attracted Garrett, but she now read books and moved in circles that took her deeper into the mystical philosophies, and it was not long before she met someone who seemed to throw more light on the nature of her visions. This person was a Spiritualist who recognised her latent mediumistic powers. He could tell, he said, that she was capable of psychic healing, psychometry, clairvoyance and clairaudience. He told her a little about Spiritualism, and invited her to accompany him to a London Spiritualist society. Garrett was unimpressed by the performance of the medium, and found the spirit messages banal, but since she wanted to discover more about the nature of her own powers, she joined a 'developing circle' at the Society. The third time she sat with the circle she found herself becoming drowsy, and soon fell asleep. When she came round, the other women said that their dead relatives had spoken 'through her' while she slept. After this episode the Secretary of the Society advised Garrett to contact a Mr Huhnli, who, she said, was knowledgeable about psychic matters. Garrett took the Secretary's advice and made an appointment to visit Mr Huhnli. During this interview, Garrett again went to sleep. When she regained consciousness he told her that she was a trance medium of great power and that her spirit-guide (an Oriental called Uvani) had spoken while she was apparently asleep. Garrett left Mr Huhnli's rooms in Lambeth in a state of consternation, 'sure that none of this experience had really occurred'. On her return home, she divulged to her third husband, James Garrett, what had happened. He became annoyed and told her she was not merely on the brink of insanity but had already lost her reason. Torn between opposing constructions of her perceptions, she became thoroughly frightened and wondered if this 'Uvani' was a figment of her imagination.[42] Nevertheless, she continued to experiment with Mr Huhnli.

As Garrett moved into Spiritualist circles, she moved away from the influence of James Garrett and his family. Her introduction to Hewat McKenzie clinched matters for the next five years. Here was somebody who had respect in the Spiritualist movement, and was deeply interested in her potential as a medium: '[He] stated that [she] had great psychic power'[43] and suggested that she have her mediumship trained at the British College of Psychic Science, under the joint direction of himself and Barbara McKenzie. She worked at the BCPS until Hewat McKenzie's death in 1929. McKenzie's enthusiasm for her psychic abilities reinforced her tenuous sense of self, and when he died she wrote: 'I felt shaken and very much alone in my work; for now the only person on whom I relied in the direction of my mediumship, had gone.'[44]

Despite her own experiences with the supernatural, and recognition of her powers from authoritative individuals, Garrett, like many mediums of the interwar period, remained painfully insecure about her identity as a medium.[45] The acceptance of the name 'medium' could, on occasions, signify the cessation of fear and uncertainty for an individual plagued by supernatural occurrences. Helen Hughes, for example, felt that the intervention of the 'old road-mender' in her life preserved her sanity, and according to her biographer, she remained comfortably within the community of Spiritualists.[46] Sylvia Barbanell painted a similar picture of Estelle Roberts, corroborated by Roberts in her autobiography.[47] But for most, mediumship was a fragile identity, constantly in the making and easily undermined. Garrett sought to understand her psychic experiences through diverse discourses: magical lore, Catholicism, cosmic consciousness, Spiritualism, telepathy, medicine, psychical research and psychology. And she was never convinced of the authenticity of her spirit-guides. Sometimes they seemed real, but she came eventually to believe that they were a dramatisation of her unconscious – an unconscious that was linked, nevertheless, to psychic processes in the cosmos.[48]

Like Garrett, Doris Stokes constructed her visions and 'voices' differently according to the relative prominence in her life of competing narratives about psychic events. Whereas her father took pleasure in her psychic abilities, and encouraged them, her mother strongly disapproved, and feared for her child's mental and moral well-being.[49] 'Mother's dark warnings', wrote Stokes, 'were firmly rooted in my mind', and she retained her fear of 'meddling' with the unknown into adulthood.[50]

When she joined the WRAF, aged twenty, her attitude towards psychic events took on the flippant, sceptical mood of her WRAF companions, who treated the local Spiritualist church as entertainment and referred to it as 'the spook show'. Although the very mention of Spiritualism 'brought all the old fears and mother's dire warnings', Stokes sat at the back of the church with her friends 'giggling and whispering and [she] convinced [herself] the whole thing was nonsense'.[51] Her view shifted again when she tried her hand at fortune-telling and gained a reputation for having 'the gift'. After the death of her son John Michael, and the scene with her dead father, she and her husband actively sought the company of Spiritualists. They went to numerous seances and started their own home circle, where she acted as medium on a regular basis. The Spiritualist Union ratified her mediumship, and her reputation spread.[52] Even so, her sense of identity as a medium was always at risk. An incident that occurred when she was working as a full-time medium illustrates her fragility in this respect. She had just given what she believed to be a successful demonstration of her abilities at a Spiritualist gathering:

> Afterwards I fetched my coat, and as I walked out I passed behind two old dears who were chatting over a cup of tea.
>
> 'Isn't she good,' said one.
>
> 'Oh she's not genuine,' the other assured her, 'she must have looked up names in the telephone book or something. She was much too good to be genuine.'
>
> I felt sick. Speechless with shock I blundered past them into the street. I'd never heard people say such things about me before – but just because I hadn't heard them didn't mean they weren't said behind my back. I was shattered.
>
> Perhaps it had all been an illusion, perhaps everybody thought I was a fraud. I thought back over the meetings I'd attended, the times I'd forced myself out in the rain and the cold, the times I'd literally waded knee-deep through snow to some remote hall. Had they been doubting me all along? Were they really laughing behind my back?
>
> To this day I don't know why that chance remark affected me so deeply. I couldn't shrug it off. I was more than hurt. In just a few seconds, my confidence had been torn to shreds.[53]

This incident so affected Stokes that she gave up work as a medium, and trained to become a nurse instead. It was several years before she appeared on a Spiritualist platform again.

Geraldine Cummins, by contrast, presents as one of the most confident and comfortable of interwar mediums. Her attitude to mediumship was unusual in that she was treated it like a profession and did not claim to have any *inherent* psychic abilities. In her biography she wrote that she had laboriously trained herself to be a medium [54] Her friend Beatrice Gibbes, with whom she lived for three-quarters of each year, helped her in this. Gibbes encouraged and organised Cummins's mediumship, and protected her against the many and potentially exhausting demands on her powers.[55] Her friend's complete confidence in the genuineness of her mediumship helped to shield Cummins against attacks of self-doubt, and she was fortunate in receiving ratification from several publicly respected figures including Sir Oliver Lodge, W. B. Yeats and the Honourable Countess Lyttelton.[56] Even so, some insecurity of identity was implied in her automatic writing, *The Scripts of Cleophas*. She produced these in a condition of trance. According to Cummins's spirit scribe, 'Messenger', the *Scripts* supplemented biblical testimony about the activities of the Apostles. In one section, the Apostles met a slave-girl, referred to simply as 'the maid', who reputedly divined the future while in trance. After meeting the Apostle Paul, her clairvoyant abilities suddenly disappeared. Her 'masters', who gained status and made money out of her ability, placed increasing pressure on her to perform. Because of her fear of them, she pretended that 'the invading spirit was once more within her, and spoke with her lips'. Her masters were pleased, and bought her presents:

> Howbeit, there was great uneasiness in the mind of this child. She lay in the darkness on the night of the quaking earth, counting as beads upon a thread her many fearful doubts concerning the words she had uttered, which were not the words of her master, the Serpent of Knowledge.[57]

The position of 'the maid' is too closely analogous to the position of the modern medium to be entirely coincidental. Tossed between a bewildering array of constructions on their identities, mediums risked loss of security in their capabilities, and consequently in their sense of 'self'. As Stokes said, this loss was capable of tearing a person's confidence 'to shreds'. Ironically, it was in contact with those who ardently desired to discover the presence of psychic life in the cosmos, psychical researchers, that mediumistic identity was most at risk. As we shall see, this happened as a function of the relationship between psychical researchers and mediums.

Psychical researchers were always on the lookout for 'new talent'. Paul Tabori, psychical researcher and the biographer of Harry Price, writes: 'It is the dream of every psychical investigator to discover a medium all by himself, to develop and test her according to his own ideas and then present her and her results to the world.'[58] The key word here is 'discover'. 'Discovery' was one way of interpellating an individual as a medium. Harry Price, for example, 'discovered' Stella C., who knew that strange things occurred in her presence but had no perception of herself as a medium before meeting Price on a train one day. It was Price who bestowed on her the name medium. Once she had agreed to take part in Price's experiments, however, the burden of proving that she was 'genuinely' mediumistic shifted on to her. In accepting fraud-proof conditions, she implicitly took on the challenge of proving that she was who *Price* said she was.

One physical medium, Ada Bessinet, had the presence of mind to resist this peculiar twist in the interpellation of mediums. According to Horace Leaf, who told the story to Muriel Hankey,[59] McKenzie had caught Bessinet out in an act of fraud during a series of demonstrations. McKenzie, who had set up secret apparatus, informed her that she was 'obviously cheating'. Then the following exchange took place:

> MR. McK: It is you, and not spirits, who produce these manifestations: In other words, you act fraudulently.
>
> MISS B: Mr. McKenzie, if you repeat those words in the presence of others, or in writing, I will sue for defamation of character. State any time when I have said, either by word spoken or written, spirits produce my phenomena. I have never made that claim. During all the seance I am unconscious, and have no knowledge of what takes place. It is *you* who call me a medium and say that spirits produce the phenomena.[60]

Bessinet confounded McKenzie on this occasion, but the continual demands psychical researchers made on mediums to *prove* their identities could have unhappy consequences for the medium in question. Sometimes the intervention of a psychical researcher in the life of a medium could be a really traumatic experience. The case of Mrs Forbes – who featured prominently in the Thornton Heath poltergeist case, described in Chapter 6 above – serves as an example.

As we know, Nandor Fodor, a keen psychical researcher, was among the curious who came to the Forbes's home on 23 February 1938, having heard of the case through a report in the *Sunday Pictorial*. The situation intrigued him. The phenomena of spontaneously flying eggs, shattered glass and crashing furniture, among other things, were sufficiently startling to attract his attention, and the Forbes family seemed to him to be 'creditable' people. He found Mrs Forbes, around whom the phenomena gathered, 'a charming, intelligent and vivacious woman of thirty-five', who did not seem to understand the disturbances in her house, and was 'badly shaken' by them. He described her husband as 'a plain, straightforward, intelligent man who works hard and has built up, by years of effort, a good business'. David, the Forbes's only son, who had joined the business, seemed equally 'sound'. Finally, Fodor described George Simmons, the lodger, as 'genial and affable, the type of man whose nerves it would take a great deal to affect'.[61]

Thus Fodor, to begin with, had no doubts about Mrs Forbes's or her family's good faith – indeed, her nervous reaction to the poltergeist seemed to underline her veracity: 'She was trembling after each crash and her heart was beating very fast. I do not think this condition was simulated.'[62] It is clear from Fodor's initial enthusiasm that he thought he had discovered a genuine medium of extraordinary power. The report of his research assistant, Mr Evans, confirmed his own impression of Mrs Forbes. On 28 June 1938, Evans wrote: 'On looking through my notes on the Thornton Heath case made on my first visit to the house (February 23rd), I experience afresh the feeling I had at that time: that is to say an utter belief in the genuineness of the phenomena and also in the good faith of Mrs. Forbes.'[63]

Over the next four months, while Fodor carried out tests, Mrs Forbes's phenomena multiplied. She produced an array of apports and projected her astral body (once she stole some small articles from Woolworth's while in this condition), she fell into spontaneous trances, was clairvoyant and clairaudient, and had olfactory psychic presentiments. When she detected the smell of violets, a bunch came out of the air; when she became aware of an animal odour, claw marks appeared down her back. She bore the mark of stigmata on her forehead, a vampire visited her at night, and all the time the violent activities of the poltergeist continued at her home.

As her phenomena became more outlandish, and Fodor became

better acquainted with her history, he began to harbour doubts about the supernatural character of the phenomena she produced. 'Showmanship was in the air', he wrote, after she had made objects appear and disappear while having tea at his flat.[64] Moreover, Fodor became increasingly doubtful about Mrs Forbes's sanity. During their four-month association, he continually asked her to take part in experimental tests. He conducted these tests, initially designed for the purpose of gathering evidential material and classifying phenomena,[65] informally at the Forbes's home. Soon, however, as his doubts about her increased, the tests became increasingly rigorous and formal, and it was not long before he thought he detected fraud.

The seance in question took place at the International Institute for Psychical Research on 22 March 1938. The pre-seance controls were routine by the standards of psychical research. Mrs Forbes was asked to remove all her clothing in the presence of three women. When she was naked, they searched her armpits; they then gave her specially prepared clothes to wear, intended to eliminate the concealment of objects. After she had dressed, the women examined her hair and shone a torch into her mouth. She was not allowed to be alone except to visit the lavatory. During the seance she was in constant physical contact with an investigator.[66] Despite these precautions, Fodor was unconvinced of the psychic origin of the objects she produced that day. When her first apport, a penny, appeared, Fodor, who was sitting next to her and controlling her movements, felt 'spasmodic jerks' in her hand, 'as if the sinews were expanding'.[67] He thought the apport might have come from inside her garment, but was unsure how. The last one, a locket, came when she seemed tired, and looked to Fodor 'like an attempt at unloading' [an attempt to get rid of concealed objects before re-dressing in the presence of witnesses].[68]

After eight weeks of investigation, his belief in her mediumship had slipped further, although he was considering the possibility that fraudulent and genuine practices may not have been mutually exclusive. After a series of eight sittings held at the IIPR between 25 March and 20 April, he speculated that:

> The more startling phenomena still took place at Mrs. Forbes's home, but so much also happened at the Institute, there was no reason to complain. Some of these happenings were self-evidential, establishing an excellent case for the supernormal range of the powers of Mrs.

Forbes's unconscious, others were of a compromising character but psychologically still very interesting. They made me incline to the analytical view that dissociated persons can work on two levels of consciousness. They may attempt fraud on one and continue it on the second in a state of genuine trance; they may also produce supernormal phenomena. In other words, the table sittings have led me to conclude that there is a genuine psychic angle in the problem of fraud and the life of a dissociated personality must be considered as a whole and not split into departments of the genuine and fraudulent.[69]

However, Fodor (like Price with Helen Duncan) was fast losing interest in *any* theory of supernatural intervention to account for Mrs Forbes's phenomena, and was pursuing her mediumship for other reasons. His interest increasingly focused on her mental condition, which he interpreted according to Freudian precepts of sexual neurosis. The emphasis of his research eventually shifted from the seance room to the couch; he carried out free-association tests with her and analysed her dreams. In 1948 he produced a paper where he repeated his – by now – firm conviction about poltergeist phenomena: 'I consider them … to be manifestations of major mental disorder of schizophrenic, though temporary, character, not the product of anything supernatural.'[70]

Ten years earlier, while Fodor still speculated about the nature of Mrs Forbes's phenomena, she had made increasingly desperate attempts to maintain his and the Institute's interest in her mediumship. She seems to have conceded to their every demand. She allowed Fodor what looks from his account like unlimited access to her home and family, she visited his home for tests, she gave any number of sittings (lasting two to three hours each) at the Institute, with varying degrees of conditions and controls placed upon her. As we have seen, some of these involved removing all her clothing in front of strangers, and remaining in what must have been their suffocatingly close presence until she reached the seance room. As Fodor noted, having to undress was doubly distressing for her because one of her breasts had been removed during an operation, and her body was 'badly scarred by repeated draining of an abscess on her kidney'.[71]

It is obvious from Fodor's notes that the strain on Mrs Forbes was becoming intolerable as her trials (in all three senses of the word) progressed. At a seance held at the Institute on 17 March, she complained that she felt sick as she approached the seance room. Her 'pulse [was] 96, her hands [were] shaking'. A little later, Mrs Forbes's heart was 'beating wildly. Pulse 120'.[72] At a seance held the following week her condition was worse. Just before she produced an apport, her 'left hand started to shake, she was sick, her face flushed and her heart beat very fast'. Later she felt faint, cold and clammy.[73] During another seance at the Institute on 1 April, while Mrs Forbes was trying to produce an apport, purportedly through her spirit-guide, she 'felt sick and her heart (tested by Dr. Willis) was beating fast'. A short while later she entered trance, and her 'pulse became very irregular … Dr. Willis felt so anxious that he wanted her brought back to normal consciousness.'[74]

One incident during these tests caused Fodor temporarily to revise his scepticism about the supernatural origins of Forbes's phenomena. On 12 April 1938 at 3.40 p.m., Fodor received a call from George Simmons, the Forbes's lodger, saying that his sister-in-law, Rose, was with him and was in a state of agitation. Although Mrs Forbes was at the Institute, she had just appeared to Rose at her home, had spoken to her and taken an eternity ring with blue stones. At 3.22 p.m. the same afternoon Mrs Forbes had entered trance at the Institute, and was apparently talking to Rose. Even more disquieting, the eternity ring turned up in Mrs Forbes's hand during the seance. Fodor commented: The 'ring apport appears to be *prima facie* genuine and … I am left wondering how far it supports Mrs. Forbes's dramatic self-projection'.[75]

In Fodor's words, Forbes was 'elated' by the enthusiasm of the Seance Committee, and she promised to project herself that night into the Institute's seance room.[76] And at about 9 p.m., he heard a knock on the door. But Mrs Forbes's success did not last. Her suspicious behaviour at tests, and the bizarre nature of her other phenomena, convinced Fodor that she produced all her phenomena fraudulently owing to her unstable psychological condition.

Over the course of exhausting seance work between February and June 1938, and as Fodor's interest in Mrs Forbes's mediumship waxed and waned, her physical and emotional condition deteriorated. She lost weight rapidly (28 lb over four months),[77] and wounds appeared on her body for which she claimed supernatural agency. She complained that her sight was beginning to fail with the strain of working at the Institute.[78] On 25 March a bleeding cross appeared on her forehead that she said her dead father had put there, but it looked to Fodor as if it had been inflicted by normal means – either a pin or a nail.[79] On

2 April she appeared at the top of the stairs at home wearing a big necklace which, she claimed, had caused severe burns on her neck.[80] Soon after this she became preoccupied with a phantom tiger which, she said, had attacked her with its claws. Soon wounds appeared on her back, neck and arms. Clearly, Fodor believed that these mutilations were self-inflicted. It is equally clear that, on some level, Mrs Forbes was aware of his doubts about her mediumship, although he had not told her. After a seance on 3 May, where Fodor appealed to Mrs Forbes's spirit-guide, 'Bremba', to allow him to tighten experimental conditions still further, Mrs Forbes was 'weak, dejected and shivering.'[81] Later she expressed her misery and resentment about the demands placed on her by Fodor and the Institute through a speech made by 'Bremba'. According to Fodor, 'Bremba' complained that the Seance Committee were:

> trying the medium, that we expected too much, that people annoyed her by staring at her, that we should not search her any more than we did, that her husband disliked the idea of her being searched, that if we were not convinced now we should never be, that her domestic difficulties were on the increase and that eventually she would have to give up the experiments.[82]

On 13 May things came to a head when Fodor (like Price) introduced X-ray equipment as part of the seance controls without consulting Mrs Forbes. When he led her to where the operators were waiting, she became 'very excited. She was determined not to be X-rayed'. Applying similar pressure to that which Price had used on Helen Duncan, Fodor pointed out how 'bad it would look if the sitters in the next room were informed that she refused to submit to being X-rayed'. It was not long before she capitulated to his demands.[83] The X-ray photograph 'showed a heart shaped thing and a brooch under her left breast'.[84] Fodor did not tell Mrs Forbes about the results of the tests, but she went to see him on 24 May about them and said: 'I feel there was something on the X-ray plate.' Fodor agreed that there was and she left him, he remembered, 'in a state of extreme distress and misery'.[85]

Fodor continued to monitor Mrs Forbes and, amazingly, continued to hold seances with her. Now she claimed that a vampire visited her at night. When this happened, she felt herself 'get weaker and weaker, sinking'. When Fodor questioned her about it, her distress poured out:

Sometimes I feel that I am not here, that I am not really alive. I feel as if I had died on the operating table [from her kidney operation]. It seems to me as if another person had taken possession of my body … I used to tell my husband after my last kidney operation, 'I am not really here. I am dead. You don't know it. You cannot really hear me.'[86]

Of course, one cannot know what the 'true' origins of Mrs Forbes's trauma may have been,[87] but there is every reason to suspect that the interest of psychical researchers in her phenomena contributed to her misery and personal disorientation. Early acclaim and *recognition* of her mediumship was followed by increasingly rigorous tests – tests that questioned the mediumistic identity she had acquired. She lost weight at an alarming rate over the period, and Fodor's seance notes reveal her considerable emotional and physiological turmoil as the tests progressed. Then there is the elation she felt when interest in her mediumship was restored temporarily through the incident with Rose, and her despair when her veracity was again undermined by the results of the X-ray tests. Fodor tells us that towards the end of the four-month period she came to believe that 'someone else had taken the place of her ego in her body'.[88]

Mrs Forbes's responses to the investigation of her mediumship were extreme, and could have been related to some prior psychosis. But her submission to intrusive and exhausting tests was not at all unusual. As we saw in Chapter 7, many mediums allowed themselves to be cast in the subordinate role of experimental object, and suffered at the hands of their investigators. It is to this disturbing aspect of mediumship that I wish to turn next.

Subordination

Mediums could – and did – gain indirect power through the authority of revelation. Mediumship could also signify resistance to the limitations of normative gender roles, and Alex Owen has suggested that the seance 'made possible the staging of [unconscious] desire' through the persona of a spirit-guide.[89] This might involve assertive, antagonistic or overtly sexual ('male') behaviour.[90] Unlike Stella Cranshawe in her waking state, her guide, 'Palma' (a child of indeterminate sex), was far from submissive and once, in 1926, violently removed a comb from the hair of a woman participant and flung it across the room.[91] Many other mediums had high-status or aggressive male figures for guides. When Louise Meurig Morris came under the control of her spirit-guide, 'Power', she assumed 'masculine and priestly mannerism[s]', her soprano voice changed 'into a ringing baritone' and, according to her supporters, she displayed a 'grasp of philosophy … far above her intellectual capacities'.[92] Eileen Garrett's two guides, Uvani and Abdul Latif, had similar personae. Helen Duncan's guide, Albert, was raucous, belligerent and flirtatious;[93] Mrs Wickland's spirit visitors were often aggressive and sometimes violent.

Mrs Wickland's mediumship traversed a huge range of spirit characters from black labourers and sailors, to drunkards and murderers, to maid-servants and orphan children. Under the control of one of these personalities, she would routinely cross the boundary of acceptable feminine behaviour. Once the spirit of an alcoholic called 'Paul Hopkins' controlled her. He regularly obsessed a 'Mrs V' and made her a 'periodic inebriate'. In the following passage, recorded in 1923, this spirit communicated 'through' Mrs Wickland and conversed with her husband, Carl Wickland:

> DOCTOR. Are you a stranger to us? Where did you come from?
> SPIRIT. (Attempting to fight.) It's too warm! Why did you pull me away when I was just going to have a drink and a good time?
> DR. Aren't you ashamed of yourself? Do you think that controlling a lady and ruining her life is a good time?
> SP. When a fellow feels so blue, what can you do?
> DR. You must overcome your old habit.
> SP. I'm so warm. I'm awfully hot!
> DR. Where did you come from?
> SP. Give me something, quick! I'm so dry.[94]

The spirit of 'Paul Hopkins' continued to demand alcohol. Later in the seance he offered to fight everyone in the room, and referred to Mrs V as 'that big, fat woman'.[95] Thus the seance, with its tacit plea of special circumstances, could sanction forbidden practices. As we saw in Chapter 3, however, the sort of flagrantly transgressive behaviour permitted in mediums like Mrs Wickland, who conducted 'rescue circles', was not tolerated at more run-of-the-mill seances. If mediumistic performance sometimes subverted normative femininity, it was more likely to entrench it in the interwar years.

Mediums often occupied powerless and subordinated positions in relation to those around them, particularly psychical researchers. Both Helen Duncan and Stella Cranshawe were, in different ways, dominated and subordinated by Harry Price and the investigation team at the National Laboratory for Psychical Research. Baron Von Schrenck-Notzig employed similar methods to Price in his research of Eva C.,[96] as did Nandor Fodor, with Mrs Forbes, and Hewat McKenzie when he 'auditioned' mediums applying to work at the British College of Psychic Science. McKenzie expected his employees to submit to his autocratic regime all the time. Of course, a medium who received ratification from a psychical research organisation enhanced her reputation and earning power, but as I have noted before, financial rewards for mediums were relatively small. I think we need to look elsewhere for an explanation of why mediums commonly adopted a submissive role in relation to their investigators.

There is a grotesque symmetry in the relation between mediums and psychical researchers: the discourse of psychical research demanded submission, while the discourse of 'true mediumship' implied self-negation, sacrifice and willingness to suffer. As we know, Spiritualist discourse valorised the martyred woman, and self-negation was made to seem a necessary part of mediumship. Mediums were expected to live on a 'higher plane', devoid of rich food, alcohol, sex and other worldly pleasures. Suffering in empathy with a spirit visitor in, for example, its memory of injuries or death pangs was a recognised part of the mediumistic function. Her body was quite literally given over to the use of a spirit entity; mediums were seen as passive channels – instruments, rather than *agents*, of the revelatory word. But we should not find such expectations strange within the Christian Judaic tradition, a tradition steeped in concepts of pain and suffering. Indeed, one historian argues that 'Western culture is permeated with sado-masochistic behaviour and each of us, as culture-bearers of past assumptions, probably have some elements in our own psyche.'[97] Nevertheless, who perpetrates and who receives pain constantly shifts and changes according to personal dynamics in specific historical circumstances. Our concern with such desires is limited to their place in interwar culture in so far as they impinged on mediumistic identity.

Novels, films, and sexology of the period wove the traditional subordination of women into images of feminine pleasure. 'Between the wars', writes Alison Light 'a whole new market of erotic literature written by women for a female audience had developed, which put the female body at its centre and drew upon the "ideals of a sexually aggressive culture" in order to imagine female pleasure.'[98] Supporting evidence for this claim is everywhere. Ethel M. Dell's novels are populated with submissive women who 'melt', and dominant, punishing men of the 'steely-eyed' variety. In E. M. Hull's bestselling novel *The Sheik*, the heroine is repeatedly raped. There is another, more subtle depiction of masochistic femininity in *The Weather in the Streets*, by Rosamond Lehmann. The plot revolves around Olivia, a middle-class woman, mistress of the aristocratic and married Roland. Lehmann's approach is unjudgemental, and she tells the story from Olivia's point of view, but the motif of the woman suffering for 'the sake of the man she loves' is unmistakable. Olivia's suffering is bound up with her pleasure and her identity. At the end of the novel, having suffered abandonment and an abortion, she returns, as if inevitably, to her faithless and feckless lover.[99] The expectancy that 'women are made to suffer' was already present in schoolgirls. Gwen Raverat, granddaughter of Charles Darwin, recalled a small but telling incident that took place at her polite girls' boarding school before the Great War: 'Once we had a debate: "that unhappiness is better for the character than happiness" … Nora and I both made impassioned speeches against the motion; but the whole school out-voted us, and, in spite of our scorn, revelled in the purifying effects of sorrow.'[100]

Such gestures towards pleasurable self-negation permeated the mediumistic persona. As others have noted, 'the vocabulary of trance mediumship oozed sexuality. Mediums were entered, seized, possessed by another'.[101] And there is an unresolved ambivalence in the medium's adoption of the 'male part', and her subordination to it. Helen Duncan's aggressive guide, Albert, said: 'During a seance Mrs Duncan is under the domination of my will … When I wish her to do anything, I suggest it. Suggestion is at the root of it all. You might say that I take control of her brain and her body.'[102] If Albert dominated his medium, human and animal entities persecuted Mrs Forbes. When a phantom tiger purportedly clawed her, her spirit control, 'Bremba', said that the tiger was his pet.[103] Another expression of masochistic fantasy emerged in her vision of a vampire visitation. During one interview with Fodor, Mrs Forbes related the following incident:

It may have been around midnight that I woke with the sensation that there was something ghastly on my left-hand side, (which is away from my husband), on top of the cover. It felt like a human body. Pressing against my head was something cold and hard, about the size of a man's head. I could not move, I could not shout, I was frozen with fear. I felt myself getting weaker and weaker, sinking. I imagine that bleeding to death would give the same sensation.[104]

Although dominant and subordinate relations between mediums and spirit-guides were typically organised around conventional gender positions, this was not always the case. Gladys Leonard's spirit-guide was 'Feda', a sentimental little-girl character with stereotypical 'spoilt child' aspects to her persona. Leonard responded to this entity in the role of the harassed mother or servant. Una Troubridge, who held many seances with Leonard for the SPR, wrote revealingly of this aspect of her mediumship. In Troubridge's experience, 'Feda' never conveyed the impression that she liked Leonard: 'She frequently indeed expresses open scorn of Mrs. Leonard's opinions, likes or dislikes, and speaks of her as of a not very satisfactory and distinctly inferior instrument.'[105] 'Feda' communicated her antagonism towards Leonard in various ways: once, when a sitter accidentally singed a few hairs of Leonard's fringe, 'Feda' suggested that a bonfire be made of the rest of her hair, which should then be replaced by a blonde wig.[106] While Leonard was in trance, she forced her to throw her wedding ring on to the fire. She 'once ordered another sitter to bestow it upon an itinerant organ grinder'.[107] Leonard told Troubridge that she went 'in fear of unpleasant consequences of some sort arising in the event of her displeasing "Feda"'. She also informed her that if 'Feda' was really annoyed, she 'simply did not come; as sittings under these circumstances could not take place, Mrs. Leonard's means of livelihood were thus removed until "Feda" considered the offence expiated'.[108]

This self-negating stance emerged in another aspect of Leonard's mediumship, involving her purported ability to travel on different astral planes. During one of these out-of-body excursions she saw the figure of a woman, apparently asleep. The sight of her depressed Leonard, for 'everything about her was brown. Her dress, hair and even her skin, were of a dull muddy brown.' Leonard felt overwhelming pity for this woman – 'She seemed to be so sad, without hope – stupid blundering'. Slowly it dawned upon her that the woman was herself: 'It was just as if I was looking at myself in a very dirty, dark, mirror.' Then a voice spoke. It informed her that the brown woman was an image of her 'lower self'. The voice listed all her faults until, wrote Leonard 'Every scrap of my self-complacency dwindled into nothingness before the beautifully modulated, even tones that thrust these unpleasant truths at me. It never entered my head to rebel, or deny any of it.'[109]

Thus psychical research did not coerce mediums into a submissive position; such a position was already implied in the mediumistic persona and in relations with spirit-guides. Victimisation and martyr-dom appear as integral aspects of mediumship in Dion Fortune's depiction of a medium in her novel *The Winged Bull*. This is a con-ventional love story in an occult setting. The heroine, Ursula, feels torn between forces for good (represented by Ted Murchison – a '[b]ig-boned, upstanding Nordic'[110]) and occult forces for evil who want to use her passive mediumistic disposition in their Black Mass rites. Ursula's brother hires Murchison as a kind of bodyguard for Ursula. He explains to him that unscrupulous occultists have already exploited her for sinister purposes, 'and pretty roughly too … things had been done to Ursula's soul'.[111] and that was why she seemed dazed: 'She isn't here at all. She's off with Hugo Astley and Fouldes [her persecutors]. She wants to do nothing but lie in a kind of day-dream and think of them.'[112]

Pleasurable martyrdom is even more explicit in Fortune's later novel, *The Demon Lover*. I noted in Chapter 4 that Fortune imagines the medium, Veronica, in several conventional masochistic postures. Lucas, her employer, uses occult means to entrap her and then binds her with an invisible chain around her neck. Veronica muses: '[Supposing] what he had said was true – supposing she were bound by an invisible chain which would tighten and strangle her if she disobeyed Lucas – why, then, she was in his hands body and soul.'[113] When Veronica becomes fully aware of Lucas's power over her, and has lost hope of escape, he takes control of her subdued, entranced body, and pushes her soul out on to the astral planes of existence to spy for him. In the character of Lucas, the roles of psychic investigator, spirit-guide and lover are fused. Like many psychical researchers, he exploits Veronica for experimental purposes of his own, yet Fortune makes it clear that this exploitation is not unpleasurable for Veronica. Indeed, by the time he is killed, halfway through the novel, she has fallen in love with him, and when he returns as a spirit entity to take control of her body, she welcomes him wholeheartedly.

If self victimisation was an aspect of mediumistic desire, then the medium cannot be seen as a simple victim of another's desire. What are we to make of people who apparently invite their own subordination? Jessica Benjamin sees the desire for submission as a 'peculiar transposition of the desire for recognition'. She writes that masochism 'is a search for recognition through an other who is powerful enough to bestow this recognition. This other has the power for which the self longs, and through his recognition she gains it, though vicariously.'[114] Conversely, the sadist's pleasure is derived through the masochist's recognition of his or her power. But:

> Since a slave who is completely dominated loses the quality of being able to give recognition, the struggle to possess [the other] must be prolonged. [The subordinate party] must be enslaved piece by piece; new levels of resistance must be found, so that she [or he] can be vanquished anew.[115]

The downward spiral continues on and on, until there is nothing left to yield.

This process has a ring of authenticity. Benjamin takes *The Story of O* as her example, but the dialectic of control she describes is equally applicable to less extreme cases. The story of the hero who pursues the heroine and breaks down her resistance bit by bit is familiar to us all. In popular interwar novels and other forms of entertainment, the progressively negated heroine was standard fare. In *The Weather in the Streets*, Olivia yields gradually to Roland's demands. Towards the end of the novel there is a period of separation, which allows her sufficient recovery time to begin the process anew. We can also view this process in the relationship between mediums and psychical researchers. Harry Price and Nandor Fodor both built up the pressure gradually on the mediums they investigated. The tests with Helen Duncan started with her giving a 'friendly demonstration'[116] and became increasingly invasive and intrusive, culminating in Price subjecting the medium to X-ray examination and pondering the possibility of lowering fish hooks into her stomach. Similarly, Fodor asked more of Mrs Forbes as the tests progressed. In *The Demon Lover*, Lucas breaks down Veronica's resistance bit by bit. Murchison's power over Ursula ebbs and flows in *The*

Winged Bull as he fends off other would-be controllers of her body and soul.

Yet it is not clear with which position different mediums identified. The aggression of some spirit-guides seems to suggest the adoption of a dominant posture, while relations with psychical researchers seem to connote conventional feminine submission. The introduction of such concepts as desire, unconscious fantasy and contingent identity into our theoretical armoury tends to blur the issue of who is doing what to whom. As Jacqueline Rose observes: 'being a victim does not stop you from identifying with the aggressor; being an aggressor does not stop you identifying with the victim.'[117] Thus the question of whether a medium is a victim or an aggressor, whether she appropriates power or yields to it, turns out to be obscure. Take, for example, the different constructions placed on Helen Duncan's mediumship. Was she the innocent victim of legal, religious and sex antagonism, or the astute and aggressive businesswoman encountered by Harry Price? Was she the unconscious manipulator of seance activity, or the instrument of collective fantasy? Did she subvert normative femininity through the persona of Albert, or was she the stereotypical submissive female, dominated in turn by Price, Henry Duncan and her own phantom, Albert? Did she alternate between these poles, or was she simply committed to a different agenda, unknown to us? Was she all, some, or none of these things?

Variability and ambivalence seem to be the only certainties in mediumistic identity – an unsatisfactory conclusion for those who are looking for certainties. For those of us who are not, there are compensations for this loss of assurance in, perhaps, perhaps a new modesty of epistemological purpose which curtails grandiose knowledge claims while simultaneously permitting the enlargement of explanatory possibilities. That the mediumistic persona is ultimately unknowable in any straightforward sense is surely unsurprising, but we can glimpse the construction of tenuous and contingent selves through attention to the dynamics of culture and unconscious desire, and through examination of the impact of a powerful Other capable of both confirming and undermining identity.

Notes

1 M. Douglas, *Purity and Danger: An Analysis of the Concepts of Pollution and Taboo* (London, Routledge & Kegan Paul, 1966), especially ch. 6.

2 Geraldine Cummins was an exception to this rule; she viewed her mediumship as a vocational profession. See G. Cummins, *Unseen Adventures: An Autobiography Covering 34 Years of Psychical Research* (London, Rider, 1951), p. 20.

3 According to the theory of interpellation, the effect of being successfully hailed in ideology as a subject is the certain belief: 'I am already who you say I am.' And we have seen this effect at work in the constitution of mediumistic identity. To be hailed or named as a medium (if accepted) produced the retroactive effect: 'This is my true identity, I have always been a medium.' L. Althusser, 'Ideology and Ideological State Apparatuses', in *Lenin and Philosophy and Other Essays*, trans B. Brewster, (London, New Left Books, 1971), pp. 123–73. There is practically an industry of commentary around this article. One of the most inventive from a Lacanian perspective comes from Slavoj Žižek, *The Sublime Object of Ideology* (London and New York, Verso, 1989).

4 Reverend G.J. MacGillivray, *What Happens after Death?* (London, Catholic Truth Society, 1929), p. 22.

5 P. Fussell, *The Great War and Modern Memory* (Oxford, Oxford University Press, 1975), ch. IV; J. Winter, *Sites of Memory, Sites of Mourning: The Great War in European Culture* (Cambridge, Cambridge University Press, 1995).

6 E. Roberts, *Forty Years a Medium* (London, Herbert Jenkins, 1959), p. 21.

7 G. Leonard, *My Life in Two Worlds*, 'Foreword' by Sir O. Lodge (London, Cassell, 1931), p. 14.

8 *Ibid.*, p. 19.

9 Cummins, *Unseen Adventures*, p. 27.

10 D. Stokes and L. Dearsley, *Voices in My Ear: The Autobiography of a Medium* (London, Futura Macdonald, 1980), p. 9.

11 *Ibid.*, p. 8.

12 *Ibid.*, p. 13.

13 *Ibid.*, p. 15.

14 *Ibid.*, pp. 52–3. Spiritualists explained inaccurate messages in several ways. Either the medium had misinterpreted the message, the spirit-guide had made a mistake, or the medium was receiving impressions from elsewhere, maybe from sitters. H. Boddington, *Psychic News Booklet 3: Trance States in Relation to Spirit Control* (London, Psychic Press, 1933), p. 9.

15 Stokes and Dearsley, *Voices in My Ear*, pp. 54–5.

16 *Ibid.*, pp. 59–60.

17 *Ibid.*, p. 62.

18 *Ibid.*, pp. 63–5 (emphasis added).

19 For information relating to Garrett's childhood, see J. Healy, *Journal of the Society for Psychical Research*, 54:806 (1986) 90.

20 E. Garrett, *My Life as a Search for the Meaning of Mediumship* (New York, Arno Press, 1975), p. 2.

21 Martha Little's Protestantism was no obstacle to her acceptance of local superstitions such as the banshee. See ch. 1 above.

22 Garrett, *My Life*, p. 23.

23 *Ibid.*, pp. 10–11.

24 *Ibid.*, pp. 25–6.

25 *Ibid.*, p. 26.

26 *Ibid.*, p. 26. Not that Garrett avoided retribution in the everyday world. For Martha Little, the killing of her ducks was the last straw in an unsatisfactory relationship with her niece, and Garrett was sent away to a boarding school.

27 D. Fortune, *Psychic Self Defence* (Wellingborough, Aquarian Press, 1973), pp. 12–13.

28 *Ibid.*, p. 13.

29 *Ibid.*, pp. 13–14.

30 *Ibid.*, p. 15.

31 *Ibid.*, p. 16.

32 *Ibid.*, pp. 17–18.

33 A. Crossley, *The Story of Helen Duncan: Materialization Medium* (Devon, Arthur Stockwell, 1975), pp. 16–17.

34 Leonard, *My Life in Two Worlds*, pp. 19, 22, 23, 40; Roberts, *Forty Years a Medium*, p. 25.

35 Garrett, *My Life*, p. 35.

36 *Ibid.*, pp. 96, 102.

37 *Ibid.*, p. 98.

38 See C. Tsuzuki, *Edward Carpenter, 1844–1929: Prophet of Human Fellowship* (Cambridge, Cambridge University Press, 1980).

39 The philosophy of cosmic consciousness was developed by R. M. Bucke in *Cosmic Consciousness: A Study in the Evolution of the Human Mind* (1901) (New Jersey, Citadel Press, 1961).

40 See ch. 4 n. 102 above for details on Rudolf Steiner.

41 Garrett, *My Life*, pp. 117–19, 120.

42 *Ibid.*, pp. 128–31.

43 *Ibid.*, p. 136.

44 *Ibid.*, p. 145.

45 Garrett's autobiographical publications repeatedly question the meaning and authenticity of her mediumship. See, for example, E. Garrett, *My Life; Many Voices: The Autobiography of a Medium* (London, George

Allen & Unwin. 1968); *Adventures in the Supernormal: A Personal Memoir* (New York, Creative Age Press, 1943).

46 B. Upton, *The Mediumship of Helen Hughes* (London, Spiritualist Press, 1947).

47 S. Barbanell, *Some Discern Spirits: The Mediumship of Estelle Roberts* (London, Psychic Press, 1944); Roberts, *Forty Years A Medium.*

48 E. Garrett, *My Life*; *Many Voices; Adventures in the Supernormal*; E. Garrett (ed.), *Does Man Survive Death?* (London, Holborn Publishing, 1958); E. Garrett, *Telepathy: In Search of a Lost Faculty*, 'Introduction' by E. R. Corson (New York, Garrett Publications, 1968); E. Garrett, *Awareness* (New York, Creative Age Press, 1943).

49 Stokes, *Voices in My Ear*, pp. 7, 14, 30, 37.

50 *Ibid.*, p. 37.

51 *Ibid.*, p. 34.

52 *Ibid.*, pp. 36–115. Stokes probably meant the Spiritualists' National Union.

53 *Ibid.*, pp. 116–17. It seems that male mediums were no less vulnerable to attacks of self-doubt in the face of a distrusting audience. A Mass-Observation reporter who attended a seance at the Marylebone Spiritualist Association in 1940 appraised the situation as follows: 'Medium exceedingly anxious to please – Ob[server] got the impression both during the seance and from conversation afterwards that he is considered to be incompetent. Only 3 people including Inv. attend though the standard number is eight' (20 August 1940). Mass-Observation Archive (University of Sussex) Topic Collection: Astrology and Spiritualism, Box 1 file B, 'Group Seance at Marylebone Spiritualist Association'.

54 Cummins, *Unseen Adventures*, p. 20.

55 *Ibid.*, p. 40. See also C. Fryer, *Geraldine Cummins: An Appreciation* (Norwich, Pelegrin Trust, 1990), especially ch. 4.

56 Cummins, *Unseen Adventures*, p. 79.

57 G. Cummins, *The Scripts of Cleophas: A Reconstruction of Primitive Christian Documents* (1928), 'Introduction' by W. P. Patterson and D. Morrison, 5th edn (London, Psychic Press, 1974), pp. 201, 229–30.

58 P. Tabori, *Harry Price Ghost Hunter* (1950) (London, Sphere Books, 1974), p. 82. Harry Price travelled the world in search of suitable subjects, as did Hewat MacKenzie, and a glance at SPR *Proceedings* over the decades shows that the organisation was prepared to go to considerable lengths to attract mediums for tests.

59 Horace Leaf was a medium and an author himself. In 1926, he published *The Psychology and Development of Mediumship* (London, Rider, 1926). He was also a staff lecturer at the McKenzies' British College of Psychic Science.

60 Horace Leaf, reproduced in M. Hankey, *James Hewat McKenzie, Pioneer*

of Psychical Research: A Personal Memoir (London, Aquarian Press, 1963), p. 142, emphasis added. Where psychical researchers had not 'discovered' the medium themselves, they were even more inclined to interrogate her as if she were an autonomous 'individual' who had founded her own identity.

61 N. Fodor, *On the Trail of the Poltergeist* (London, Arco, 1959), pp. 29–30.

62 *Ibid.*, p. 34.

63 Quoted by Fodor, *ibid.*, p. 26.

64 *Ibid.*, p. 53.

65 *Ibid.*, chs 2, 4.

66 *Ibid.*, pp. 75–6.

67 *Ibid.*, p. 76.

68 *Ibid.*, p. 78.

69 *Ibid.*, p. 81.

70 N. Fodor, 'The Poltergeist Psychoanalysed', *The Psychiatric Quarterly*, 22 (April 1948) 196.

71 Fodor, *On the Trail of the Poltergeist*, p. 167.

72 *Ibid.*, p. 72.

73 *Ibid.*, p. 76.

74 *Ibid.*, pp. 141–2.

75 *Ibid.*, p. 93.

76 *Ibid.*, p. 94.

77 *Ibid.*, p. 171.

78 *Ibid.*, p. 128.

79 *Ibid.*, pp. 130–31.

80 *Ibid.*, pp. 124–7.

81 *Ibid.*, p. 163.

82 *Ibid.*, p. 166.

83 *Ibid.*, pp. 175–6.

84 *Ibid.*, p. 177.

85 *Ibid.*, p. 187.

86 *Ibid.*, pp. 192, 194.

87 Fodor believed that her phenomena were associated with a repressed memory of rape (*ibid.*, pp. 207–22). See ch. 6 above.

88 *Ibid.*, p. 201.

89 A. Owen, *The Darkened Room: Women, Power and Spiritualism in Late Victorian England* (London, Virago, 1989), p. 222.

90 *Ibid.*, especially ch. 8 and A. Owen, 'Women and Nineteenth Century Spiritualism: Strategies in the Subversion of Femininity', in J. Obelkevich (ed.), *Disciplines of Faith* (London, Routledge, 1987), pp. 130–53.

91 Price, *Stella C.*, p. 130.

92 N. Fodor, *These Mysterious People* (London, Rider, 1935), p. 232. See

also Leslie Sharp (ed.) *Encyclopedia of Occultism and Parapsychology*, vol. 1, 2nd edn (Detroit, Gale Research Company, 1984), p. 894.

93 H. Price, *Regurgitation and the Duncan Mediumship* (London, Council at the Rooms of the National Laboratory of Psychical Research, 1931). See also James Leigh, 'Mrs Duncan's Mediumship', *The Two Worlds*, XLV: 2320 (May 1932) 305–6.

94 C. Wickland, *Thirty Years among the Dead* (London, Spiritualist Press, 1924), p. 170.

95 *Ibid.*, p. 173.

96 See Baron Von Schrenck-Notzig, *Phenomena of Materialisation: A Contribution to the Investigation of Mediumistic Teleplastics*, trans. E. E. Fournier d'Albe (London, Kegan Paul, 1920).

97 V. L. Bullough, D. Dixon and J. Dixon, 'Sadism, Masochism and History, or When is Behaviour Sado-Masochistic?', in R. Porter and M. Teich (eds), *Sexual Knowledge, Sexual Science* (Cambridge, Cambridge University Press, 1994), p. 59. See also L. Segal, *Slow Motion: Changing Masculinities, Changing Men* (London, Virago, 1990), p. 152.

98 A. Light, *Forever England: Femininity, Literature and Conservatism Between the Wars* (London, Routledge, 1991), p. 175.

99 R. Lehmann, *The Weather in the Streets* (1936) (London, Collins, 1945). A similar theme is found in the Noël Coward film *The Astonished Heart* (1949), except that this time the story is told from the wife's perspective. Christian and Barbara Faber (Noël Coward and Celia Johnson) are a happily married and successful couple until Christian falls in love with Leonora (Margaret Leighton), an old school friend of Barbara's. Although Barbara continues to love her husband, she encourages him to leave her for Leonora. She seems to take a kind of bitter pleasure in sacrificing herself for his happinesss.

100 G. Raverat, *Period Piece: A Cambridge Childhood* (London, Faber & Faber, 1952), p. 73.

101 Owen, *The Darkened Room*, p. 218.

102 J. Leigh, 'Dramatic Interview with Materialised Spirit Form', *The Two Worlds*, XLV: 2340 (September 1932) 626.

103 Fodor, *On the Trail of the Poltergeist*, pp. 134–5.

104 *Ibid.*, p. 192.

105 U. Troubridge, 'The Modus Operandi in So Called Mediumistic Trance', *Proceedings of the Society for Psychical Research*, XXXII (January 1922) 352.

106 *Ibid.*, p. 353.

107 *Ibid.*, pp. 353–4.

108 *Ibid.*, p. 354.

109 Leonard, *My Life in Two Worlds*, pp. 124–5.

110 D. Fortune, *The Winged Bull* (Wellingborough, Aquarian Press, 1989), p. 18.

111 *Ibid.*, p. 95.

112 *Ibid.*, p. 94.

113 D. Fortune, *The Demon Lover* (Wellingborough, Aquarian Press, 1987), p. 31.

114 J. Benjamin, *The Bonds of Love: Psychoanalysis, Feminism, and the Problem of Domination* (London, Virago, 1990), p. 56. *Cf.* J. Rose, *The Haunting of Sylvia Plath* (London, Virago, 1991).

115 Benjamin, *The Bonds of Love*, p. 58.

116 H. Price, *Regurgitation and the Duncan Mediumship*, p. 13.

117 Rose, *The Haunting of Sylvia Plath*, p. 122.

Afterword

> The disturbed relationship with the dead – forgotten and embalmed
> – is one of the symptoms of the sickness of experience today … The
> respect for something which has no market value and runs contrary
> to all feelings is experienced most sharply by the person in mourning,
> in whose case not even the psychological restoration of labour power
> is possible. It becomes a wound in civilization, asocial sentimentality,
> showing that it has still not been possible to compel men to indulge
> solely in purposeful behaviour. That is why mourning is watered down
> more than anything else and consciously turned into social formality;
> indeed, the beautified corpse has always been a mere formality for the
> hardened survivors. In the funeral home and crematorium, where the
> corpse is processed into portable ashes – an unpleasant item of prop-
> erty – it is not considered proper to show emotion, and the girl who
> proudly described the first-class burial of her grandmother, adding "a
> pity that Daddy lost control" (because he shed a few tears), accurately
> reflects the situation. In reality, the dead suffer a fate which the Jews
> in olden times considered the worst possible curse: they are expunged
> from the memory of those who live on. Men have ceased to consider
> their own purpose and fate; they work their despair out on the dead.[1]

This passage from Theodor Adorno and Max Horkheimer's, *Dialectic of
Enlightenment*, written during the Second World War, highlights the sharp
contrast between Spiritualist values and modern social imperatives to
sever relations with the past and with the dead. It also suggests possible
reasons for the decline of Spiritualist numbers after the Second World
War.[2] Adorno and Horkheimer trace modern attitudes to death and

dying to narcissistic individualism and commercial values;[3] others have taken a broader approach. The impact of secularisation, the privatisation, medicalisation and hospitalisation of the sick body, have all been recognised as influences in changing attitudes to death over time and place.[4] In the routine removal of the dying person from the company of relatives and friends to the hospital in the twentieth century, he or she becomes a 'patient' to be cured. 'When death arrives', writes one historian, 'it is regarded as an accident, a sign of helplessness or clumsiness that must be put out of mind.' [5]

In the midst of World War I bereavement and the proliferation of literary, visual and other kinds of memorials to the dead,[6] the erosion of traditional mourning rites and articulations of piety had already begun. Dead servicemen had colloquially 'bought it', 'got it', or 'gone West'. Robert Graves remembered a horrifying incident at the battle-front involving the corpse of a recently dead soldier: 'His arm was stretched out stiff when they carried him in and laid him on the fire-step; it stretched right across the trench. His comrades joke as they push it out of the way to get by. "Out of the light, you old bastard! Do you own this bloody trench?" Or else they shake hands with him familiarly. "Put it there Billy Boy."'[7] Such seemingly callous responses did not so much reject the dead as reject traditional sentiment and religious piety. '[W]hat many soldier-poets could not stomach were the loftier versions of civilian romance about the war', which could not comprehend such horrors as the battles of Passchendaele and the Somme.[8] In civilian life, too, particularly in modernist writing, the weakening of stable mourning codes and ritual helped to produce a new prohibition on grief.[9] In more 'popular' publications there were also attempts to maintain emotional distance from the dead. In Agatha Christie's bestselling thrillers, for example, murder victims were rarely mourned by their relatives or friends. Such shows of indifference or lightheartedness may have helped the war bereaved to defend themselves against the pain of recent loss.[10]

What might have begun as rebellion and/or psychological defence against the pain of bereavement increasingly became the norm. During the Second World War, in the interests of 'morale' and the 'war-effort', people encouraged each other to put individual feelings of fear, loss and grief in the background, and 'carry on regardless'.[11] One 'morale' story, printed by the *Daily Sketch*, told of Tony, who was too affected by the death of his brother: 'A telegram from the War Office told him that his brother had been killed … Tony hadn't taken it very well … But you could understand that. He'd been sort of fond of Bryan. But it had got worse, and, on the day of the medical [for the RAF] Tony hadn't turned up.' Since then, his girlfriend could think of him only with loathing.[12] The message was clear: to grieve was 'unmanly'; it resulted in cowardice, and reduced one's sex appeal.

The tendency to minimise or deny the emotional impact of death was made visible in the simplification of funeral rites after the war. In 1961 a Mass-Observation publication noted that more people were opting to cremate their relatives than ever before;[13] tombstones tended to be smaller, plainer and less religious in design than they had been in the 1930s, and funerals were more modest. One funeral director said: 'People want *simpler* coffins now, it's natural wood instead of varnished. *The whole occasion is lightened* … Another big difference is that they don't go in for having a meal now after a funeral, just *get it over nice and quietly*, and then all go home.'[14]

Greater simplicity in funeral rites need not connote indifference to the dead. Spiritualists themselves discouraged mourning, elaborate funerals and the cult of the cemetery, because they saw death as a joyful and quite literal transition to a 'better place'. In 1932, Hannen Swaffer reported in *Psychic News* that one Spiritualist had left instructions that 'there was to be no mourning' at his funeral; 'the flowers were to be "gay"; and people were 'to wear their ordinary clothes'. With some justification, Swaffer concluded that it was Spiritualist influence that was 'gradually … robbing the English funeral service of its terrible gloom'.[15]

If Spiritualism conformed to modernist inclinations to streamline and simplify funeral rites, it obviously countered the trend to ignore death. Its protest against the tide of modernist and rationalist ideology lay primarily in its sentimental and domesticated relationship with the deceased. It was these aspects, at least, which were among the most offensive to its critics.[16] As we have seen in earlier chapters, Spiritualists were pathologised in various medical and literary circles as deluded, weak-minded hysterics who suffered from dissociated consciousness or, more generally, from a morbid attachment to their deceased loved ones. Among psychical researchers and occultists, it was not so much that Spiritualists claimed to communicate with the dead that offended as the way they did so. Cosmic reality apparently deserved more dignity than Spiritualism offered, with its homely setting, mundane messages, anthropomorphic and grossly materialist version of the afterworld.[17]

But it was precisely the warmth of Spiritualist community, its material and anthropomorphic heaven and, above all, its promise to meet and speak with dead relatives and friends about familiar day-to-day things, which appealed to many people in the interwar years and beyond. If the cultural dominance of modernist and rationalist currents of thought after the Second World War made anthropomorphic and literal heavens of the type promoted by Spiritualists seem increasingly unlikely, the desire to see and speak with lost loved ones retained some appeal, even if fewer people were prepared to admit it. While war films like *The Way to the Stars* (1945) and *Mrs Miniver* (1942) were playing down the impact of death on the population,[18] there was an upsurge between 1939 and 1945 in the popularity of films showing 'the dead in heaven still looking very much the same as they always had been and taking a deep interest in their loved ones below'.[19] After the war, in 1955, Morey Bernstein caused a minor sensation in both America and Britain with the publication of *The Search for Bridey Murphy*.[20]

Although it was primarily about the discovery of past lives through hypnotic regression, this book relied heavily on Spiritualist concepts and images. Bernstein, an advertiser by trade, became keenly interested in hypnosis and its possibilities for psychical research after studying the work of the prominent psychical researcher J. B. Rhine. The Bridey Murphy personality appeared while Bernstein was conducting a hypnosis session with an acquaintance of his, Ruth Simmons. During this session Simmons described her own life and childhood, then she 'regressed' further to reveal another, long-dead person, 'Bridey Murphy'. Having asked 'Bridey' about her life in Ireland in the early years of the nineteenth century, Bernstein questioned her about her death. She died when she was sixty-nine years old, but retained consciousness. In the spirit world, which she described as 'one place, but ... spread out',[21] she spoke to her brother, who died when he was a baby, and to Father John, her husband's priest. She also visited her living husband and brother and tried to speak to them – she tried to talk to many people still on earth, but, she said they just *'won't listen'*.[22]

Of course, this is what Spiritualists have been saying since the last century: the dead can communicate with the living, if only the living will listen. Thus, in *The Search for Bridey Murphy* we find again an affirmation of the survival of the individual in recognisable form, and the hope of reunion with dead loved ones. This hope has persisted into recent times. In 1994, an *Everyman* television documentary revealed that the desire to speak with dead relatives in familiar terms can still draw the bereaved into Spiritualist circles.[23]

Today, the Arthur Findlay College in Stansted, Essex, is the centre of Spiritualist activity in Britain. Formerly the home of Arthur Findlay, Stansted Hall is an imposing building now used by the Spiritualists' National Union (SNU) as a residential college. The courses offered are diverse, and include aromatherapy, yoga and astrology as well as the more traditional studies on mediumship and healing techniques.[24] Courses come and go, but what is always offered is the chance to speak with dead relatives and friends through the auspices of a medium. The format is familiar. Take this fragment of a demonstration given by the College's former principal, Gordon Higginson, recorded by a journalist in the slightly ridiculing tone characteristic of outsiders:

> Higginson proceeded to give messages to the audience from their dead relatives. Again messages of best wishes or the 'you've been going through a difficult period' sort predominated. Finally the [Irish spirit control] gave way to a faint, husky West Country whisper:
>   'Mary,' said the voice. 'Mary, can ye hear me?'
>   One of the students answered in a shaky voice: 'It's you, Harry.'
>   'Mary.'
>   'Yes, Harry.'
>   'I love you.'
>   'It's me. Can you hear me?'
>   'Yes, I can.'
>   'I wish [the rest inaudible] … '
>   'Oh, that's lovely … '
> At this point transmission failed. Shortly afterwards Higginson came to his senses and the party broke up for tea. Mary, slightly shaken by her conversation with her dead husband, disappeared on her own into the garden.[25]

The influence of Spiritualist thought and practice is still evident in modern esoteric movements. Olivia Robertson, founder of the Fellowship of Isis and teacher and writer on occult subjects, trained at the London College of Psychic Studies 'with a famous medium'.[26] She retains much of what she learned there in her philosophy of the unseen

world. In *The Call of Isis* (1975), she refers to different levels of existence as spheres. Humans have a physical body, a duplicate etheric body
and a soul, and trance continues to play an important role in spirit
communication between different spheres.

Fascination with the 'unseen' and esoteric subjects has increased
since the Second World War, but the demand for traditional mediumistic
skills has declined. In 1970, Paul Tabori questioned several leading
psychical researchers about contemporary mediumship.[27] All noted that
although interest in occult subjects such as reincarnation and magic
seemed to have increased, physical mediums had practically disappeared
after the war. Reasons given for this included the development of better
equipment for detecting fraud, and the notion among Spiritualists that
physical mediumship is of 'a low order, an inferior level' to trance
mediumship.[28] Trance mediums, particularly healing mediums, continued to practise, but ones with good reputations were scarce, and they
were normally unwilling to take part in tests. One interviewee, Mrs
Goldney of the SPR, said that in the 1930s there 'seemed to be no
difficulty in obtaining interesting mediums for investigation; whereas
now, and for a long time, it has been impossible to get, or even hear
of a worthwhile physical medium'. In response to her enquiries about
mental mediums, she was told by individual Spiritualists that there was
now nobody who could compare with the famous mediums of the past
like Gladys Leonard or Eileen Garrett.[29] In 1963, Muriel Hankey noted
a similar trend. Physical mediums were extremely scarce, and she considered that mental mediums were no longer of the same calibre as
those who operated in the 1920s and 1930s. Hankey thought that the
'different *tempo* of modern life' accounted for the dearth of credible
mediums after the war: 'Fifty years ago people had more time; the
average working days were longer, but there was less to occupy the
leisure hours. The development of mediumship was carefully nurtured
in the regular home circles, sometimes continued for years before the
mediumship blossomed in maturity.'[30]

Of course, any detailed enquiry into the reasons for the decline of
traditional Spiritualist mediums, and loss of status for those that remained, would require further study. But we can speculate that alternative entertainments, the increasing emphasis on expertise and modern
responses to bereavement, have all reduced the demand for their
services. The spate of prosecutions against mediums during World War

II also suggests increased ideological intolerance towards them at this time.[31] Maurice Barbanell said that officials from the Criminal Investigation Department of Scotland Yard visited him and implied that he was damaging 'morale' by approaching the parents of deceased soldiers with messages from their sons via mediums.[32] According to *Psychic News*, it was also official BBC policy not to broadcast information on unorthodox religions such as Spiritualism, Theosophy and Christian Science.[33] In my view, however, changing attitudes to women are of greater significance in the decline of Spiritualist mediums.

During the interwar period, the medium served many discursive purposes in negotiations and disputes over the meaning of femininity and the place of women. We have seen that mediumistic relations with psychical researchers parodied not only relations between experimenters and experimental objects, but also those between master and slave. Mediumship also served as a means of expressing ideologies concerning reproduction and mothering. For Spiritualists, a medium's credibility was based on her 'feminine' attributes: her passivity, domesticity, simplicity and her personal proximity to Mary, the exemplary mother. In other negative discourses she represented the vampire mother – 'the mother of fright and lust' – or, conversely, her mysticism could be related to the 'sexual frustration of the old maid', who turned out to be, in some contexts, another variation on the vampire mother. Such representations of motherhood and spinsterhood, and women as willing slaves, have clearly lost ideological ground with the success of modern brands of feminism and with the furious debates surrounding women in their reproductive, mothering, and sexual roles. So what has become of mediums in this rapidly changing social landscape?

Ideologies of femininity and motherhood in the second half of the twentieth century have been unconducive to the development of the traditional Spiritualist medium.[34] Whether we refer to the kind of feminism that simply demands the same rights and privileges as men, or to more complex varieties that seek to analyse the historical, linguistic and psychological sources of patriarchal power, all (broadly speaking) reject traditional assumptions that men should occupy the public sphere, women the private; that men are active, women passive; and that maternity is the sole function and destiny of women. I have argued that the Spiritualist discourse conformed, in many ways, to traditional assumptions about gender; others have noted that mediumship could involve their subversion.[35] But whether we are talking about conformity or subversion, the efficacy of either strategy relied on traditional discourses of femininity retaining their ideological currency. With the weakening of such discourses, mediums have been deprived of their historic sources of legitimation and models of identity. Occasionally a medium achieved international success in the 1960s and 1970s within the frame of traditional mediumship,[36] but ideologies surrounding mysticism have developed in directions that reflect the new and multifaceted ways in which women understand their own spiritual experiences.[37]

Within this diversity, one strand of mystic feminine consciousness has grown significantly in popularity. Instead of the sacrificing Mother of Christ deployed by Spiritualists, this variety of mysticism deploys the sign of the primordial mother as powerful goddess. An example of this shift in consciousness is evident in one of Dion Fortune's later novels, *The Sea Priestess* (1938). Whereas the mediumistic heroines of *The Demon Lover* (1927) and *The Winged Bull* (1935) are portrayed as passive and dependent, the medium/priestess of *The Sea Priestess* is active and independent. Morgan Le Fay is a woman of indeterminate age (probably old), but glamorous appearance, who solicits the help of the weak and asthmatic Wilfred in the magical rites she performs. Her purpose is to invoke the goddess of the sea, and Wilfred, who has fallen in love with her, acts as her priest. The book is not so much a traditional romance as an assertion of the timeless mystical, sexual and reproductive power of 'Woman':

> Morgan Le Fay told me [Wilfred] that she had chosen for her part the cult of the Great Goddess, the primordial Mother. And this goddess was symbolized by space and the sea, and the inmost earth. She was Rhea, and Ge, and Persephone, but above all she was our Lady Isis in whom all these are summed up; for Isis is both corn goddess and queen of the dead – who are also the unborn – and the lunar crescent is upon her brow. Under another aspect she is the sea, for life first formed in the sea, and in her dynamic aspect she arose from the waves as Aphrodite.[38]

Towards the end of the book Isis appears to Molly, Wilfred's young wife, and tells her that in ancient times 'it was the women who were dynamic, and it was not until corruption came upon the pagan world that the priests took all the power'.[39] Assuming Wilfred's character, as narrator, Fortune adds:

> Our conventions have so stereotyped the polarity between a man and
> a woman that it has got stuck and no one knows how to shift it. But
> what we want in the part of marriage that is behind the veil is the
> dynamic woman, who comes in the name of the Great Goddess,
> conscious of her priesthood and proud of her power, and it is this
> self-confidence that the modest woman lacks.[40]

This summoning of 'powerful femininity' in the name of the Great
Goddess has had widespread application in recent times. From about
the 1970s, movements such as Womanspirit in the United States have
flourished,[41] any number of books and articles have been written on
the historical origins of matriarchy,[42] and dozens of groups have come
into existence that are devoted to the exploration of the 'self' through
veneration of the goddess. Then there are those who have developed
theories concerning the role of the primordial mother in the psyche;[43]
others, like Olivia Robertson, have been more eclectic in their approach.
Robertson incorporates theories from Theosophy, multiconsciousness,
cosmic consciousness, dream experience and modified Spiritualist ideas
into her spiritual ethos, to produce a feminine image that is more like
the goddess than the medium. The shift from medium to goddess is
accomplished in her book *The Call of Isis* through several simple moves.
More emphasis is placed on the individual imagination and less on
spirit guides. The psychic goal, as Robertson sees it, is to move from
'the passive world of dreams and trance to the active domain of manipulating power'.[44] And she notes the contrast in outlook between
traditional mediums and modern occultists: faced with a problem, they
[the latter] would say: 'I am going to do something about this'!'[45] In
this psychic setting, the self-erasement of the traditional medium is
replaced by puposeful intent.

The success of prewar mediums in this changing spiritual landscape
has been uneven. Helen Duncan and Eileen Garrett represent the two
ends of the spectrum. Duncan, like many physical mediums, was almost forced out of business after two highly publicised court cases
where she was accused of fraud, one in 1933 and one in 1944. In 1933,
the prosecution alleged that the manifestation of the spirit-guide, Peggy
Hazeldine, was really a woman's undervest manipulated by the medium.
Duncan was found guilty and fined ten pounds. The Spiritualist community was divided over the affair. At her trial in May, the president of
the SNU, J. B. McIndoe, said that he had once detected Duncan in

fraudulent acts. A month later – no doubt under pressure from the Committee of the SNU, which supported her – he issued another state-ment where he expressed regret for his first.[46] The controversy sur-rounding Helen Duncan's mediumship came to a head again on 31 March 1944, when she was convicted at the Old Bailey of 'pretending to exercise conjuration',[47] and sentenced to nine months' imprison-ment. Portsmouth police arrested her after they received information about Spiritualist activities in the area. In his statement at Duncan's trial, a War Reserve policeman said he went to Copner Road, Ports-mouth, where a seance was in progress, and discovered her covered in a white shroud, pretending to be a spirit-guide.[48] Spiritualists were again divided over the affair. The influential journal *Light* endorsed the court decision that she was fraudulent,[49] and referred readers to Harry Price's book *Regurgitation and the Duncan Mediumship* (1931), where he published his theory that the Duncan manifestations were merely cheese cloth, stored in her 'secondary stomach'. Others, like Maurice Barbanell of *Psychic News*, strenuously opposed all charges against her, and led the campaign for her vindication and release from prison.[50] In 1956, five weeks after another police raid at one of her seances, she died. Her supporters insisted that 'shock had caused the death of the medium'.[51]

Why did Helen Duncan's mediumship seem so implausible? To say that she was convicted of fraud only begs the question. Her mediumship was of the kind most likely to offend modern aesthetics, and the cult of rationality and expertise. Duncan's unromantic background in a working-class area of Perthshire, where she bore nine children, did not conform to dominant ideals of spirituality, beauty and knowledge. As I noted in Chapter 5, the physical phenomena that mediums like Duncan produced strongly evoked images of repellent maternity. Her stout figure must have reinforced this effect. Harry Price, at least, visualised her as a cow, performing her mediumistic feats through the benefit of a second stomach. Her raucous spirit-guides and style of demonstration gave the impression of an old-fashioned music-hall act, far removed from the 'cold clear light' of 'progressive' scientific knowledge. Unintellectual, domestic, anthropomorphic and materialistic, Duncan personified stigmatised working-class and female culture.

Eileen Garrett, on the other hand, enjoyed a good reputation among psychical researchers and Spiritualists until her death on 17 September 1970.[52] From the beginning, her mediumship and persona were perceived as worlds apart from Duncan's. Her credibility seems to have been based partly on her 'rational' and 'modern' approach to her mediumship. Psychical researchers found her 'surprisingly different in appearance and manner from any other medium'. In 1927, one investigator described her as 'very modern, Eton-cropped and humorous'.[53] Better still, her perceived modernity did not prevent her from following the self-negating rules of conduct demanded by both Spiritualists and psychical research-ers. Garrett managed to maintain a tension between the positions of subject and object in her working life as a medium. Although she allowed herself to be the passive object of experimental and Spiritualist enquiry, she was, simultaneously, a participant in those enquiries. She never claimed that her 'voices' and visions had objective reality of their own (except as a child), but treated them as unusual phenomena that she wished to understand according to scientific as well as mystic precepts. Thus she was never placed in the position of having to 'prove' her claim to mediumship.

In 1940, her life changed dramatically. She moved to America, where she unambiguously asserted her own speaking voice (independent of her spirit-guides) by establishing the publishing house Creative Age Press and the journal *Tomorrow*. During the years 1941 to 1951, she wrote 120 editorials, 30 book reviews and 4 books. In 1951, with the assistance of her friend, Frances Payne, she opened the Parapsychology Foundation, devoted to the scholarly exploration of parapsychology.[54] To put it briefly, her approach shifted from the traditional self-negation expected of women in the interwar years to the self-assertion, increasing-ly demanded of them and asserted by them (who knows which came first?) in the post-World War II years. With her authoritative position as publisher and founder of a scholarly institution, Garrett came to exemplify powerful femininity. Paradoxically, her reputation as one of Britain's best mediums was at its most secure after she had ceased to practise regularly.[55] In 1963, her lifetime friend Muriel Hankey spoke of her mediumship in the past tense. Referring to the lack of good mediumistic subjects for research in the present, Hankey wrote:

> Where are the willing guinea-pigs of the subject to assist the work of the parapsychological specialists now examining the *modus operandi* of the seance room? And will there ever be another Eileen Garrett?[56]

*

Like all writing, this book has been a personal journey. Embedded in my historical consideration of Spiritualism and mediumship are the traces of private fixations and desires. I was made painfully aware of modern imperatives to forget the dead when my six-year-old brother died. Shocked, appalled and heartbroken, my immediate family and near relatives struggled to deal with this crisis in our lives. But no meaning could be wrung from it. Having no religious framework but the ghost of rejected Christianity, we railed at the arbitrary cruelty of a God in whom none of us believed. Friends and acquaintances were horrified and deeply embarrassed by the event. Spurning traditional platitudes about God and heavenly reunion, they muttered about time and its healing power. This was inadequate, and they knew it – that was why they were embarrassed. I suspect, too, that their avoidance of us was not just linked to feelings of personal inadequacy, but associated with a new superstition associated with death and mourning: that mourning is a sentimental affront to the modern cult of the invincible individual – an affront precisely because it exposes human mortality. It was as if we were infected or tainted by association with death.

In a way, the writing of this book has been a cathartic exercise for me – a chance to experience (albeit vicariously) the comfort and succour offered by Spiritualism to the bereaved. But for many people today, Spiritualism is an outmoded, rather ridiculous belief that is irrelevant to the secular preoccupations of the 'enlightened' twenty-first century. In keeping with this assumption, historians have tended to confine them-selves to commenting on its impact and meaning for Victorian culture. But as I have tried to show, the hegemony of the secularist thesis has frequently obscured the persistence and influence of Spiritualist thought in interwar Britain, and its influence persists in indirect ways beyond this period. Post-World War II interest in the supernatural is displayed in the popularity of books like *The Search for Bridey Murphy*, and tele-vision programmes dealing with supernatural themes. Despite wide-spread scepticism about the existence of an afterworld, many people still hope to 'see' their dead loved ones again. Surely, the continuing popularity and emotional impact of the opening lines of Vera Lynn's wartime song – 'We'll meet again, don't know where, don't know when' – connotes something beyond the expectation of mundane reunion. Similarly, the continued appeal of J. M. Barrie's *Peter Pan* (1904) may be the fact that Peter *returns* from Never Never Land.[57] The hope that the dead are not lost for ever, and may still be present in some form, is expressed in many small ways. Maybe the room of the deceased is preserved, or an arrangement of flowers is placed beside their photograph. My own father (who has no knowledge of, or interest in, Spiritualism) keeps fresh flowers by my brother's photograph to this day.

Notes

1 T. Adorno and M. Horkheimer, *Dialectic of Enlightenment* (1944), trans J. Cumming (London, Verso, 1979), pp. 215–16. The modern distaste for death and dying, and the perception of mourning as an asocial and somehow indecent activity, have been noted elsewhere. In his autobiographical introduction to *Death, Grief and Mourning*, Geoffrey Gorer writes that after the death of his brother he refused invitations to cocktail parties, explaining that he was in mourning:

> [T]he people who invited me responded to this statement with shocked embarrassment, as if I had voiced some appalling obscenity. Indeed, I got the impression that, had I stated that the invitation clashed with some esoteric debauchery I had arranged, I would have had understanding and jocular encouragement; as it was, the people whose invitations I had refused, educated and sophisticated as they were, mumbled and hurried away. (*Death, Grief and Mourning in Contemporary Britain* [1965] [London, Cresset Press, 1965], p. xxxii)

2 G. Nelson, *Spiritualism and Society* (London, Routledge & Kegan Paul, 1969), p. 157. In 1993, Gordon Higginson of the SNU claimed that there were over 400 Spiritualist churches in Britain: 'Beyond the Barrier', *Open Space,* Channel Four, 1993. This is considerably fewer than in 1937, when over 500 churches were affiliated to the SNU alone. The presiding secretary at the time estimated that there were twice as many meeting places not connected with the Union: 'Archbishop's Committee on Spiritualism: Report of the Committee to the Archbishop of Canterbury', chaired by the Right Reverend Francis Underhill, DD (unpublished, certified copy, 1947), Harry Price Library, University of London.

3 C. Lasch, *The Culture of Narcissism: American Life in an Age of Diminishing Expectations* (New York, Norton; 1979); see Juliet Flower MacCannell for a psycho-feminist interpretation of the modern imperative to sever ties with the dead. Building on Adorno's work, Flower MacCannell associates this process with the rise of the narcissistic individual, which, she argues, has replaced the patriarchal family as the dominant social unit in modern Western society: *The Regime of the Brother: After the*

Patriarchy (London, Routledge, 1991). In an effort to counter an un-critical nostalgia for the Victorian death, David Cannadine argues that the very extravagance of the Victorian funeral was less to do with psychological support than with commercial greed and exploitation: 'War and Grief, Death and Mourning in Modern Britain', in J. Whaley (ed.), *Mirrors of Mortality: Studies in the Social History of Death* (London, Europa, 1981).

4 C. Gittings, *Death, Burial and the Individual in Early Modern England* (London, Croom Helm, 1984) Philippe Ariès traces attitudes to death from the Middle Ages to the present in *The Hour of Our Death*, trans. H. Weaver (New York, Alfred Knopf, 1983). For an immensely useful collection of historical essays on death and culture, see R. Houlbrooke (ed.), *Death, Ritual, and Bereavement* (London, Routledge, 1989).

5 Ariès, *The Hour of Our Death*, pp. 586–7.

6 J. Winter, *Sites of Memory, Sites of Mourning: The Great War in European Culture* (Cambridge, Cambridge University Press, 1995). See also Paul Fussell, who writes:

> The whole texture of British daily life could be said to commemorate the war still. It is remembered in the odd pub-closing hours, one of the fruits of the Defence of the Realm Act; … [it] persists in many of the laws controlling aliens and repressing sedition and espionage. 'D' – notices to newspapers … are another legacy. So is Summer Time. So are such apparent universals as cigarette-smoking, the use of wristwatches (originally a trench fad), the cultivation of garden 'allotments' ('Food Will Win the War'). So is the use of paper banknotes, entirely replacing gold coins. The playing of 'God Save the King' in theatres began in 1914 and persisted until the 1970s, whose flagrant cynicisms finally brought an end to the custom.
>
> Every day still the *Times* and the *Telegraph* print the little 'In Memoriam' notices – 'Sadly missed,' 'Always in our thoughts,' 'Never forgotten,' 'We do miss you so Bunny' – the military ones dignified by separation from the civilian. There are more on July 1 than on other days, and on that day there is always a traditional one. (*The Great War and Modern Memory* [Oxford, Oxford University Press, 1975], p. 315)

7 R. Graves, *Goodbye to All That*, 4th edn (London, Cassell, 1969), p. 100.

8 Winter, *Sites of Memory, Sites of Mourning*, p. 204. At the Front, soldiers like Graves found it hard to tolerate the official clergy, 'bible-wallahs' and new arrivals 'who talked patriotism': *Goodbye to All That*, pp. 167–8.

9 Nevertheless, grief could reappear in sublimated form. See, for example, Mark Spilka's analysis of Virginia Woolf's seeming inability to grieve the death of those close to her in *Virginia Woolf's Quarrel with*

Grieving (Lincoln, University of Nebraska Press, 1980). In his discussion of Barrie's *Peter Pan* (1904), David Holbrook connects the return of the boys from the Never Never Land to the fear 'of going out of existence': 'Woman, Death, and Meaning in *Peter Pan* and *Mary Rose*', in *Images of Woman in Literature* (New York, New York University Press, 1989), p. 75.

10 A. Light, *Forever England: Femininity, Literature and Conservatism between the Wars* (London, Routledge, 1991), especially ch. 2. In a recent publication about people's experiences of death, a fireman noted that, like Graves's soldiers, he and his colleagues used humour as a standard means of distancing themselves from their emotional responses to death:

> We tend to joke about death, or injuries, which is a way of alleviating it, alleviating your feelings. You know, just a way of putting a blank face on it. You tend to cover it, mask it, with humour which helps everyone out of the situations. I can think of – not thousands – but hundreds of incidents where people have been killed, members of the public, I mean, and we've joked about it. Not within the public's hearing. We joke about it because its the only thing that can keep you sane. (Assistant Divisional Officer Dick Clisby, in R. Dinnage, *The Ruffian on the Stair: Reflections on Death* [Harmondsworth, Penguin, 1990], p. 148)

11 See, for example, D. Sheridan (ed.), *Wartime Women; An Anthology of Women's Wartime Writing for Mass Observation* (London, Mandarin, 1991), especially ch. 10.

12 J. E. Verbeke, 'Behind the Barrier', *Daily Sketch*, 5 October 1940, p. 8.

13 Mass-Observation, *Britain Revisited* (London, Gollancz, 1961), pp. 44–5.

14 *Ibid.*, p. 43.

15 H. Swaffer, 'No Mourning for Dennis Terry; Spiritualism's Effect on Funerals', *Psychic News*, 13 August 1932, p. 3.

16 Modernist and rationalist traditions are, of course, opposed in many other respects, but 'modernist', 'naturalist' or 'rationalist' perceptions have overlapped historically, and proved notoriously difficult to define as separate entities. See M. Bradbury and J. McFarlane, *Modernism, 1890–1903* (Harmondsworth, Penguin, 1976); D. Lowe, *History of Bourgeois Perception* (Chicago, University of Chicago Press, 1982); S. Kern, *The Culture of Time and Space 1880–1918* (Cambridge, MA, Harvard University Press, 1983); R. Williams, *The Politics of Modernism: Against the New Conformists*, ed. and introduced by T. Pinkney (London, Verso, 1989).

17 With respect to nineteenth century responses to Spiritualism, Daniel Cottom observes:

> Outsiders and opponents might seize on the freakishness of spir-
> itualist manifestations: speaking tables, writing appearing out of
> nowhere, bodies possessed by ghostly controls, turtles and freshly
> cut flowers dropped into locker rooms, departed spirits tugging on
> gentlemen's trousers. They laughed, though, only because the mani-
> festations were not marvellous enough. They were ridiculous, not
> marvellous, because they insisted on clinging to common objects
> such as tables, turtles and trousers.

As well as being an affront to modern sensibilities, Spiritualism, as
Cottom further notes, 'abandoned traditional conceptions of sublimity'
('On the Dignity of Tables', *Critical Inquiry*, 14 [Summer 1988] 771,
770).

18 *The Way to the Stars* (1945) is set on an English air base during the
Battle of Britain. Michael Redgrave plays an experienced pilot who is
married to 'Toddy' (Rosamund John). The couple have a baby son.
One day, the pilot fails to return from a raid on Germany. His death
is treated as 'bad luck', and no space is given to scenes of mourning.
It is implied that Toddy's contribution to the 'war-effort' is to bear
her bereavement 'without fuss'. Similarly, the death of Mrs Miniver's
daughter-in-law is treated as an occasion for renewed inspiration for
the 'war-effort'.

19 L. England, quoted from J. Richard and D. Sheridan (eds) *Mass Observation at the Movies* (London, Routledge & Kegan Paul, 1987), p. 292.

20 As a contribution to parapsychology the book was unsuccessful. One
reviewer said:

> We are given practically no information about the current life of
> the subject so we cannot surmise how easily she might have
> invented 'Bridey'. We may be reasonably sure, however, that a
> searching psychological study of the subject would take all the
> 'mystery' out of this case. It would also reveal the remarkable power
> of unconscious mental life to bilk, not only a naive hypnotist, but
> also the subject herself. (J. Dollard, *New York Herald Tribune*, 12
> February, 1956, p. 4)

Another, for *The New York Times*, wrote: 'For those who know the
literature of parapsychology, Morey Bernstein is anything but an experienced investigator' (*New York Times*, 8 January 1956, p. 22). Bad
reviews did not detract from its popular success. A full-length feature
film based on the book was released in 1956.

21 M. Bernstein, *The Search for Bridey Murphy* (London, Hutchinson, 1956),
p. 124.

22 *Ibid.*, p. 124.

23 'The Happy Medium', *Everyman*, BBC, 1994.

24 *The Arthur Findlay College: 1993 Program.* The 1999 Program is available from Stansted Hall, Stansted, Essex CM24 8UD. See also 'Beyond the Barrier', a film account of Spiritualism produced by Spiritualists associated with the Arthur Findlay College. The film was shown by Channel 4, *Open Space*, 1993. For a journalist's view of the college's personnel and their activities, see Amanda Mitchinson, 'Blythe Spirits', *The Independent Magazine*, 198, 20 June 1992, pp. 44–8.

25 Mitchison, 'Blythe Spirits', p. 48, col. 1.

26 O. Robertson, *The Call of Isis* (1975), 2nd edn (Clonegal, Cesara, 1990), p. 14. Robertson's other publications include: *St Malachy's Court* (London, Peter Davies, 1950); *Field of the Stranger* (London, Peter Davies, 1948); *Miranda Speaks* (London, Peter Davies, 1950); *It's an Old Irish Custom* (London, Dennis Dobson, 1953).

27 They included Mrs K. M. Goldney, a vice-president of the SPR with forty years' experience in the various branches of psychical research; Peter Underwood, President of the Ghost Club; and George Medhurst, another SPR member: P. Tabori and P. Raphael, *Beyond the Senses: A Report on Psychical Research and Occult Phenomena in the Sixties* (London, Souvenir Press, 1971).

28 *Ibid.*, p. 202.

29 *Ibid.*, pp. 191–2.

30 M. Hankey, *James Hewat McKenzie, Pioneer of Psychical Reserch: A Personal Memoir* (London, Aquarian Press, 1963), p. 63.

31 In 1942 the mediums Austin Hatcher and Emily Little were prosecuted and sentenced to three months' imprisonment. Helen Duncan was also prosecuted in 1944, as were Jane Yorke and Emily Johnson. See Nelson, *Spiritualism and Society*, pp. 165–7.

32 M. Barbanell, *Psychic News*, 21 September 1940, p. 1.

33 P. Miller, *Psychic News*, 3 February 1940, p. 1.

34 Ursula King makes a similar point on a broader level. She finds that as 'far as traditional religions are concerned, many feminists find the historically available models of spirituality too restricting and oppressive, too one-sided and male-dominated for their new understanding of self and community' (*Women and Spirituality: Voices of Protest and Promise* [Basingstoke, Macmillan, 1989], p. 119).

35 A. Owen, *The Darkened Room: Women, Power and Spiritualism in Late Victorian England* (London, Virago, 1989); J. Walkowitz, *City of Dreadful Delight: Narratives of Sexual Danger in Late Victorian London* (London, Virago, 1992); V. Skultans, 'Mediums, Controls and Eminent Men', in P. Holden (ed.), *Women's Religious Experience* (London, Croom Helm, 1983), pp. 15–26; C. Kahne, 'Hysteria, Feminism, and the Case of *The Bostonians*', in R. Feldstein and J. Roof (eds), *Feminism and Psychoanalysis* (Ithaca, NY, Cornell University Press, 1989), pp. 280–97.

36 Doris Stokes became quite famous in the 1970s in Britain. She spoke

on platforms up and down the country, and appeared on television. She also performed on television in Australia. She maintained a subordinate posture towards her spirit-guides and insisted that her role in the communication of spirit messages was an entirely passive one: D. Stokes and L. Dearsley, *Voices in My Ear: The Autobiography of a Medium* (London, Futura Macdonald, 1980).

37 King, *Women and Spirituality*.

38 D. Fortune, *The Sea Priestess* (Wellingborough, Aquarian Press, 1989), pp. 159–60.

39 *Ibid.*, p. 261.

40 *Ibid.*, p. 265.

41 The journal *Womanspirit* was first published in the United States in 1974.

42 See, for example, M. Stone, *The Paradise Papers*, new edn (London, Virago, 1979); M. Gimbutas, *The Goddesses and Gods of Old Europe 6500–3500 BC: Myths and Cult Images*, new edn (Los Angeles, University of California Press, 1982). Ursula King's *Women and Spirituality* covers a cross-section of titles that deal with the historical and psychological significance of the goddess figure.

43 See, for example, N. Hall, *The Moon and the Virgin: Towards Self-Discovery and Healing* (London, The Women's Press, 1980), which draws explicitly on Jungian concepts in order to imagine a feminine ethos of the future.

44 Robertson, *The Call of Isis*, p. 36.

45 *Ibid.*, p. 50.

46 A. Crossley, *The Story of Helen Duncan: Materialization Medium* (Devon, Arthur Stockwell, 1975), pp. 47–9.

47 She was also convicted of 'causing money to be paid by false pretences and creating a public mischief': 'The Case of Mrs. Duncan', *Light*, LXIV:3288 (1944) 144–7.

48 M. Barbanell, *The Case of Helen Duncan* (London, Psychic Press, 1945), p. 22.

49 'The Case of Mrs. Duncan'.

50 Barbanell, *The Case of Helen Duncan*.

51 Crossley, *The Story of Helen Duncan*, p. 180.

52 M. Hankey, 'Obituaries', *The Journal of the Society for Psychical Research*, 45:746 (1970) 406–8.

53 Quoted by B. Inglis, *A History of the Paranormal, 1914–1939* (London, Hodder & Stoughton, 1984), p. 276.

54 J. D. S. McMahon, *Eileen J. Garrett: A Woman Who Made a Difference* (New York, Parapsychology Foundation, 1994), pp. 20–24.

55 In her 1968 biography, *Many Voices*, Garrett wrote that she now used her mediumistic gifts mainly for healing purposes. Her other activities as author and publisher claimed most of her attention: *Many Voices:*

The Autobiography of a Medium (London, George Allen & Unwin. 1968), p. 231.

56 Hankey, *James Hewat McKenzie*, p. 63.

57 Holbrook, 'Woman, Death, and Meaning in *Peter Pan* and *Mary Rose*', p. 78.

Index